Ideologies in Education

⟨COUNTERPOINTS▶

Studies in the
Postmodern Theory of Education

Joe L. Kincheloe and Shirley R. Steinberg
General Editors

Vol. 319

PETER LANG
New York • Washington, D.C./Baltimore • Bern
Frankfurt am Main • Berlin • Brussels • Vienna • Oxford

Ideologies in Education

Unmasking the Trap of Teacher Neutrality

EDITED BY
Lilia I. Bartolomé

PETER LANG
New York • Washington, D.C./Baltimore • Bern
Frankfurt am Main • Berlin • Brussels • Vienna • Oxford

Library of Congress Cataloging-in-Publication Data

Ideologies in education: unmasking the trap
of teacher neutrality / edited by Lilia I. Bartolomé.
p. cm. — (Counterpoints: studies in the postmodern
theory of education; v. 319)
Includes bibliographical references and index.
1. Discrimination in education—United States. 2. Teachers—
United States—Attitudes. 3. Postmodernism and education—United States.
4. Critical pedagogy—United States. I. Bartolomé, Lilia I.
LC212.2.I33 371.001—dc22   2007003553
ISBN 978-0-8204-9704-4
ISSN 1058-1634

Bibliographic information published by **Die Deutsche Bibliothek**.
Die Deutsche Bibliothek lists this publication in the "Deutsche
Nationalbibliografie"; detailed bibliographic data is available
on the Internet at http://dnb.ddb.de/.

Cover design by Clear Point Designs

The paper in this book meets the guidelines for permanence and durability
of the Committee on Production Guidelines for Book Longevity
of the Council of Library Resources.

© 2008 Peter Lang Publishing, Inc., New York
29 Broadway, 18th floor, New York, NY 10006
www.peterlang.com

All rights reserved.
Reprint or reproduction, even partially, in all forms such as microfilm,
xerography, microfiche, microcard, and offset strictly prohibited.

Printed in the United States of America

To all those teachers whose political clarity ruptures all forms of discrimination, social injustices, and undemocratic classroom practices

Table of Contents

Introduction: Beyond the Fog of Ideology ix
    Lilia I. Bartolomé

Section I. White Supremacist Ideologies Challenged

Chapter 1. Hysterical Blindness and the Ideology of Denial:
    Preservice Teachers' Resistance to Multicultural Education 3
    Ricardo E. Gonsalves

Chapter 2. Shooting the Messenger: The Consequences of Practicing
    an Ideology of Social Justice 29
    María V. Balderrama

Section II. The Invisible Pervasiveness of Dominant Ideologies

Chapter 3. Underprepared "Veteran" Special Education Teachers' Reliance
    on Racist and Classist Ideologies 49
    Felicity A. Crawford

Chapter 4. Teachers' D/discourses and Socially Situated Identities:
    Literacy Practices in a Mexican High School 73
    Guadalupe López Bonilla

Section III. Hegemonic Ideologies in U.S. History Curricula

Chapter 5. Unlearning the Official History: Agency and Pedagogies
of Possibility 97
Panayota Gounari

Section IV. Promising Practices Based on Praxis

Chapter 6. Critically Examining Beliefs, Orientations, Ideologies,
and Practices Toward Literacy Instruction: A Process of Praxis 117
Karen Cadiero-Kaplan

Chapter 7. Sharing the Wealth: Guiding All Students Into the
Professional Discourse 135
Stephanie Cox Suárez

Section V. Gaining Greater Ideological Clarity

Chapter 8. "I'm White, Now What?" Setting a Context for Change
in Teachers' Pedagogy 161
Paula S. Martin

Chapter 9. Reflections from Beneath the Veil: Mainstream
Preservice Teachers (Dis)Covering Their Cultural Identities 181
Nelda L. Barrón

Chapter 10. Mapping the Terrain(s) of Ideology in New Urban
Teachers' Professional Development Experiences 207
Paula Elliott

Section VI. Ideologically Clear Teachers: Two Case Studies

Chapter 11. Developing Ideological Clarity: One Teacher's Journey................. 231
Cristina Alfaro

Chapter 12. Politicized Mothering: Authentic Caring Among
African American Women Teachers 251
Tamara Beauboeuf-Lafontant

Afterword: The Importance of Ideology in Contemporary Education 265
Joe L. Kincheloe

Contributors... 271

Index.. 275

Introduction: Beyond the Fog of Ideology

LILIA I. BARTOLOMÉ

> [A] ruling ideology does not so much combat alternative ideas as thrust them beyond the very bounds of the unthinkable. Ideologies exist because there are things which must at all costs not be thought, let alone spoken. How we could ever know that there were such thoughts is then an obvious logical difficulty. Perhaps we can just feel that there is something we ought to be thinking, but we have no idea what it is.
> (EAGLETON, 1991, P. 58)

The invisible yet pervasive nature of oppressive dominant ideologies and the urgent need to clearly perceive and speak of their existence and the harmful impact they have on education are courageously taken up by the contributors to this volume, *Ideologies in Education: Unmasking the Trap of Teacher Neutrality*. Educators and the general public typically do not understand that the solutions to many of the educational challenges facing subordinated students are not purely technical or methodological in nature, but are instead rooted in typically unacknowledged discriminatory ideologies and practices. In this book, readers are invited to confront the continuing existence and vigorous resurgence of not easily named discriminatory perspectives toward students from subordinated cultural groups, as well as their numerous manifestations in schools. However, it is not enough to struggle to name and critique these discriminatory ideologies and practices; there is also an urgent need to identify effective counter-hegemonic orientations and pedagogical interventions that work to neutralize unequal material conditions and biased beliefs. The authors presented in this book do just that—address hegemonic and counter-hegemonic ideologies at both the practical and theoretical levels.

As Eagleton expresses explicitly in the epigraph, the insidious invisibility of dominant ideologies prevents educators from more accurately identifying and analyzing current challenges in the education of subordinated and marginalized populations. A solution to a problem cannot logically be imagined until one has a firm grasp of the particular problem or challenge. In the field of teacher education, it is particularly urgent that preservice educators develop the ability to analyze educational challenges critically and thoroughly so as to develop equally critical and comprehensive solutions.

In much of the current teacher education literature on preparing teachers to deal effectively with diversity, scholars focus on increasing teachers' cultural responsiveness and their knowledge about various ethnic cultural groups; their familiarity with second-language acquisition processes and second-language pedagogy; their ability to utilize constructivist teaching and mediating approaches; and their knowledge of best practices with diverse student populations. These and other efforts to prepare teachers effectively are certainly necessary, despite the fact that most programs concentrate on these areas without addressing the ideological and political dimensions of educating subordinated students. For example, in multicultural education courses across the country, teacher educators toil diligently to provide their students with the information necessary to effectively work with minority students in a relatively short period of time—usually a semester. Despite good intentions, I maintain that the invisible foundation—hegemonic ideologies that inform our perceptions and treatment of subordinated students—needs to be made explicit and studied critically in order to comprehend the challenges presented in minority education—and possible solutions—more accurately.

Paulo Freire (1985) encouraged educators to uncover the influence of dominant ideologies when they confront educational problems or obstacles faced by subordinated student populations. He argued that in order to solve an educational problem, educators must first comprehensively and historically situate the problem—that is, "construct" the problem. After situating the problem, the next step is to critically analyze or "deconstruct" the issue, and in so doing make the oppressive ideologies evident. The final step is to imagine realistic alternative possibilities, to envision and then dare to implement more humane and democratic solutions—solutions that lead to the reconstruction of the problem as a means to develop liberatory solutions.

The precise intent of this book is both to expose hidden and invisible hegemonic ideologies and their myriad manifestations in education and to offer potential intervention strategies that reflect a more democratic and counter-hegemonic ideological orientation. Before delving into the book's content, however, it will be useful to discuss the concept of ideology.

WHAT IS IDEOLOGY?

Before addressing the concept of ideology, I want to share an example of the tendency in education to embrace technical solutions and to reject discussions of ideology and its possible influences on teaching and learning. At an educational conference on linguistic minority education held at the Harvard Graduate School of Education, a visiting professor challenged my focus on ideology and argued that, based on her teacher education research, ideology has very little to do with the effective preparation of preservice teachers. Instead, she argued, the focus lies on providing preservice teachers with technical knowledge and skills such as second-language acquisition theory and methodology. This professor maintained that in her research on preservice teachers and practicing teachers, the teachers clamored for more technical knowledge, not greater understanding of ideology. While I certainly recognize the need to provide preservice teachers with expertise in theory and instructional methods, I found her protest that ideology is not relevant especially disturbing and somewhat disingenuous given that she teaches and conducts research in California—a state that has recently passed numerous legislative propositions that clearly reflect racist ideologies meant to subordinate Latino/Mexican immigrants. For example, in 1986, Proposition 63, which required that all official documents be printed solely in English and all government proceedings be conducted solely in English, passed in California. This initiative sparked similar English-only and anti-bilingual education initiatives and policies in other states. A few years later in California, Proposition 187, which passed in November 1994 (though declared unconstitutional in 1997), was known as the anti-immigration and anti-immigrant bill. It advocated banning undocumented immigrants, especially those from Mexico, from public education and other state-provided social services. In 1996, Proposition 209, also known as the anti-affirmative action legislation, prohibited gender- and race-based preferences in public education, employment, and contracting in California, thus reversing civil rights gains made by Latinos since the 1960s. Finally, in June 1998, Proposition 227 outlawed bilingual education and prohibited the use of languages other than English for instructional purposes in California public schools.

John Halcón (2001) powerfully points out the harmful ideologies that inform these laws and their consequences at the school and classroom levels:

> While these legislative initiatives in California may seem far removed from the classroom and irrelevant to the teaching of literacy, they have had a far-reaching influence

in shaping negative public attitudes toward Latinos and toward the use of Spanish in the classrooms. The truth is, we live in a society that currently boasts of its intolerance for non-English speakers through passage of English-only amendments, anti-immigrant, anti-bilingual education, and passage of anti-affirmative action amendments to keep "foreigners," especially Mexicans, in check. This negative rhetoric does not remain in the public domain, but filters down from the mass media and the larger sociopolitical context to Mexicano/Latino homes, to parents and their children who embrace it, subconsciously and uncritically, without understanding it. The result is, at best, ambivalence toward one's language and culture, and, at worst, a self-hate that hinders learning. (pp. 72–73)

I would add that these negative ideologies do not merely affect the victims of these harmful belief systems, but are also internalized by educators and manifested in their teaching and their treatment of Latino and other immigrant and minority students. Given the importance of recognizing and interrogating discriminatory ideologies and their manifestation in classrooms, I was taken aback at the insistence of this Harvard visiting professor that ideology was not a significant factor in teacher education. This seemingly progressive academic's resistance to acknowledging the significance of ideology exemplifies what Macedo and Freire (forthcoming) label as the predominance of educators' willingness to "kill ideology ideologically."

This tendency to "kill ideology ideologically" signals an urgent need to study ideology in education. I begin my discussion of ideology by first providing an accessible definition and then answering questions that I believe readers may ask when they approach this book. Many readers might respond to the title of this book by asking, "What is ideology?" "Is it important for educators to study ideology?" "If ideology is significant, what can educators do to develop a greater understanding of it?" "What are some of the challenges that teacher educators face in assisting their preservice teachers' development of ideological understanding?" Furthermore, importantly, "What are the characteristics of educators who have increased their understanding of ideology and what effects does it have on their teaching?" The book's eleven contributors eloquently address one or more of these questions in their courageous and powerful chapters. In this introductory chapter, I address the first two questions, and direct you to the various authors' chapters for their responses to the others.

The primary challenge is responding to the first question, "What is ideology?" In his book on ideology, Andrew Heywood (2003) explains that "the word ideology was coined during the French Revolution by Antoine Destutt de Tracy (1754–1836) and was first used in public in 1796. For de Tracy, *idéologie* referred to a new 'science of ideas,' literally an idea-ology" (p. 6). However, the original meaning of the term had little impact on later use. In fact, Heywood informs us that "[t]he first problem confronting any discussion of the nature of ideology is the fact that there is no settled or agreed definition of the term, only a collection of rival definitions" (p. 5). He lists various definitions that have been attributed to ideology and that have a direct impact on this book's use of the term. Heywood's list includes the ideas of the ruling class, the worldview of a particular social class or social group, and an officially sanctioned set of ideas used to legitimize a political system or regime (p. 6). Terry Eagleton (1991) also takes on the "tangled conceptual history of the notion of ideology" (p. xiii). Like Heywood, he emphasizes the conceptualization of ideology as legitimizing the power of a dominant social group or class. Eagleton quotes John B. Thompson when he explains that "[t]o study ideology is to study the ways in which meaning (or signification) serves to sustain relations of domination" (p. 5).

For our purposes, ideology refers to the framework of thought constructed and held by members of a society to justify or rationalize an existing social order. Dominant ideologies are typically reflected in both the symbols and cultural practices of the dominant culture that shape people's thinking such that they unconsciously accept the current way of doing things as "natural" and "normal." Although this definition conveys the position that various social classes, and not just the ruling class, hold and perpetuate particular ideologies, a key focus of this book is to identify and interrogate hegemonic ideologies that generally reflect dominant class values and interests and that are detrimentally imposed on subordinate classes in schools. In other words, the focus of this book is on ideological hegemony and its manifestations in various educational contexts. The aim of the book is to help educators perceive the influences of hegemonic ideologies in the teacher education literature more clearly. For example, the literature on teacher beliefs and attitudes tends to treat these matters as separate and unrelated to discriminatory hegemonic ideologies, such as white supremacist ideologies that mark nonwhite and poor student populations as "deficient." If one does not uncover the influence such hegemonic ideologies have on teachers' thinking, then teachers often "normalize" these racist and classist ideological orientations and treat them as "natural."

Hegemonic ideology was defined by Antonio Gramsci (1935/1971) as the power of the ideas of the ruling class to overpower and eradicate competing views and become, in effect, the commonsense view of the world. Furthermore, "Gramsci emphasized the degree to which ideology is embedded at every level in society, in its art and literature, in its education system and mass media, in its everyday language and culture" (Heywood, 2002, p. 8). He explained that it is precisely because of schools' and other institutions' success in perpetuating dominant ideologies and legitimizing the existing social order that dominant groups need not deliberately oppress people or alter their consciousness (although this can happen). Instead, given their pervasiveness, ruling cultural ideologies as perpetuated in schools are generally unseen, and if they are perceived they are deemed "natural." Thus, unconscious acceptance is perceived as legitimate and normal.

Eagleton (1991) lists five different strategies employed by dominant cultures to legitimize and render hegemonic ideologies "invisible":

1. Promoting beliefs and values congenial to the dominant culture
2. Naturalizing and universalizing such beliefs so as to render them self-evident and apparently inevitable
3. Denigrating ideas that might challenge the dominant culture
4. Excluding rival forms of thought, perhaps by some unspoken but systematic logic
5. Obscuring social reality in ways convenient to itself

It is precisely these strategies that render discriminatory hegemonic ideologies invisible and thus difficult to name and identify. Eagleton further explains that because hegemonic ideologies are perceived by members of a society as natural and self-evident, alternative ideas are not considered because they are perceived to be beyond the bounds of the thinkable. He maintains that dominant "[i]deologies exist because there are things which must at all costs not be thought, let alone spoken" (p. 58). Gramsci (1935/1971) also made the crucial transition from ideology as a system of beliefs to ideology as concrete lived social practices reflecting the unconscious lived social experience and the influences of societal institutions. This shift and focus on the lived and personal dimensions of ideology has been taken up more recently by Antonia Darder, Rodolfo Torres, and Marta Baltodano (2002).

IDEOLOGY AT THE PERSONAL LEVEL: WHY IS IT IMPORTANT FOR EDUCATORS TO STUDY AND BETTER UNDERSTAND IDEOLOGY?

Darder et al. (2002) discuss how seemingly invisible hegemonic ideologies and explanations of existing social hierarchies are internalized and manifested at the individual level. They explain how important it is to identify these unconsciously accepted social worldviews and to make them concrete for teachers so they can learn to consciously resist accepting ideologies that can potentially translate into discriminatory classroom practices. In their discussion of ideology, Darder et al. explain that in addition to understanding ideology as a societal level phenomenon,

> [Ideology must also] be understood as existing at the deep, embedded psychological structures of the personality. Ideology more often than not manifests itself in the

inner histories and experiences that give rise to questions of subjectivity as they are constructed by individual needs, drives, and passions, as well as the changing material conditions and social foundations of a society. (p. 13)

Darder et al. make a strong case for studying the ideological dimensions of educators' views and experiences. Although there is no research that definitively links teachers' ideological stances with particular instructional practices, many scholars suggest that a teacher's ideological orientation is often reflected in his or her beliefs and attitudes and in the way he or she interacts with, treats, and teaches students in the classroom (Bartolomé, 2004; Cochran-Smith, 2004; Nieto, 2003; Sleeter, 1994). Interestingly, while there is a plethora of writings that examine educators' beliefs and attitudes, there have been few systematic attempts to examine the political and ideological dimensions of these beliefs and attitudes and how these worldviews reflect particular ideological orientations. Indeed, in the literature teachers' beliefs and attitudes tend to be treated as apolitical, overly psychologized constructs that magically spring from the earth and "merely" reflect personality types, individual values, and personal predispositions that have little to do with the existing larger political, social, and economic order. In other words, we know little about whether or how teachers view and rationalize the existing social order in terms of race, ethnicity, socioeconomic status, gender, and so on, and whether or not their views influence how they treat and teach subordinated students. Moreover, it has not yet been acknowledged that teachers' conscious and unconscious beliefs and attitudes regarding the legitimacy of the greater social order and the resulting unequal power relations among various cultural groups at the school and classroom level are significant factors to take into account in order to improve the educational processes and outcomes of minority education.

Given this lack of research, critical educators such as Henry Giroux maintain that exposing and interrogating dominant ideologies is fundamental to any discussions of education, pedagogy, and teacher preparation. According to Giroux (1983), there is an urgent need for additional research that identifies teachers' ideologies and explores the possible harmful effects of uncritical and narrow ideological belief systems. Preservice and practicing teachers too often emerge from teacher education programs having unconsciously absorbed assimilationist, white supremacist, and deficit views of nonwhite and low-income students. This ideological stance often constitutes the foundation upon which future teacher education efforts are built. In teacher education programs, aspiring teachers are typically not required to reflect critically on their ideological orientations, and thus may bring with them unconsciously held racist and xenophobic views that have the potential to taint teacher-student teaching and learning. This reality is especially disturbing because, despite demographic shifts and dramatic increases in the number of students of color, the majority of teachers continue to be white females. Sherry Marx and Julie Pennington (2003) warn of the detrimental possibilities of unchecked racist ideologies in this teacher population:

> White, female, preservice teachers strongly influenced by and readily perpetuating white racism ... were not "hood-wearing Klan members or name-calling Archie Bunker figures." ... However, the ways in which they perpetuated racism were even more destructive that the hateful, virulent rants of a white supremacist. (pp. 101–102)

EXPOSING DOMINANT DISCRIMINATORY IDEOLOGIES: MERITOCRACY, WHITE SUPREMACY, AND DEFICIT VIEWS OF MINORITY STUDENTS

Teacher education research studies like Marx and Pennington's suggest that prospective teachers, regardless of their ethnic background, often uncritically and unconsciously tend to hold beliefs and attitudes about the existing social order that reflect dominant ideologies that are harmful to many students (Bloom, 1991; Davis, 1994; Gomez, 1994; Gonsalves, 1996; Haberman, 1991; Marx & Pennington, 2003; Sleeter, 1992, 1993, 1994). Key dominant ideologies include the belief that the existing social order is fair and just—a meritocracy—and that disadvantaged cultural groups are responsible for their own disadvantages. Educators and the general public tend to view nonwhite and poor students as cognitively, genetically, and/or culturally deficient (Valencia, 1997; Valencia & Solórzano, 1997). Furthermore, most educators believe that students from subordinated groups—both immigrant and domestic minorities—must assimilate into the dominant culture and be schooled solely in English.

THE IDEOLOGY OF MERITOCRACY

Meritocracy refers to a "form of society in which educational and social success is the outcome of ability and individual merit" (Jary & Jary, 1991, p. 303). John Farley (2000) elaborates on a key component of meritocracy ideology—the belief that blacks and Latinos are responsible for their own disadvantages. Farley writes that this belief "appears deeply rooted in an American ideology of individualism, a belief that each individual determines his or her own situation" (p. 66). Implicit in this ideology is the belief that the socioeconomic hierarchy resulting from this system is appropriate and fair and need not be questioned by educators. Educators operating according to this ideology generally believe that the socioeconomic hierarchy is based on merit, and that nonwhite and linguistic minority students who want to achieve simply need to learn English and adopt the mainstream culture. All we have to do is look at the situation of African

Americans and Native Americans to understand that proficiency in English in and of itself does not guarantee first-class citizenship: English has been rendered the dominant language by the forced loss of their native languages. Interestingly though, both prospective and experienced educators often resent having to take courses that challenge their meritocratic views of society (Gonsalves, 1996; also see Gonsalves chapter 1 and Elliott chapter 10 in this book). Even when teachers recognize that certain minority groups historically have been economically worse off than Whites, have academically underachieved, and have higher mortality rates than Whites, their explanations for such inequalities are usually underdeveloped or nonexistent (Bartolomé, 1998; King, 1991; also see Balderrama, chapter 2 of this book).

ASSIMILATION AND DEFICIT IDEOLOGIES: TWO DEEPLY EMBEDDED DOGMAS

Assimilationist ideology, as used here, is treated as synonymous with the Anglo conformity model, which refers to the belief that immigrants and subordinated indigenous groups should be taught to conform to the practices of the dominant Anglo-Saxon culture.

Despite the fact that the dominant culture tends to equate the assimilation experiences of nonwhite minorities with those of European White immigrants of the past, it is crucial to highlight the reality that the United States has indigenous groups and people of African origin who are essentially colonized subjects, and that this history of internal colonization is very much evident today. In particular, when we examine assimilation efforts related to domestic minority groups, such as Native Americans, Native Hawaiians, Mexican Americans in the Southwest, and descendents of enslaved Africans, we find that the sanctioned practice of cultural assimilation to achieve domestication and linguistic suppression has been the historical norm, rather than assimilation to achieve integration as has been the case for most white immigrant groups.

According to Ronald Schmidt (as cited in Wiley, 1999), the experience of linguistic minorities of color in the United States has been noticeably different from that of European immigrants in several respects:

- Nonwhite linguistic minorities were extended the benefits of public education more slowly and grudgingly than were European Americans, despite the fact that they too were taxed for this.
- When education was offered to nonwhite linguistic minorities, it was usually done in segregated and inferior schools.

- Nonwhite linguistic minority groups' cultures and languages were denigrated by public educators and others. In addition, these groups were denied the opportunity to maintain and perpetuate their cultural heritage through the public schools.
- Reflective of these visible forms of rejection and exclusion by the dominant group in the society, the education that was offered was exclusively assimilationist and functioned not to integrate the groups into the dominant culture, but to subordinate and socialize them for second-class citizenship.

It is important to reiterate that, even though educational and language policies aimed at European immigrants and nonwhite linguistic minority groups can also be described as assimilationist, in the case of nonwhites they involved a domestication rather than an integration dimension. However, despite this long history of assimilation to achieve subordination, many educators continue to negate this reality and cling to the ideological myth that assimilation is a desired goal in the education of minority students. In fact, when preservice educators are confronted with this well-documented history of subordination, they often violently rebel and blame minorities for their subordination and continue to insist that assimilation is a most desired goal of schooling (Gonsalves, 1996; King, 1991).

A second belief system related to an assimilationist orientation is the deficit ideology, also referred to in the literature as the social pathology model or the cultural deprivation model, which has the longest history of any educational perspective or "theory." Richard Valencia (1997), who has traced its evolution over three centuries, finds that the deficit model explains disproportionate academic problems among minority students as being due largely to pathologies or deficits in their sociocultural background (e.g., cognitive and linguistic deficiencies, low self-esteem, poor motivation). Barbara Flores (1993) documents the effect this deficit ideology has had on schools' past and current perceptions of Latino students. Her historical overview chronicles descriptions used to refer to Latino students over the last century, which range from mentally retarded, linguistically handicapped, culturally and linguistically deprived, and semilingual to the more current euphemism for Latino and other poor and minority students: the at-risk student. Valencia (1997) explains that deficit explanations continue to be the most prevalent in education:

> The most common understanding of school failure among low-income children of color and the one deeply embedded in the individual consciousness of teachers, scholars, and policy-makers "blames the victim." (p. 38)

Furthermore, by not unmasking deficit thinking for what it really is—hegemonic ideology—it continues to exist and mutate in teacher education classrooms because, even though multicultural education efforts attempt to "interrupt notions of deficit thinking, [they] are often 'contaminated by other forms of deficit thinking'" (Pearl, 1997, p. 215).

The combination of a meritocratic view of the social order combined with an assimilationist ideology and a deficit orientation proves to be an especially deadly one because it rationalizes disrespect for minority students' native languages and primary cultures, misteaching them English and about the dominant culture, and then blaming their academic difficulties on the students themselves. Unfortunately, teachers' lack of understanding of these hurtful ideologies often translates into their uncritically accepting the status quo as "natural" and refusing to question if, how, and when they subscribe to and replicate these ideologies. This lack of educator clarity can also lead them down a path to teaching that includes assimilation for subordination and unknowingly perpetuating deficit-based views of poor and nonwhite students. Educators who do not identify and interrogate their negative racist and classist ideological orientations may often unknowingly reproduce the existing social order (Bartolomé, 1998; Bloom, 1991). Even master methodologists with the best of intentions can unknowingly end up perverting and subverting their work because of unacknowledged and unexamined harmful ideologies, such as dysconscious racism (King, 1991) and other discriminatory tendencies—tendencies that in the end reproduce the very dominant oppressive ideologies that created the need for the latest teaching methodologies.

FORMAL AND EXPLICIT STUDY OF IDEOLOGY

It is important that educators formally study ideology and learn about the harmful manifestations various ideologies can have in the school context. Furthermore, they should be challenged to increase their ideological clarity so they can improve their own teaching, and thus increase their students' chances of having academic success. In earlier writing (Bartolomé, 2000), I describe ideological clarity as the process by which individuals struggle to identify and compare their own explanations for the existing socioeconomic and political hierarchy with those propagated by the dominant society. I argue that when teachers are forced to name and juxtapose ideologies, they can better understand if, when, and how their belief systems uncritically reflect those of the dominant society, and thus unknowingly serve to maintain the unequal and unacceptable conditions that so many students experience on a daily basis.

I further describe political clarity as a never ending process by which individuals achieve an ever-deepening consciousness of the sociopolitical and economic realities that shape their lives and their capacity to transform such material and symbolic conditions. It also refers to the process by which individuals come to understand the possible links between macro-level political, economic, and social variables and subordinated groups' academic performance in the micro-level classroom (Bartolomé, 1994). Given the dramatic changes in student demographics and diverse student needs, it behooves us as teacher educators to help our students increase their political and ideological clarity and teach them to resist racist and classist deficit views of their own students, and to prevent them from hiding behind these views to explain why their students do not respond to their instruction.

My own research on teachers suggests that many successful teachers hold counter-hegemonic ideological orientations that allow them to question unfair and discriminatory practices in schools. In one study on successful high school educators of linguistic minority and immigrant students, I found that the educators rejected discriminatory ideologies such as white supremacy, deficit views of minority students, and assimilation as a goal for their minority students (Bartolomé, 2004). Furthermore, because they also perceived their minority students as not operating on a level playing field, these educators emphasized their role as advocates and their responsibility to level the playing field for their students. These findings highlight the power that teachers and other educators possess and can potentially wield in their work to create more just and democratic schools. They also suggest that formal study of ideology should be an essential component of any teacher education course of study. By unmasking and critically studying dominant ideology and its manifestations in schools, preservice teachers can potentially begin to develop critical thinking similar to that articulated by the target educators in the study. It is only through the development of critical thinking skills, coupled with a necessary ethical posture, that teachers, as agents of change, can take revolutionary steps to improve their students' educational chances.

THE HOPE AND POWER OF HUMAN AGENCY

Critical educators such as Michael Apple, Antonia Darder, Henry Giroux, and Donaldo Macedo remind us that additional work needs to be done in order to better understand the multiple ways in which dominant ideologies are manifested in educational settings in order to be able to intervene on behalf of the students when these ideologies emerge in hurtful and discriminatory ways. In his seminal book *Ideology and Curricula,* Michael Apple (1990) argues for a more comprehensive understanding of how "institutions of cultural preservation and distribution like schools create and recreate forms of consciousness that enable social control to be maintained without the necessity of dominant groups having to resort to overt mechanisms of domination" (p. 3). Apple suggests that multiple dimensions of schooling be examined as part of the effort to understand how dominant ideologies are maintained in schools and that they include the school as an institution, the particular knowledge forms inculcated and valued in schools, and *the educator him or herself*.

Bessie Dendrinos (1992) highlights the complex and dynamic nature of ideology and contends that we must keep in mind the hopeful power of human agency in challenging and transforming discriminatory dominant ideologies. She reminds us that ideology is not a fixed and static entity and cautions against perceiving ideology as a "unified, shared concept shared by an entire society or subculture" (p. 78). Dendrinos maintains that it is important that educators grasp this complex and tension-filled view of ideology because it argues against simplistic claims that institutions such as schools are uncontested in their reproduction of dominant ideologies. While it is true that dominant ideologies in educational institutions include values about what constitutes legitimate authority, high status, appropriate behavior, and official knowledge, the successful imposition of dominant ideologies is not a given since different groups who subscribe to differing and sometimes contentious ideological beliefs come into contact in this sphere. As a result, while attempts are made to impose or resist ideologies in schools and in the greater society, new ideologies are also constantly being negotiated and reconstructed.

The reality that human beings possess tremendous agency to challenge and transform harmful ideologies cannot be underestimated, especially in the case of prospective teachers who work with students from subordinated cultural groups. If teachers learn to unmask and question hurtful dominant ideologies as they manifest in their classrooms, they can work on behalf of their students to transform their schools into more humane and democratic places. This hopeful yet realistic stance is the one taken by the authors of this book because, while they brilliantly examine the multiple ways that dominant ideologies are manifested in various educational contexts, they also identify counter-hegemonic interventions that can be made in schools to render them more democratic and just institutions.

INTRODUCTION TO BOOK CHAPTERS

I hope that I have thus far satisfactorily answered the questions, "What is ideology?" and "Why is it important to for educators to understand ideology and develop ideological clarity?" I now ask the readers to shift their focus to the last three questions listed at the beginning of this chapter: "What can educators do to develop greater ideological clarity?" "What are some of the challenges that teacher educators face in assisting their preservice teachers' development of ideological understanding?" and "What do ideologically clear teachers look like?" The eleven authors respond to these questions in the book's six sections:

1. White Supremacist Ideologies Challenged
2. The Invisible Pervasiveness of Dominant Ideologies
3. Hegemonic Ideologies in U.S. History Curricula
4. Promising Practices Based on Praxis
5. Gaining Greater Ideological Clarity
6. Ideologically Clear Teachers: Two Case Studies

The authors in section one present key strategies for helping preservice teachers to overcome their resistance to counter-hegemonic concepts in order to more clearly perceive and challenge hurtful dominant ideologies, such as white supremacy ideology. In section two, the authors discuss seemingly invisible and deeply entrenched ideologies deemed almost commonsensical by the dominant society that range from state-imposed definitions of literacy to deficit views of high school minority special education students. The need to prepare preservice educators to critically analyze state-sanctioned textbooks, such as those used to teach U.S. history, as one strategy to uncover hegemonic ideological content is presented in section three. The fourth section focuses on praxis as a key strategy to help educators develop critical reflection-action abilities to both name and challenge dominant ideologies, as well as their own acceptance of such beliefs and collusion with resulting discriminatory practices. The chapters in section five focus on current efforts to challenge white preservice educators to understand their cultural identities, especially in terms of white privilege and differential power relations among cultural groups. The various authors document their preservice teachers' developmental processes and their struggle to develop greater ideological clarity by both naming white supremacist ideologies and practices and identifying strategies for rendering their teaching more democratic and just. Finally, in section six, the authors answer the question, "What do ideologically clear teachers look like?" In their discussion of teachers—experienced African American female teachers and one relatively novice Chicano educator—the authors highlight the commonality between the teachers: a fine-tuned awareness of discrimination in the classroom and strategies for combating such injustice. A more detailed discussion of each section and its chapters follows.

SECTION ONE: WHITE SUPREMACIST IDEOLOGIES CHALLENGED

In this first section, Ricardo Gonsalves and Maria A. Balderrama urge educators to come bravely face-to-face with dominant ideologies, such as white supremacist views of the world, and to interrogate them seriously as one strategy for developing preservice teachers' understanding of the significance of ideology in education.

In "Hysterical Blindness and the Ideology of Denial: Preservice Teachers' Resistance to Multicultural Education," Gonsalves offers a psychoanalytic model for better understanding the phenomenon of white student resistance in courses such as multicultural education. His model helps educators understand more clearly why preservice teachers often unconsciously yet violently deny and resist counter-hegemonic explanations of the social order. He then brilliantly explains why resistance constitutes a necessary stage in any learner's learning process. As a way to help teacher educators understand this stage in their students' learning process more clearly, Gonsalves provides a four-stage model of political and social consciousness that allows for consideration of the path through which preservice teachers may acquire critical consciousness and begin to name and interrogate previously held racist and classist beliefs.

In "Shooting the Messenger: The Consequences of Practicing an Ideology of Social Justice," María Balderrama describes various resistant behaviors her white preservice teachers have exhibited in reaction to her course coverage of social justice and democratic principles. Balderrama eloquently describes her white graduate students' surprisingly bold attempts to subordinate her, a Chicana professor, and put her in "her place" in order to correct the "incorrect" and "inappropriate" social order created in the classroom that has her at the top of the classroom social hierarchy and in the role of expert professor. By challenging the instructor both directly and indirectly, the students work hard to delegitimize her authority and expertise and to revert the classroom's social order to one where they, as whites, once again reign supreme. Perhaps without being fully aware of their efforts, the students unwittingly collude to return the Chicana to her "rightful" subordinate place—a place that most Chicanos assume in the greater society, particularly in the Southwest. Balderrama categorizes and describes a typology of resistance that students have exhibited over the years in her courses.

SECTION TWO: THE INVISIBLE PERVASIVENESS OF DOMINANT IDEOLOGIES

In the book's second section, Felicity Crawford and Guadalupe López Bonilla capture the stubborn intransigence of dominant ideologies. Despite the fact that these studies were carried out in different countries, both researchers powerfully chronicle how the teachers' discourse "gives away" their ideological stances.

In "Underprepared 'Veteran' Special Education Teachers' Reliance on Racist and Classist Ideologies," Felicity Crawford describes the classroom practices and beliefs of four white U.S. high school special education teachers as they relate to their black and Latino students. Crawford's ethnographic study vividly captures how special education teachers, underprepared despite decades of classroom teaching experience, rely on dominant "commonsense" classist and racist explanations to account for their minority students' academic underachievement. It is interesting to note that, although the target teachers were not initially well prepared to work with special needs students, they did not make significant efforts during their twenty-plus years in the schools to increase their special education knowledge base and expertise. Crawford concludes that the teachers' inadequate initial special education training, their unexamined deficit views of minority students, and their lack of opportunities to develop reflective skills created a pedagogical context in which the teachers taught in an unplanned and unstructured manner, tended to rely on deficit classist and racist views to evaluate their students, and regularly used exclusionary language to "invite" their students to leave school.

Guadalupe López Bonilla, in "Teachers' D/discourses and Socially Situated Identities: Literacy Practices in a Mexican High School," describes a similar teacher tendency to unknowingly slide into dominant cultural ideologies. In her work with public school teachers at a Mexican international baccalaureate high school, López Bonilla probes the teachers' perspectives on literacy and their beliefs about teaching literacy skills in two content areas, history and literature. Using discourse analysis, López Bonilla discovers the teachers' acceptance of the dominant, nationalistic ideologies promulgated by the Mexican secretary of education and how they allow these state-sanctioned ideologies to override their knowledge of pedagogically sound practice.

SECTION THREE: HEGEMONIC IDEOLOGIES IN U.S. HISTORY CURRICULA

The third section presents Panayota Gounari's contribution, "Unlearning the Official History: Agency and Pedagogies of Possibility." In it, Gounari examines the U.S. history curriculum and instruction and points out the dangers in teaching American history in an ideologically uniform and canonical manner. She eloquently explains that hegemonic history, as it is taught in schools, becomes a powerful tool that regulates the way people live and provides paradigms for mimesis, rather than creating structures in which new social and cultural spaces emerge. The author recommends that curricular materials and teacher instructional approaches reflect what she calls a "conflictual consensus approach" that encourages students to consider various versions of history rather than parroting one official version.

SECTION FOUR: PROMISING PRACTICES BASED ON PRAXIS

The fourth section of the book consists of two chapters contributed by Karen Cadiero-Kaplan and Stephanie Cox Suárez. In "Critically Examining Beliefs, Orientations, Ideologies, and Practices Toward Literacy Instruction: A Process of Praxis," Cadiero-Kaplan shares her interview/dialogue protocol used to guide teachers as they reflect on and analyze their beliefs about biliteracy instruction and their actual practices. The potential of this heuristic is illustrated in Cadiero-Kaplan's description of one high school teacher's reflection process as she juxtaposed her beliefs regarding the optimal bilingual and biliteracy development of English language learners with her current monolingual English-only instructional practice.

Through a process of dialogue and authentic reflection, Cadiero-Kaplan demonstrates how teachers can become more aware of the congruencies and incongruencies between their articulated beliefs and their actual practices—practices often determined by school district and statewide mandates. She concludes with recommendations for increasing the coherence between teachers' beliefs and good intentions and their actual instructional practice.

In "Sharing the Wealth: Guiding All Students Into the Professional Discourse," Stephanie Cox Suárez describes how she, a college-level teacher educator, assumes the role of cultural mentor so as to guide her students, particularly her minority and working-class students, into the teaching profession. She integrates her personal history as a Mexican American from a working-class background and reflects on how her own journey—as one from the outside the mainstream—influences her work as a teacher educator. Cox Suárez describes the tension in her dual role as teacher as cultural mentor and teacher as gatekeeper, and chronicles her struggle to help students acquire the academic culture and discourses they need in order to "cross the border" into the profession.

SECTION FIVE: GAINING GREATER IDEOLOGICAL CLARITY

Section five of the book contains the work of three authors: Paula S. Martin, Nelda Barrón, and Paula Elliott. These authors describe the particular learning processes their predominantly white students undergo in multicultural education and antiracism courses that focus on white racial identity development.

In "'I'm White, Now What?' Setting a Context for Change in Teachers' Pedagogy," Paula S. Martin shares her research on a particular brand of antiracism education that highlights white racial identity and white privilege as core concepts for students to identify and critically examine. Martin demonstrates the success of this approach with suburban white teachers. She describes teachers' increased racial identity development and awareness of white privilege. In addition to demonstrating increased awareness, Martin's teachers articulate concrete plans for incorporating their new learning into their teaching.

Nelda L. Barrón describes her teacher training efforts in a small private college in "Reflections from Beneath the Veil: Mainstream Preservice Teachers (Dis)Covering Their Cultural Identities." Using ethnographic observation, interviews, and student journal data, Barrón describes key White students' development in her introductory course on identity and race. The goal of her research was not to determine the particular course's effectiveness in changing the preservice teachers' beliefs but to identify the deeply rooted ideology from which these participants approach learning about such concepts as identity, culture, race, and oppression.

Barrón offers encouraging findings since her students display ideological shifts that suggest that they have begun to perceive and question their own sense of white supremacy and the role it plays in their work with students of color. After reading this chapter, the reader will walk away not only with descriptions of successful preservice teacher case studies, but also with an understanding of the cultural and ideological elements required in teacher preparation course- and fieldwork.

Paula Elliott shares her similar work with White preservice teachers. In "Mapping the Terrain(s) of Ideology in New Urban Teachers' Professional Development Experiences," Elliot describes her teacher educator involvement in a pilot project initiated to support and sustain new teachers in urban schools. She describes her efforts to help teachers critically examine hegemonic ideologies by eliciting their questions, expectations, and beliefs about teaching and learning in urban and diverse schools; analyzing their questions and concerns for implicit hegemonic influences; and engaging the teachers in both pedagogical and ideological discussions in light of their questions and concerns. Elliott's preliminary findings suggest that "starting where the teachers are at" in order to discuss ideological matters is a promising teacher education strategy.

SECTION SIX: IDEOLOGICALLY CLEAR TEACHERS: TWO CASE STUDIES

The last section of the book chronicles teachers' developing understanding of the political and ideological dimensions of their work with working-class students of color. While it is clear that no one can ever achieve complete political and ideological clarity, it is through praxis that individuals enter a never-ending cyclical action-reflection process that is sure to increase their understanding of the political and ideological dimensions of education in general and minority education in particular.

In "Developing Ideological Clarity: One Teacher's Journey," Cristina Alfaro describes one young Chicano teacher's awakening and his growing realization of the influence racist and classist belief systems have on his teaching during his participation in a U.S.-Mexico international teacher education program. Alfaro powerfully captures the young teacher's growing understanding and his acceptance that definitions of education and culture must necessarily address unequal power relations and social hierarchies if one plans to work with marginalized student populations. Using interviews and journal data, Alfaro learned that the teacher was able to apply his experience with racism and discrimination in the United States to a Mexican sociocultural context. Although he had previously romanticized Mexican culture, his more comprehensive understanding of discriminatory ideologies and classroom practice allowed him to readily detect how classist and racist ideologies were manifested in Mexican classrooms. Alfaro describes the teacher as realistically hopeful in his desire to return to the United States and to incorporate more democratic and critical teaching practices into his culturally diverse classroom.

In the final chapter, "Politicized Mothering: Authentic Caring Among African American Women Teachers," Tamara Beauboeuf-Lafontant similarly addresses the political and ideological dimensions of culture and teaching. Beauboeuf-Lafontant describes experienced African American female teachers' understanding of the political nature of "caring" and discusses the difference between aesthetic and authentic caring. She maintains that a key characteristic of authentic caring is a teacher's understanding of minority group subordination, its effects on students of color—both psychologically and academically—and the serious commitment to undo the harmful effects of subordination via culturally and politically responsive education.

The authors in this volume attempt to address the ideological dimensions of educators' beliefs, attitudes, and thinking and their actual practices. Together the eleven chapters paint a complex portrait of the myriad of ways in which discriminatory hegemonic ideologies are manifested in teacher preparation programs and other educational contexts. More importantly, that authors capture and describe their counter-hegemonic efforts to create more democratic and socially just learning contexts for all students in general, but in particular for students from cultural groups that have historically been mistreated and mistaught in our schools.

The chapters that follow offer more detail in their descriptions and explanations of hegemonic ideologies and their varied manifestations in teacher education and other educational contexts. Taken together they elaborate on my response to the first three questions asked at the beginning of this chapter: "What is ideology?" "Is it important for educators to study ideology?" and "What are some of the challenges that teacher educators face in assisting their preservice teachers' development of ideological understanding?" Furthermore, they provide research that powerfully responds to the two questions presented earlier in this introduction: "What can educators do to develop a greater understanding of it?" and "What are characteristics of educators who have increased their understanding of ideology and what effects does it have on their teaching?" It is my hope that this book reflects Paulo Freire's (1985) contention that in order to transform education for subordinated students, educators must first clearly and courageously apprehend and see through the disorienting fog of ideology and unmask its oppressive elements. I also hope that the reader will come away clearer regarding the political and ideological nature of education that Paulo Freire (1985) so powerfully conveys:

> [S]eparating education from politics is not only artificial but dangerous. To think of education independent from the power that constitutes it, divorced from our concrete world where it is forged, leads us either to reducing it to a world of abstract values and ideals (which the pedagogue constitutes inside his consciousness without even understanding the conditioning that makes him think this way), or to converting it to a repertoire of behavioral techniques ... (p. 170)

REFERENCES

Apple, M. W. (1990). *Ideology and curriculum* (2nd ed.). New York: Routledge.
Bartolomé, L. I. (1994). Beyond the methods fetish: Toward a humanizing pedagogy. *Harvard Educational Review, 64*, 173–194.
Bartolomé, L. I. (1998). *The misteaching of academic discourses: The politics of language in the classroom.* Boulder, CO: Westview Press.
Bartolomé, L. I. (2000). Democratizing bilingualism: The role of critical teacher education. In Z. F. Beykont (Ed.), *Lifting every voice: Pedagogy and politics of bilingualism* (pp. 167–186). Cambridge, MA: Harvard Education Publishing Group.
Bartolomé, L. I. (2004). Critical Pedagogy and Teacher Education: Radicalizing Prospective Teachers. *Teacher Education Quarterly, 31*(2), winter.
Bloom, G. M. (1991). *The effects of speech style and skin color on bilingual teaching candidates' and bilingual teachers' attitudes toward Mexican American pupils.* Unpublished doctoral dissertation, Stanford University.
Cochran-Smith, M. (2004). *Walking the road: Race, diversity, and social justice in teacher education.* New York: Teachers College Press.
Darder, A., Torres, R., & Baltodano, M. (2002). Introduction. In A. Darder, R. Torres, & M. Baltodano (Eds.), *The critical pedagogy reader* (pp. 1–23). New York: Routledge Falmer.
Davis, K. A. (1994). Multicultural classrooms and cultural communities of teachers. *Teaching and Teacher Education, 11*, 553–563.

Dendrinos, B. (1991). *The EFL textbook and ideology.* Athens, Greece: N. C. Grivas.
Eagleton, T. (1991). *Ideology: An introduction.* London: Verso.
Farley, J. E. (2000). *Majority-minority relations* (4th ed.). Upper Saddle River, NJ: Prentice Hall.
Flores, B. M. (1993, April). *Interrogating the genesis of the deficit view of Latino children in the educational literature during the 20th century.* Paper presented at the annual meeting of the American Educational Research Association, Atlanta.
Freire, P. (1985). *The politics of education: Culture, power, and liberation.* New York: Bergin & Garvey.
Giroux, H. (1983). *Ideology, culture and the process of schooling.* London: Falmer.
Gomez, M. L. (1994). Teacher education reform and prospective teachers' perspectives on teaching "other people's children." *Teaching and Teacher Education, 10,* 319–334.
Gonsalves, R. (1996). *Resistance in the multicultural education classroom.* Unpublished manuscript, Harvard Graduate School of Education, Cambridge, MA.
Gramsci, A. (1971). *Selections from the prison notebooks* (Q. Hoare & G. Smith, Trans.). New York: International. (Original work published 1935).
Haberman, M. (1991). Can culture awareness be taught in teacher education programs? *Teacher Education, 4,* 25–31.
Halcón, J. J. (2001). Mainstream ideology and literacy instruction for Spanish-speaking children. In M. de la Luz Reyes & J. J. Halcón (Eds.), *The best for our children: Critical perspectives on literacy for Latino students* (pp. 65–77). New York: Teachers College Press.
Heywood, A. (2003). *Political ideologies: An introduction* (3rd ed.). New York: Palgrave Macmillan.
Jary, D., & Jary, J. (1991). *The Harper Collins dictionary of sociology.* New York: HarperPerennial.
King, J. E. (1991). Dysconscious racism: Ideology, identity, and the miseducation of teachers. *Journal of Negro Education, 60,* 133–157.
Macedo, D. and Freire, P. (forthcoming). *Ideology matters.* Rowman & Littlefield.
Marx, S., & Pennington, J. (2003). Pedagogies of critical race theory: Experimentations with white preservice teachers. *International Journal of Qualitative Studies in Education, 16,* 91–110.
Nieto, S. (2003). *What keeps teachers going.* New York: Teachers College Press.
Pearl, A. (1997). Cultural and accumulated environmental deficit models. In R. R. Valencia (Ed.), *The evolution of deficit thinking: Educational thought and practice* (pp. 211–241). Washington, DC: Falmer.
Sleeter, C. (1992). Restructuring schools for multicultural education. *Journal of Teacher Education, 43,* 141–148.
Sleeter, C. (1993). How white teachers construct race. In C. McCarthy & W. Crichlow (Eds.), *Race identity and representation in education* (pp. 157–171). New York: Routledge.
Sleeter, C. (1994). A multicultural educator views white racism. *Multicultural Education, 1*(39), 5–8.
Valencia, R. R. (Ed.). (1997). *The evolution of deficit thinking: Educational thought and practice.* Washington, DC: Falmer.
Valencia, R., & Solórzano, D. (1997). Contemporary deficit thinking. In R. R. Valencia (Ed.), *The evolution of deficit thinking: Educational thought and practice* (pp. 160–210). Washington, DC: Falmer.
Wiley, T. G. (1999). Comparative historical analysis of U.S. language policy and language planning: Extending the foundations. In T. Huebner & K. Davies (Eds.), *Sociopolitical perspectives on language policy and planning in the U.S.* (pp. 17–38). Philadelphia: Benjamins.

Section I. White Supremacist Ideologies Challenged

CHAPTER ONE

Hysterical Blindness AND THE Ideology OF Denial: Preservice Teachers' Resistance TO Multicultural Education

RICARDO E. GONSALVES

INTRODUCTION: PRESERVICE TEACHERS AND RESISTANCE TO MULTICULTURAL EDUCATION

Each year thousands of students enter teacher training programs to become the next generation of educators for our children, and each year these preservice teachers encounter new and, at times, radical information about how urban schooling undermines the academic potential of children of color. While many of these preservice teachers hold the possibility of instituting a positive change in the lives of children, others will replicate the institutional imperative that relegates "minority" children to a lifestyle of poverty and servitude. After two decades of implementing courses that attend to the learning styles and cultural resources of diverse communities, Multicultural Education (MCE) remains a volatile issue at the center of debate on educational policy and pedagogical approach (Greenman & Kimmel, 1995; Obidah, 2000). To intervene against the process of miseducation requires that teacher educators address the issue of resistance to instruction that focuses on ethnic, class, and linguistic diversity.

The discussion about resistance presented here refers to opposition to those forms of multicultural education that are defined as critical (McLaren, 1995), progressive, or as defined by Sleeter and Grant (1995) "Education That Is Multicultural and Social Reconstructionist." These approaches to MCE emphasize a concern for social justice and offer techniques that link critical knowledge with social activism. It is an approach that focuses on the historical and contemporary aspects of oppression, combined with a mandate to teach toward the empowerment of children of color. Teaching MCE from a critical perspective provides a context for integrating issues related to inequity such as race, class, gender, and sexual preference. The content of MCE courses is often controversial as it exposes the tacit or implicit contradictions in our society, directly challenging the beliefs of many pre-credential teachers. Progressive approaches to MCE make explicit the links between the history of oppressed minorities and the current state of schooling in America. Information about academic tracking, the misuse of intelligence tests, continued segregation, forced deportations, and many other topics reveal an underworld of American society of which most preservice teachers have never been aware.

Progressive approaches to MCE seek to train preservice teachers as advocates for the poor and dispossessed. Course materials that explore immigration, bilingual education, racism, and affirmative action illustrate the connections between schooling and institutionalized oppression. Some preservice teachers may find the experience of discussing these issues to be anxiety producing as they require dialogue about volatile political topics in the public domain of the classroom. There is risk involved when divulging one's opinions and examining deeply held personal beliefs. On more than one occasion I have heard preservice teachers attempt to diffuse potential conflict and respond defensively to the issue of racial bias in the classroom by saying, "I don't see children of color, I only see children."

A review of the literature in the field of multicultural education indicates that resistance to its concepts and content has become a focus of concern and continues to be a problem in providing instruction in this topic (Carson & Johnston, 2001; Wallace, 2000). The current discourse about what constitutes resistance to MCE relies on general terms; as in a bad attitude, opposition, or defiance. A more dynamic approach to the problem of resistance to instruction acknowledges student resistance as both a psychological defense of the individual ego and the ideological values of the dominant culture. In essence, the dual nature of resistance as a simultaneous defense of personal identity and dominant ideology has not been thoroughly considered.

I approach the problem of resistance to MCE by using the metaphor of hysterical blindness in describing how preservice teachers block out any contradictions to personally held beliefs and values. As in the phrase "I don't see children of color," there is much more that is not being seen because a great deal of emotional energy is invested in keeping troubling issues out of sight and out of mind. This form of defense represents a deeper ideology of denial that simultaneously represses public and individual awareness about the inequities in our educational systems. It is a resistance developed during early socialization and operates as a form of collusion between the individual and society, ensuring that the ideological imperative of dominant culture is well defended and replicated without distortion.

Hysterical blindness is a psychosomatic disorder in which an individual defends against a stressful situation by converting psychological distress into a physical disability, the loss of sight. The experience of a physical affliction deflects attention from the source of the trauma to the symptoms associated with immediate physical incapacity. This situation allows any awareness of the original stressor to be repressed. It also absolves the person from culpability in the situation as the individual is recast as a victim who is suffering from a disability. As used here hysterical blindness refers to a symbolic form of denial at the level of social-cognitive functioning. In this context hysterical blindness is a national affliction and a cultural norm. It operates as a defense against critical awareness of how educational inequality against others is intrinsic to maintaining individual privilege for some. In other words, the defense of hysterical blindness functions to repress knowledge that racial violence and social trauma are prerequisites to secure our personal comfort.

RESISTANCE TO MCE AND THE PUBLIC DISPLAY OF EMOTIONAL DISTRESS

In reviewing the literature on resistance to multicultural education, I found examples of how students were expressing strong emotional responses to information that was in contradiction to their understanding of how society functions. The authors consulted describe students' reactions as hostile, angry, feeling shame, feeling guilt, and being confused (please refer to Table 1). In a study that focused on the effectiveness of teaching techniques in multicultural education the students' journal entries revealed emotional responses such as feelings of "being attacked" and subsequently "turning off" to anything the instructor had to say (Ladson-Billings, 1991, p. 151). In reflecting on college students' reactions to subjects concerning racism and social structure, Beverly Daniel Tatum (1992) described students' self-reported responses of guilt, shame, anger, and despair as emotional obstacles that block the "cognitive understanding and mastery of the material" (Tatum, 1992, p. 1). In an essay on the teaching of antiracist pedagogy, Ahlquist (1991) inventoried students' beliefs and values during the first three weeks of a class and found examples of "mechanistic thinking" (Ahlquist, 1991, p. 160) that replicated negatively held beliefs about minorities in the context of "common knowledge." This mechanistic reflex relies on available cultural scripts (Wierzbicka, 1999) found in

TABLE 1. Emotional and behavioral examples of resistance

Author	Type of Course	Students Responses
Ahlquist (1991)	Multicultural Foundations	Expressed feelings of guilt, shame, fear, anger. Denial of existing social inequality.
King (1991)	Social Foundations	Hostility, anger, fear confusion, guilt, shame.
Ladson-Billings (1991)	Introduction to Teaching in a Multicultural Society	Reports of being attacked, feelings of guilt, hostility. "Turning off" to receiving negative information.
Tatum (1992)	Psychology of Racism	Absenteeism, withdrawal, denial, passivity, non-completion of assignments. Feelings of guilt and anger.
Solomon (1995)	Social Foundations	Anger, hostility. Reports that the literature and research was anti-white and based on faulty methodology.

the broader social sphere to explain why inequality and poverty continue to plague people of color and working-class Anglos. This form of thinking is a default to popular "wisdom" as an escape from critical thinking and emotional investment in the issues.

The new information provided in MCE courses carries with it the expectation that the loyalties and beliefs of the preservice teacher will be altered in favor of a more equitable approach to multicultural relations. However, sudden exposure to challenging views may create confusion regarding the preservice teacher's self-concept and can hinder progress toward comprehending the general ideal of tolerance that multicultural education hopes to fulfill (King, 1991). This behavior may occur when the previously held beliefs are rooted in the self-concept of the preservice teacher and the expected shift in perspective may initiate difficulty in adapting to new expectations of cultural competence as an educator. At times this exposure to new ideas occurs while the preservice teacher is still immersed in so-called "lay knowledge" typically characterized by preconceived notions about minorities. Some students enter into coursework without exposure to alternative views and have as a point of reference the reactionary and conservative perspective that is offered as the norm for our society.

Even so, it may be the challenges to previously held beliefs and a person's sense of self that spur the confusion some preservice teachers' experience, resulting in a defensive reaction to alternative explanations of how our society functions. For example, when discussing the rationale for bilingual education some students will rely on nativistic arguments that newcomers should assimilate and learn English. Some proclaim that the children of undocumented workers should not be educated with American taxpayers' dollars. This type of response shifts the discussion from the pedagogical benefits of bilingual education to the political sphere where immigrants are criminalized, and the taxpaying citizen becomes the victim. New information that is discordant with previously held beliefs may engender a defense against a perceived threat to the foundation and essence of an individual's worldview. The very act of questioning established norms may in itself be an emotionally disturbing process that triggers feelings of shame, disobedience, and guilt. However, this scenario raises questions about resistance as a response to an immediate event or as a symptom that masks deeper levels of conflict.

PSYCHOSOCIAL DEVELOPMENT AND RESISTANCE TO MCE

Recent discourse about resistance to MCE presents opposition by preservice teachers in very general terms without consistent definitions or descriptions that contextualize the conditions under which the opposition occurs. Resistance in these studies is treated as an *a priori* component of courses in MCE rather than a particular phenomenon viewed in relation to other influences such as the model of multicultural education being presented, specific topics being discussed, or the teaching characteristics of the instructor. In attempting to understand resistance, it is helpful to consult the literature in psychodynamic theory that defines the phenomenon in terms of a defense mechanism and provides insight as to how the process is manifested and expressed in various forms. Briefly, resistance is defined as a "conscious or unconscious psychological defense against bringing repressed (unconscious) thoughts to light" (Werner, 1984, p. 119).

As to how this defense operates against psychological distress and disequilibrium, Paolino (1981) indicates that resistance may be an unconscious belief that there is no alternative to one's current situation, and all that therapy or any intervention (such as MCE) will accomplish is to deprive individuals of any security provided by their current psychological state. While that emotional state may be problematic and dysfunctional, it is at least a secure reference point to a known social and psychological context. It is important to note that during therapy, resistance is a sign that the patient is making progress. In other words, when a topic is found to be emotionally challenging, a client's resistance to further exploration indicates that the issue is close to the source of the patient's distress.

Resistance as a defense is illustrated in the literature of human development as an integral part of the transformation process occurring when a new stage of development is initiated. Borrowing from constructive-developmental theorist Robert Kegan, the individual operates in a state of equilibrium and balance that eventually deteriorates when change, as an adaptive response, is a requisite to restore well-being (Kegan, 1982). This dynamic occurs when new sociocultural expectations render a previous stage no longer functional and a structural transformation with regard to how we operate in and with the world must take place.

Possibly preservice teachers resist multicultural education because of a need to defend dominant social values that are experienced on a personal level and are integral to the sense of self. Again the work of Kegan illustrates how at a particular developmental stage the core issue is adapting to ideological imperatives. Specifically, to fully transform one's identity at a particular stage of adulthood the individual must choose "either the tacit ideological support of American institutional life, which is most supportive to the institutional evolution of white males, or the more explicit ideologies in support of a disenfranchised social class, gender or race" (Kegan, 1982, p. 102). As the very essence of previously held truths is shaken by the possibility of error and rival interpretations, cognitive dissonance emerges, and some preservice teachers may experience anxiety and emotional distress.

Resistance by the preservice teacher may indicate a necessary phase of conflict and resolution before a broader understanding of people of color can be appreciated and new possibilities of sociocultural relations can be considered. However, when assessing the stability of newly acquired levels of cultural awareness, Tatum (1992) indicates that resistance may run deep and prevent any long-lasting change as students may regress to earlier stages of racial bias. This situation creates a context where students may naturally defend against a threat to their values and block further consideration of the material.

DISSONANCE AND THE MORAL DILEMMA

Resistance to new information and the interrogation of personal beliefs may spark an ethical and moral dilemma in which the preservice teacher must reconcile competing values about education, equality, and privilege. The problem of contradiction between personal beliefs and ethical behavior has long been a focus of study in the area of human development (Kohlberg, 1976). The essence of a moral dilemma is that a person must make a choice and take action that supports one or another set of contradictory values and beliefs. However, much of the information used in decision-making to resolve such dilemmas relies on the individual's limited knowledge structure. In attempting to arrive at a correct decision, individuals realize that they cannot satisfy the requirements of both expectations, and as a result they are left with a sense of moral failure.

The difficulty in resolving a moral dilemma is central to the process of transforming one's beliefs and values about racial and ethnic minorities, a process that is also marked by stages of development. The substantive research by Janet Helms (1990) provides a six-stage model of White interethnic relations. Each stage illustrates a dramatic change in social consciousness regarding self-Other interaction. The stages are defined as Contact, Disintegration, Reintegration, Pseudo-Independence, Immersion/Emersion, and Autonomy. The Disintegration stage identifies the point at which preservice teachers may experience emotional conflict when they encounter information contrary to their beliefs. The Disintegration stage is described as an experience of conflict when acknowledging the meaning of being White. This awareness triggers a moral dilemma between the tacit assumptions about whiteness and the social consequences of privilege afforded to such an identity. As Helms describes it, "the Disintegration stage may be the first time in which the person comes to realize that the social skills and mores he or she has been taught to use in interacting with Blacks rarely works. Thus, the person in Disintegration may not only perceive for the first time that he or she is caught between two racial groups, but may also come to realize that his or her position amongst Whites depends on his or her ability to successfully 'split' her or his personality" (Helms, 1990, p. 58). As an illustration of the conflict experienced during the disintegration process Helms posits four components of a moral dilemma presented below:

The desire to be a religious or moral person versus the recognition that to be accepted by the dominant culture one must treat minorities immorally

The belief in freedom and democracy versus beliefs in racial inequality

The desire to show love and compassion versus the desire to keep minorities and immigrants in their place at all costs

The belief in treating others with dignity and respect versus the belief that minorities are not worthy of respect

The belief that each person should be treated according to his or her individual merits versus the belief that minorities should be evaluated as a group

This moral dilemma, also described as a state of conflicted consciousness (Helms, 1990), could apply to any individual being presented with new information about others who are culturally different. This scenario particularly applies when the preservice teacher is confronted by historical and contemporary examples of oppression with the explicit goal of intervening against injustice. Unlike courses on pedagogical theory, instruction on multicultural diversity in the classroom embodies an expectation that the preservice teacher will experience a change in beliefs about ethnic differences, which will in turn affect their behavior. This change should direct White people away from stereotypical assumptions about people of color and toward an understanding of how a child's language and ethnicity is a vehicle for achievement (Bartolomé, 1994).

Individuals must summon the courage to question their own beliefs and re-evaluate their assumptions about those who are different from them. This change in attitude requires careful introspection and a reassessment of one's own ethnicity and social position. However, contradictory information about one's previous beliefs about others' ethnicity could spur a negative reaction to the information and possibly to the messenger. As explained by Bracher (1999), "Self-knowledge can also threaten students' identity and thus courses and materials that produce or entail threatening self-knowledge are often resisted and defended against. Many students, for example, resist studying aspects of their own culture because the knowledge that such study provides will demonstrate that they do not really embody certain of their most cherished identity-bearing master signifiers" (p. 174). The defense against "threatening self-knowledge" also suggests a process where individuals' unconscious commitment to their ethnic or national identity operates as a system of beliefs and decision making rules for interethnic relations. It is a tacit belief system that is suddenly laid bare and submitted for inspection and critique in the context of MCE coursework.

HYSTERICAL BLINDNESS AND THE IDEOLOGY OF DENIAL

Some forms of resistance, such as denial, consist of blocking any awareness of reality in an attempt to evade the impact of traumatic recollections or current events. In the context of the MCE classroom, this defense may take the form of repeating commonly held racist beliefs as commonsensical or as a truth that "everybody knows," blaming minorities for their state of impoverishment or the criticizing the instructor for biased teaching practices (Solomon, 1995). For example, when conducting research on preservice teachers' approaches to instruction in multicultural education, I observed students who would offer the opinion that "This is just a bunch of liberal-Marxist propaganda. We just have to endure this PC bullshit until we get our credential." On one occasion when teaching at a local university, I was told that if I was so concerned about the poor, that perhaps I should "go back to Mexico" and teach there (I am an American of Portuguese ancestry). Other students assume a defensive position and offered comments such as "No one cares that White people have become a minority without rights in their own country." At times some preservice teachers may indicate that they already have attained a multicultural awareness and attempt to divert attention to issues of teaching techniques (Bartolomé, 1994), while others rely on religious or popular clichés about all children being equal.

Attempts to block out information that is contradictory to previously learned beliefs is akin to the defense of hysterical blindness in which the experience of psychic trauma is repressed and converted to an involuntary loss of sight. This defense is similar to the process of "psychic numbing" discussed by Robert Lifton (1968) as a condition where individuals are emotionally blocked and unresponsive to the trauma surrounding them. As a defense of social identity, hysterical blindness allows for the process of blaming the victim, maintaining stereotypes about people of color and Social Darwinist notions about the survival of the fittest. In essence, the formula for resolving ethical contradictions develops into "In case of moral dilemma—go blind." However, while hysterical blindness functions to repress forbidden knowledge at the unconscious level, this attempt at concealment is always fraught with the possibility of discovery. Borrowing from Lacan (1977), "The unconscious is that chapter of my history that is marked by a blank or occupied by a falsehood: it is the censored chapter. But the truth can be rediscovered; usually it is written down elsewhere" (p. 50).

Hysterical blindness in the service of dominant ideology is a very tenuous defense as everyday contradictions threaten to reveal a harsh view of historical and current atrocities that serve to sustain economic stability. To maintain denial at the level of social and individual awareness, the institutions of dominant culture must replicate an illusion (and delusion) of racial equality on a daily basis and to do so in a very personal way. As noted by Adler, human beings have a fundamental link to the social realm that is always available to awareness. However, "This does not mean that social feeling is constantly in our conscious thoughts; but it does require a certain amount of determination to deny it and set it aside" (Adler, A. 1998, pp. 139–140). Dominant culture engages in a relentless barrage of propaganda executed at every level of contact between the individual and the social structure to set aside historical evidence and the contemporary assault on humanity. In a sense, the process of denial established by the dominant culture is a form of psychological warfare upon the citizenry. The ultimate goal is to institutionalize hysterical blindness as an ideological norm and erase the possibility of critical thinking. A better understanding of how ideology guides social and psychological development would greatly assist in comprehending the preservice teachers' identification with the dominant culture and resistance to MCE.

SOCIALIZATION AND THE HEGEMONY OF EXPERIENCE

The socialization process is a means through which children acquire the language, norms, values, and beliefs of their culture. It is both a formal and informal process that guides our acquisition of particular roles and expected behaviors according to social standards. Successful socialization implies that we will share the same beliefs and values of the larger culture. This is precisely why national elites, federal, state, and local governments enforce compulsory education according to rigidly defined cultural standards. The internalization of external rules, values, and beliefs helps to ensure that individuals will not question or rebel against established authority. Much of what constitutes formal education is simultaneously a means of socializing children into the dominant culture and also a vehicle for delivering "corrective guidance" to those who cannot or do not conform to social norms. This dynamic, though, raises the question at what point is socialization a healthy adaptation to reality and at what point does it become coercive and contrary to the individual's best interest? As illustrated by Erik Erikson, "We must never stop inquiring by what inner mechanisms the young can be made to participate in acts of cowardly extermination. The answer is that they, too, are ... members of nations and classes which are denied the promise of a certain wholeness of national and economic identity, and thus they grasp at, or let themselves be grasped by, what one may call totalistic ideologies" (1964, p. 91). This insight in turn raises the question of the role of the teacher as an agent who can either reify an oppressive and harmful ideology or "de-ideologize" (Martin-Baro, 1994) and empower young children.

Focusing on how socialization allows for the internalization of prevailing values provides some insight about the source of distress exhibited by some preservice teachers. The literature about resistance to MCE suggests that preservice teachers come to the training experience perceiving the act of teaching as an uncritical replication of what and how they were taught (Artiles, 1997) and that many preservice teachers have limited exposure to people of color and experience in inner-city environments. In a study by Howey and Zimpher (1989), college faculty described preservice teachers as a homogeneous group of middle-class youths with little experience or contact with non-White populations and a restricted frame of reference on minority issues. The individual preservice teachers' sociocultural history, the level of diversity of the college attended, and the teaching-internship experience are forces that shape the core beliefs of preservice teachers, including expectations for the academic achievement of minority children.

Many preservice teachers unconsciously rely on commonly held beliefs as explanations for current social inequality and operate on the assumed truth of these ideas. The basis for these beliefs is preserved and advanced through prevailing interpretations of history, by stereotypes found in the mass media, or the myth of common knowledge about others (Aguilar & Pohan, 1996; Haymes, 1995; hooks, 1992). Discourse about cultural diversity in the United States is restricted to an unctuous spectacle of unconvincing concern usually derided as forced political correctness. This form of denial and distortion may well be the bedrock of American values. Philip Slater states that, "Escaping, evading, and avoiding are responses which lie at the base of much that is peculiarly American ... These responses also contribute to the appalling discrepancy between our material resources and our treatment of those who cannot care for themselves" (1970, p. 14). While resistance may be a cultural script at the social level, from a psychoanalytic perspective resistance can be viewed as a defense of an ego subsumed by dominant social norms (Alcorn, 2001; Bracher, 1999; Carson & Johnston, 2001).

This interpretation implies that resistance to MCE is predetermined by an ideological imperative that is internalized during early socialization. It is a form of hegemony via self-regulation that is imposed through the subtle process of child-rearing practices and training in self-censorship. Donaldo Macedo (2006) defines this condition as autocensorship, a process that is further elaborated by Noam Chomsky as "a form of indoctrination that works against independent thought in favor of obedience. Schools function as a mechanism of this socialization. The goal is to keep people from asking questions about important issues that directly affect them and others" (Chomsky, 2000, p. 24). Resistance to progressive ideals and critical thought is a fundamental building block of socialization. This realization in turn exposes the tremendous amount of energy needed to disavow and suppress information about how social inequality serves as the foundation for stability and economic success.

IDEOLOGY AND THE COLONIZATION OF CONSCIOUSNESS

As stated previously, hysterical blindness is a form of resistance inherent in the practices of dominant culture and the ideology in which we are socialized. The impact of prior socialization and the chronic problem of resistance indicate that brief exposure to MCE will do little to change people's attitudes and beliefs. The short-term exposure to counter-hegemonic ideas occurs in a nanosecond relative to a lifetime of immersion in reactionary norms and standards of behavior. The emotional and cognitive impact of such exposure is quickly dispersed as the social machinery of the dominant class resumes the work of colonizing individual consciousness according to the dictates of empire. That is, public consciousness, manufactured by social institutions and the media, supplants individual awareness and negates the possibility of spontaneous critical thought. To attempt any intervention against prior socialization requires an appreciation of how social and individual resistance is intertwined at the level of individual consciousness and precludes critical thinking. It is precisely the confluence of ideological imperatives with individual cognitive functioning and belief systems that comprises the dual nature of resistance.

The work of Althusser (2001) illustrates this process which he describes as interpellation, a means by which ideology, via its institutions, "hails" or calls out to individuals in a very personal way and recruits the individual into the ideological community of true believers (Althusser, 2001). Through this process, the subjective experience of expressing the dictates of ideology is accomplished by supplanting the individual's authentic emotions, reactions, and thoughts with the scripted responses provided by mass culture. The result is a seamless and mutual defense through which the individual experiences hysterical blindness in everyday life and allows ideology, as an abstraction, to be materialized in the flesh and enacted through our behavior. This link between ideology and individual action is elaborated by Massumi who notes that "society is a dissipative structure with its own determining tension between a limitative body without organs and a non-limitative one. Together, in their interaction, they are called a 'socius' (the abstract machine of society)" (Massumi, 1996, p. 75). This view also exemplifies the process through which resistance is secured via internalized beliefs and externalized activity carried out in the fulfillment of social roles.

Borrowing from the work of educator Joyce King (1991), and psychosocial theory I suggest that ideology operates at four levels of individual and social consciousness and at each level dominant culture is at work enculturating the individual with reactionary beliefs and values. Each level of public and private consciousness constitutes an arena in which individual action is negotiated according to the demands of society. Table 2 below illustrates the shared levels of consciousness that comprise a symbiotic dependence and interaction between the individual and the social structure. In terms of social and political awareness the individual has little opportunity to think beyond the parameters set by ideological imperative imposed by the state (Althusser, 2001; Fanon, 1963, King, 1991; Macedo, 1994; Marcuse, 1996).

In the social domain, the values of dominant culture operate across all forms of consciousness to maintain the social order. The dissemination of dominant values extends to the realm of personal subjectivity creating a false consciousness that exists in complicity with society (the superego) and enforces the rules of dominant culture through individual experience. This relationship could be considered as a social extension of a symbiotic ego. As noted by Koenigsberg, "Based on thirty-five years of research on the psychological sources of politics, I have found

TABLE 2. Shared levels of social and individual consciousness (Gonsalves, 2002)

Social	Individual
conscious	awareness and reaction to ideas
preconscious	emerging awareness of unconscious striving
dysconscious	uncritical habit of mind and behavior
unconscious	repressed fantasies/fears/desires/knowledge

that the fantasy of symbiosis or 'oneness' is a central motive compelling people to project their desires and lives into the political arena. People seek to 'identify' with nations, cultures and ideologies. They aspire toward a sense of omnipotence through the fantasy that it is possible to fuse their bodies and selves with a 'body' politic" (Koenigsberg, 2005). In a sociocultural nexus this reciprocity allows the individual to remain innocent and guilt-free as they are merely following orders according to the dictates of a supposed moral authority.

The process of symbiosis as discussed here consists of the individual's allegiance to ideology in return for being allowed to survive within the current social order. It is collusion with power for the sake of personal gratification. As a defense and denial of this collusion, hysterical blindness and what passes as naïve ignorance is actually the individual's repressed awareness of her or his cooperation with a racist and terrorist state apparatus. This mutual denial of oppression and exploitation is experienced as a delusion of oneness with the social order. The symbiotic compatibility between individual and social norms is accomplished through a relentless barrage of ideological and cultural directives. The creation and enforcement of this delusion is the main function of popular culture, including educational institutions that operate as a vehicle through which the practice of oppression is recast as normal behavior.

Dominant ideology, inescapable by its relentless imposition upon our consciousness, has established a means by which an authentic self is subverted and seduced into an allegiance with alien economic and cultural imperatives. In this scenario, our frame of reference is an ongoing event composed of seamless images and ideas broadcast by sources ranging from mass media, educational institutions, and parents. It is the rule of ideology manifest as a daily ritual of belief and action. As stated by Guy Debord in *The Society of the Spectacle*, "Understood in its totality, the spectacle is both the outcome and the goal of the dominant mode of production. It is not something *added* to the real world—not a decorative element, so to speak. On the contrary, it is the very heart of society's real unreality. In all its specific manifestations—news or propaganda, advertising, or the actual consumption of entertainment—the spectacle epitomizes the prevailing model of social life" (Debord, 1983, p. 3). During the process of lifelong socialization the individual experiences the rules of society as personally authored beliefs. As a result, individuals may feel that they have independently acquired these standards when in fact the beliefs and values are imposed upon them to maintain and reproduce the social order.

This reflection of the value system seeks to fragment social solidarity and isolate the individual in a state of insecure dependence on authority. Throughout our history reactionary forces have attempted to purge free-thinking and democratic beliefs from the American psyche, replacing any capacity of critical thought with an inventory of mindless responses supplied by pop culture and conservative pundits. However, at times repressed knowledge of collusion with an immoral state apparatus is exposed and sensations of guilt and shame emerge. In the context of preservice teacher training the MCE or antiracist courses the moral dilemma may create the possibility for a critical consciousness to emerge. It could be that an uneasy conscience is the first step toward critical awareness.

CRITICAL CONSCIOUSNESS AND TRANSFORMATIONAL RESISTANCE

To counter years of socialization and inherent resistance to progressive ideas requires a deeper and sustained effort to introduce an alternative worldview. I suggest that a preservice teacher must pass through the four levels of consciousness and resistance before developing a critical perspective. That is, thinking critically is part of a developmental process where the individual is introduced to alternative views of how society functions and to the relationship between social inequity and personal privilege (Fox & Prilleltensky, 1999; Freire, 1970). This process necessitates that the fears and desires repressed at the unconscious level must be named, confronted, and raised to the level of critical consciousness. To thoroughly address the problem of ideological resistance requires a comprehensive approach to undo the effects of previous socialization. However, to move beyond hysterical blindness requires a shock to the system to break out of complacency and develop the courage to interrogate previously held values and beliefs. To accomplish this transition requires a consistent effort by instructors to assist the individual in moving from a location of oppressor or oppressed and toward a position of egalitarian relations and empowerment.

The concept of critical consciousness, as developed by Paulo Freire, exemplifies this new state of awareness. Critical consciousness is a psychological state in which the individual has political clarity in understanding the social and political relations that drive oppression and the structure of their own life. It also implies that the individual has sufficient moral determination and passion to act on this understanding. That is, critical consciousness liberates altruistic motives, initiating hope and aspirations for a just world. This link between passion and knowledge is prerequisite for social change. The question is how to awaken that desire when any emotion that spurs critical thinking has been suppressed? Specifically, how can MCE instructors overcome a socialization process that is dedicated to maintaining a monocultural perspective? In Figure 1 below I illustrate the various stages of consciousness and how an MCE (or Anti-Racist) course is a crucial juncture in the process of transforming predetermined beliefs and values and contributes to overcoming resistance based on prior socialization.

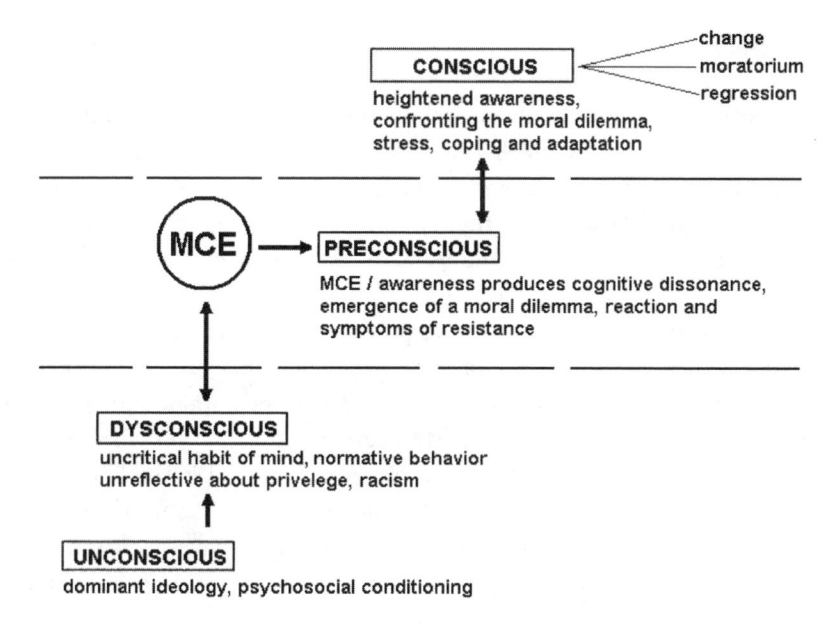

```
                    ┌───────────┐   ← change
                    │ CONSCIOUS │ ←── moratorium
                    └───────────┘   ← regression
                    heightened awareness,
                    confronting the moral dilemma,
                    stress, coping and adaptation
                              ↑
        ┌─────┐     ┌──────────────┐
        │ MCE │ ──→ │ PRECONSCIOUS │
        └─────┘     └──────────────┘
           ↑        MCE / awareness produces cognitive dissonance,
                    emergence of a moral dilemma, reaction and
                    symptoms of resistance
                              ↓
        ┌──────────────┐
        │ DYSCONSCIOUS │
        └──────────────┘
        uncritical habit of mind, normative behavior
        unreflective about privelege, racism
                ↑
        ┌─────────────┐
        │ UNCONSCIOUS │
        └─────────────┘
        dominant ideology, psychosocial conditioning
```

Figure 1. Stages of social consciousness and resistance (Gonsalves, 2002).

The path to developing critical consciousness requires that at each stage of consciousness a particular form of resistance is encountered and must be addressed. In this context, resistance by the preservice teacher may be a necessary phase of development en route to a deeper understanding of how oppression is implemented via educational practice. In Figure 1 above, the MCE course is a context in which dissonant information is a trigger for unconscious and dysconscious thoughts to emerge into a preconscious awareness that a moral dilemma is developing. This moral dilemma can be emotionally challenging and at times be very distressing. In other words, the experience of encountering information that is discordant with deeply held beliefs initiates a visceral and intuitive sense that repressed knowledge is about to be exposed. The preservice teacher must grapple with personal beliefs, the expectations of the instructor, experiences presented by minorities and evaluate the new information in relation to personal identity. Attempts to resolve the moral dilemma rests on three options: changing one's views, entering into a moratorium, or regressing to earlier ethnocentric and possibly racist beliefs. In the context of an emerging political awareness, consciousness, and resistance are interdependent forces that guide development. In the section below, I describe each of the levels of consciousness and how resistance operates at the level of individual experience. The two-way arrows at the preconscious and conscious stages indicate that, as new information is encountered, there is a re-visiting of the prior stage as a point of reference and comparison.

UNCONSCIOUS

At the unconscious stage the individual is immersed in dominant culture and is socialized according to the ideology of the dominant order. Examples of these ideals are a belief in meritocracy, individualism, the melting pot, and justice under the rule of law. Resistance to alternative views or revisionist history is based on enforced ignorance to maintain the standards of dominant culture. Resistance at this level is characterized as unconscious because the individual is not able to reflect upon his or her life in relation to power or to contemplate the process of domination and subjugation as applied to personal experience. The actual relations of power are unavailable for inspection or consideration, and this reality, in turn, perpetuates the myth of an irrefutable totality that presents dominant culture as a natural order. As pointed out by Franz Fanon (1963), "The collective unconscious is not dependent on cerebral heredity; it is the result of what I shall call the unreflected imposition of culture" (p. 191). Fanon makes it clear that what we hold in the unconscious is not just the memories of infancy and childhood, but also the disfigurement of an authentic human experience.

DYSCONSCIOUS

The term *dysconscious* is derived from the concept of Dysconscious Racism developed by educator Joyce King (1991). King defines Dysconsciousness as "an uncritical habit of mind (including perceptions, attitudes, assumptions, and beliefs) that justifies inequity and exploitation by accepting the existing order as a given." In her description of Dysconscious Racism, King emphatically points out that this condition is not an absence of consciousness but rather a form of *impaired* consciousness. For example, students who automatically refuse to critically examine the social construction of racism by relying on assumptions such as "humans have always been that way, it will never change," exhibit reliance on pat answers and unarticulated reasoning.

The concept of dysconsciousness is similar to that of mindlessness, defined by Ellen Langer as a form of thought characterized by "entrapment in old categories; by automatic behavior that precludes attending to new signals; and by action that operates from a single perspective" (Langer, 1997, p. 4). Dysconsciousness is the process of embracing the standards of dominant culture, thereby allowing impunity for our actions. At the dysconscious level, there is an aspect of collusion operating between the individual and society. This arrangement compels the individual to shun critical thinking and avoid reflection. It also indicates a very superficial "unawareness" that may actually be a semi-conscious defense, such as hysterical blindness, working against the threat of exposure to contradictions between ideological ideals and beliefs about equality and freedom.

PRECONSCIOUS

The concept of the *preconscious* refers to a form of consciousness that holds ideas, thoughts, or memories not currently active in conscious awareness. Preconscious thoughts are present but dormant and can be recalled by prompting from the environment. The preconscious can be thought of as a holding area for material from the unconscious or dysconscious before it is fully realized in consciousness. Emerging awareness is designated as a preconscious experience because there is a sensation, perhaps a precognition of conflict, as the individual begins to realize that a moral dilemma is developing and must be resolved. This sensation indicates that exposure to information in an MCE course is bringing forth the tacit and repressed knowledge about social inequity. At this point preservice teachers are expected to reflect on their personal behavior and make choices about what to believe, what commitments to make, or which loyalties to discard. The new information provides a clue as to the values and beliefs that are expected to be in accordance with the goals of MCE. It also implies a standard of professional competence that is made explicit through the materials provided in the MCE course and implicit as a criterion for a passing grade. The pressure to meet the new demands intensifies the conflict of choosing loyalties and making a commitment to new ideals.

CONSCIOUS

This designation indicates that the preservice teacher is fully cognizant of social inequality and the expectation that multicultural education is a vehicle to address these issues. However, to be conscious and aware of sexism and racism does not guarantee that the individual will change his or her views. At this stage of consciousness the preservice teacher has three options on how to address the moral dilemma: change, moratorium, or regression. I will hold the discussion about a change in consciousness for last, as that option holds the possibility for developing a critical consciousness.

The option of choosing a moratorium in making a commitment to MCE indicates that the preservice teacher cannot proceed beyond the current level of awareness and will not make any further progress at this time. For example, one student responded to a film about racism with the following comment: "I was moved by the pain and anger caused by racism … as a white male it was something I have never felt and I know I will never really understand. I came away from that film especially wanting to be part of the solution. I at least in a small way began to feel the pain of racism. But I came away a little bit confused about what to do." This stage may indicate the need for an extensive period of re-assessment and reflection upon the moral dilemma. It is likely that many preservice teachers may remain in this stage as it takes time to evaluate and absorb the impact of emotionally challenging information. As noted by one teacher-educator, students like to "tinker" with their new ideas and previous values before making any decision or commitment to new values. It is also unlikely that a preservice teacher will shift from dysconscious resistance to critical consciousness within the time span of one semester.

If the awareness gained through exposure to MCE is more than the preservice teacher can tolerate he or she may regress to a previous form of defense and resistance. In this scenario the preservice teacher may have exhibited resistance throughout the semester but at a level that obscured the depth of the preservice teacher's emotional conflict. As a result of previous exposure to MCE, regression to a prior defensive position may be accomplished with greater sophistication in the preservice teacher's ability to conceal racist views. As Alcorn (2001) illustrates, "students are expected to learn about race or class and, as a result, change their practices as subjects. But once again, this assumption that learning about something will change human practice ignores the defensive nature of subjectivity. Defensive subjects can 'learn about' many things, and yet this learning may have no effect on their practices other than strengthening their modes of defense against such knowledge" (p. 177). This statement indicates that the preservice teacher's attitudes are not exactly unchanged, but rather a deeper and more sophisticated resistance emerges to defend the preservice teacher's identity. For example, some preservice teachers will agree that inequality has always existed but adopt the point of view that it is simply a fact of human nature and therefore pointless to try and intervene. This shift in defensive posture implies that resistance is an ongoing and dynamic process that adjusts according to one's emotional investment in the issues.

CHANGE, CRITICAL CONSCIOUSNESS, AND TRANSFORMATIVE RESISTANCE

The category of change refers to a progressive modification of attitudes, values, beliefs, and opinions that occurs as a result of exposure to MCE. At this particular stage, the preservice teacher is capable of voicing criticism of the dominant culture and breaking the cycle of silence and hysterical blindness. After confronting and resolving the moral dilemma, the preservice teacher accepts the implications of this new level of understanding. If individuals achieve and maintain critical consciousness, they may find themselves in an ironic situation where they are now consciously resisting, at a personal and social level, an ideology that was previously defended and unconsciously acted upon. More precisely, as preservice teachers acquire a critical consciousness, there is also the development of a *transformative resistance* that counters hysterical blindness, allowing preservice teachers to acquire political clarity and sustain new opinions.

As a psychological defense, transformative resistance is a form of vigilance directed toward prior beliefs and values. It could be considered a state of metacognitive functioning as the individual experiences a heightened awareness of their relation to the community, the world, and to history. It is both a state of critical consciousness and a political act that helps individuals gain clarity about their relationship to the dominant culture. In this context, transformative resistance becomes a conscious experience that is linked to altruistic behavior as a form of struggle against oppression. This dynamic in turn fosters the development of social activism and *political resistance*, a healthy response to living under conditions of oppression.

The following text, an excerpt from a young woman's report on her experience in Europe during the 2004 presidential election, is provided as an illustration of the painful confrontation with one's inability to see the self in connection to politics. She was confronted by other young people who could not understand how Americans could re-elect George W. Bush. The result was introspection about her lack of awareness and a shift toward critical consciousness and transformational resistance.

> For the first time in my life, I realized I was a "sleeping" American. Experiencing an "awakening" as an American has not been a pretty process. I am appalled at much of what I am learning about our government, ashamed as to how our military treats prisoners, confused as to why we are even in a war and unsure as to how to live my life with all this new information. My first tendency is to want to run and escape from it—I want to move—relocate to a country that doesn't have these kinds of problems. Maybe a higher calling is to stay and help other sleeping Americans wake up. Maybe that is how change will happen. As an "awakened" American I see that I have a responsibility to know what is going on in our country and in the world and to act accordingly. I must say I feel like a novice in this area of my life and do not know yet know how to respond appropriately—but I am learning and I am willing to change.

The comments above indicate that this individual has experienced a profound transformation, one that is both painful and exhilarating. This person has moved from a state of unawareness to a desire for more information and a commitment to work for the greater good. It is the type of transformation that we hope to see in antiracist and MCE courses.

In discussing the psychological benefits of political awareness and activism, Sullivan (1990) states that "Resistance becomes an agent process when it fosters the

TABLE 3. Stages of resistance

Unconscious compliance	Socialization and internalization of reactionary ideals, values and standards. Resistance as an integral component of the self.
Dysconscious resistance	Automatic opposition to progressive ideas. Hysterical blindness operating in the domain of social interaction. Mindlessness.
Preconscious resistance	Emerging awareness of conflict and a moral dilemma. Vigilance and strengthening of resistance and defenses.
Transformative resistance	Resolution of the moral dilemma. Vigilance and awareness of prior reactionary beliefs and motivation to gain political clarity and maintain critical consciousness.

development of community and solidarity. When a personal world appears to be sustained by resistance, one can see that there is an authentic cultural project, which is not deviance, but a community of what one might say is a different order" (p. 139). Again, there is the process by which internal psychological resistance is expressed in real time as an act of political opposition. However, at this stage of awareness, there is an additional component of building an alternative community that creates a social support for those who consciously oppose the dominant culture.

The process of changing long held values and beliefs is marked by resisting new information at various levels of awareness. The table below illustrates the various stages of resistance as a developmental shift from unconscious motive and dysconscious behavior through a transformative phase ending in conscious political action.

Through the identification of the four stages of consciousness and types of resistance, teacher-educators may be able to assess the opposition to course content and tailor activities to utilize resistance as a point of dialogue and discovery. This activity would allow for exploration of the issues with sensitivity and respect for the respective preservice teacher's frame of reference. It is important to reiterate that frequently resistance is a precursor to change. It is a process that can become the focus of attention and be used as a vehicle for exploring an individual's relationship to a multicultural world.

CONCLUSION AND RECOMMENDATIONS: THE CURRICULUM AS CONTESTED SPACE

The complex process of challenging prior socialization illustrates why a one-semester course is not sufficient to have a long-term impact on beliefs and values. To counter prior socialization and the cult of mass culture requires that teacher-educators implement a comprehensive approach to untangle the intricate ties that bind individual identity to the dominant social order. Such a process would provide multiple points of exposure to alternative views combined with social support to assist the preservice teacher in traversing the four levels of consciousness. To more effectively address the problem of resistance, I would suggest an approach that consists of

1. a prerequisite course on the psychology of racism
2. a critical MCE course with attention to resistance as a psychological defense
3. a challenge to schools of education to change the training curriculum and fulfill the ideal of providing MCE across the teacher training program, i.e., in literacy and reading instruction courses.

A course on the psychology of racism, prior to instruction about MCE, is necessary to allow full consideration of how socialization and racism affect the psychology of individuals from all ethnic groups and how they can impact children in urban schools. This type of class would assist preservice teachers in understanding their own social history and political identity in comparison to the impact of racism and inequality upon children of color. It would be an opportunity to "work through" these conflicts before engaging the study of MCE as theory and technique. Such a course would provide a comprehensive understanding of the relationship between the demands of the social structure and the formation of individual identity. There are many examples of antiracist courses available on Internet sites such as the Radical Psychology Network and the Society for the Psychological Study of Social Issues that could assist in developing a confluence of methods.

Teaching a critical MCE course with a focus on resistance is an approach that recognizes the problem of reactionary opposition as a mutual ideological defense of the person and the social order. This approach would consist of drawing from the fields of critical pedagogy and critical psychology to address issues of social justice and personal transformation (Martin-Baro, 1994; Sullivan, 1990). Instructors could also become familiar with psychodynamic techniques of group relations and employ these tools during the process of instruction (Jay, 1987; Robertson, 2000). This training should include methods that assist the instructor in identifying issues of resistance and transference combined with techniques to utilize resistance as a pivotal juncture in the learning experience (Davis, 1987; Keeley, 1995). Although not identified as a utilizing psychodynamic technique, the work of Gay and Kirkland illustrate how the instructors use varied modalities to maintain preservice teachers' engagement with the process of critical thinking. "In addition to actually exhibiting multicultural self-reflection and critical consciousness in our teaching behaviors, we use ... related techniques to help our students understand what is going on. During teaching episodes we routinely stop the substantive discussion and shift attention to debriefing the process that has just occurred. Initially, we assume responsibility for telling students what just happened, using conceptual, analytical, and interpretative descriptions, as well as pointing out textual and functional shifts in the discourse" (Gay & Kirkland, 2003).

There should also be a post-course MCE support system consisting of mentors and organizational contacts to assist preservice teachers in implementing MCE in the classroom. This involvement would model the ideal of community building and allow the preservice teacher to create a personal network of allies. A community connection would provide a means of emotional sustenance that many progressive preservice teachers feel is lacking after they leave the halls of the academy. As pointed out by other researchers (Guillaume, Zuniga-Hill, & Yee, 1995), once they are assigned to a classroom, many preservice teachers do not implement multicultural education. This raises the possibility that with only one semester of exposure to MCE, they remain immersed in, or are just barely emerging from, the belief structure of the dominant culture, and that resistance in the institutional environment blocks their progress.

Regarding teaching MCE across the curriculum, this last point is exactly what MCE advocates say should be done in the schools, but it is not applied to the teacher-training programs (Gonsalves, 2002; Wallace, 2000). That is, in the literature on multicultural education, the phrase "writing across the curriculum" is frequently used to describe the process of including an MCE perspective in all subjects at the elementary and secondary school levels. However, in schools that train future educators this standard does not always apply. In many teacher-training programs, MCE is a special course and the issues of cultural diversity are not integrated into other courses on pedagogy.

This dynamic raises the issue of why only one or two courses that cover ethnicity, language, and class diversity are implemented as part of the teacher training program. Indeed, to have a special course that is dedicated to diversity is to marginalize the topic from the rest of the curriculum, condemning it to irrelevance. In a sense, there is a stigma of uselessness attributed to courses of MCE and this attitude reinforces the process of hysterical blindness. Stigmatizing the topic creates a situation where a course on MCE is designed to fail, and this failure reinforces the notion that such knowledge is irrelevant to the "real world." It also illustrates how the overall curriculum of professional training is an arena for the displacement of critical views. The curriculum of graduate schools of psychology and education exist as a contested space where the affliction of hysterical blindness is spread through the institution as a defense against progressive change (Mio & Awakuni, 2001; Sue et al., 1998; Wallace, 2000). If the function of graduate training is to replicate the pathology of denial and resistance, than it should be the priority of progressive academics to provide the antidote of critical consciousness at every opportunity.

REFERENCES

Ahlquist, R. (1991). Position and imposition: Power relations in a multicultural foundations class. *Journal of Negro Education, 60*(2), 158–168.

Alcorn, M. (2001). Ideological death and grief in the classroom: Mourning as a prerequisite to learning. *Journal for the Psychoanalysis of Culture and Society, 6*(2), 174.

Aguilar, T. E., & Pohan, C. A. (1996). Using a Constructivist approach to preservice teachers' thinking about diversity in education. In F. Rios (Ed.) *Teacher thinking in cultural contexts.* (pp. 260–281). Albany, N.Y. SUNY.

Alfred, A. (1927). *Understanding human nature* (C. Bret, Trans.). Century City, MN: Hazedlen Foundation.

Althusser, L. (2001). *Lenin and philosophy and other essays.* New York: Monthly Review Press.

Artiles, A. J. (1995). Learning to teach in multicultural contexts: exploring preservice teachers knowledge change [Part 2]. Paper presented at the annual meeting of the Council for Exceptional Children, Indianapolis, IN.

Bartolomé, L. I. (1994). Beyond the methods fetish: Toward a humanizing pedagogy. *Harvard Educational Review, 64,* 173–194.

Bartolomé, L. I. (1998). *The Misteaching of academic discourses: The Politics of language in the classroom.* Boulder, CO: Westview Press.

Bracher, M. (1999). Psychoanalysis and education. *Journal for the Psychoanalysis of Culture and Society, 4*(2), 177.

Carson, T., & Johnston, I. (2001). Cultural difference and teacher identity formation: The need for a pedagogy of compassion. *Journal for the Psychoanalysis of Culture and Society, 6*(2), 259–264.

Chomsky, N. (2000). *Chomsky on miseducation.* D. Macedo (Ed.). Lanham, MD: Rowman and Littlefield.

Cross, W. E., Jr. (1991). *Shades of black: Diversity in African-American identity.* Philadelphia: Temple University Press.

Davis, R. C. (1987). Pedagogy, Lacan, and the Freudian subject. *College English, 49*(7), 749–755.

Debord, G. (1983). *The society of the spectacle.* Detroit: Black and Red Publishers.

Erikson, E. (1964). *Insight and responsibility: Lectures on the ethical implications of psychoanalytic insight.* New York: W. W. Norton & Co.

Fanon, F. (1963). *The Wretched of the Earth.* New York: Grove Press.

Fox, D., & Prilleltensky, I. (1999). *Critical psychology: An introduction.* Thousand Oaks: Sage.

Freire, P. (1970). *Pedagogy of the oppressed.* New York: Continuum/Seabury Press.

Gay, G., & Kirkland, K. (2003, summer). Developing cultural critical consciousness and self-reflection in preservice teacher education. *Theory Into Practice.* The Ohio State University. http://www.findarticles.com/p/articles/mi_m0NQM/is_3_42/ai_108442644.

Gonsalves, R. E. (1998). *Resistance to instruction on multicultural education: A pilot study of instructors' experiences at five California State universities.* Unpublished qualifying paper. Harvard Graduate School of Education.

Gonsalves, R. E. (2002). *A qualitative study of pre-credential teachers' responses to instruction in multicultural education.* Unpublished dissertation. Harvard Graduate School of Education.

Grant, C. A. (1994). Challenging the myths. *Multicultural Education*. v2 n2 p4-9 Win.
Greenman, N. P., & Kimmel, E. B. (1995). The road to multicultural education: Potholes of resistance. *Journal of Teacher Education, 46*(5), 26–41.
Guillaume, A. M., Zuniga-Hill, C., & Yee, I. (1995). Prospective teachers' use of diversity issues in a case study analysis. *Journal of Research and Development in Education, 28*(2), 69–78.
Harris, A., Carney, C., & Fine, M. (2001). Counter work: Introduction to "Under the covers: Theorizing the politics of counter stories." *The International Journal of Critical Psychology,* (4), 14–37.
Haymes, S. N. (1995). White culture and the politics of racial difference: Implications for Multiculturalism. In C. Sleeter & P. McLaren (Eds.), *Multicultural education, critical pedagogy and the politics of difference*. Albany: State University of New York Press.
Helms, J. E. (1990). *Black and white racial identity: Theory, research and practice*. Westport, CT: Greenwood Press.
hooks, b. (1992). *Black looks: Race and representation*. Boston: South End Press.
Howey, K. R., & Zimpher, N. L. (1989). *Profiles of preservice teacher education: Inquiry into the nature of programs*. Buffalo: State University of New York Press.
Jay, G. S. (1987). The subject of pedagogy: Lessons in psychoanalysis and politics. *College English, 49*(7), 785–800.
Keeley, S. M. (1995). Coping with student resistance to critical thinking: What the psychotherapy literature can tell us. *College Teaching, 43*(4), 140–145.
Kegan, Robert (1982). The evolving self: Problem and process in human development. Cambridge, MA. Harvard University Press.
King, J. E. (1991). Dysconscious racism: Ideology, identity, and the miseducation of teachers. *Journal of Negro Education, 60*(2), 133–146.
Koenigsberg, R. (2005). *Making conscious the unconscious in social reality: The psychoanalytic interpretation of culture*. Retrieved May 30, 2005, from http://home.earthlink.net/~libraryofsocialscience/making_conscious.htm.
Kohlberg, L. (1969). Stage and sequence: the cognitive developmental approach to socialization. In D. Goslin (Ed.), *Handbook of socialization: Theory and research*. New York: Rand McNally.
Lacan, J. (1977). *Écrits: A selection* (A. Sheridan, Trans). New York: W. W. Norton.
Ladson-Billings, G. (1991). Beyond multicultural illiteracy. *Journal of Negro Education, 60*(2) 147–157.
Langer, E. J. (1997). *The power of mindful learning*. Cambridge, MA: Perseus Books.
Lifton, R. J. (1968). *Death in life: The survivors of Hiroshima*. London: Weidenfeld and Nicolson.
Macedo, D. (2006). *Literacies of power: What Americans are not allowed to know*. Boulder, CO: Westview.
Mahler, M., Pine, F., & Bergman, A. (1975). *The psychological birth of the human infant: From symbiosis to individuation*. New York: Basic Books.
Marcuse, H. (1966) Eros and civilization: A philosophical investigation into Freud. Boston, Beacon Press
Martín-Baró, I. (1994). *Writings for a liberation psychology*. Cambridge: Harvard University Press.
Massumi, B. (1992). *A user's guide to capitalism and schizophrenia: Deviations from Deleuze and Guattari*. Cambridge, MA: MIT Press.
McLaren, P. (1995). White terror and oppositional agency. In T. Goldberg (Ed.), *Multiculturalism: A critical reader*. Cambridge, MA: Blackwell.
Mio, J., & Awakuni, G. I. (2000). *Resistance to multiculturalism: Issues and interventions*. Philadelphia: Bruner Mazel.

Nieto, S. (1996). *Affirming diversity: The sociopolitical context of multicultural education* (2nd ed.). White Plains, NY: Longman.
Obidah, J. (2000). Mediating boundaries of race, class and professional authority as a critical multiculturalist. *Teachers College Record, 102*(6), 1035–1060.
Paolino, T. R., Jr. (1981). *Psychoanalytic psychotherapy: Theory, technique, therapeutic relationship and treatability*. New York: Brunner/Mazel.
Radical Psychology Network. (n.d.). *Teaching materials syllabi—Readings*. Retrieved from http://www.radpsynet.org/teaching/index.html.
Robertson, D. L. (2000). Enriching the scholarship of teaching: Determining appropriate cross-professional applications among teaching, counseling, and psychotherapy. *Innovative Higher Education, 25*(2), 111–125.
Slater, P. (1970). *The pursuit of loneliness*. Boston: Beacon.
Sleeter, C. E. (1992). *Keepers of the dream: A study of staff development and multicultural education*. Washington, DC: Falmer.
Sleeter, C. E., & Grant, C. A. (1987). An analysis of multicultural education in the United States. *Harvard Educational Review, 57*(4), 421–444.
Sleeter, C. E., & Grant, C. A. (1995). *Making choices for multicultural education. Five approaches to race, class, and gender* (2nd. ed.). New York: Merrill Publishing Co.
The Society for the Psychological Study of Social Issues (n.d.). Teaching Materials Development Program 2002. Retrieved from http://www.spssi.org/teach.html.
Solomon, P. R. (1995). Why teach from a multicultural and anti-racist perspective in Canada? *Race Gender & Class, 2*(3), 49–66.
Sue, D. W., Carter, R. T., Casas, J. M., Fouad, N. A., Ivet, A. E., Jensen, M., LaFromboise, T., Manese, J. E., Ponterroto, J. G., & Vasquez-Nutall, E. (1998). *Multicultural counseling competencies: Individual and organizational development*. Thousand Oaks, CA: Sage.
Sullivan, E. V. (1990). *Critical psychology and pedagogy: Interpretation of the personal world*. Toronto: The Ontario Institute for Studies in Education.
Tatum, B. (1992). Talking about race, learning about racism: The application of racial identity development theory in the classroom. *Harvard Educational Review, 62*(1), 1–24.
Wallace, B. (2000, December). A call for change in multicultural training at graduate schools of education: Educating to end oppression and for social justice. *Teachers College Record,* (6), 1086–1111.
Werner, A. (Ed.). (1984). *The American psychiatric association's psychiatric glossary*. Washington, DC: American Psychiatric Press.
Wierzbicka, A. (1999). *Emotions across languages and cultures: Diversity and universals*. New York: Cambridge University Press:

CHAPTER TWO

Shooting the Messenger: The Consequences of Practicing an Ideology of Social Justice

MARÍA V. BALDERRAMA

Well the oppressors are trying
To get me down

—JIMMY CLIFF, "THE HARDER THEY COME"

INTRODUCTION

The quote above by the reggae singer Jimmy Cliff aptly captures the essence of this chapter: that the process of oppression often includes the attempts of dominant culture persons to discredit those individuals whom they see as not fitting into the status quo. Furthermore, as Cliff later sings, oppression does not end with merely discrediting the individual, but also by "them trying to get me down, trying to drive me under the ground;" that is, by permanently silencing the individual. The metaphors of oppression described in Cliff's reggae song "The Harder They Come" are useful in discussing students' resistance to their Chicana professor's attempts to link teacher education coursework to social justice concepts and issues.[1]

The research presented in this chapter documents the manifestation of student oppositional behaviors in courses in which I expose students to an ideology of social justice. I identify types of student resistance that is reflected in their attempts to "shoot the messenger" and discredit me, the professor. I use the metaphor of "shooting the messenger" to capture the consequences that professors from subordinated cultural groups often face when they challenge the ideological beliefs of their dominant culture students.

MY POSITION AS A CHICANA SOCIAL JUSTICE EDUCATOR

I teach in southern California in the largest county in the United States, which also has the dubious distinction of having the lowest college attendance rate in the state. People of Mexican origin or Chicanos have been inhabitants of this county, and California, for hundreds of years (Acuña, 1998; Barrera, 1979). Mexicans are active participants in all facets of life, yet they have been given few opportunities to have a legitimate presence in political arenas. Los Angeles, after Mexico City, is the second city in the world with the largest Mexican population. However, only recently, and after 130 years has this city elected a mayor of Mexican ancestry, Antonio Villaraigosa. This is a vivid example of how the political power of the Mexican community has been historically limited and relegated to a lower status.

Historical academic underachievement tends to be one indicator of the consequences of the social policies mediating this disempowerment. Academic underachievement is normative for Chicano youths with high school dropout rates hovering at approximately 50% to 60% in California. Thus, few Chicanos/ Chicanas are given opportunities to acquire higher education degrees, and Chicana/Chicano college professors in California remain few in number.

An informal poll of approximately 150 students in the teacher education courses I teach revealed that approximately 90% of these students had never been taught by a bilingual Chicana in all of their schooling experiences. I was the first "educated Mexicana" most of my students had faced. My students, similarly to my colleagues, lack experiences in seeing Mexicans (particularly women—Chicanas) in positions of power and authority.

In 1994, the California Commission for Teacher Credentialing legislated a curriculum that required prospective K-12 teachers to take courses that addressed diversity explicitly and directly in teacher preparation courses. That is, before 1999 students were required to take *a course* (typically a multicultural education course) that examined cultural issues and their connections to schooling, teaching, and learning. Although students were required to fulfill a multicultural requirement, many remained resistant to enrolling in such a course. It was not uncommon to hear students question the "relevance and importance of culture" in teaching and learning and to demand "more important courses that teach methods—like how to do math or enforce discipline." Frequently, prospective teachers state they do not need a class on culture and argue, "I need a class to learn how to handle *those* kids."

The majority of the students enrolled in my multicultural education courses have been prospective secondary school teachers. Data about student background collected from these approximately 150 students revealed the profile of the typical student in these classes as male and White. On average, they were between 30 and 45 years old and pursued teaching as a second career.[2] Many of these students were economically displaced and had lost their jobs because nearby large military bases had closed down during the Bill Clinton presidency or to corporate "downsizing." Some students confessed that they had been disillusioned by their inability to get rich with their degree in business, and teaching seemed to be a viable alternative with their earned bachelor of arts degree. Frequently, students mentioned that their mothers were teachers and entered the credential program upon their family's advice. Approximately 95% were monolingual English speakers with some indicating they spoke a "little Spanish." Most grew up in semi-rural conservative communities, were born-again Christians, and were part of the lower middle class but aspired to middle-class status.[3]

CULTURAL ENCOUNTERS AND DENIAL OF ASYMMETRICAL POWER RACE RELATIONS

I generally carry out introductions on the first day of class, which includes asking the students to situate themselves culturally and politically. I typically request that students identify their ethnicity or culture, and most of my White students indicate not having ethnicity or culture. "I'm an American," or "I have no clue where my family is from," or "European mutt" are common ways White students introduce themselves. Culture tends to be perceived as belonging to "other people" because students perceive culture or ethnicity to be held by non-White "others," such as Blacks, Native Americans, Asians, and Chicanos, and other Latinos, for example. It was not uncommon to hear White students express seeing culture as existing apart and external from them.

A denial-discourse concerning cultural realities (including cultural background, ethnicity, color, or phenotype) is part of the resistance that students quickly infuse into the classroom discussion. While many students complain about having to take the course, their discourse of denial frequently initiates explicit acts of resistance toward me, the professor, as well as other students—in other words, those "messengers" who actively seek to identify and name inequality in academia and schooling.

The predictability of some White students' challenges and resistance to my teaching led me to categorize types of student resistant behaviors. Throughout the years, I have discovered that these resistance manifestations, while at first appearing to be random incidents, become part of a consistent and systematic form of behavior. The four manifestations of student resistance that emerged from my observations include the following:

1) resistance at first sight
2) role reversal: the arrogance of resistance
3) culture as superficial knowledge
4) challenging the Professor's grading system

All of these manifestations have the goal of discrediting the professor, or in the words of Jimmy Cliff, making the professor look like a clown and trying to shoot her down. In categorizing these manifestations of resistance, I note that within my teaching context "not all resistance is created equal." In other words, resistance varies from cohort to cohort and from class to class. The degree of intensity of White students' resistance is highly dependent on the blend or composition of the class, their level of politicization, and the nature of the specific topic, including the use of "shock" terms (i.e., racism, oppression, social justice) used in class. For example, when resistant students make up the majority of the enrollment in the class, they find support and ideological comfort in their numbers and express their resistance more overtly by frequently suggesting bias on the part of the professor while also questioning the relevance of controversial political topics to the class. These dynamics create a situation where resistant students feel safe expressing anger and disgust. When the class composition is more balanced by the presence of a significant number of non-resistant students, there is a tendency for more extended and open discussions to take place whereby students make genuine efforts to contemplate different perspectives. In these more ideologically balanced contexts, it is not uncommon to hear the resistant student say "I'm not gonna say anything anymore in this class, as I see no one wants to hear my point of view."

RESISTANCE AT FIRST SIGHT: CHALLENGING THE PROFESSOR'S POSITION OF AUTHORITY

Resistance at first sight characterizes the behavior of many students when they realize that their professor is not White. In the beginning of the semester, I always put my name on the board and introduce myself by pronouncing my name with the proper Mexican Spanish accent, including rolling the "rr"s in my last name. I am a petite woman with olive skin and have been socialized by my alma maters, Wellesley College (undergraduate degree) and Stanford University (M.A. and doctorate), to assume appropriate classroom and teaching behaviors, such as speaking clearly, standing in front of the class, and making eye contact with my audience. Given that most students (certainly by the time they are in graduate school) have been socialized to recognize and accept these teacher/student behaviors as appropriate, makes it even more outrageous when they attempt to ignore my role and legitimate authority. I vividly recall on one occasion entering the classroom and walking toward the front of the room to occupy the traditional designated teacher space. As I approached the head of the class, the informal chatter turned to silence, until one student asked with disbelief in his voice. "Are *you* the teacher?" I responded with a proud yes, and he immediately laughed.[4] On another occasion, students ignored me until I called the class to order. They kept talking over and around me until I resorted to a management strategy used by many elementary teachers—I turned the classroom lights off. Turning on and off the lights in the room forces students to be quiet and give you their attention, as they are stunned by the lights going on and off.

Seeing a Chicana occupy the role of authority in a university classroom seems hard for many dominant culture students to accept. Their experiences with segregated schooling and housing, as well as the stereotyping of Chicanas/Chicanos by the mass media have provided ample characterization and personal experience regarding who is where in the societal socioeconomic ladder. Furthermore, it is clearly evident that, at least for my students, a Chicana does not have the right to be a university professor! Students have been effectively socialized to know and to expect that in university contexts, positions of power are held by White males, and with some exceptions, White females. Thus, their subsequent behavior, characterized by anger and resistance, is consistent with what many White students have been socialized to accept as part of their White privilege and social position.

In examining literature of student resistance, Shor's (1992) work discusses how he, too, experienced resistance upon entering the classroom. He was surprised and taken aback by his students' resistance, but after talking with his students, he found their resistance was valid. The school was forcing the students to take a standardized placement test which the group found unfair and meaningless. Shor described his success in turning this unfair testing practice into an act of student empowerment, where he ultimately bonded with his class. Upon reading this account, I judged his context of resistance to be totally different from mine for several reasons. First, Shor's experience with resistance was due to unfair institutional practices; second, his legitimacy to occupy the teacher space was not an issue in his context of resistance.

In my context, my students appear to experience "status anxiety" (Kincheloe, Slattery, & Steinberg, 2000) because my mere presence reestablishes and redefines status orders which do not match many of the students' ideological expectations.

For example, recently, several master's degree students complained to my department chair about my Stanford degree, telling her they did not like me telling them ("bragging" is the word they used) that I had attended Stanford. They failed to tell my department chair that my studies at Stanford were mentioned within the context of teaching them about the groupwork model (Complex Instruction) developed by my mentor Elizabeth Cohen at Stanford University. I was merely citing the source for this strategy and my direct involvement with the development of this specific groupwork model. I found it interesting that my chair also questioned the necessity of informing my students that I was a Stanford graduate. Her line of questioning, and the fact that she took the time to talk with me about this matter and make it an issue, is a clear example of status anxiety operating at various levels within academia.

Shor does not report that his students asked in disbelief if he was the professor or complained about having an Ivy League educated professor. These were not relevant issues in his profile of student resistance. The student resistance he experienced was more procedural than ideological. His physical characteristics (gender and race) are associated with privilege and authority. University professors are expected to be male and White, not female and Brown.

As Kincheloe et al. (2000) explain,

> Hispanic women and Latinas, of course, face special forms of crypto racism encodement, as literature and the media depict them as powerless and sometimes pathological. As subjugated, subservient, loyal daughters, wives and mothers ... often portrayed as unresistant to their positions as sex objects and be frilled consorts with a culturally backward proclivity to excessive praying. (p. 376)

The following story by a colleague from sociology places the "status anxiety" issue in context of my teaching situation.

> I would walk my granddaughter around my middle class neighborhood and would frequently be approached by white neighbors about how much I charged for child care. The more frequently I walked her, the more frequently I was approached and asked about my nanny services. It got to where I didn't want to walk my granddaughter anymore! (Conversation with E. E. Valdez, 1998)

The "nanny story" above captures the ideological base grounded in White privilege, which many White prospective teachers bring to the classroom, provides concrete examples of status anxiety and in understanding White students' resistance. In their eyes, Chicanas are expected by many to be "nannies" not "profesoras." This special form of "crypto racism encodement" automatically places Chicanas as subordinates within the Southwest's social pyramid of economic power. Within the context of the university classroom, the Chicana professor is not viewed as a legitimate intellectual source of knowledge, but instead a type of "clown" or a fool employed to entertain students and not to be taken seriously. This dynamic in turn has consequences for the message being voiced, making it vulnerable and susceptible to questioning.

Not being viewed as a legitimate source of knowledge has direct consequences on the professor's ability to teach anyone because the teacher is part of the curriculum. Teachers cannot deny that the teacher's mere presence (gender, race, class, language, phenotype, culture) is an integral part of the teaching and learning context. Simply being present as a specific identity undoubtedly colors or de-colors, politicizes or de-politicizes, educates or miseducates, clarifies or mystifies schooling and educational practices. My students in this context were candidly cruel when they realized they were to be taught by a member of a group whom they have been taught to view and **treat** as subordinate.

I believe this is why progressive White male and female educators are more palatable and experience less resistance from students during discussions of social justice in comparison to scholars who are themselves members of historically subordinated groups. As one of my White male counterparts suggests, "I am white and male, and because of that I can afford the privilege to be wrong when I teach. But you're brown and female, you aren't given *any* privileges."

Resistance, within this context, is a political act with issues of power and White privilege at its core. Resistance is also resilient and, if necessary, can adapt quickly to maintain power and privilege, even with what appear to be innocuous questions. Attempts to make me look like a clown continued but this time by reclaiming and renaming my position of power by attempts to redefine my earned "messenger" title.

"Any questions?" I remember asking students after welcoming them to class.

"I have a question," said a male student from the back of the room. I poised myself for a challenging question. "What are you? I mean, what do you want to be called?" he disingenuously asked.

In all of my experiences in undergraduate and graduate school I had never experienced any of my professors being asked this question, "what they wanted to be called." At that moment in time, I was not clear as to what he was asking, but intuitively I knew there was more to his query than met the eye. I knew from my studies in sociology and anthropology that formal and informal titles are symbolically important in all societies.

"What do *I* want to be called?" I felt awkward and defensive. "What are other **professors** called? You can call me as you call my colleagues. Professor is fine," I remember answering. This "simple" name/title calling question constitutes another example of resistant White students' attempts to make me look like a clown—an attempt that would unfortunately repeat itself throughout the semester.

An informal conversation with several female African American and Chicana professors confirmed my experiences with and observations of student resistance in my classroom.[5] In our talk, we shared our observation that our male (White and color) colleagues are frequently referred to as Dr. or Professor, while women are usually called by their first name. Titles before the name of women of color tend to produce status anxiety because significant social rankings and public displays of power take place based on names. Eliminating my title effectively equalizes any hierarchy which disprivileges them as White students. In other words, eliminating my title "cuts me down to size" and realigns social roles by placing me in a subordinate role and raising them to their "rightful" superordinate position. This behavior is another indication of how localized classroom political acts operate within a broader social context. I accepted the implicit challenge and took it further by asking several of my White male and White female counterparts if they were asked what they wanted to be called. My colleagues seemed surprised by my question and indicated that they had never been asked this question and responded, "It's always assumed 'Professor' or 'Doctor,'" they responded.

Feminist research tends to indicate that "students often respect male professors more than they do females" (Jackter & Flemming, cited in Maher et al., 1994, p. 155). Chicana feminist Aida Hurtado suggests,

> Gender alone does not determine whether a woman holds a super ordinate or subordinate position in society. Rather "socially constructed markers" determine placement and relative power. (cited in Goldberger et al., 1994, p. 189)

This chapter extends feminist theories presented by Stephanie Jackter and Leslie Flemming, on the one hand, and Hurtado on the other, by suggesting that social markers such as gender and ethnicity be named explicitly and be included as an integral part of the social context (including political and sociohistorical factors). Tip O'Neil's famous line that "all politics is local" captures my point. That is, the local politics and the political power occupied by groups (American Indian, Chicano/Chicanas, Latinos, Asians, African Americans, for example) determine the degree of legitimacy accorded members from such groups. In some contexts, African American women may be seen as occupying a higher status than Chicanas, or Asians may have more credibility than Black female scholars. Many of the students have been effectively socialized to internalize the psychology of White privilege, and their behavior has an internal logic which grounds their ideological base and motivates their resistance at first sight. To deny these social status variables (gender, phenotype, ethnicity, last name, cultural background, bilingualism) operating, only limits our understanding of the variations in models of resistance.

ROLE REVERSAL: THE ARROGANCE OF RESISTANCE

Role reversal as an overt act of resistance is another example of the salient behavioral manifestations of an internalized ideology reflective of the dominant social order. In this manifestation of resistance, White students attempt to usurp and assume the position of professor or "expert" in the classroom as a way of correcting the faulty social order in the classroom and reasserting White superiority. For example, resistant students frequently demand being the voice of authority in the classroom about "culture and schooling," a topic that they have previously admitted to knowing very little about.

Examples of this role reversal are a way for White students to reclaim their perceived loss of White privilege at the hands of their non-White professor. Students' efforts to reclaim their rightful white superiority frequently revolve around the course syllabus. I continue to find that students' sense of loss of privilege is a clear and strong indicator of the levels of student resistance in my courses. Resistant White students frequently question the structure of the curriculum, the relevance of the readings, the choice of the readings (including voices of the non-White authors), and the assignments. Many times the students' arrogance of resistance is obvious when they ask if they can alter the reading list and customize it, for example, by incorporating an ethnic story they read as high school students. The syllabus represents the professor's expertise of the subject area so it should not be surprising that when students attempt to impose their supposed "expertise," the course outline becomes a symbolic struggle for power and authority in the classroom.

Other points of contention include student resistance to state-required field observations. It is not uncommon to hear students state that, since they are not planning to teach in a diverse school, they should not have to carry out their observation in a diverse school setting. I have informally noted that many of the students who resist carrying out public school visits also say they plan to teach in a private, religious school. These students, one might recall, initially reveal in their student background questionnaires that they have limited theoretical and practical knowledge about the topics related to culture, ethnicity, teaching, and academic achievement. Nevertheless and without fail, it is precisely these students who resist learning about issues related to historically subordinated youths, particularly those of Mexican origin. Furthermore, they insist on challenging my expertise, "taking over" the course, and "making me look like a clown." Their attacks on my competency range from minutiae such as noting that the pages on the syllabus are not numbered at the center (as they prefer) to "telling me" to put copies of selected texts on reserve (this has already been done and is indicated on the syllabus). Furthermore, they also "tell me" how to organize classroom activities (also addressed specifically in my syllabus). Admittedly, this role reversal deals with the more technical aspects of the course, yet it remains a power struggle nonetheless, particularly when observable patterns persist and are examined in relationship to other classroom interactions.

CULTURE AS SUPERFICIAL KNOWLEDGE

A unique challenge in multicultural education courses is imparting knowledge to students who come in with only a small foundation to build upon and who resist learning new concepts that present multicultural education for social justice and, in the process, challenge the status quo. Many students can accept the culture-school connection if it is embedded in the single-group model, which includes addressing culture by focusing on one group at a time and frequently only once per year (Sleeter & Grant, 1999).[6] That is, many students are willing to accept the notion that all that is needed to equalize achievement is to sprinkle cultural activities such as a Mexican Mariachi or tacos in the curriculum. Integration of culture in the curriculum in this superficial manner is palatable and safe, when it is "celebrated" once per year, minimizing the role, presence, historical contributions and existing subordination of many cultural groups, including women. This approach also provides an "out" as these one-day, once per year festivals allow teachers to meet the requirement of integrating culture in their curriculum. Indeed, this approach is far from the model of social justice that I discuss in class. As mentioned above, the multicultural model I propose is closer to the social transformation model in Sleeter and Grant's (1999) typology. In this approach schooling inequalities are examined within a broader social context, and these discussions are followed by developing plans for strategic actions to change those processes that perpetuate academic failure of historically subordinated students. This multicultural model challenges resistant students' ideological dimensions of culture and is another aspect of the social justice curriculum I implement in this course.

The students' preference for a more superficial and uncritical cultural orientation is consistent with their conservative/reactionary ideological base because the single relations model lends itself to de-politicizing the classroom as a sociocultural arena. The single-relations model allows for "Taco Tuesday," which attempts to infuse culture through often meaningless isolated, prepackaged, one-shot-deal activities. More importantly though, the teacher is let off the hook about developing a deep understanding of the role of culture (particularly of the dominant culture) and its causal relationship to academic achievement and ultimately life chances. This is why many of my White students actively and overtly reject the ideological perspective that insists upon a model of educational transformation that includes examining schooling, classrooms, and teaching within a political and sociohistorical context dominated by a hegemonic ideology, resulting in unequal distribution of educational attainment, wealth, and power. Predictably, discussions and group activities that critically examine disproportionate academic failure by Chicanas/Chicanos is the turning point for resistance to begin to ooze out of the classroom, spill into the offices of administrators, and end up in overt and intentional attempts to "shoot the messenger."

It is my commitment to help students see how ideology distorts reality by keeping privilege hidden, but this initiative bothers many White students in my classroom. If I were to approach multicultural education as a bag of teaching tricks that would allow these students to exoticize the other, perhaps they would feel more comfortable receiving instruction from a Chicana professor. The level of resistance and discomfort students experience in these classes is clearly related to the message of social justice, the degree to which counter-hegemonic processes are named and articulated in class, and my unapologetic stance as their professor—the superordinate authority in charge of the course.

Figure 1 below shows levels of resistance along a continuum of social justice issues. The greater the focus on class, race, gender, and language, the more resistance the students exhibit in class. The more the curriculum and discourse are sanitized by emphasizing methods and techniques, the less the resistance. The more the discussions make students accountable about the work they must undertake to be humanistic, democratic, bilingual, and multicultural educators, the greater their resistance. The less the discussions make them accountable by focusing on external issues such as individual student issues, self-esteem, standards, and cultural holidays, the less the resistance exhibited by students.

The theoretical framework that informs my teaching and discussion of social justice is grounded in critical theory and the sociology of education. My discussions with students include how I view and treat them as thinkers, problems solvers, doers, and intellectuals—not technicians (Giroux, 1988)—examining the "big picture" of schooling while examining and focusing on how the dominant culture prevails and oppresses youths from subordinated groups. Readings and activities are framed by examining the school and classroom as social systems oiled by differential status relations (if untreated). I challenge them to think about their work, while infusing state-of-the-art knowledge, pedagogy, and practice that provide teachers with the skills to democratize classrooms by including all the children present.

My field notes reveal that the days when we discuss "shock concepts" such as critical pedagogy, ideology, status relations in the classroom and society, are those days when students articulate the most resistance and verbalize their frustration. Tying schools and classrooms to the wider social structures and order and explaining that schools often mirror society's inequalities unless teachers make

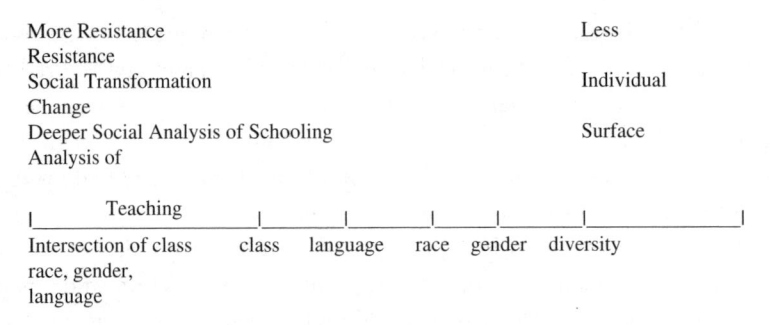

```
More Resistance                              Less
Resistance
Social Transformation                        Individual
Change
Deeper Social Analysis of Schooling          Surface
Analysis of

         Teaching
|_____|_____|_____|_____|_____|_____|
Intersection of class    class   language  race  gender   diversity
race, gender,
language
```

Figure 1. Continuum of resistance.

conscious efforts to intervene, proves very difficult for many students to grasp or even consider since they tend to see teaching taking place in a vacuum and as an activity that is neutral and apolitical.

The strength of resistant students' ideologies sustains an extensive array of explanations justifying their myopic understanding of the world around them. For example, a frequent comment articulated by students is that the school they attended was fair and they never witnessed unfair social hierarchies in their classroom. In addition, personal stories that deny social stratification and schooling inequality are common. These stories tend to be embedded in beliefs about living in a meritorcratic social system that rewards an individual's hard work regardless of race, language, gender, or cultural or socioeconomic background. Their resistance is partially due to their unconscious belief that their unacknowledged privileged social position has provided them with all of the acceptable and correct explanations. Classic student resistant behavior includes insisting that teaching is a politically and ideologically neutral activity and that classrooms are, and should be, isolated from the politics of the school, district, state, country, and the world. One student who admitted her ideological base had been shattered commented to me privately: "Your class has rocked my boat. I will never see schools the same again. I thought we were going to get a list of cultural how-to's when I took this class. Instead I have learned to always see schools connected to everything else, even politics!"

CHALLENGING THE PROFESSOR'S GRADING SYSTEM

Grades are also a major symbol of power and authority in schools, and this is where, as suggested earlier, students want to discredit my ability to evaluate their work. I have learned when to expect anger, confrontation, and outright challenge about my ability to assess my students' work. These events generally take place after returning the first written assignment or after a quiz or examination when some students do not get "perfect" scores. Many of the students' arrogance of resistance about their knowledge of the topic—culture and schooling—is manifested by a preconceived notion about the "easiness" of the course.

One student, a prospective English teacher, when asked to rewrite a section of a paper that was incomprehensible, scheduled an appointment with the Chair of my department and initiated her discussion by inquiring about my credentials, why I had been hired, who had hired me, and basically questioning my ability to evaluate her. "I am an English teacher, have excellent writing skills, grew up speaking English and after all, she's bilingual, isn't she?" she shouted, pointing to me. My department Chair could not believe the arrogance and racism of this student. She quickly interrupted the student's accusations, came to my defense, and reminded this student of her student status. Again, I remind my reader of my preparation at two of the most prestigious institutions in the country, Wellesley College and Stanford University. This crystallizes this student's racism as her outrageous allegations are unfounded and merely that—racist. The midterm tends to mark the time when resistant students have reached high levels of anger, status anxiety, and their ideological discomfort forces them to tap into the university mechanisms as the one sure way to "shoot the messenger." Because White students know that institutions have historically been responsive to their needs, they turn to institutional level mechanisms to obtain support for their ideological stance and maintenance of their position of privilege.

Repeatedly, resistant students seek support by going around the professor and outside the classroom for ideological support by using "grading" as a symbol for resistance. As the final grading period approaches, resistant students fear a loss of power if the minority professor (a subordinate) assigns them a low grade. I believe that they know their own limitations in the field, including their lack of relevant cultural knowledge and fear their grade will accurately reflect their weaknesses, and so they attempt to prevent me from grading them by complaining about my (in)ability to grade fairly. One of the privileges of being a schooled White is knowing how institutions work and which buttons to push in order to get things done. So, when administrators ask the students why they have not first talked to me about their concerns related to their grade in the course, the students respond that they are afraid their complaints will have negative ramifications on their grades. Some have even mentioned their fear that I may get violent if they confront me personally! I found this "fear factor" allegation amusing and also replete with racist overtones as one of the students who made this allegation was one foot taller than I in height, male, and approximately 150 pounds heavier than I! Fortunately, my many years as professor/messenger have taught me to create and provide explicit and fair grading procedures and evaluations. What is more, my grading policies are all clearly outlined in my syllabus.

My experiences with resistance have resulted in intentional attempts by students to silence my message of social justice by trying to gain institutional support to remove me from the classroom. The attempts to "shoot the messenger" are typically more frequent during the implementation of policies stemming from racist State legislation such as Proposition 187 and 209.[7] Many students do not want to engage in discussions that challenge them to think and reexamine their worldview, their ideology, and their positions of privilege and power. Students refuse to enter into the discourse of social justice and become outwardly hostile when oppressive and institutional racism is explicitly named. For example, they begin to raise their voice, become emotional and incoherent in their logic, their breathing becomes heavy, they cross their arms on their chest, and many leave the room. They become even more hostile by my refusal to "sanitize" my discussions, assignments, and activities. That is, students prefer that I talk solely about how to teach or about methods and not about how our inability to teach all students equitably and its implications for teaching for democracy and social justice. It is during this time that their loyalty to their conservative/reactionary ideology results in their attempts to obtain institutional support of their views. My students turn into soldiers of ideology with a sense of duty to protect others from hearing this teacher speak about schools as sites of oppression. Their attempts to shoot me down include going to college and university administrators and filing complaints, including writing letters, suggesting that they "want to protect other students" from my bias, as they felt harmed by me. Even as a courtesy, I have never received copies of these letters, although I was once allowed to examine them briefly while one administrator informed me of students' complaints. Some students have even gone as far as to say that while I talk about humanity, I have violated their humanity by not treating them with respect (which actually means that I have not approached them with the deference they expect as Whites when dealing with a Chicana). This is yet another interesting phenomenon: They learn to appropriate the liberatory language I use in class against me and with a clear intent to silence me.

DO NOT ENTER: THOSE TALKING JUSTICE MAY BE SHOT!

For every action, there is a reaction. So it is with politicized teaching, because this approach uses a political analysis to examine schooling and education. Thus, when the professor suggests that teaching is not neutral but is grounded in a specific political ideology, she initiates an action. Naming, teaching, learning, and practicing an ideology of social injustice are not without negative consequences. Professors must expect students' disapproving reactions when ideologies of oppression are challenged. Given specific social and historical contexts, instructors need to be cognizant that discussions of social justice may result in the message and the messenger being "shot." Institutional support is essential for not getting "shot."

My story attempts to include clarity in voice in the discussion of multicultural education lacking in many academic and educational circles. Many teacher educators and teachers believe the social justice "thing" was resolved in the previous century. Talk of equity has been replaced with more fashionable and profitable discussions of standards and certification. In many social and educational circles, there is complicity in the silence about the core issues of the growing educational apartheid, particularly for historically subordinated students of Mexican origin in the Southwest.

My message intends to remind those listening that resistance to social justice and economic democracy does not manifest itself in the same way across contexts and among various historically subordinated groups. History has demonstrated that racism, sexism, and classism are highly resilient and adaptive to specific contexts. I suggest that it is this adaptability that is responsible for the maintenance and perpetuation of social mechanisms of oppression.

Another lesson learned and useful to me in my survival as a university professor has been to comprehend that the teaching context and the students' backgrounds are part of a broader social structure in which the "isms" such as sexism, classism, and racism are perpetuated and allowed to operate on a daily basis and at all levels of social interaction. This clarity and understanding also grounded me and prevented me from the "crazy making." The feminist literature suggests that when women encounter difficulties, problems, or opposition, they have a tendency to blame themselves.

Equally important is that through systematic observation and note-taking, I was able to discern and establish patterns of resistant behavior useful in informing my own practice. While initially I failed to see and understand these patterns, over the years it became clearer that many students in my classes, particularly White students, engaged in a power struggle designed to silence a female professor of color with a message of social justice (Fairclough, 1989, 1995). Resistant students' attempts "to drive me underground" powerfully captures their attempts to realign their positions of power because their preconceived ideological notions have been toppled. Again, Jimmy Cliff's lyrics capture my own experiences, because, I have "gotten what's mine" as I still teach the message of social justice. I have also learned to better understand my role, my students, their resistance, and to be clear about the signs that lead to "shooting the messenger," as well as the consequences and the cost of practicing an ideology of social justice.

NOTES

1. Student resistance is defined as those behaviors, including verbal and non-verbal communication, and actions demonstrating overt opposition to dialogue and discussion to topics related to social justice. The social justice component of my coursework includes critique and articulation of existing inequalities in schools along social class, race, language, and ethnicity using a sociohistorical analysis. Another aspect of this social justice curriculum includes scholarly articles and data collected from multiple sources and disciplines (sociology, economics, history, anthropology, political science); this curriculum does not merely name, but it describes, articulates, and documents social and academic inequality as integral elements of ideological and hegemonic processes. Opposition to this social justice curriculum (student resistance) is observable, and manifests itself at both individual and group levels and is characterized by a palpable and ongoing unwillingness on the part of the student(s) to consider multiple perspectives and alternative explanations—other than blaming the victims and their respective cultures—to systemic academic underachievement by historically subordinated groups. Student resistance frequently results in attempts to sabotage classroom discussions and activities, as well as discrediting the professor whenever social justice issues are put on the table.
2. Field notes, journal entries, and student background forms (see note below) were collected for approximately 150 students enrolled in the prerequisite course, "Culture and Schooling" for the Single Subject Teaching Credential. Observations and data were collected between 1995 and 1997.
3. My teaching practices include getting to know my students, their background, and the experiences they bring to teaching. I have developed a "Student background form," which I use to inform my practice. Students are asked questions such as where they attended school, what language(s) they speak, about multicultural education, what they would like to learn and previous course work in culture and/or ethnic studies, including personal and professional experiences with student diversity.
4. In presenting a paper at the National Conference of Race and Ethnic Relations in American Higher Education, New Orleans, 2002, I shared with the participants how students laughed at me when I told them I was the professor. One of the participants (identifying herself as a graduate student from a university in the southern United States) corroborated my experience; she had experienced and seen this with her computer science professor (East Indian, female) whereby many of her White students laughed when she responded affirmatively to a student's question inquiring about her being the instructor for the course.
5. The use of titles is a phenomenon reflecting vividly the ideology of a hierarchical social order, with women (White and of color) being relegated to subordinate roles by the way in which they are addressed. My students in this study crystallized the subtleties (that were not so subtle) of relegating women to a lower status by how they address us. Many of my colleagues, particularly women from historically subordinated populations, and I have observed a distinct pattern in the difference in how students and staff address us. Male professors (regardless of ethnicity) are generally addressed with a formal title preceding their name, usually Professor, Dr., or Mr. Women tend to be addressed by their first name. I have been conducting an informal experiment, whereby I purposefully use my title of Dr. in all my correspondence, message, and interactions. I have found that female staff at our college are most resistant to using my professional title, perhaps reflecting their own internalized sexism. Again, I have tallied that the male professors are affectionately called Dr. G (short for Gonzalez, for example).
6. Sleeter and Grant (1999) present a typology for teaching multicultural education that includes five approaches that address unequal power relations in the United States. These include teaching the exceptional and culturally different, human relations approach, single-group studies, multicultural

education, and education that is multicultural education and social reconstructionist. My social justice curriculum used in these courses utilizes the latter approach as it names and deals with oppression and social structural inequality based on social class, gender, and race. It also *strongly* encourages teachers to be agents of change and reform in their classrooms, schools, and communities.
7. Proposition 187 and 209: The anti-immigrant sentiment, supported by Governor Pete Wilson and his administration began to blame immigrant and ethnic minorities for the economic problems of the state.

In November 1994, Californians passed an initiative, Proposition 187, cutting off some health and social services, including access to public education to illegal aliens and their children. That initiative was put on "hold" by a federal court, but the vote helped set the stage for a national debate on immigration and major legislation in Congress. It was described in the official ballot argument as "the first giant stride in ultimately ending the ILLEGAL ALIEN invasion."

Prop 209 was passed in California in 1996 and fundamentally banned affirmative action: "The state shall not discriminate against, or grant preferential treatment to, any individual or group on the basis of race, sex, color, ethnicity, or national origin in the operation of public employment, public education, or public contracting." After legal challenges were settled the proposition went into effect in 1997, with the 1998 freshman class within the University of California system being the first to feel the effects of the ban on affirmative activities.

REFERENCES

Acuña, R. F. (1998). *Occupied America* (3rd ed.). New York: Harper & Row.
Balderrama, M. V. (2002). *Calling out white academe: Power and ideology in higher education.* Paper presented at 15th Annual National Conference of Race and Ethnic Relations in American Higher Education." June 1, 2002. New Orleans, LA.
Balderrama, M. V., Texeira, M., & Valdez, E. (2004). Una lucha de fronteras (A struggle of borders: Women of color in the academy). *Race, Gender, and Class, 11*(4), 135–154.
Barrera, M. (1979). *Race and class in the Southwest.* South Bend, IN: University of Notre Dame Press.
Cliff, J. (1973). "The harder they come." Canada: Island Records. Lyrics retrieved from www.stlyrics.com/lyrics/hardertheycome/thebiggerttheycometh. June 26, 2007.
Fairclough, N. (1989). *Language and power.* London: Longman.
Fairclough, N. (1995). *Critical discourse analysis: The critical study of language.* London: Longman.
Giroux, H. (1988). *Teachers as intellectuals. Toward a pedagogy of learning.* New York: Bergin & Garvey.
Goldberger, N., Tarule, J., Clinchy, B., & Belenky, M. (Eds.). (1996). *Knowledge, difference and power: Essays inspired by women's ways of knowing.* New York: Basic Books.
Kincheloe, J. L., Slattery, P., & Steinberg, S. R. (2000). *Contextualizing teaching: Introduction to education and educational foundations.* New York: Addison-Wesley.
Maher, F. A., & Tetreault Thompson, M. K. (1994). *The feminist classroom: An inside look at how professors and students are transforming higher education for a diverse society.* New York: Basic Books.
Shor, I. (1992). *Empowering education: Critical teaching for social change.* Chicago: The University of Chicago Press.
Sleeter, C. E., & Grant, C. (1999). *Making choices for multicultural education: Five approaches to race, class, gender.* Upper Saddle River, NJ: Prentice Hall.

Section II. The Invisible Pervasiveness of Dominant Ideologies

CHAPTER THREE

Underprepared "Veteran" Special Education Teachers' Reliance ON Racist AND Classist Ideologies

FELICITY A. CRAWFORD

Special Education high school teachers in urban schools today are challenged to improve the academic outcomes of students with a vast array of needs, many of which stem from students in urban schools being under-taught, mis-educated (Orfield, 2004), misunderstood, and mis-placed in special education settings (Brophy, 1998; Deno, 1970; Good & Brophy, 2003; Oswald, Coutinho, & Best, 2002; Rist, 1970; Rosenthal & Jacobson, 1968; Valenzuela, 1999). In particular, there is a high percentage of Black and Latino students in special education because teachers (most of whom are White females) are unfamiliar and under-prepared to respond to the social, cultural, and linguistic differences that exist between them and their students. Furthermore, misunderstandings between teachers and students often escalate, here in the United States, because both our society and our system of education have continually perpetuated racist and classist ideologies[1]—most notably through media and texts—that are sustained by stereotypical messages of deficiency on the account of perceived ability, socioeconomic, cultural, and linguistic differences (Harry, Klingner, Sturges, & Moore, 2002; Valencia, 1997; Valenzuela, 1999). Stereotypical messages of deficiency have become commonly acceptable explanations for failure among students of color (Valencia, 1997; Valenzuela, 1999). As such, when students of color are placed in special education, their academic starting point becomes even more tenuous, primarily because special education has historically been informed by the medical/deficit model

(Mehan, Hartwick, & Meihls, 1998). In fact, students of color in special education programs are often thought of as "doubly deficient" (Fierros & Conroy, 2002; Harry, 1992; Harry, Klingner, Sturges, & Moore, 2002).

I embarked on a study to learn from experienced special education teachers about their pedagogy in self-contained special education classrooms with students of color. I was surprised to find, despite these teachers' veteran status, they were underprepared and, more surprisingly, unreflective and disinclined to analyze their teaching, especially in classrooms with students of color. This chapter describes these teachers, some key beliefs they hold about Latino and Black students, some pedagogical practices that give way to their deficit orientations, and their inability to engage in reflection. I argue that any efforts to change the outcomes of students in the self-contained special education classroom would continue to fall short if teacher educators do not provide preservice and inservice teachers with opportunities to gain up-to-date knowledge of subject-specific content and develop their "ideological clarity"[2] (Bartolomé, 2004, p. 98). Ideological clarity here refers to an individual's understanding of how his or her own attendant ideas, beliefs, attitudes[3] (audible and visible expressions of what people feel, expect, and do about another or about an issue) intersect with prevailing societal beliefs and shape their everyday practice toward groups of students marginalized by race, language, and ability.

RESEARCH QUESTIONS

The purpose of this study was to understand if and how veteran special education teachers' attitudes and beliefs influenced their instructional practices and were reflected in their actual teaching of Black and Latino students. Thus, the research questions:

1. How do veteran special education teachers' attitudes and beliefs about Black and Latino students manifest in their initial conversations about students in general and these students in particular?
2. What actions and language (both verbal and nonverbal) do veteran Special Education teachers exhibit during instruction? The chapter's report is a small part of a larger study that examined how veteran special education teachers' attitudes and beliefs about students in special education, and Black and Latino students in particular, manifest in their lesson plans, their curricula, and in their actions as they taught in urban self-contained special education classrooms with primarily Black and Latino students.

RESEARCH METHODOLOGY

I used an ethnographic approach to this qualitative study because I wanted to generate data that were rich in detail and embedded in the context I wanted to study (Maxwell, 1996; Miles & Huberman, 1994, 1996; Spindler & Spindler, 1987). Specifically, I used purposeful sampling to select four (n = 4) participants (Gall, Borg, & Gall, 1996) and conducted 48 teacher interviews, 20 classroom observations, and reviewed teachers', school, and state curricular documents. Next, I used Strauss and Corbin's (1998) grounded theory analysis to make sense of and derive themes from the study and Gee's (2002) discourse analysis technique to explicate the teachers' verbal and non-verbal language (see Appendix A: Research Methodology).

THE STUDY

St. Augustine High School

The four veteran special education teachers whom I interviewed and observed all worked at St. Augustine High School,[4] a large comprehensive public high school located in a small industrial city, Smalltown, Massachusetts. Founded in the 1800s, St. Augustine High served immigrants who, until the 1980s, came mostly from Europe. Beginning in the late 1980s, the student population changed rapidly until in 2004, approximately 55% were students of color who collectively spoke close to fifty different languages. In targeted self-contained special education classrooms, the percentage of students of color was disproportionately higher than the percentage represented in the student population. Between 75% and 79% of the students in special education were either Blacks or Latinos, and 13% to 25% were White or from other racially and culturally diverse backgrounds, as were Southeast Asians. Contrary to the demographic changes among students, the teaching staff remained relatively unchanged; consisting mostly of White teachers from working class Irish or Italian immigrant families. One of the reasons that the majority White teaching staff remained relatively unchanged was the fact that funding cuts in Massachusetts in the 1980s precipitated a hiring freeze of educators and school closings in several districts across the state for a number of years.

The Special Education Department at St. Augustine High

The special education department at St. Augustine High was a relatively small department, consisting of approximately 300 students in a school with a population of 1,600 students. St. Augustine used a numerical system to track students in special education. The numerical system in use at St. Augustine was derived from a now defunct numerical system, or prototypes, which was used by the state to identify the amount of time students needed outside of the general education setting.

FOUR VETERAN SPECIAL EDUCATION TEACHERS: THEIR IDEOLOGICAL ORIENTATIONS

The four target teachers, Esme, Marlene, Joss, and Julian (pseudonyms), had long-standing connections with the city. Esme is a White woman in her mid-fifties who began her tenure as a teacher in special education classes thirty-three years ago. Born to working-class immigrant parents in one of the largest cities in the Northeast region of the United States, Esme spent her early years of elementary school in a large urban school system and her high school years in a small rural agricultural town. Esme chose to become a special education teacher because she felt that there were not many career options for women so she decided to seek a master's in education at a local university:

> When I got to the master's level, there was no way to major in that [dance therapy] except to major in gym and I said, "I don't think so." Being the cultural snob that I am, I am not majoring in gym. And I did not plan on sports so that more or less did it.

Esme pointed out that, although "there were special education classes in the building" of her high school, whom she recalled as "TMRs and MRs,"[1] her first real connection with students in a special education program occurred during her internship while still a dance major at a four-year undergraduate institution.

Marlene is a White woman in her late forties who had been teaching for twenty-four years in self-contained special education classrooms. She spent the first eight years teaching at elementary schools and the last 16 at St. Augustine High School. Marlene grew up in a working-class "conventional family": a two-parent household with two children. Her father worked as a teacher, her mom stayed at home. Marlene described herself as one who "did as she was supposed to do." She entered the profession at a time when there were numerous job openings in Massachusetts after the state passage of its first major special education law Chapter 766 (1972), or the General Law Chapter 71B, which required the state provide programs for school-age students with disabilities be granted opportunities to maximize their potential.

Julian, a White male in his mid to late fifties had been teaching for 30 years, 20 of which he spent at St. Augustine High. Julian comes from a working-class Italian family. Both of his parents "did not have a lot in terms of financial assets" or education but instead came from families that placed high value on work in their daily comportment. Julian recalled one of his grandfather's sayings: "if you don't work, you don't eat—[it's] as simple as that!" Julian believes that from his family he inherited a very strong "work ethic." He identified one of his key sayings as, "you don't do the job you don't get paid— simple."

Joss is a White woman in her late forties with more than 25 years of teaching experience. The daughter of working-class Italian immigrants, Joss became the first in her family to attend college where she studied education and became licensed as an elementary school teacher. She came to special education because she was attracted by the "99.4%" job placement rate. She entered the system as a special education teacher despite admitting to "never seeing a special needs child in her life."

Apart from the similarities in the aforementioned characteristics, the four special education teachers shared similar professional credentials. Three of the four teachers began their careers as unlicensed special education teachers and were subsequently granted licensure on account of the length of time they spent in the profession as a special educator of record, and their participation in professional development seminars to maintain licensure. Three of the four teachers (the women in the study) came into the profession soon after Chapter 766 (1972) was passed. This statute required "that districts identify, evaluate, determine services, and provide programs for school age children who—because of their disabilities—are unable to progress effectively in regular education and require special education to develop their individual potential" (§§1–3). Chapter 766 resulted in lots of job openings in special education at schools across the state of Massachusetts. The fourth, Julian, came into special education because he empathized with students with disabilities. None of the four teachers pursued additional college level courses after they graduated college more than 20 to 33 years before. Instead, their professional development opportunities were mostly geared toward managerial issues and compliance with federal and state laws that governed special education, which, when combined with their lack of content mastery as special educators, and their deficit views of the students proved detrimental to their students. In the sections that follow I discuss teachers' descriptions, explanations for student underachievement, and their actions and language during instruction.

TEACHERS' DESCRIPTIONS OF STUDENTS

In this next section, I identify the differences between teachers' descriptions of the White students they taught in special education prior to the 1980s and the descriptions and explanations for underachievement among the Black and Latino students they were teaching at the time of the study. I also provide some insight into teachers' actions in classrooms with Black and Latino students.

"Underdogs": Teachers' Sympathetic Beliefs About White Special Education Students

Having embarked on a teaching career more than 20 years earlier, most of the students the teachers taught in their earlier years were predominantly White students from working-class backgrounds. The teachers described these White students as needing assistance or else empathized with them. Julian, for example, indicated:

> [Children in] the area we grew up in were always kind of considered the underdog and most special ed kids are also viewed as underdogs. The[re] were kids who didn't have opportunities and kids who didn't see themselves going beyond a certain point, [but] I saw myself going beyond a certain point. I have to help them do the same.

In this instance Julian was talking about the population of students he met at the high school 33 years earlier, at the beginning of his tenure as a teacher when the student population consisted of primarily White students. Similarly, in her early professional life, Esme saw herself as working to provide services for students who needed her help:

> No one was really sure what my mandate was—I really didn't have one. It was like, "Well let me see what I think the needs are." And from there, it seemed to me that there were really a lot of kids who needed help …

Here again it is worth noting that Esme applied these descriptions to White students whom she taught in her early years. The teachers also described their students at that time as dependent on their families after they left high school because most "had difficulty finding work." Teachers' descriptive language underwent a marked change when the racial and cultural make of the student body reflected greater numbers of Black and Latino students.

"I close my eyes; I don't even know how many Black students I have"

All four teachers responded to the increase in students of color at the high school by deliberately eschewing the relevance of their students' race and culture in their classrooms. For instance, Marlene said:

> Across all five of my classes there is a lot of diversity: there're Haitian students, they're students from El Salvador … we have Colombian students, Brazilian students. We have all of them. I think this probably isn't right but … I don't get off too much

on the cultures because I am trying to build a basic writing, reading, skills for surviving here ...

Similarly, Joss intimated:

> I close my eyes ... I don't even know how many Black kids I have. I don't know how many Spanish kids I have. I have a couple of Indian kids—they are the smallest of the minorities. You know, we just don't see it.

In like manner, Esme said, "I don't think about that. I focus more on the basics—can they read and understand—things like that." Julian echoed similar sentiments, "All these kids merge, and it doesn't matter. Their backgrounds do not predetermine how far they go in school." To these teachers, purporting to "not see" differences in students' race or culture was an appropriate response to students' differences. Race, because it is socially constructed, does not exist in a vacuum. To people of color, race is an important factor in determining their social identity. To hear the teachers say repeatedly that race did not matter was a serious attempt (either conscious or not) to de-politicize and dismiss the uniqueness that students of color bring to the classroom.

TEACHERS' EXPLANATIONS OF BLACK AND LATINO STUDENT UNDERACHIEVEMENT

When asked specifically about the achievement levels of Black and Latino students, all four of these teachers referred to readily available racist stereotypical images that pervade U.S. society.

"I try to build them up ... [but] they are going home to something ... less than adequate." Teachers repeatedly indicted Black and Latino students and their families for being at the root of the challenges they faced in school. Esme, for example, declared that students were unmotivated in part because they did not view themselves as capable and neither did she:

> By expecting them to engage with the content you are telling them that [they] can really do this. ... Sometimes I have to sell myself on the idea. ... Academically, for them to know they can carry a notebook around and be responsible for their own work materials ... helps them build that idea that they can do things.

In this instance, Esme was making a case for why it was best to focus on vocational rather than on academic pursuits. In doing so she co-opted students' thoughts to strengthen her own notion that the students felt insecure about their own intellectual capacities. Similarly, Marlene felt strongly that her efforts in the classroom would never make a difference in the academic outcome of her students because of their home environments:

> No matter how much I try to build them up during the day, they are going to go home to something that is less than perfect, less than adequate. It's just more what they have, what they have to draw on, and what they have to go home to that makes it different.

Here again, Marlene's reference to students' inadequate home lives resonates with racist/classist images of Black and Latino students. Whether conscious of the ways in which they were constructing students of color or not, these four teachers continually described Black and Latino students in an irreverent manner. For example, Joss said in her first interview:

> It's the exception—the learning disabled kid who is bright and comes from a really educated family. It's the exception rather than the rule for the kids I am dealing with. So in many cases the parents are less educated and they see their kids unrealistically. We still tend to have a lot of parents from different cultures where education isn't as important as it is here.

To Joss, the level of work she was going to get from students was decided long before students entered her class. She assumed that being born with a disability into a family from a different cultural background was a strong indicator of intellectual deficit.

Julian's ideas were similar to Joss's in that he identified a portion of his students as deprived before they entered the classroom:

> Some of the students have been culturally [and] academically deprived. A lot of the kids don't get reading like a lot of middle class do now. The parents work and that's not their fault—it's their economic position. Some parents may not have the intellectual ability to do these things either.

The teachers' outlook during the second and third stages of interviews (i.e., the pre- and post-observations) did not subside. In fact, their beliefs about their students' inability intensified over time in their descriptive statements.

Slow, low-functioning, and lethargic. The teachers often used one of the three terms to describe Black and Latino students as "slow," "low-functioning," and "lethargic." It also appears as if the teachers believed that school knowledge was innately acquired. If kids didn't possess it, they evaluated them negatively. For instance, Esme indicated:

> Sanchez is really slow. He is just now learning that the earth is round. He does not know the things we take for granted. So yes, he is really one of my slower students.

In another instance, she highlighted her minority students' low academic potential and shared her beliefs that an academic track for these students was not a realistic undertaking:

> People make the case for saying that [they] will never have another chance in their life again, like in high school, to build as much academics as [they] can—and many do make that case. I just don't buy that case. Not with the kids I work with, you know. It is true for kids who have some academic potential, but it is not true for kids who have no concept formation and abstract ability.

Similarly, Julian said, "They are so low-functioning—most of them read at a fifth grade level." For instance, in the midst of a discussion about the irrelevance of student race and culture to learning, Julian compared students in suburban schools with his students at St. Augustine. He noted that suburban "students and their parents are more interested in education so you get a better type of student—better meaning more motivated." Moreover, all four teachers indicated that everything they tried to give their students to do was "too difficult." Consequently, what students were learning in all of their classes was a far cry from what their peers were learning in regular classrooms. The teachers also believed that students' intellectual incapability and lethargy were unavoidable or normal traits. By the end of my data collection processes, teachers had used the words, "slow," "low-functioning," "lethargic," "unmotivated" in more than 251 separate instances.

In general, the four teachers' beliefs and attitudes toward Black and Latino students reflected a misrepresentative yet long inherited system of ideas that eschewed the intellect and social competence of Blacks and Latinos. Students were frequently described as inept, lazy, and disinterested in school, and teachers repeatedly abdicated their responsibility for changing their students' outcomes. The thought that these teachers might unknowingly replicate prevailing negative patterns raises the importance of ensuring that teachers have ample opportunities to question and to discuss the origins of the assumptions they make about their students.

ABSENCE: AN ISSUE AT ST. AUGUSTINE HIGH

The teachers' beliefs about Black and Latino students manifested themselves in their language and actions toward these students during instruction in ways that placed students' opportunities to learn in great peril. In particular, one of the most striking outcomes of teachers' interactions with students was the teachers' ability to facilitate different kinds of students' absence. In this section, I share how teachers' language and actions gave way to students' absence from the classrooms.

The National Center for Education Statistics (2002) indicates that up to 72% of students in grade 12 miss at least one day of school per month. Further, they assert that absence hinders not only the absentee's learning but that of their peers when it leads to repetition of a lesson or particular topics. At St. Augustine, for example, all four teachers accepted students' absence as a given and reported that three to four in a class of approximately 12 students were absent from school each day. Marlene, for instance, indicated that a few of her students "showed up once, perhaps twice in the last two months." Similarly, Julian stated quite matter-of-factly that four of his students "just stopped coming." In other words, the teachers just accepted that approximately one-third or more of their students were going to be absent, and this attitude unwittingly gave way to teachers facilitating two types of student absence: physical absence and mental absence. Physical absence—when students who are marked present are absent from the classroom at the time of instruction at the behest of school educators. Similarly, mental absence also stems from, although less directly, educators' negative treatment of the students and occurs when students who are present at the time of instruction but disengaged from instruction. Together, these two types of absences proved to be a barrier to students' access to education. This finding was significant, given that the four teachers at Augustine had already indicated to me that they were experiencing problems with students who did not come to school very often. What follows are definitions and descriptions of the characteristics of the physical absence and mental absence as it occurred in the classrooms I visited.

Physical Absence

I define physical absence as the phenomenon whereby students are recorded as present in the school attendance records but are actually absent from individual classes for a variety of reasons that include being summoned by school administrators, sent from class by their teachers, and leaving their classrooms for a variety of reasons with the teachers' permission.

Characteristics of physical absence. Students who left classrooms did so because they were sent by teachers to the office for disciplinary and or administrative purposes (most often to get a temporary school identification card). In addition, students were also summoned by school administrators, or else excused themselves from classrooms for varying lengths of time (e.g., from 3 minutes to the whole 66 minute class period) with their teachers' permission. Further, in more than 50% of the cases of the physical absence phenomena, the teachers issued consecutive passes for students seeking permission to leave the class.

Mental Absence

I define mental absence as occurring in students who are physically present in a classroom but mentally disengaged from the lesson at hand or from the activities that are initiated by the teacher. In other words, this concept describes students, who are absent in every other way except for their physical presence in a classroom. An equally important criterion to both these concepts is that the teacher is physically present in the room and facilitating the occurrence of either phenomenon by doing nothing or by initiating behaviors that lead to one or the other. Combined, physical absence and mental absence are particularly dangerous because they represent significant barriers to student learning and academic achievement. Students who are either physically or mentally absent at the time of instruction stand no chance of learning.

TRACKING PHYSICAL ABSENCE AND MENTAL ABSENCE

In each observation, I took detailed notes of lessons. For instance, I recorded the time (e.g., 8:00 a.m.) when students departed and re-entered classrooms. I also recorded their race and gender; and, if known, the reasons why they left the room. For example, I recorded the number of students and the amount of time each was physically absent from all of the classes I observed because they were summoned by the school disciplinarians (see Figure 1: Sample of Time Black and Latino males lost to physical presence/absence). I tracked mental absence by taking detailed notes of teacher actions and student engagement during instruction. In particular, I tracked the amount of time teachers spent lecturing; the types of questions they asked; the types of responses their instructional strategies elicited from students. For example, in four out of five observations in Julian's class, six of the seven students never responded to, or asked questions, during instruction. In fact, two Black females spent all of their class time conversing. Another African

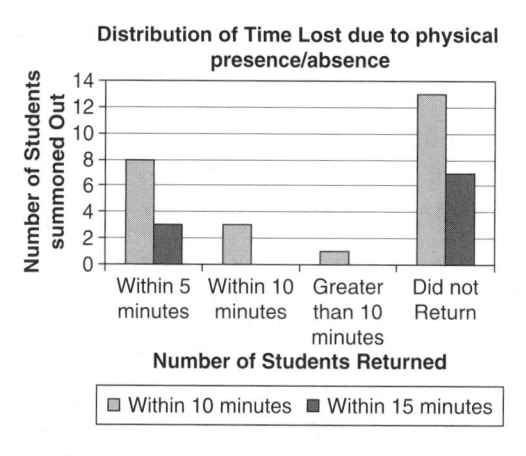

Figure 1. Sample of time Black or Latino students lost due to physical presence/absence.

American female kept her head on her desk throughout each lesson. In both cases, Julian did not interrupt students. Instead he directed his attention elsewhere.

TEACHER TACTICS FOR FACILITATING PHYSICAL ABSENCE

Once inside the target classrooms, it became evident to me that teachers and members of the school administration were the key contributors to the pattern of persistent physical absence among students.

Physical absence from the classroom was precipitated in one of two ways: by a call from St. Augustine's building disciplinarians or administrators; or by teacher initiated action to dismiss a student from the classroom. Each class observation lasted for 66 minutes. In the 20 observations (or 22 hours) I made in classrooms, students were summoned a total of 53 times to the school disciplinarian's office. In 51 of those instances, the students who called out were Black and Latino males. Specifically, of the 51 Black and Latino students who were summoned to the school disciplinarian, 25 were called out of the classroom within 10 minutes of the beginning of the class. Thirteen of those 25 students did not return. Those students who did return to class did so at varying times. For example, eight of the 25 students who left after the first 10 minutes of class came back within five minutes; three came back within 10 minutes; and one came back in 13 minutes of time due to being summoned by the school disciplinarian. Further exacerbating the learning time lost among students who were physically present at school were teacher tactics that facilitated students' disengagement. The teachers' tactics included encouraging students to leave the classroom; silencing students through humiliation and reprimand, or doing very little to engage students in the learning process during actual instruction.

Underlying the problem of student absence, either physically or mentally, was the fact that the four teachers held low expectations of the Black and Latino students who did make it to school each day. More troublesome was the fact that teachers' expectations of Black and Latino students gave way to intolerance, impatience, and disrespect, all of which were evident in tactics (such as humiliation, reprimand, avoidance, and exclusion) they used.

TEACHER TACTICS FOR FACILITATING MENTAL ABSENCE: ANYONE READY TO GO YET?

Most of the Black and Latino students who were left in classrooms after their peers were eliminated demonstrated signs of disengagement during instruction.

In Julian's class, for example, one Black female kept her head on the desk throughout each class, and two Black females spent most of the time during each lesson carrying on a conversation. Instead of interrupting the students' negative behaviors, Julian persisted in providing them ready access to the exit.

The problem of persistent mental absence among students was compounded when teachers invited students to leave the classroom. In one of Julian's classes, for example, he invited students to leave a total of 14 times during a single 66 minute period by repeatedly asking variations of the question, "anyone ready to go yet?" Below is an excerpt from notes that I took within the first 23 minutes, of a 66-minute lesson in Julian's class that provides several examples of mental absence as they occurred:

> **7:53** The bell rings, signaling the start of the period. There are seven students in the room (3 Black females, 2 Black males, 1 White female and 1 White male). In a somewhat hurried and slightly muffled tone, Julian begins class by saying, "What we [are] going to do today is talk about—he moves over to the board and quickly picks up a stick of chalk from the ledge of the board—he draws a stick figure representing a person and then quickly, some backwards Cs emitting from the figure's ears to mimic sound waves—then continues to speak, "what we are talking about is vibration … sound vibration." He looks away from the chalkboard and back at the students and says, "Anyone ready to go yet?" No one responds. Julian continues on.
>
> **7:55** White female in front of the room is the only one who opens up a notebook. None of the other six students has changed what they were doing before Julian began: Two Black females are still talking in Haitian Creole; the other Black female put her head on the desk from the moment she sat down and has not looked up since; the lone White male in the room is still thumbing through a magazine; while the two Black males are sitting silently in the back of the class with their attention seemingly drawn to the conversations of the two females seated in front of them. No one speaks except Julian.
>
> **7:58** Julian pauses and says to the two Haitian girls, "speak English, speak English—I can't understand what you are saying." One of the students says in a matter-of-fact-tone—"we are not talking to you!" Julian turns to the others and asks a question about sound vibration. No one answers. He says, "Don't want to wake you, but are you ready to go yet?" Still no one responds.

While the tone of voice the students used as they addressed Julian conveyed antagonism and disrespect and Julian's lack of response spoke much more loudly. Could it have been that he did not expect any better of them? Alternatively, did it mean that he was unprepared to work with this population of students? While one might speculate on which explanation is plausible, Julian's cryptic question about whether or not the class was awake or ready to leave conveyed that he neither expected much from his students nor did he believe they cared enough to pay attention in class.

62 | IDEOLOGIES IN EDUCATION

> **8:00** Julian continues on talking in a hurried, slightly muffled tone about sound and writing on the board. About three minutes elapse.
>
> **8:05** (10 minutes into the lesson). Julian looks up and says "Is everyone awake?" No one responds. He says, "You guys need to go to bed early, or you could always leave if you get too sleepy" Julian continues with the lesson.
>
> **8:10** Julian suddenly stops talking and looks up with a slightly bewildered look as if he is only just now realizing that no one is responding. He looks away from the chalkboard and at the students. He pauses and then speaks, "Are you ready to leave yet?" When no one responds, he says, "You guys need some energy." He walks over to the windows nearest him and begins opening them amidst loud complaints from the two Haitian females, "Don't open the window! We are going to catch a cold. We are not used to this weather!" [It is March, but on this day the temperature is well below 40 degrees]. Julian says, "Just want to wake you up in case you are ready to leave."

Again, one gets the impression that Julian felt there was no point in trying to engage his students because he believed they were disinterested in school. Opening the window instead seemed to be the only plausible way to elicit a response from his students.

> **8:12** The phone rings (every class has an extension). One student says he hopes that it is for him. Julian walks over to the phone answers it very quickly and then gets back to teaching.
>
> **8:13** He continues asking and answering after waiting a few seconds for students to respond. He also continues giving examples of how sound travels and encourages students to jump in at anytime. Julian pauses and says, "so you all ready to go yet?" He glances over toward me, seated on the opposite side of the room and says in a seemingly apologetic tone, "This is a tough audience."
>
> **8:15** He continues on with questions like "anybody knows how vocal chords work?" he encourages them by saying "tell me and I'll give you a reward."
>
> **8:16** He bangs a piece of wood on to his desk and says "I don't want to wake anybody up, but tell me how it is you can hear this sound." He asks one student, who visibly jumped, "Christine, you all right?' again he looks across at me and explains, "Just trying to entertain them a little bit. So anyone ready to get away yet?"

Within the span of 23 minutes Julian had not only repeated the question, "are you ready to go yet" approximately 8 times or once every 2.3 minutes but had also done nothing to stop those who were clearly disengaged from the lesson. In addition, within the identified span of 23 minutes, 6 of Julian's 7 students lost all of their learning time for that 66-minute class period which equaled 6.6 hours, which I calculated by multiplying the number of students who engaged in off-task behaviors with the length of the class time, 66 minutes. More compelling was the fact that Julian's verbal exchanges remained unchanged for the duration of my observations in this class. Specifically, the total cumulative hours I observed Julian's class was 5.5 hours, or approximately one school-day. Within those 5.5 hours, 6 of 7 of Julian's students lost the equivalent of one week of class (or 33 hours) due to their uninterrupted off-task behaviors. I also observed similar outcomes (student disengagement) occurring with great frequency in the other three teachers' classes.

SUMMARY AND DISCUSSION OF PHYSICAL AND MENTAL ABSENCE FINDINGS

Teachers' language and actions toward Black and Latino students together suggest a strong connection between the two. For instance, the four teachers believed that the Latino and Black students in their classes were intellectually incapable and cared little about school. They expected Black and Latino students to be disengaged and disrespectful in their demeanor. As a result, they unwittingly conveyed, by their verbal behaviors (threat, humiliation, reprimand) and actions—excluding students from class which resulted in the dangerous habit of mental and physical absence among students at the behest of teachers. While there were approximately three to four students in each of their classes who did not attend school each day, those who were there became the recipients of negative behaviors and actions from teachers. If absence among students contributes to negative academic outcomes, then it seemed counter-intuitive for teachers to consciously facilitate the same among Black and Latino students on a regular basis.

SUMMARY AND DISCUSSION OF THE CHAPTER

The aim of the study presented in this chapter was to understand if and how veteran special education teachers' attitudes and beliefs influenced their instructional practices and were reflected in their actual teaching of Black and Latino students. In general, I found that the teachers believed these students were intellectually incapable and cared little about school. They expected students to be disengaged and disrespectful of learning. As a result, their verbal behaviors and actions conveyed much disregard for Latino and Black students. Further, the teachers' beliefs and expectations of Black and Latino students with disabilities manifested itself in several ways: First, the teachers accepted failure as given among their students. Second, they expected that their students would not come to school. Third, the teachers expected that students who did attend school would misbehave or be disengaged, and thus they spent much time reprimanding and/or threatening them with exclusion and other disciplinary measures. Fourth, by allowing themselves to locate the problems within their students, they succeeded in abdicating their ethical responsibilities as teachers. For instance, the teachers did not plan their lessons. Instead they relied on a mechanistic approach to teaching and insulted and or excluded students who did not participate. Even more striking was the fact that they did not refer to any of the sophisticated strategies that are part of the knowledge-base in special education. This latter issue reflects their unpreparedness as special educators. As a result, teachers, through their attitudes and actual teaching practices, appear to perpetuate the perniciousness of racism. Students with disabilities who might have thought of trying would have been hard pressed to respond differently if they were met each day with teachers' pessimism. The question is, what might teacher preparation programs do to prepare teachers to act in the best interest of the students they teach?

IMPLICATIONS/RECOMMENDATIONS FOR SPECIAL EDUCATION PREPARATION PROGRAMS AND SPECIAL EDUCATORS: THE ROLE OF IDEOLOGY IN SHAPING TEACHER PRACTICE

It is evident that the four veteran teachers' unwavering acceptance of the socially constructed notion of a superior/inferior worldview placed students with disabilities and Black and Latino students at a disadvantage as learners. These findings suggest the need for special education teacher preparation programs to be deliberate about applying critical pedagogical practices that are aimed at helping preservice teachers to examine the connections between taken-for-granted ideas, their assumptions, and their instructional practice.

Ideology—or schemes for making sense of one's reality—reflect particular predetermined patterns of thought (or mental steps); inherited ideas (legacy), and social factors (such as where we live, how we are socialized, our cultural frames of reference, our professions, and our daily interactions) (Mannheim, 1936). Unless questioned, the ways in which we are shaped by ideology remains tacit. We only become aware of them when confronted by radically different models of thinking that cast doubt on that which we hold to be true. Then, depending on our group affiliation, we respond collectively to either maintain the status quo or work for change. For special educators to fully understand how to help students in special education classrooms succeed, it becomes important that they have ample opportunities to:

- engage in explicit study of ideology;
- develop teacher reflection/praxis;
- explicitly study of deficit ideology legacy in Special Education and in minority education in general.

To move special educators toward changing the outcomes for students who are marginalized in schools means beginning with an explicit study of ideology, which in turn necessitates a commitment to making critical literacy central to the work of teaching. Critical literacy must be practiced in preservice special education programs and among K-12 educators. Bartolomé (2004) advocates for teachers to be able to make the connections among ideology, power, and culture (Leistyna & Woodrum, 1996) in order for them to challenge, resist, and interrupt oppressive practices (Darder, Torres, & Baltodano, 2002 as cited in Bartolomé, 2004). A first step in educators developing the strategies to interrupt oppression would be for teachers to demonstrate their critical reflective abilities through reflection on action or praxis (Freire, 1970).

Second, praxis, or constantly reflecting on one's actions and justifications in any situation, would pave the way for teachers to "see" discriminatory practices, like racism, clearly and to construct ways to counter such hegemonic practices. Teachers who have spent considerable time developing their reflective abilities are much more deliberate and conscious of their thoughts and actions; they are more likely to catch themselves or retract from a stance that could impede students' performance. Engaging in reflection on action could provide teachers an excellent opportunity to become aware of the times they facilitate mental absence among their students.

Third, teachers need to engage in explicit study of the deficit orientation ideology in special education and in educating students of color in order to fully understand its impact on students of color with disabilities. In addition, teachers must develop the political clarity that would enable them to understand the adverse realities that their students face and to work more effectively on their behalf (Bartolomé, 2004). Moreover, it is crucial to ensure that special educators acquire the appropriate knowledge and skills (like language acquisition, teaching reading, and differentiating instruction) for working with diverse student populations.

Ideally, special education was intended to provide students with disabilities the supports and strategies they needed to rightly access the same level of public education as their peers without disabilities. In fact, the 1997 amendments to the Individual with Disabilities in Education Act make clear the rights for students with disabilities. The question is what is it that special educators need to do differently to ensure that all students, including those from culturally and linguistically diverse backgrounds have the best possible outcomes?

The State of Massachusetts, for example, requires, in their licensure regulations that preservice teachers have opportunities to teach in inclusive education classrooms. Such a move holds much promise for providing special educators opportunities to collaborate with colleagues in general education classrooms in ways that would enhance their own professional growth as well as secure positive academic outcomes for students with disabilities. One teacher in the study, Joss, found that working with a general educator afforded her multiple opportunities to learn new pedagogical strategies that she otherwise would not have learned or applied to her work with students in self-contained classrooms. A system of team-teaching across general and special education settings sets up a self-checking system where no *one* teacher is free to do as she or he wants. Further, sustaining inclusive education means that special education teacher educators and special education teachers must work to uncover, examine, and rethink their racist and classist assumptions and biases that guide practices that isolate these students from the general curriculum in the first place. This approach is particularly important given that there is a wealth of literature (see for example, Bartolomé, 2004; Freire, 1997; Giroux, 1994; Macedo, 1994; Sleeter, 1992), which indicates that teachers (irrespective of race, class, and culture) tend to unquestioningly and unconsciously perpetuate racist and classist beliefs and attitudes that replicate prevailing ideologies that prove detrimental to students.

APPENDIX

RESEARCH DESIGN AND METHODOLOGY

Overview of Research Design and Methodology

I wanted to understand what four (n = 4) veteran special education teachers planned for, taught, and reflected on their lessons in self-contained classrooms with a majority of Black and Latino students at one urban high school. The central concept that I examined was teachers' attitudes, or audible and visible expressions of how they thought, felt, and behaved toward Black and Latino students. To do so, I conducted 48 interviews with veteran teachers, 20 classroom observations, and then analyzed their verbal and non-verbal communication and behavioral patterns for themes and provided an interpretation of the meaning I derived from the data I collected (Creswell, 1998; Miles & Huberman, 1994, 1996; Strauss & Corbin, 1987).

Interpretation of Findings

After returning the transcripts to the participants for review (Miles & Huberman, 1994, 1996) I applied several analytical measures to interpret the data I collected. First, I applied Strauss and Corbin's (1998) grounded theory analysis process to begin my data analysis.

Strauss and Corbin (1998) describe analysis as the interplay between researchers and data (p. 13). Given that I was a Black woman trying to study teachers' (in this case, White teachers') attitudes in classrooms with a majority of Black and Latino students, I thought that it was important that I inculcated a process that allowed me, from that type of analytic process, to apply a systematic method for looking deeply at the data to try to gain a sense of what was happening. Strauss and Corbin's three-tiered grounded theory analytic process afforded me that opportunity.

Moreover, Strauss and Corbin (1998) defined analysis as both an art, because of the level of creativity that the researcher has to apply to the process, and a science, because of the rigor and the need to substantiate any claims with data. Coming from an artistic background, it was easy for me to move fluidly between letting go—or trusting the process and to allowing the data to take me where I needed to be as well—and applying a system that ensured the rigor of the study.

Next, I used Strauss and Corbin's three-tiered grounded theory approach to analyzing the six sets of data I collected. The first tier, "open coding" (Strauss & Corbin, 1998, p. 119), set the stage for eliciting rich information from the text by repeatedly asking a fundamental question, "What is happening here?" To respond to that question meant doing a line-by-line analysis of all of my data (which equaled approximately 200 single-spaced pages of interview transcriptions and documents, which were compiled as a book with line numbers and divided into separate sections by data sets) each time, asking the same question.

Delving into the raw data by asking the same question repeatedly resulted in an extensive list of specific phenomena (e.g., incidents, events, actions, interactions, issues) and conceptual codes. For example, at one point in her initial interview (lines 354–355) Esme said, "I don't do lesson plans, you know. I generally know where they are headed and what they'll be doing. It's loose, very loose." Applying the first-tier open coding, I asked the question, "What is happening here?" I first responded to the question by using key words in the respective participant's sentence to create "in vivo" codes (e.g., "I don't do lesson plans"), after which I applied a "labeled phenomenon" (Strauss & Corbin, 1998, p. 103). Applying these elemental labels allowed me to stay open to exploring all kinds of possibilities.

Letting go and allowing the process to take me where I needed to be often meant going over the same section of transcript repeatedly in this first round to really open up the ideas in the text. So, for example, in going over the same text, "I don't do lesson plans. ..." I looked for other characteristics (e.g., issues, expectations, assumptions, and feelings). So to the text, "I don't do lesson plans ..." I added the following labels: issue: no prior planning and over-reliance on experience; assumption: that teaching was static. This repeated and intensive open-coding process yielded approximately 235 pages of labeled phenomena, which I again compiled into a book (with each line identified by number, quote, and open codes).

At the second tier, "axial codes" (Strauss & Corbin, 1998, p. 123), I read and re-read specific data sets to establish higher level, or abstract, categories and subcategories to group concepts that related to the same phenomenon. I systematically developed and linked subcategories. Specifically, I identified properties and dimensions by asking questions like why, how come, where, when, how, and with what results. For example, the first in-depth interviews teachers described pivotal events that shaped their schooling experiences. Often these changes were precipitated or came with attendant emotional responses. Trying to understand antecedent conditions meant looking, for example, at what participants were using as referents, how they viewed their social contexts at the time, the kinds of feelings that these situations elicited, and then at the beliefs, values, and attitudes that manifested in their conversations over time.

I also made constant comparisons across participants to gain a sense of the similarities and differences and broader themes that existed. By using this layer of analysis, I significantly reduced the data to approximately 50 pages and narrowed the number of the explanatory codes to three themes: change, difference, and conflict. Next I used analytical memos as a way to work through my interpretations. What was more important at this level was having a clear understanding of how the categories were related to each other (Strauss & Corbin, 1998). To demonstrate my understanding of the relationships, I identified patterns that occurred under particular conditions over a period of time.

The intent at the third tier, selective coding, was to "integrate and refine" (Strauss & Corbin, 1998, p. 143) the categories I identified. In doing so, I first identified a central or core finding or a broad sense of what my interpretation of the information of the study yielded. Thus, the question I asked myself: What was the main analytic idea in the study? The key criteria for determining a response was to ensure that the central finding emerged frequently from the data; and that it was sufficiently linked to the categories I identified. Patterns were also coded by color to distinguish between participants. I also asked myself: How can I explain the variations between and among categories? To respond adequately, I again compared data across themes while constantly moving backward and forward in the raw and coded data to ascertain teachers' motivations, interactions, as well as the consequences of their actions.

To further integrate and refine my understanding of the categories I identified, I applied Gee's (2002) Discourse Analysis Technique at strategic points to examine the reflexive relationship between teachers' language and their situations. For example, after repeatedly reading through sections of the transcripts,

I recognized that in their discussions of their work with students, teachers did not use any language that demonstrated any expertise in special education. To deepen my understanding of the phenomenon, I isolated phrases from sections of teachers' responses specific prompts and asked them to tell me about their students. One teacher responded:

> ... most of the [teachers in the special education department] do ... extra things for these kinds of kids ... but they are willing to draw the lines: sometimes they pat them on the back and yell at them when they think they are not really correct ... I'll give them a boot in the pants when they really need that too ... I think a lot of kids come from disorganized homes ...

To this extract I applied the six questions from two of Gee's (2002) six building tasks: semiotic building and socioculturally situated relationship building. Thus, the first question I asked was, "What sign systems are relevant (and irrelevant) in the situation (e.g., speech, writing, images and gestures)? How are they made relevant (and irrelevant) and in what ways?" (Gee, 2002, p. 93).

The sign system that is relevant here is the teacher's speech. Specifically, he used vague language (e.g., "extra things," "willing to draw the lines") without identifying what these might have been when discussing the strategies that he and his colleagues used to assist students who have difficulty responding correctly. Next, I asked, "What sign systems of knowledge and ways of knowing are relevant (and irrelevant) in the situation? How are they made relevant (and irrelevant), and in what ways?" (Gee, 2002, p. 93). It was clear from their statements that the teachers relied on their experiential knowledge of working with students, thereby making irrelevant any strategies they might have learned in formal programs. What was evident was that nothing in the teachers' language indicated their understanding of the special education strategies that they could have used to differentiate instruction and/or make accommodations for students who had difficulty processing information.

Continuing with the semiotic building task I asked, "What social languages are relevant (and irrelevant) in the situation? How are they made relevant (and irrelevant), and in what ways?" (Gee, 2002, p. 93). It was clear that the teacher was subscribing to the prevailing cultural models of students that accessed over-used stereotypical language that would have been acceptable to those who subscribed to the superior/inferior worldview as it pertained to Blacks and Latinos. Moreover, the very fact that they could not communicate any of the students' strengths rendered any they might have had irrelevant because teachers increasingly relied on the cultural models, or first thoughts, they created as a reference for Blacks and Latinos. Also evident was that the social language of deficit was uppermost in teachers' thinking about the students. In this case, their deficit was their students' intellectual inability.

Another question I raised, using Gee's Analysis Technique was, "How are these relationships stabilized or transformed in the situation?" From the teachers' statements, it also became apparent that they had little or no previous experience with students form culturally and linguistically diverse backgrounds and that their prior experiences were more or less restricted to students who were also White.

Of this same extract I also asked, "In terms of identities, activities and relationships, what Discourses are relevant (and irrelevant) in the situation? How are they made relevant (and irrelevant), and in what ways?" (Gee, 2002, p. 93). The teacher's insistence on focusing only on what this student did not or could not do served to distance him from building substantive connections with students. In addition, this teacher's reference to students as "they," "these," and "them" coupled with the cultural models they referenced minimized any characteristics that were unique to them and instead relegated them to the impersonal status of "other."

Moreover, using Gee's Data Analysis Technique provided me a way to analyze teachers' other social language systems, which Gee (2002) proposes is unique to particular groups and are designed to carry out specific functions" (p. 95). For example, one of the teacher's frequent eye-rolling responses coupled with her staccato-like repetition of the phrase "come on, come on" in my judgment communicated an attitude of impatience while it also silenced the student to whom her attention was directed. After this particular lesson, I checked in with the teacher to gain an inside perspective and learned that she was feeling impatient with the student who, she indicated, gave the same incorrect answer over and over again. While it may appear as though validity is a subjective proposition using this type of analysis, Gee concedes that when convergence occurs on a series of 18 questions that it would be highly unlikely that the judgments of insiders and outsiders will unite without good reason.

NOTES

1. Ideology here refers to the explanations and justifications that an individual draws on to construct meaning for him/herself in any context (Yeboah, 1998).
2. Bartolomé (2004) defines ideological clarity as the "process by which individuals ... define and compare their own explanations of the existing socioeconomic and political hierarchy with the dominant society's" (p. 98).
3. The word attitude has often been used with disparate meaning. For example, popular use of the word (e.g., to have an "attitude") insinuates a negative orientation. In the dominant U.S. culture where self-control and impenetrability have high value in the workplace, attempts to focus on attitudes are rejected because they are cast as an emotional expression most closely associated with being female. Further, when methodically applied to relations between groups, one much studied attitude, prejudice, for example, generates feelings of superiority and inferiority that unearth stereotypical beliefs that often lead to adverse consequences (Johnson, 1991). Sociologist, Johnson (1991)

in his book *The Forest for the Trees: An Introduction to Sociological Thinking*, readily agrees that the term *attitude* involves emotion that prompts us to feel and act in particular ways. He nonetheless argues, more importantly, that attitudes uncover core beliefs and values which ultimately become the basis upon which we, as people, enact behavior. Furthermore, I use the word *attitude* to imply intentional ways of thinking that emerge from conscious or unconscious sources, made obvious by one's feelings that surface in verbal and nonverbal language exchanges that incorporate tone of voice and physical expressions to delimit expectations and subsequent behaviors toward the subject or object of consideration.

4. The names of the school and city and other identifying names were changed to protect the confidentiality of the participants.

REFERENCES

Bartolomé, L. I. (2004). Critical pedagogy and teacher education: Radicalizing prospective teachers. *Teacher Education Quarterly, 39*(1), 97–122.

Brophy, J. (1998). *Advances in research on teaching: Expectations in the classroom.* Greenwich, CT: JAI Press.

Creswell, J. W. (1998). *Qualitative inquiry and research design: Choosing among five traditions.* Thousand Oaks, CA: Sage.

Darder, A., Torres, R., & Baltodano, M. (2002). Introduction. In A. Darder, R. Torres, & M. Baltodano. *The critical pedagogy reader.* New York: Routledge Falmer.

Freire, P. (1970). *Pedagogy of the oppressed.* New York: Continuum.

Freire, P. (1997). *Mentoring the Mentor: A Critical Dialogue with Paulo Freire.* New York: Peter Lang.

Gee, J. P. (2002). *An introduction to discourse analysis: Theory and method.* New York: Routledge.

Giroux, H. (1994). Educational reform and the politics of teacher empowerment. In J. Kretovics & E. J. Nussell (Eds.). *Transforming urban education* (pp. 396–410). Boston: Allyn Bacon.

Good, T. L., & Brophy, J. E. (2003). *Looking in classrooms.* Boston: Allyn and Bacon.

Harry, B. (1992). *Cultural diversity, families and the special education system.* New York: Teachers College Press.

Harry, B., Klingner, J. K., Sturges, K. M., & Moore, R.F. (2002). Of rocks and soft places: Using qualitative methods to investigate disproportionality. In D. J. Losen & G. Orfield (Eds.), *Racial inequity in special education* (pp. 71–92). Cambridge, MA. Harvard University Press.

Johnson, A. G. (1991). *The forest for the trees: An introduction to sociological thinking.* Orlando, FL: Harcourt, Brace, Jovanovich.

Leistyna, P., & Woodrum, A. (1996). Context and culture: What is critical pedagogy? In P. Leistyna, Woodrum, & S. Sherblom (Eds.), *Breaking free: The transformative power of critical pedagogy* (pp. 1–7). Cambridge: Harvard Education Publishing Group.

Losen, D. J., & Orfield, G. (Eds.). (2002). *Racial inequity in special education.* Cambridge, MA: Harvard University Press.

Losen, D. J. (2004). Graduation rate accountability under the No Child Left Behind Act and the disparate impact on students of color. In G. Orfield (Ed.), *Dropouts in America. Confronting the dropout rate crisis* (pp. 41–56). Cambridge, MA: Harvard University Press.

Macedo, D. (1994). *Literacies of power: What Americans are not allowed to know.* Boulder, CO: Westview.

Mannheim, K. (1936). *Ideology and Utopia.* New York: Harcourt, Brace, Jovanovich.

Maxwell, J. A. (1996). *Qualitative research design: An interactive approach.* Thousand Oaks, CA: Sage.

Mehan, H., Hartwick, A., & Meihls, J. (1986). *Handicapping the handicapped: Decision-making in students' educational careers.* Stanford, CA: Stanford University.

Miles, M. B., & Huberman, A. M. (1994). *Qualitative data analysis: An expanded sourcebook.* Thousand Oaks, CA: Sage.

Orfield, G. (2004). Losing our future: Minority youth left out. In G. Orfield (Ed.), *Dropouts in America: Confronting the graduation rate crisis* (pp. 1–11). Cambridge, MA: Harvard University Press.

Oswald, D. J., Coutinho, M. J., & Best, A. M. (2002). Community and school predictors of overrepresentation of minority children in special education (pp. 1–13). In D. J. Losen & G. Orfield (Eds.), *Racial inequity in special education.* Cambridge, MA. Harvard University Press.

Rist, R. C. (1970). Student social class and teachers' expectations: The self-fulfilling prophecy in ghetto education. *Harvard Educational Review, 40*, 411–451.

Rosenthal, R., & Jacobson, L. (1968). *Pygmalion in the classroom.* New York: Holt, Reinhart and Winston Inc.

Rubin, D. (1999). *The power of English: Basic language skills for adults.* Upper Saddle River, NJ: Prentice Hall.

Sleeter, C. (1992). Restructuring schools for multicultural education. *Journal of Teacher Education, 43*(2), 141–148.

Spindler, G., & Spindler, L. S. (1987). *Interpretive ethnography of education: At home and abroad.* Mahwah, NJ: Lawrence Erlbaum.

Strauss, A., & Corbin, J. (1998). *Basics of qualitative research: Techniques and procedures for developing grounded theory.* Thousand Oaks, CA: Sage.

Takaki, R. (1993). *A different mirror: A history of multicultural America.* Boston: Little, Brown, and Company.

Valencia, R. R. (1997). *The evolution of deficit thinking: Educational thought and practice.* London: Falmer.

Yeboah, S. K. (1988). *The Ideology of racism.* London: Hansib Publishing Limited.

CHAPTER FOUR

Teachers' D/discourses AND Socially Situated Identities: Literacy Practices IN A Mexican High School

GUADALUPE LÓPEZ BONILLA

The current educational program under Mexico's Secretariat of Public Education (SEP, by its Spanish acronym) called for a profound reform at the high school level with the purpose, among others, of improving students' learning and their command of information and communication technologies (SEP, 2001). In reality, experience shows us that the hidden agenda in these reforms has been the reduction of educational expenditure (Carnoy & de Moura, 1997; Díaz Barriga & Inclán, 2001). In general, educational reforms have meant a stricter control over teachers' in-class performance and have placed higher demands on their work: an increase of their teaching load (larger groups per class), and a heavy amount of administrative duties. For the educational system in general, and high school education in particular, these policies have been translated into an emphasis on enrollment, and an unspoken policy of quasi-automatic grade promotion that seeks to diminish the high drop-out rate and educational attrition at this school level; that is to say, educational reforms have been a cosmetic and superficial process with little or no impact on educational practices. This situation is not any different from the findings more than a decade ago about the state of education in Mexico: an increase in the numbers of students enrolled in the system at the expense of academic quality and a broader access for all (Comisión Económica para América Latina, 1992).

For high school education, a crucial aspect of this recent reform effort is the proposal to implement a national teacher development program in order to provide teachers with "new competences and skills to promote significant learning experiences" (SEP, 2001, p. 167, the original is in Spanish). Studies about reform and teacher development programs, however, have found that these efforts are bound to fail if they approach teachers' development without taking into consideration teachers' existing beliefs, intentions, and attitudes (Haney, Czerniak, & Lumpe, 1996; Poulson, Avramidis, Fox, Medwell, & Wray, 2001). This is more so in the case of Mexico where, according to recent studies, teachers perceive teacher development programs within the context of educational reforms as improvised and lacking academic rigor, and serving the purpose to merely "inform teachers of what is new in the system" (Sandoval, 2001, p. 99). Thus, it appears that for many teachers, these programs function as 'bogus programs' where "teachers often remain under tight control and [are] limited in the scope of their power to influence the conditions of their work" (Zeichner, 1992; as cited in Smyth, 1997, p. 1113).

In the current reform initiative teachers are once again conceived as subjects implementing the ideas of others (Díaz Barriga et al., 2001), and no attention is given to their working conditions, their beliefs and attitudes about the existing curriculum, and in general, about what actually goes on inside high school classrooms. These social elements are but some of the aspects articulated in the complex process of the social practice of teaching (Fairclough, 2004).

In order to gain access to teachers' beliefs about those elements that shape their teaching activities, it becomes necessary to establish a distinction between the activities in the classroom and the social practices inherent in them. In the case of literacy, Barton and Hamilton (2000) make a clear distinction between literacy events and literacy practices: The former are observable activities in which reading and writing are involved, whereas the latter constitute cultural ways of using written language. Contrary to literacy events, literacy practices are not observable, as these implicate beliefs, values, and attitudes which are internal to the individual (Street, as cited by Barton & Hamilton, 2000). As such, "practices are shaped by social rules which regulate the use and distribution of texts, prescribing who may produce and have access to them" (Barton & Hamilton, 2000, p. 8). Social institutions, such as schools, establish procedures and expectations that are expressed in routine activities involving written and oral texts. Because these are practices that involve different discourse communities, the study of literacy events as they emerge in specific social contexts can help to identify literacy practices associated with different domains of life.

In this chapter I explore teachers' beliefs about literacy in two specific content areas: History and Literature. Two literature and two history teachers from a public high school were interviewed for the study. The purpose of the interviews was to elicit teachers' beliefs about literacy and subject matter. The interviews were analyzed taking into account the context of the situation and the three variables identified in Functional Systemic Linguistics (FSL) as relevant to instances in which language is being used: field, tenor, and mode of discourse (Halliday, 1978). Briefly speaking, field alludes to "the institutional setting in which a piece of language occurs"; tenor "refers to the relationship between participants," and mode to the "channel of communication adopted" (Pearce, as cited in Halliday, 1987, p. 33). In FSL the categories of field, tenor, and mode are associated with three semantic functions of language: Field activates the representation of experience (experiential function), tenor the subject positions (interpersonal function), and mode the information focus (textual function). Treating the interviews as texts constituting "systems of knowledge and belief" (Fairclough, 1995, p. 6)—in their experiential, interpersonal and textual functions—I was able to discern teachers' beliefs about literacy and subject matter. In addition, transcripts of actual lessons were analyzed in order to find out to what extent teachers' beliefs and perceptions guide their teaching activities in the classroom. The study was conducted in the border town of Tijuana, in Northern Mexico.

Central to this study is the notion that literacy, conceived as the "mastery of a secondary Discourse" (Gee, 1996, p. 143), can be a powerful source of meta-knowledge that leads to the critique of other literacies. Thus, a key purpose in this study was to identify teachers' perceptions of "dominant literacies" (as they are present in national curricular mandates) and the ways these are adapted or questioned in their teaching practice. The research questions guiding the analysis were: What are teachers' beliefs about subject matter, literacy, and dominant literacies? What aspects of teachers' experience and background influence these perceptions? How do such beliefs and perceptions guide their teaching practice?

In order to address these questions three aspects of teachers experience were considered: teachers' disciplinary background and formal training in the teaching profession; the Discourses (Gee, 1999) present in teachers narratives about their own experience; and the teaching situation of each of the participants in the study and the constraints placed upon them by the institution (Bourdieu, Passeron, & de Saint Martin, 1995). In light of a dominant Discourse that insists on treating schools as industries pursuing effective, "narrowly utilitarian objectives" (Smyth, 1997, p. 1091), it is important to look at teachers' beliefs, perceptions, and attitudes taking into account the different and sometimes opposing Discourses that are present in their teaching practice. Addressing these issues provides a glimpse of teachers' ideologies about themselves as members of a particular professional community, and about the system in which their teaching practices are embedded.

THEORETICAL FRAMEWORK

Teachers' Beliefs and Knowledge

In recent years, studies addressing the role of teachers' beliefs in their teaching practice have grown considerably (Marcelo, 1987; Pajares, 1992; Borko, Flory, & Cumbo, 1993; Calderhead, 1996; Borko & Putnam, 1996; Richardson, 1996; Tatto, 1998; Moni, van Kraayenoord, & Baker, 1999; Miras, Solé, & Castells, 2000; Poulson et al., 2001; van Driel, Beijaard, & Verloop, 2001; Brindley & Schneider, 2002). A common topic in some of these works is the theoretical difficulty in distinguishing between beliefs and knowledge (Pajares, 1992; Borko & Putnam, 1996; Calderhead, 1996; Richardson, 1996). In clarifying this distinction, I will draw upon the work of Norman Fairclough (1995, p. 44), who states:

> ['K]nowledge' implies facts to be known, facts coded in propositions which are straightforwardly and transparently related to them. But 'ideology' [...]... involves the representation of 'the world' from the perspective of a particular interest, so that the relationship between proposition and fact is not transparent, but mediated by representational activity.

Thus, a subject's values, beliefs, and ideology cannot be reduced to that subject's knowledge.

Building up on the work of Foucault and Michel Pêcheaux, Fairclough (1995, p. 39) argues that social institutions impose on the subjects they construct "ideological and discoursal constraints [...]... as a condition for qualifying them to act as subjects." As an example, Fairclough mentions that "to become a teacher, one must master the discursive and ideological norms which the school attaches to that subject position"; that is to say, one must talk in certain ways which entail a particular way of looking at things that, ultimately, is the ideological norm for that ideological discursive formation.

D/discourse and Situated Identities

Akin to Fairclough's work, the work of James Gee on discourse analysis offers a sound theoretical framework for looking at the way individuals use language "to enact activities, perspectives, and identities" (Gee, 1999, pp. 4–5). For Gee, Discourses (with a capital D) are "socially accepted associations among ways of using language, of thinking, valuing, acting, and interacting, in the 'right' places and at the 'right' times with the 'right' objects (associations that can be used to identify oneself as a member of a socially meaningful group or 'social network')" (Gee, 1999, p. 17); whereas discourses (with a lowercase d) refer to language in use.

A central aspect of Discourses, Gee argues, is recognition; as such, they are crucial in understanding different identities enacted by individuals through (but not only) language. Gee argues that "making visible and recognizable *who* we are and *what* we are doing always involves a great deal more than "just language" (Gee, 1999, p. 17). This "more than just language" is another way of looking at Discourses; whereas the "who" projected through language and Discourse is a "socially situated identity."

Situational Elements and Semantic Features of Text

Any linguistic expression is determined by its immediate social situation; every utterance, the product of social interaction; that is to say, a linguistic expression is a product of the circumstances of the interaction, and the conditions under which the speakers function (Vološinov, 1973). Building on Malinowski's concept of "context of the situation," Halliday (1987) identifies three variables determining any instance in which language is being used: field, tenor, and mode. Field refers to the activity taking place and the purposes for using language in that activity (for example, a math class, a seminar, a game); tenor refers to the role relationships among the participants (questioner, informer), and mode refers to the symbolic organization of text and the channel of communication (oral versus written, thematic structure of the text). These three situational elements are associated with specific semantic components of text: field with the experiential or ideational function of language, tenor with the interpersonal function, and mode with the textual function. Thus, field determines the "range of meaning as content," tenor "the range of meaning as participation," and mode the "range of meaning as texture" (Halliday, 1987, p. 117). In Fairclough's words, texts function "ideationally in the representation of experience and the world, interpersonally in constituting social interaction between participants in discourse, and textually in tying parts of a text together in a coherent whole" (1996, p. 6) Due to ideology's impact on all three levels of the context (field, tenor, and mode), as it is actualized in linguistic choices, texts become linguistic evidence of beliefs, biases, and positions encoded in them (Eggins, 1994).

METHOD

Context of the Study

Tijuana is one of the fastest growing cities in Mexico. Its population grew from close to 250,000 inhabitants in 1970 to over one million inhabitants in 2000.

Migration has traditionally been an important part of Tijuana's fast population growth. The border area and the industrialization program in Tijuana have attracted a large number of immigrants from different parts of Mexico. Tijuana's population has a relatively high education level, higher than in other parts of Mexico and similar to that in Mexico City (INEGI, 2000).

I began doing research on literacy practices at the Preparatoria Federal Lázaro Cárdenas in Tijuana in July of 2000. With a student population of nearly 4,000 students, Lázaro Cárdenas is unique in that it is totally funded by the Federal government, whereas other high schools have mixed or state funding. It is also one of two public institutions in the country that offer the international baccalaureate as an alternative program to the national curriculum for obtaining a high school diploma. Due to the costs and high academic standards of this program, however, only a handful of students (less than 3% of the total school population) have access to this option.

In order to explore the possibility of interviewing and doing in-class observations of history and literature teachers, I approached the school administrators and explained my research interests. After careful consideration they suggested that I work with four teachers who agreed to participate in the project, and who were regarded as some of the most experienced in their field by the teaching community of this institution. Thus, I began my work with Mr. González, Ms. Osuna, Ms. Camacho, and Mr. Torres.

Data Collection

The interviews were conducted in the teachers' cafeteria during their free periods between classes. All the teachers had read a brief description explaining the purpose of the study and the activities planned for the duration of the project. In it, I stated that my main interest was to become familiar with the way history and literature are taught in the context of a public high school, and that I was particularly concerned with literacy practices in these two subjects. The interviews were described as a way of tapping into their views on teaching, literacy, and subject matter.

One semi-structured interview lasting an average of 75 minutes was conducted with each of the participants. These were recorded and later transcribed in their entirety. The interview addressed questions regarding the teachers' previous experiences; their beliefs about subject matter, literacy, and national curricular mandates; and problems encountered in their teaching experience. Because sequence and grammar are very important when doing discourse analysis, I provide a close translation in English for each excerpt cited, and the Spanish original at the end of the chapter (see appendix).

In order to have a clearer perspective on teachers' beliefs about literacy and if and how these perspectives guide their teaching practice, in-class observations of one lesson taught by each of the participants were conducted and recorded. These were later transcribed and coded according to the nature of the literacy events observed, and the types of student-teacher interaction in them. I followed Mary Hamilton's (2000) description of literacy events and identified four aspects: the participants, the setting, the artifacts, and the activities in each literacy event.

Data Analysis

I use Halliday's concepts of field, tenor, and mode to describe the interviews and to explore the semantic features activated by these situational elements: Thus, I analyze the referents expressed in the teachers' interviews (experiential function), my role as researcher/interviewer and the interpersonal relations between myself and the participants (interpersonal function), and the textual features of the language used: oral discourse, themes, and situational deixis (textual function).

Gee's conception of socially situated identity, on the other hand, allowed me to explore how different members of a professional community construct their own sense of self in relation to other members of the same and other communities, depending on the context of the situation. With this in mind, it is important to consider that for this study the participants were selected with a set of criteria that identified them from the onset: they were teaching professionals working in a prestigious public high school, and they were considered good teachers in their field by their peers and school administrators. To these overlapping identities set forth before the interviews took place, other voices (Bakhtin, 1986), identities and Discourses emerged during the interviews, as will become evident in the following discussion.

RESULTS

Teachers' Disciplinary Background and Experience: The Case of Two History Teachers

Mexico has basically had only one teacher training program for all elementary, middle, and a large number of high school teachers: the teacher training colleges known as *Escuelas Normales*. By attending this type of government funded school, teachers (elementary, and in some cases middle and high school) are not required to have a college degree since they obtain their teaching credentials from the *Escuela Normal*, a credential that is now considered equivalent to a college degree.

The *Escuelas Normales* are controlled by Mexico's Secretariat of Public Education (SEP), and have always played a major role in national affairs through the teachers powerful union (Sindicato Nacional de Trabajadores de la Educación, SNTE). This role was exacerbated after the Mexican Revolution with the introduction of a "nationalist approach in the school curriculum, reflected later on in the free-text policy" (Morales-Gómez & Torres, 1990, p. 66). It was only as recently as 1984 that enrollment in the *escuelas normales* began requiring that prospective teachers hold a high school diploma, and, during that same year, they started awarding a *licenciatura*, i.e., an educational degree equivalent to a B.A. degree to their graduates. Before then, in-service teachers could obtain a university degree from the *Universidad Pedagógica Nacional* (Pedagogical National University), which was created for this purpose in 1978 by a presidential decree.

For the teaching professional, the *escuela normal* has become a clear path for obtaining the teaching credentials that allow a teacher's insertion into the public school system. Thus, trainer and employer are one and the same entity. It is important to note that the only other pathway to teaching is by being a university graduate who, by choice or necessity, decides to teach. These professionals are not required to cover any teacher training program prior to their insertion in schools.

Ms. Osuna: The Discourse of a "Maestra Normalista"

Ms. Osuna, a history teacher with 17 years of teaching experience at the school where the research was conducted, embodies a typical profile of the *maestra normalista*. Trained in the *Escuela Normal Federal* in her native state (Nayarit, in Central Mexico), she received her credentials with a specialty in history in 1975 and worked as an elementary and middle school teacher in schools along the western states of Mexico (Nayarit, Sinaloa, Baja California). Because she had been trained and was working in the federal school system, she declared not encountering any obstacles when she moved from one state to another, easily reinserting herself in different federal schools where she taught at every level: elementary, middle, and finally high school. When she moved to Tijuana she began working at the Preparatoria Federal where she was, at the time the interview took place, one of only a handful of full-time teachers. Her typical teaching load was three courses (nine hours per week).

I met Ms. Osuna for the interview in the teachers' cafeteria in September 2001. I began by introducing myself and briefly explained the purpose of the interview. In these declarative statements, I provided information about the research I was conducting and stated that I wanted to learn from experienced teachers their views on literacy and the kinds of problems they encountered in their teaching practice (tenor, interpersonal function). This introduction was followed by questions and answers about six main topics: professional background and previous teaching experience, opinions on the importance of teaching/learning history, her goals in teaching this subject, her opinion about the national curricular program, the kinds of literacy events her class promoted, and the challenges she encountered in her teaching practice (field, experiential function). This same approach was employed in each teacher interview.

Ms. Osuna's responses included recurrent comments about her vocation as a teacher and her commitment to the federal system. For instance, when asked about her teaching experience, Ms. Osuna offered the following comment:

> I am thrilled about being a teacher ever since the moment I chose this profession … my experience has always been within the federal system, I have tried to defend the federal system because I feel it's very beneficial for teachers … that is why it's wonderful to belong to the federal system. (excerpt 1)

For the most part, the experience encoded in Ms. Osuna's answers describes what Halliday refers to as "mental processes," with a high number of verbs that allude to affection (experiential function).

At first, Ms. Osuna was a little hesitant with her answers, and it was evident that I, a researcher from a public university, was an outsider in a higher position within the hierarchy of the educational system (tenor, interpersonal function). This role was even more obvious when she mentioned a previous study conducted by my university, where students from this high school were identified as poor students. When I asked her how she assigned papers to her students, she was evasive as the following example illustrates:

> GLB: How often do you assign papers to your students?
>
> MO: Well right now I only have three groups of students [I teach to three different classes], but I have always worked, when I've taught ten groups … and I didn't have anything in the office. That's why I say that if one is really interested in education, if one really wants Mexico to go forward, we [teachers] are responsible of doing this about constantly overseeing what our students are doing … (excerpt 2)

In her answer, Ms. Osuna's declarative I-statements (interpersonal function) did not provide the information demanded in the question, but she shifted to a recurrent referent in her discourse: the good of the country (experiential function). The shift in field illustrated above was punctuated by circumlocutory utterances where Ms. Osuna became the topical theme in every clause (mode, textual function).

Very early in the interview, Ms. Osuna's socially situated identity became apparent: a committed federal teacher (*maestra normalista*) with a clear mission in her work. As a result, her past experience was represented as a smooth transition from one place/level to another within a system that rewards her dedication with good working conditions: a full-time position with a light teaching load.

This representation of her own experience seemed to have a big influence on the beliefs and values guiding her teaching practice: When asked about her beliefs and perceptions about history as a high school subject, Ms. Osuna stated that her history class served the purpose to inculcate in students the love for their country (*amor patrio*) and "historical values" that confer a sound national identity. Arguing that students are direct beneficiaries of the country's history (as evident in their right to public education), and perceiving herself as a product of that history, Ms. Osuna's history class is conceived as a privileged space for shaping the values of Mexican adolescents: a strong ideology of nationalism and patriotism.

When asked about the readings she chose for her class, Ms. Osuna declared that her students were free to choose from different sources in order to form their own opinion, but later she added:

> They know that they need to be very careful about what they read because sometimes the texts do not fulfill our expectations about what we want Mexico to be ... because sometimes writers are very radical and they write history according to their own perspective, right? What's convenient for them. (excerpt 3)

Therefore, reading, in Ms. Osuna's history class, is a highly sanctioned activity, where students have access to the kinds of texts that imbue in readers the ideology of patriotism.

Not surprisingly, the literacy events observed in Ms. Osuna's history class were students reading a short biography of Benito Juárez (a Mexican president famous, among other things, for his Indian heritage) followed by their written comments on Juárez's contributions to the growth of the country. In Ms. Osuna's words, plagued with hyperbolic expressions, the history of Mexico becomes a sort of hagiographic discourse praising the lives and deeds of the country's national heroes, while the tenor observed in her class was scattered with emotional appeals (interpersonal function) encoded in imperative clauses such as the following: "I say no! Let's not blame the government! ... Search for your own truth! ... You can do it!" (excerpt 4).

One can argue that Ms. Osuna's highly ideologized beliefs about history are part of a dominant representation of the role that teachers have in Mexican society, institutionalized as clear norms, rituals, and routine activities ever present in elementary and middle schools, as well as in the *Escuelas Normales:* singing the national anthem every Monday, paying homage to the Mexican flag (*honores a la bandera*), and a strong respect for discipline and authority. As part of this dominant ideology, the beliefs and perceptions of Ms. Osuna about her own role as a history teacher have become naturalized and are perceived as the right course of action.

Mr. Gonzalez: A Public Servant in Disgrace

Mr. Gonzalez holds a degree in law from the prestigious National Autonomous University of Mexico (UNAM, by its Spanish acronym). A native of Mexico City, he had been teaching history at the research site for 13 years. At the moment the interview took place, his average teaching load was 30 hours per week (10 three-hour per week courses with 45 to 50 students in each course). Formerly, he had worked for 17 years at the Secretariat of Public Education (SEP) in Mexico City. While at the SEP, he was promoted from a low level clerk to secretary and advisor to several middle- to high-level functionaries. Throughout the interview, Mr. Gonzalez's discourse was filled with narratives about his past experience as a public servant in Mexico City. It was his experience at the SEP Mr. González highlighted from the outset when I asked him about his background and teaching experience (field, experiential function):

> I have been teaching, one could say, for 13 years. Because, actually, more than teaching, I was into educational planning, consulting, as far as education is concerned, advising functionaries over there at the Secretariat for Public Education. That's what I was, analyst for the Ministry of Education, planning the national educational system. (excerpt 5)

When I asked him about his previous teaching practice, he mentioned several times that while at the SEP, he suffered an "unfortunate mishap" due to political circumstances and was demoted and forced to teach social sciences at a junior high school in the outskirts of Mexico City:

> Ah, well! I suffered, along with my boss, an unfortunate mishap (*caí en desgracia*) due to political circumstances, and I (was sent) went to a technical school as the coordinator of social sciences; I taught there ... (excerpt 6)

Thus, his teaching career began as an imposition by a bureaucratic system that promotes or demotes employees according to the political whims of those in positions of power.

It is interesting to note that Mr. Gonzalez encoded his present condition as a history teacher through the lens of his past experience in higher places. In this sense a Discourse of displacement/exile was dominant in his interview. This scenario was evident in his frequent use of time and space deictics (mode: I was, down there, up here), and in the continuous shifting in his voice. For instance, when he described his past experience, the voice of authority was quite distinct:

> *I was in charge* of operations ... *I noticed* that some school principals and vice principals ... were not well prepared for school management ... so other colleagues and *I designed* school management courses ... and they were so good that the

Undersecretary asked us to teach those courses to every middle school ... and so *I almost became national coordinator* of those courses. (excerpt 7)

However, his voice changed noticeably when he spoke about his current experience as a history teacher,

It's unbelievable but my experience is that *students* are not interested in this subject ... teachers don't have any resources to pressure students into learning, and *teachers* are regularly *blamed* when things go wrong ... *students* don't like us. (excerpt 8)

These responses can be analyzed in light of the shift in thematic pattern (textual function) and the types of processes (experiential function) when one compares his discourse about the past with his discourse about the present: In excerpts 5 and 7, there are several material/action processes (consulting, advising, planning, designed) where he is the main actor; and several relational processes (was, became) that describe "good" attributes about him (in charge, national coordinator). In both these instances, he was the topical theme, i.e., the narratives were clearly about him and his good deeds and attributes (textual function).

By contrast, his discourse shifted to the topical theme of "others" (students) when he talked about his present experience (excerpt 8), and through the passive voice, he appears indirectly (teachers) as the recipient of negative actions (blame). Taking into account this continual shift in voice, one can say that Mr. Gonzalez's situated identity was marked by his Discourse of exile/resentment: His current struggle as a not much liked history teacher working under poor conditions was perceived through the lens of a former successful public servant fallen prey to the system.

As to his views on literacy, Mr. Gonzalez declared that Mexican history was like a novel plagued with heroes and villains, but he stressed the importance of learning the facts expressed in any text, because "History is written the same way in every book." In the literacy events observed in Mr. Gonzalez's class, students read out loud from a text containing brief historical entries and episodes, and this activity was followed by Mr. Gonzalez's interpretation of what had just been read to the whole class. The interpersonal distance and hierarchical relation in the act of teaching observed during his class confirmed Mr. Gonzalez's poor opinion about his students when I asked him if he promoted group discussions in class. His answer provided more evidence of the poor expectations he had about his students: "The problem is that a lot of time gets wasted in an analysis that I suspect won't get done ...."

Ms. Osuna's and Mr. Gonzalez's Beliefs About History

Mr. Gonzalez expressed his belief that history as a subject was highly formative for students because it allowed them to become familiar with the nation's problems. For Mr. Gonzalez, history serves the purpose to "promote national unity and solidarity with our country's problems." It was clear that Mr. Gonzalez shared Ms. Osuna's belief that history as a subject matter provides the ideological cohesion for developing a "national identity" in students, yet the two teachers privileged different subject matter content in their class: love for the homeland (*amor patrio*) in Ms. Osuna's class (attitudinal content), and facts and figures in Mr. Gonzalez's class (declarative content). One could say that both Mr. Gonzalez and Ms. Osuna expressed beliefs deeply ingrained at the institutional level and at the personal/professional level, for

> [a]s institutions actively engaged in forms of moral and social regulation, schools presuppose fixed notions of cultural and national identity. As educators who act as agents in the production, circulation, and use of particular forms of cultural and symbolic capital, teachers occupy and inescapable political role. (Giroux, 1996, p. 43)

It was not surprising that Mr. Gonzalez's and Ms. Osuna's superficial critiques of the dominant literacy was expressed in terms of the extent of the program and not the content.

THE EXPERIENCE OF TWO LITERATURE TEACHERS

Ms. Camacho: The Privatization of Public Schooling

Of the four teachers interviewed, Ms. Camacho was the best educated teacher with the most years of experience. Similar to Ms. Osuna, Ms. Camacho studied to be a *maestra normalista,* but she continued her schooling at the public university in her native Nuevo León, where she graduated with a degree in Spanish literature, and a master's degree in linguistics. Spanning 26 years, her teaching experience covered every level in the system: elementary school, middle school, high school, and university, with the last 16 spent at this high school. While in Nuevo León, she authored two composition textbooks for university students.

Ms. Camacho was a founder of the International Baccalaureate (IB) at this school, the first public high school to offer it in the country, where she had been teaching literature for the past 16 years. At the moment the interview took place she had a teaching load similar to that of Mr. Gonzalez: 10 courses with 45 to 50 students in each course of 30 hours, and it was the first time she taught literature to students enrolled in the national program.

From the beginning Ms. Camacho was very assertive in her responses, providing precise answers to every question (tenor, interpersonal function). In contrast with Ms. Osuna and Mr. Gonzalez, Ms. Camacho immediately began talking about the importance of literature for high school students:

> Students need to learn to express themselves orally and by writing, but they also need to learn different facets of reading; they need not just to understand what they read, [but] they need to learn to read critically so that they can really interpret what they read when they go to the university. That's why here in high school, students have to learn to read between the lines, and most importantly, learn to be a critical student, and that it's something that you only learn when you read. (excerpt 9)

She was also very critical when asked about her current experience with students in the national program and complained that "they don't see how useful this subject is, it's kind of like I'm talking to a wall." This attitude was reinforced by her open criticisms of the dominant literacy as it was expressed in the national program:

> If the curriculum was designed so as to help students develop a love of reading, that should be the main purpose of the program, unfortunately, this is not the case because the program is too technical, too oriented towards theory ... the program imposes these technical aspects that we are forced to teach. (excerpt 10)

However, it is important to note that this criticism was expressed in the context of a constant comparison between her experience teaching in the national program and her experience in the IB program. In her answers, it was evident that being an IB teacher gave her a critical stance toward the national curriculum:

> It's difficult for me to establish some kind of parameter of comparison between the national and the international program, because they're two different programs with different goals; the objectives of the international program are for the long run whereas the objectives of the national program are for the short run. (excerpt 11)

Thus, one could say that her beliefs about subject matter and literacy were the product of her experience as an IB instructor.

Her teaching experience in two contexts within the same high school was also perceived in terms of private versus public schooling as it became clear in some of her comments regarding her perceptions of the difference in quality of instruction provided in private schools in comparison to public schools. Having worked in the private school system in the past, Ms. Camacho emphasized the critical reading and writing skills development opportunities in private schools. Given the fact that students enrolled in the IB program have to pay for the program fees (which cover IB materials and evaluations and are charged in U.S. dollars), it was not surprising that the distinction between private versus public schooling was a constant element in Ms. Camacho's discourse, a metaphor perhaps of the privatization of a public school that the IB program seemed to embody in this particular context.

Her identity as an IB/private teacher was most evident when she referred to students in both programs, as it was highlighted by clear markers in her discourse:

> I grade their notebooks ... but *these* students are not used to this experience, I worked for a long time in a private school and grading *their* notebooks was taken for granted, but not *here*, and this is the first time that I work with *students in the national program*, I have always worked with the IB students. (excerpt 12)

In a way, Ms. Camacho's discourse was similar to that of Mr. Gonzalez's in her constant use of deictics ("these students," "their notebooks": mode, textual function), but her perceptions about her current struggle with students in the national program were expressed in terms of a flawed public system when compared to the private system, as both her past experience in private schools and her long experience with the IB students (a highly selective, expensive program) in this school seemed to attest.

In spite of her criticism of the national program and of her high qualifications as a literature teacher, Ms. Camacho complied with the national mandates as it was evident in the interview and class observations, where students read and worked with the only book assigned for the whole semester: a textbook covering the technical content recommended in the program. Thus, she seemed to be convinced there was nothing she could do to change the institutional practices of the public educational system. Her criticism, however, was very clear in pinpointing crucial problems of Mexico's public high school education: curricular content, group size, time spent in class, and teachers' teaching load. Of particular interest was her criticism regarding literacy skill instruction and the differences/inequalities when compared with a program such as the IB or private schooling.

MR. TORRES: LOCAL VERSUS DISTANT LITERACIES

Mr. Torres was born in the central state of Jalisco but moved to Tijuana when he was a youngster and considered himself a native of this border town. His educational background included a degree in teaching from Tijuana's *Escuela Normal Estatal*, with a major in Spanish, and some postgraduate work on reading. His teaching experience spanned 22 years of teaching reading (*Taller de Lectura y Redacción*) and literature in this high school, and one year of teaching language at the middle school located next door, where he had been a student in the past. His average teaching load was 30 hours per week.

Similar to Ms. Camacho's responses, Mr. Torres's answers were short and very much to the point. Although Mr. Torres expressed his frustration with students' lack of motivation with reading in general and with literature in particular, he was the only one of the four teachers interviewed who seemed to be actively searching for ways to get students involved in the literacy activities his class promoted. For instance, when I asked him what he thought about the national curricular program, Mr. Torres seemed to think the program was well-suited for the needs of his students: "I think that the program, even though it's designed by people 2000 miles away from here, I think that it's appropriate, I think it's good ..." (excerpt 13); however, he also emphasized the fact that the program was part of "distant literacy practices," as opposed to the "local literacies," to which he seemed to adhere during his classes (Street, 1995).

Although the program Mr. Torres was referring to does not require any particular readings, he made sure that his students read, along with three works recommended in the program (a textbook and two novels by renown Latin American authors), a collection of short stories written by a local author. This regionalization of the national program was a point he explicitly stressed several times during the interview. He explained that "[he was] in the process of seeing how to implement and regionalize the information about the topic/genre of the legend" (excerpt 14), a process he would accomplish by including regional folktales in the required readings. By teaching a literary genre through the writings of a local author, Mr. Torres subverts the literary canon inherent in the national program, as well as in students' cultural expectations with regards to literature as a subject: "[students] get 'blocked' when it comes to literature; they think, right? *El Quijote de la Mancha* ... " (excerpt 15). In fact, Mr. Torres's emphasis on this topic was expressed as a shared obligation between him and his students:

> I was just telling students yesterday: *we have* to read texts that are more regional, and that it's why they [the students] are now going to analyze *Las Leyendas de Tijuana*, by Sor Abeja, which is an excellent book. (excerpt 16)

In this last example, Mr. Torres encodes a verbal process followed by direct speech in which, through a modulated declarative ("we have to read texts that are more regional"), he expresses a command to his students. Even so, he briefly eliminates the hierarchical relationship between himself and his students by sharing this responsibility with them.

These examples illustrate a dominant Discourse in Mr. Torres's interview: Through his strong identification with the region where he taught, one could hear the voice of a committed teacher somehow different from Ms. Osuna's Discourse (in her case, a teacher loyal to the public system in general, and the federal system in particular); or to Ms. Camacho's commitment to good education under the "right" circumstances. The referents expressed in Mr. Torres's interview encoded the strong commitment of a teacher for *these/his* students. In fact, it was this same identity that emerged at one point toward the end of the interview when he questioned my knowledge about regional literature and local folklore (interpersonal function):

> By the way, have you read *Las Leyendas de Tijuana*? No? It's very interesting, the students get excited. There's this very pretty story that takes place here, where we are. I've lived here since I was one year old ... I grew up here ... I used to swim in that swimming pool, and when I get that story and I began to read it I was so scared ... and then imagine, I tell all this to the students, now read it and we begin to comment and discuss; that's what has allowed me to get them interested in literature ... (excerpt 17)

Mr. Torres's interview was different from the others' in several other aspects: The informal tone adopted by him in his use of the pronoun *tú* (as opposed to the formal *usted* used by the rest of the participants) when he addressed me minimized the interpersonal distance between us. This lack of formality was reinforced by the reversal of roles introduced by him when he questioned my knowledge of regional literature, thereby reducing any hierarchic relation between us (interpersonal function).

In spite of Mr. Torres's apparent compliance with national curricular mandates about subject matter, his insistence on the need to teach regional authors showed a different picture: Instead of teaching theory, he made sure his students read a few novels during the semester, instead of reading the "classics" (e.g., *El Quijote*), he preferred to share his knowledge about local traditions and folklore. These activities were a clear corollary to Mr. Torres's beliefs about literacy and subject matter: the need to start by reading about one's own reality.

DISCUSSION

Through the interviews, teachers' D/discourse provided an access to some of their beliefs about subject matter, literacy, and dominant literacies: For both history teachers, the content in their classes was a powerful tool for inculcating in students a strong national identity, although this perspective took a different shape in their teaching. In line with this kind of thinking, content literacy for Ms. Osuna meant uncritical reading of texts praising the lives and good deeds of national heroes, whereas Mr. Gonzalez leaned more toward memorization of certain facts: names, dates, and figures. Both teachers seemed to comply with the national curriculum, although they expressed their frustration with the amount of information required to teach; content was apparently not a problem.

A different picture emerged from the interviews of the two literature teachers: Both teachers defined subject matter in terms of critical literacy, yet only one (Ms. Camacho) overtly criticized the national program as being too technical. Her criticism, however, encompassed the public school system, and her constant comparison between IB program/students and her current students (enrolled in the regular/national program) seemed to reach the students as well. This perception was reinforced by her reluctance to teach critical literacy to students enrolled in the national program, as her compliance with curricular mandates seemed to attest. By contrast, Mr. Torres seemed to agree with the content of the national program, yet his strong regional identity imbued his Discourse with clear undertones of non-compliance with dominant/distant literacies embodied in canonical literature or removed from the local context. This apparent contradiction was resolved by teaching content (literary genres) through local folklore, a clear indication of his commitment to the school and students' regional context.

CONCLUSION

The context of the situation (*field*: interview about teachers' beliefs about subject matter and literacy; *tenor*: hierarchical relationship between a researcher from the state university and four high school teachers, formal in three instances, relatively informal in one; *mode*: spoken face-to-face communication) was highly determinant of the four teachers' discourse as it was expressed in their representation of experience (experiential function), their relationship with me as an interviewer/researcher, and with the students as objects of their discourse (interpersonal function), and their use of narratives, questions, answers, and situational deixis (textual function).

In the case of this study, I, a researcher from a public university, was an outsider in a higher position within the hierarchy of the educational system. Furthermore, as it is a common practice with a lot of public universities in Mexico, the contact between my university and this particular high school was at best scarce and superficial. This fact was palpable in two of the teachers' misgivings about the interviews, as it was evident through their distancing from the social context (Ms. Osuna and Mr. Gonzalez), and at least in one case, the act of teaching (Mr. Gonzalez).

Although only one teacher (Ms. Camacho) overtly criticized the dominant literacy as expressed in the national curriculum, her referent in this criticism was her successful experience in private education (the IB program and her past experience), and attributed her failure in promoting critical literacy in students to a flawed public system. In contrast, one teacher (Ms. Osuna) expressed her satisfaction with the educational system in general, and with her experience in particular. This attitude, in turn was reflected in her teaching practice, where history became an opportunity to develop in students a "strong national identity," and reading a highly censored activity with no opportunity for dissent or critical thinking.

Conversely, contrary to his explicit approval of the national curricular mandate, one Literature teacher's Discourse (Mr. Torres) and teaching experience subverted the dominant literacy through his regionalization of the content, and at least on one occasion, inverted the roles of interviewer/interviewee to question my knowledge on this subject (interpersonal mode).

Through the narratives of displacement (Mr. Gonzalez, Ms. Camacho) and the institutionalized discourse on teaching (Ms. Osuna), three of the teachers seemed to comply with the dominant literacy. Just one teacher, as it was clear in his strong regional and professional identity, questioned in his practice the pertinence of the dominant ideology.

APPENDIX: THE EXCERPTS IN THE ORIGINAL SPANISH

MO—A mí me emociona ser maestra desde el momento mismo que elijo esta profesión ... mi trayectoria siempre ha sido dentro del sistema federal, he tratado de defender el federalismo porque siento que lo práctico es de mucha ventaja para los profesores ... por eso es maravilloso estar en la federación. (excerpt 1)

GLB—¿Con qué frecuencia les pide usted trabajos?

MO—Fíjese y ahorita solamente tres grupos ... pero todo el tiempo he trabajado, cuando he tenido diez grupos, y no tenía nada aquí en la oficina. Por eso yo digo que si realmente le interesa a uno la educación, de verdad quiere uno avance y la transformación de México, los maestros somos los obligados a hacer esto de estar constantemente viendo qué están haciendo nuestros alumnos. (excerpt 2)

MO—También ellos saben, los alumnos que están conmigo, que deben tener mucho cuidado en lo que leen; porque hay conceptos que en ocasiones no llenan las expectativas de lo que realmente quisiéramos que fuera México, verdad? ... Entonces hay gente como muy radical, gente que escribe historia pero que como a su manera, no? A su conveniencia ... (excerpt 3)

MO—*Digo no! no culpemos al gobierno! ... busca tu verdad! ... Tú puedes!* (excerpt 4)

MG—Efectivos de clase, se puede decir que trece años aquí. Porque en realidad yo, más que dar clases me dedicaba a la planeación educativa, a asesoramiento, también en el aspecto educativo, a funcionarios de allá de la Secretaría de Educación Pública. Eso era lo que hacía yo, analista de la Secretaría de Educación Pública, planear el sistema educativo nacional. (excerpt 5)

MG—Ah, bueno! Caí como mi jefe en desgracia políticamente y me fui como coordinador del área de ciencias sociales en una escuela técnica; ahí di clases. (excerpt 6)

MG—Era coordinador operativo ... Porque yo advertí que los directores y subdirectores de escuelas secundarias ... no tienen técnicas y conocimientos sobre administración ... entonces junto con otros maestros diseñamos un primero y un segundo nivel que se llamaban cursos de actualización administrativa para directores y subdirectores ... Fueron tan buenos estos cursos que más tarde Aquiles Caballero, que era subsecretario, nos solicitó que se ampliara a secundarias generales ... Entonces me convertí casi en coordinador operativo a nivel nacional de esos curso. (excerpt 7)

MG—Es increíble pero la experiencia es que [a los alumnos] no le llama la atención la materia ... el maestro ya casi no tiene armas para presionar al alumno a que aprenda, y regularmente se le culpa siempre al maestro cuando salen mal las cosas ... [los estudiantes] no nos quieren ... [a los maestros de Historia]. (excerpt 8)

MC—El estudiante necesita aprender a expresarse primeramente y tanto en forma oral como en forma escrita, pero también necesita aprender todas las fases de la lectura, necesita no nada más la lectura de comprensión, necesita llegar hasta la lectura crítica para que realmente pueda interpretar los textos a los que se va a enfrentar durante su carrera universitaria, entonces aquí en la preparatoria se deben sentar las bases para que el alumno aprenda a ser un alumno crítico, y solamente eso se logra mediante la lectura. (excerpt 9)

MC—Si los programas [curriculares] estuvieran más encaminados a que el alumno ... a despertarles el amor por la lectura, yo pienso que ese sería el objetivo final del programa; desgraciadamente en parte se cumple pero en una buena parte es muy técnico, muy teórico ... el programa nos obliga a cubrir aspectos más técnico. (excerpt 10)

MC—A mí se me hace un poco difícil establecer, digamos algunos parámetros de comparación entre el nacional y el internacional, porque son dos programas diferentes y la finalidad de ellos también es ... son objetivos algunos a largo plazo como el internacional y a corto plazo el del nacional ... (excerpt 11)

MC—Les corrijo la libreta ... por ejemplo estos alumnos no están acostumbrados a esta famosa libreta, yo porque trabajé muchos años en el colegio particular y pues la libreta era así como algo de cajón, pero aquí no, y yo éste es el primer semestre que trabajo con el nacional, yo siempre he trabajado con el internacional ... (excerpt 12)

MT—Me parece que el programa, aunque lo hagan a tres mil kilómetros de distancia me parece que en su conjunto está ajustado ... es bueno. (excerpt 13)

MT—Ahora mismo estoy en el proceso de ... de ver cómo voy a implementar y regionalizar el conocimiento sobre el tema leyenda ... (excerpt 14)

MT—Tienen bloqueado aquí literatura; piensan, ¿no? "El Quijote de la Mancha." (excerpt 15)

MT—Ayer se los decía a los alumnos: tenemos que ver a veces materiales que sean más regionales y en ese sentido ahora van a analizar *Las leyendas de Tijuana*, de Sor Abeja, que es un libro excelente. (excerpt 16)

MT—A propósito, ¿ya leyeron las *Leyendas de Tijuana*? ¿no? Está interesante, a los chamacos les emociona. Hay una leyenda muy bonita que se desarrolla aquí justamente donde estamos ... yo viví aquí desde un año de edad ... aquí crecí, ... me tocó bañarme en esa alberca que está aquí, y cuando yo agarro esa leyenda y la empiezo a leer viví con ella con un susto ... entonces imagínate, todo eso se los digo a los chamacos, ahora léanla y ya, empezamos a comentar y discutir, eso es lo que a mí me ha permitido interesarlos en la literatura ... (excerpt 17)

REFERENCES

Bakhtin, M. M. (1986). *Speech genres & other late essays*. Austin: University of Texas Press.

Barton, D., & Hamilton, M. (2000). Literacy practices. In D. Barton, M. Hamilton, & R. Ivanič (Eds.), *Situated literacies: Reading and writing in context* (pp. 7–15). London: Routledge.

Borko, H., Flory, M., & Cumbo, K. (1993). Teachers' ideas and practices about assessment and instruction: A case study of the effects of alternative assessment in instruction, student learning and accountability practices. Technical Report. Los Angeles: National Center for Research and Evaluation, Standards, and Student Testing (CRESST).

Borko, H., & Putnam, R. (1996). Learning to teach. In P. Berliner & R. Calfee (Eds.), *Handbook of educational psychology* (pp. 673–708). New York: Macmillan.

Bourdieu, P., Passeron, J. C., & de saint Martin, M. (1994). *Academic discourse: Linguistic misunderstanding and professorial power*. Stanford: Stanford University Press.

Brindley, R., & Schneider, J. J. (2002). Writing instruction or destruction: Lessons to be learned from fourth-grade teachers' perspectives on teaching writing. *Journal of Teacher Education, 53*, 328–331.

Calderhead, J. (1996). Teachers: Beliefs and Knowledge. In P. Berliner & R. Calfee (Eds.), *Handbook of educational psychology* (pp. 709–725). New York: Macmillan.

Carnoy, M., & de Moura, C. (1997). *¿Qué rumbo debe tomar el mejoramiento de la educación en América Latina? Informe del Banco Interamericano de Desarrollo*. Retrieved July 15, 2002, from http://www.iadb.org/sds/doc/Edu-CCastroS.pdf.

Comisión Económica para América Latina, CEPAL. (1992). *Educación y conocimiento: eje de la transformación productiva con equidad*. Santiago de Chile: Author.

Díaz Barriga, A., & Inclán, C. (2001). El docente en las reformas educativas: Sujeto o ejecutor de proyectos ajenos. *Revista Iberoamericana de Educación, 25*, 17–41.

Eggins, S. (1994). *An introduction to systemic functional linguistics*. London: Continuum.

Fairclough, N. (1995). *Critical discourse analysis: The critical study of language*. London: Longman.

Fairclough, N. (2004). Semiotic aspects of social transformation and learning. In R. Rogers (Ed.), *An introduction to Critical Discourse Analysis in education* (pp. 225–236). New Jersey: Lawrence Erlbaum Associates.

Gee, J. P. (1996). *Social linguistics and literacies: Ideology in discourses*. New York: Falmer.

Gee, J. P. (1999). *An introduction to discourse analysis: Theory and method.* New York: Routledge.

Giroux, H. (1996). Is there a place for cultural studies in colleges of education? In H. Giroux, C. Lankshear, P. McLaren, & M. Peters (Eds.), Counter narratives. *Cultural studies and critical pedagogies in postmodern spaces.* New York: Routledge.

Halliday, M. A. K. (1978). *Language as social semiotic: The social interpretation of language and meaning.* London: Edward Arnold.

Hamilton, M. (2000). Expanding the new literacy studies: using photographs to explore literacy as social practice. In D. Barton, M. Hamilton, & R. Ivanič (Eds.), *Situated literacies: Reading and writing in context* (pp. 16–34). London: Routledge.

Haney, J. J., Czerniak, C. M., & Lumpe, A. T. (1996). Teacher beliefs and intentions regarding the implementation of science education reform strands. *Journal of Research in Science Teaching, 33,* 971–993.

Instituto Nacional de Estadística, Geografía e Informática, INEGI. (2000). *Censo nacional de población y vivienda.* México: Author.

Marcelo, C. (1987). *El pensamiento del profesor.* Barcelona: CEAC.

Miras, M., Solé, I., & Castells, N. (2000). Evaluación en el área de lengua: pruebas escritas y opiniones de los profesores. *Lectura y Vida: Revista Latinoamericana de Lectura, 21*(6).

Moni, K., van Kraayenoord, C., & Baker, C. (1999). English teachers; perceptions of literacy assessment in the first year of secondary school. *Australian Journal of Language and Literacy, 22,* 1–25.

Morales-Gómez, D., & Torres, C. A. (1990) *The State, Corporatist Politics and Educational Policy Making in Mexico.* Westport: Praeger.

Pajares, M. (1992). Teachers' beliefs and educational research: Clearing up a mecí construct. *Review of Educational Research, 62,* 303–332.

Poulson, L., Avramidis, R., Fox, R., Medwell, J., & Wray, D. (2001). The theoretical beliefs of effective teachers of literacy in primary schools: An exploratory study of orientations to reading and writing. *Research Papers in Education, 16*(3), 271–292.

Richardson, V. (1996). The role of attitudes and beliefs in learning to teach. In J. Sikula, T. J. Buttery, & E. Guyton (Eds.), *Handbook of research on teacher education* (pp. 102–119). New York: Macmillan.

Sandoval, E. (2001). Ser maestro de secundaria en México: Condiciones de trabajo y reformas educativas. *Revista Iberoamericana de Educación, 25,* 83–102.

Secretaría de Educación Pública. (2001). *Programa Nacional de Educación, 2001–2006.* México: Author.

Smyth, J. (1997). Teaching and social policy: Images of teaching for democratic change. In Biddle, B., T. Good, & I. Goodson (Eds.), *International handbook of teachers and teaching* (pp. 1081–1143). London: Kluwer.

Street, B. (1995). *Social literacies: Critical approaches to literacy in development, ethnography and education.* New York: Longman.

Tatto, M. T. (1998). The influence of teacher education on teachers' beliefs about purposes of education, roles, and practice. *Journal of Teacher Education, 49,* 66–77.

van Driel, J., Beijaard, D., & Verloop, N. (1999). Professional development and reform in science education: The role of teachers' practical knowledge. *Journal of Research in Science Education, 38,* 137–158.

Vološinov, V. (1973). *Marxism and the Philosophy of Language.* Cambridge: Harvard University Press.

Section III. Hegemonic Ideologies in U.S. History Curricula

CHAPTER FIVE

Unlearning the Official History: Agency and Pedagogies of Possibility

PANAYOTA GOUNARI

Remembrance of the past may give rise to dangerous insights, and the established society seems to be apprehensive of the subversive contents of memory. Remembrance is a mode of dissociation from the given facts, a mode of "mediation" which breaks, for short moments, the omnipresent power of given facts. Memory recalls the terror and the hope that passed.
—Herbert Marcuse, One Dimensional Man (1974, p. 98)

DISCURSIVE CONSTRUCTION OF AN IDEAL HISTORICAL MODEL

The present obsession with "historical literacy" has reached unprecedented proportions in the United States, both in the education debate and in the public arena. We are witnessing an intellectual battle over a redefinition of history—ranging from support to programs that teach traditional American history by those in charge of disbursing federal funds and proclamations by conservative groups of a widespread "historical illiteracy," to the very death of history as it is illustrated in the notorious *End of History* by Francis Fukuyama.

This historical moment is by no means coincidental. As the United States assumes the role of a megapower aspiring to become the referent for the reading of the rest of the world and insists upon setting the context in which world histories should be interpreted, there is a tremendous need to rewrite and promote history from a hegemonic point of view, thereby securing a world order to be legitimized through the construction of a discourse of common sense. Thus, there exists the attempt, on the one hand, to create new "mnemonic frameworks of definition"[1] that impose an understanding of subsequent histories through dehistoricizing spaces, places, and social locations. On the other hand, the conservatives accuse youths of historical illiteracy, as a form of ignorance of what is hegemonically deemed "important," as stated by Lynne Cheney:

> We are not doing a very good job of teaching [American history] now, as a recent survey of seniors at the nation's top liberal arts colleges and research universities reveals. Scarcely more than half, the survey found, "knew general information about American democracy and the Constitution." Vast majorities were ignorant of facts that high school seniors should know: Only a third could identify George Washington as the American general at Yorktown; fewer than a quarter knew that James Madison was the "father of the Constitution."[2]

In a similar tone, the ultra-conservative American Council of Trustees and Alumni (ACTA) has been warning that "As we move into the 21st century, our future leaders are graduating with an alarming ignorance of their heritage—a kind of collective amnesia—and a profound historical illiteracy which bodes ill for the future of the republic."[3]

While conservatives are eager to penalize youths for ignorance of what they call "basic historical facts," they produce their own version of "true" history that

a. is limited to the history of the United States and ignores its own, inextricable links to world histories, the ways in which the United States radically affects them and is affected by them;
b. has a "canonical" virtue to the degree that it is characterized as "shared," "homogeneous," and "worthy" and is promoted accordingly;
c. is western-centered and marginalizes other histories;
d. presents itself in disconnectedness with the current socio-historical order and the ideological weavings it entails; and
e. uses a dehistoricized language manifested through specific discursive practices that legitimize its supposed accuracy.

This obsession with an assimilationist and homogeneous notion of history that is necessarily dehistoricized—because it needs to erase history in order to rewrite it—gave rise to a number of works that proposed "cultural literacy" and "historical consciousness" as an antidote to what has been perceived as a series of crises in our modern western civilization. The propagation of these mythical crises reached their apogee with the publication of Allan Bloom's *The Closing of the American Mind*,

E. D. Hirsch's book, *Cultural Literacy: What Every American Needs to Know*, and Arthur Schlesinger's *The Disuniting of America: Reflections on a Multicultural Society*, among others. What these authors share is their obsession with the construction of a so-called crisis in U.S. history that, in their view, has been degraded into a useless, anathematic, and irrelevant narrative since it has been stripped from what they consider its canonical context. These conservative scholars, however, purposely fail to link the canonical base of U.S. history with a western, Eurocentric, patriarchal framework. They claim to be concerned with a form of historical amnesia that is spreading like a virus in contemporary societies that fail not only to remember the past, but also to celebrate history in its supposed triumphant truth—a quality that they perceive as making history "didactic" and "transparent." At the same time, while accusing youths of historical illiteracy, they hold the ideological conviction that gives primacy to western civilization while attacking other forms of cultural identifications and memories, which, nevertheless, are historical as well. Along these lines one can understand the ongoing assault on ethnic, race, and gender studies, among other fields because these are seen as not purely "historical." However, our understanding of the "historical" should move beyond the institutionally sanctioned official version to include diverse forms of knowledge, dangerous memories, and experiences that mark the extent of our unfinishedness as human beings and our sense of agency as intervention in the world.

The idea of a homogeneous and non-threatening narrative of U.S. history, one that has been sterilized from racial conflicts, gender tensions, and subjugated histories, has been essential to the reproduction of a culture of consensus where citizens passively and uncritically accept the fateful relationship of their country to the rest of the world. As Edward Said notes, "History is what as Americans we are supposed to believe about the U.S. (not about the rest of the world, which is "old" and therefore irrelevant)—uncritically, unhistorically. There is an amazing contradiction here. In the popular mind the U.S. is supposed to stand above or beyond history."[4] This concept leads to the creation of a false dichotomy between "old" versus "new" history, which is never lost on policy makers, who often rely on historical disconnectedness to forge distorted realities that promote their respective version of history. This dynamic was abundantly clear when now former U.S. Secretary of Defense Donald Rumsfeld attempted to dismiss the European opposition, spearheaded by France and Germany, to the Iraq war, which he characterized as the "old" Europe that is no longer relevant. The "new" visionary Europe is made up of countries that remain obediently aligned with U.S. hegemonic principles. The old versus new Europe false dichotomy also attempts to create a context that brooks no dissent or discussion concerning the preemptive war against Iraq, the violation of world regulatory bodies such as the United Nations, and the ethics and values of multilateralism and international consensus. Having failed to find moral and ethical grounds to launch a pre-emptive and illegal war condemned by most of the world, Rumsfeld's only recourse was to rely on the manipulation of discourse strategies and to arrogantly dismiss world opinion, historical facts, and international laws. This attitude became evident in his statement when he was asked by a crowd of European journalists "for proof for the assertion that weapons of mass destruction confronted the United States with a clear and present danger." Rumsfeld said, "The absence of evidence is not evidence of absence."[5]

The use of false dichotomies such as old versus new Europe by Rumsfeld, and George W. Bush's "You're either with us or against us,"[6] is in line with Said's thinking, which suggests that in the construction of "common sense," the United States appears as an extra-historical entity to the degree that it supersedes history while at the same time using it to legitimize its own (dis)order. Here common sense needs to be understood in conjunction with the thinking of Antonio Gramsci. According to Gramsci, common sense is

> the conception of the world which is uncritically absorbed by the various social and cultural environments in which the moral individuality of the average man [sic] is developed. Common sense is not a single unique conception, identical in time and space. Its most fundamental characteristic is that it is a conception which, even in the brain of one individual, is fragmentary, incoherent and inconsequential, in conformity with the social and cultural position of those masses whose philosophy it is.[7]

If common sense is the assimilation of the dominant ideology to the degree that it seems natural and is uncritically believed, then the discourse of common sense used by the dominant order can be understood as the uses of language in the form of discourses as forms of social practices that work to neutralize language and therefore the ensuing practices, institutions, assumptions, and presuppositions. This way of thinking results in "developing a type of moral individuality" that is deeply immune to human suffering and injustice. All this is shaped through historical, social, cultural, and ideological practices that, in the case of common sense, are either erased or invisible, making the discourse of common sense a powerful tool to justify policies, political decisions, and practices that are largely designated to oppress, stupidify, and block dissent. Along these lines, the selection of a specific historical discourse does not allow any possibility for interrogation, which might lead to the opening up of history or historical difference. In other words, instead of viewing the "crisis of history" as containing the possibility for developing multiple referents for its understanding, conservative scholars and policy makers recoil into a fixed, predetermined treatment of history that is "descriptive rather than anthropological and political. ... Its meaning is fixed in the past, and its essence is that it provides the public with a common referent for communication and exchange."[8]

However, in their urge to make a common historical referent "transparent" and "didactic," conservative scholars and ultra-right think tanks achieve "nothing less and nothing more than a veiled [historical] information-banking model based on a 'selective selection' of Western [historical events],"[9] designed to devalue, dismiss, and degrade the daily lived experiences that constitute the historical referents for those people who are never included in their so-called history. This process of evaluating and understanding history not only "dismisses the notion that [history] has any determinate relation to the practices of power and politics,"[10] but it also creates a false binarism between what constitutes the official history and what "is largely defined as a part of an on-going struggle to make history, experience, knowledge, and the meaning of everyday life in one's own terms."[11]

The current challenge for critical educators and progressive policy makers is to reinvent history to include multiple histories and experiences that reflect the lives, struggles, aspirations, and dreams of both dominant and subjugated groups. This will help move these subjugated groups from the periphery of our school curricula into a center stage where they will be able to recount their own histories while at the same time questioning and redefining the dominant version. In this chapter I juxtapose the official version largely promoted by the conservative agenda against other equally important, albeit marginalized histories. At the same time, I am attempting to deconstruct the conservative notion claiming that a level of historical literacy can be reached by simply parroting or reciting "important" historical facts. Uncritical assimilation of historical facts achieves nothing more than a reproduction of the official version that stops short from mobilizing any type of intervention into the public sphere. Unfortunately, as this chapter demonstrates, conservative educators and policy makers have been successful in promoting their own fatalistic romanticism through a historical discourse of common sense that reproduces an ideology of consensus.

HISTORY AS CONTAINMENT: THE CONSERVATIVE AGENDA

The understanding of history as the reproduction of the official version is best illustrated in a relatively recent survey entitled "Losing America's Memory: Historical Illiteracy in the 21st Century," conducted by the ultra-conservative American Council of Trustees and Alumni (ACTA). ACTA defines itself as a "non-profit organization based in Washington D.C., dedicated to academic freedom, quality and accountability." According to their survey, 81% (four in five) of the senior students from the "top 55" universities and colleges of the United States failed a history test that included questions such as, first, "identify the basic principles of the U.S. constitution," second, "who is the father of the U.S. constitution," or third, "identify a line from the Gettysburg address," and so forth, while 99% of the students asked could positively identify Beavis and Butthead as cartoon characters and 98% knew that Snoop Doggy Dog was a rap singer.[12] The analysts of the survey unleashed a harsh critique against today's youths accusing them of historical illiteracy to the degree that, according to them, it jeopardizes the "belief that a shared understanding, a shared knowledge, of the nation's past unifies a people and ensures a common civic identity" (ACTA, 2000). Seen through this conservative prism, the "failure" of the senior students in history was for ACTA analysts a failure to assume a type of civic identity that is "common" for everybody living in the United States.

Such surveys, through their discourse, the presence as well as the absence of specific content, attempt to legitimize a specific type of historical literacy. In order to achieve this end, they recur to a wide range of discursive tactics; ACTA presents itself as a non-profit organization, which resonates in the public's mind with institutions such as churches or church associations, schools, charities, medical providers, legal aid societies, volunteer services organizations, research institutes, museums, and so forth. ACTA's nonprofit organizational character aims at two things: to promote a politically neutral profile, thus creating the assumption that there is no political agenda behind its goals and action, and to legitimize its discourse and practices. At this juncture, ACTA's ideology disguises its ideological nature by becoming naturalized and perceived as "common sense." However, a close analysis of its discourse, including both events and their structures, unveils its political and ideological agenda.

Take for instance the title of the 2002 ACTA survey "Restoring America's Legacy: The Challenge of Historical Literacy in the 21st Century." The assumptions are that history is some form of mental restoration of events, a revival of the dead. The word *legacy* conjures an image of glory while it carries a worthiness, presupposing that history has to be glorious to be important, that it is about luminous times and great contributions, rather than about genocides, wars, tensions, and ideological conflicts as well. This is illustrated in the glorification of other early European arrivals or the celebration of Columbus Day. Lynne Cheney insists that "We should teach our children how hard the establishment of this country was. One of the documents they should read is *Of Plymouth Plantation*, in which William Bradford describes how the pilgrims 'brought safe to land ..., fell upon their knees and blessed the God of heaven, who had brought them over the vast and furious ocean."[13] Cheney forgets to mention, of course, that where the Pilgrims settled was the land of the Wampanoag, a Native American tribe who welcomed them. Here is how Frank James, a tribe member selected as a speaker for the 350th anniversary of the Pilgrim's landing described the same event:

> The Pilgrims had hardly explored the shores of Cape Cod four days before they had robbed the graves of my ancestors, and stolen their corn, wheat and beans. ...

Massasoit, the great leader of the Wampanoag, knew these facts; yet he and his People welcomed and befriended the settlers ... , little knowing that ... before 50 years were to pass, the Wampanoags ... and other Indians living near the settlers would be killed by their guns or dead by diseases that we caught from them ... Although our way of life is almost gone and our language is almost extinct, we the Wampanoags still walk the lands of Massachusetts ...[14]

James's speech was censored because it presented a version of history that went against the "official story."

Along the same lines and in contrast to Lynne Cheney's westernized curriculum ideas, Zinn for example, gives a different perspective for the ventures of Columbus, less glorious and noteworthy:

The policy and acts of Columbus for which he alone was responsible began the depopulation of the terrestrial paradise that was Hispaniola in 1492. Of the original natives, estimated by modern ethnologists at 300,000 in number, one-third were killed off between 1494 and 1496. By 1508, an enumeration showed only 60,000 alive ... in 1548 Oviedo doubted whether 500 Indians remained.

When we want to teach our students about "how hard the establishment of this country was" following Cheney's advice, we should make sure to include the decimation of indigenous peoples and the atrocities committed against them. According to Zinn, "The same misguided values that have made slaveholders, Indian killers, and militarists the heroes of our history books still operate today."[15] It becomes obvious that there are groups of people who are usually absent from the "gloriousness" of American history—"our history" according to Cheney—and from history textbooks: the Native Americans, the Mexicans, the African slaves, the women, the immigrants, and so forth. In the conservative agenda of writing history, there is almost never a space to talk about their histories. Even when marginalized groups are present, all conflicts and tension are erased or silenced to promote a more "politically correct" harmonious picture of co-existence.[16]

The purported "political correctness" is part of the same discourse that ACTA uses in its report. Following the phrase "America's Legacy" in the main title of ACTA's report, the subtitle serves to reiterate and affirm that historical literacy is, in fact, the restoration of the American legacy. Here ACTA celebrates a revival of history by erasing it. The report completely neglects the fact that there are six billion people on this planet with their own histories and lived experiences, 6 billion offspring of people who lived before us and tracked their own histories, creating diverse historical memories. Nevertheless, according to ACTA, history starts and ends in the United States, and historical literacy is equated with American history literacy. Even so, ACTA employees not only select the history that is worthy from the vast array of historical events and realities, they also suppress entangled histories from this selected version. For instance, while they promote learning American history, they exclude discussions of race relations, slavery, and oppression, and the genocide of Native Americans. Despite their purported commitment to academic freedom they unleash an overt attack on multiculturalism and race studies accusing universities that "instead of broad courses on the full sweep of American history, … [they] require a narrow focus on racism and inequality." They insist that "while knowledge of these topics is surely commendable, it is woefully incomplete when most students bring to the classroom a virtual ignorance of America's history and its contributions to freedom and democracy."[17] There is a noticeable paradox: ACTA creates a false dilemma in that educational institutions are either going to teach American history or they are going to teach about racism and inequality—as if the former can possibly exist without the latter and vice versa. Conservative scholars refuse to teach the inextricable connection between the two as well as their consequential relation. In this respect, they advocate a commonsense styled pedagogy that does not extend beyond a certain comfort zone and does not call into question their "facts." Furthermore, the call to teach "America's history and its contributions to freedom and democracy" excludes the entangled histories of America's support to *coups d'etats,* dictatorships, paramilitary organizations, and so forth. The result is the creation of a false binary: America in its totality and grandeur or unworthy local histories of its people.

The missing elements in the title and the ensuing text in the ACTA survey are remarkable because not only is there no reference to the worth of other histories in contributing to our understanding of the world but also everything "American" is squeezed under "*our* shared past," or "*our* democracy's origins" never really explaining or identifying those whose identities are casually collapsed under "we." Can we truly talk about a "common civic identity" in a multicultural society like the United States? In order to understand this version of American history, we need to look both at the inclusions and exclusions and ask why one event may have been excluded at the expense of the other, who participated in the decision process, and what does that choice imply pedagogically for our students who read and try to understand their world given their multiplicity of origins. In addition, ACTA blatantly ignores the fact that people outside the United States lived in organized free societies that—for their historical time—were extremely democratic and participatory, as is the case with governments in most European countries. It also ignores the essential fact that a discussion of U.S. history is not complete without its incorporation into world history. By failing to "read" different historical texts (as both events and discourses) in their dialectical relations, the survey misses a great opportunity to challenge not what the students know or do not know, but rather in what ways this knowledge obscures their understanding of the world or illuminates some aspect of their civic life and therefore helps them move toward the agency and subjectivity necessary for every democratic society.

The survey goes into great lengths to suggest that "after September 11, it is particularly urgent that *we* know what *we* are fighting for, not just whom *we* are fighting against" but fails to raise the question "why are we fighting?" and "who is *we*"? Interestingly, here we see a tension between private and public histories as they collapse into each other; "we" is used where there is a call for total consensus in order to legitimize political decisions and irrational or illegal wars—yet the cultural histories of "we" are not at all included in ACTA's "official story." ACTA chairwoman, Lynne Cheney, insists that "knowledge of the ideas that have molded us and the ideals that have mattered to us function as a kind of civic glue. Our history and literature give us symbols to share; they help us all, no matter how diverse our backgrounds, feel part of a common undertaking." Anyone who has taken the time to read the long list of atrocities committed with U.S. support would call into question Cheney's "symbols to share." In addition, Cheney's use of "us" alludes to an illusionary consensus and a common culture. Her sentence is quite contradictory. On the one hand, she acknowledges that there are diverse backgrounds while on the other she claims that "our history and literature give U.S. symbols to share," failing to qualify to whose history and literature she refers. Clearly Cheney does not refer to the quasi-genocide of the Native Americans, appropriation of Mexican land, the round-ups of Japanese during WW II, or the enslavement of Africans. What Cheney really wants to suggest is that people from diverse backgrounds should unite under an umbrella of "commonality," with western or westernized memories functioning as the link. This approach implies celebrating a version of history where all of these diverse backgrounds are silenced or excluded, allowing the glory (real or imagined) of the West to shine as a process that reproduces dominant values.

It would be naïve to believe that ACTA actually advocates historical literacy. A "firm grounding in American History," as they so strongly promote, would mean learning about innumerable histories of massacre, bloodshed, inequality, undemocratic decisions, and unpopular policies while unlearning myths. It would mean a learning process designed to rupture the flawless picture of harmonious living in a model democratic society. It would mean questioning the reasons for going to war, as well as the U.S. involvement and military interventions in many countries around the hemisphere, the U.S. support of dictatorships, *coups d'etats*, paramilitary organizations, and the training of terrorists around the world.[18] It would mean exposing students to the huge divide between the rich and the poor, creating spaces to talk about racial inequalities and explaining how these inequalities have been historically shaped and reproduced. The survey insists that "if we are to preserve our Republic and keep faith with those who established it, each of us must understand our rights and responsibilities—literally we must restore America's legacy,"[19] a process whereby civic rights and responsibilities are collapsed into the restoration of American legacy. This is a highly contradictory claim for a country whose history provides abundant examples of a disregard for democratic institutions both at home and abroad. In addition, the fundamental principle in any democracy is to raise questions, rather than accepting "our legacy" and "keep faith with those who established it." A strong democracy is one that asks as many questions as possible about itself, its instauration, and survival. As opposed to teaching a traditional history of consensus and imposing a distorted common sense, a more honest and democratic account would advocate an unsettling pedagogy that promotes a conflicted consensus. Conflicted consensus is dangerously absent from U.S. society. Anyone who raises questions or tries to develop a critical understanding outside the dominant paradigm and is willing to perceive history as a possibility is usually accused of being a revisionist or unpatriotic.

ACTA's accusation that this "lack of understanding and suffering from historical illiteracy bodes ill for the future of our Republic" hides a more pernicious agenda of consensus and passivity. Instead of viewing the past as opening up space for other possible histories, the conservative discourse around remembering (as it is manifested in the ACTA Survey) focuses on history as common ground, a statistical collection of shared facts and institutions that attempt to create some sort of absolute consensus—a consensus that provides the bedrock upon which U.S. civic identity is constructed. Along these lines Donaldo Macedo suggests that

> the conservative cultural agenda fails to acknowledge ... that the reorganization of "our common culture" points to the existence of "our uncommon culture," for commonality is always in a dialectical relationship with uncommonality. Thus, one cannot talk about the centeredness of our "common culture" without relegating our "uncommon" cultural values and expressions to the margins creating a de facto silent majority.[20]

In their call to bring American history back to colleges and universities as an antidote to Snoop Doggy Dog, Beavis and Butthead, and the crisis of cultural literacy and democracy, conservative educators fail to understand that what is at stake in the present so-called crisis of history and in the young people's "resistance" or "inability" to remember is larger than simply historical literacy as competence and fact banking. The true crisis does not lie in the inability of students to memorize "worthy" historical events, but in their inability (which is consciously and intentionally maintained by the school curricula) to critically look at the past and the present and understand them in dialectical relationship as evolving rather than closed processes.

Similar to ACTA's call for "historical literacy" as facts-acquisition and memorization, the reauthorization by the U.S. Department of Education of the

Teaching American History program as part of the Elementary and Secondary Education Act,[21] also engages in a selective processing of history. Under the provisions of this program, $119 million dollars in grant money was given to 122 local school districts during 2004 with the aim of "rais[ing] student achievement by improving the quality of teaching by strengthening teachers' knowledge, understanding and appreciation of American history."[22] As announced by U.S. Secretary of Education Rod Paige, "from the Mayflower Compact to the Articles of Confederation to the civil rights marches of the 1960s, American history is alive with stories of discovery, bravery and ideas about how we live."[23] Paige insists that "students who know and appreciate the great ideas of American history will be well prepared to understand and exercise their civic rights and responsibilities."[24] Already there is the assumption that American history contains only great ideas, which closes down any pedagogical intervention to learn from unsettling memories. This proposal not only equates again history with American history, but it also legitimizes an official version of American history, excluding other intertwined histories. This sanitized American history is defined as an accumulation of "great ideas" and "bravery," a register of events that are to be transmitted to produce a specific type of civic identity. However, this structural and positivistic perception of history fails to explain a number of pertinent issues. For instance, how are students to participate in a global world armed only with knowledge of American history, as if it held some transcendental knowledge or power? Can students question the "great ideas" contained in American history? What types of representations and assumptions does this type of history create about "us" and the "others"? Who is "us" anyway? Finally, what sort of agency is to be produced when history is held hostage through a prescribed method of remembering in a closed-down space that not only minimizes possibilities but also fails to provide alternative choices in terms of historical narratives?

The true agenda of the *Teaching American History* grants is revealed in their information section where it states that grants are to be awarded to local educational institutions in order "to carry out activities to promote the teaching of *traditional* American history in elementary schools and secondary schools as a separate academic subject (not as a component of social studies)" (emphasis added).[25] Practically speaking, what this means is that the schools that receive federal funding should dedicate more time, energy, special activities, and resources to teaching a version of canonical traditional American history and, for this, these schools will be rewarded. It is ironic that under these guidelines, it would appear that teaching Howard Zinn's "People's History of the Unites States" would result in being eliminated from federal funding. The teaching of traditional American history is designed as a band-aid for what is perceived as historical illiteracy. It will, in turn, close down any possibility of interrogating historical narratives or the very notion of what is "traditional." Again, the choice of wording points to the construction of a discourse of common sense where so-called traditional American history remains unproblematic. At stake here is more than a blatant return to a canonical version of American history and a conservative attack on the school curriculum. The indisputable reign of tradition eclipses any possibility of an American identity outside these strictly prescribed historical parameters.

Tradition in the conservative view, denotes the "recording of events," a linear order of particular ways, means, representations, and institutions shared in some temporal locus in the past and deemed important as a mimetic pattern for the present and the future. It functions as a paradigm of correctness for how to live one's life, as well as with a rigid guideline for any type of individual decision making. In this sense, tradition "is perceived as having a built-in institutional quality: the assumption that there is nothing that people currently alive can do to change the institutions they inherited, and that if oblivious to their impotence they try to meddle with the legacy—then unimaginable disasters will follow, whether brought about by divine punishment or by the laws of nature which neither admit nor bear any violation."[26]

It becomes obvious that both ACTA's surveys and these touted educational policies concerning the teaching of history are an attempt to redefine history and force a return to what is called "basics." Consequently, this information-banking approach leaves out important questions that are necessary for a more critical understanding of this redefined history. What are the consequences for a democratic society of teaching a homogenized, sterilized version of history? What does it mean to create consensus among citizens? In what ways does our "common culture" create more uncommonality and difference? In fact, it is an oxymoron to speak of a "common culture" or absolute consensus in a cultural democracy where, according to Chantal Mouffe, "there can never be a completely inclusive consensus. ... The very condition of the possibility for consensus is at the same time the condition of the impossibility of consensus without exclusion."[27] Mouffe suggests that in a democracy we should witness a "conflicted consensus," that is, some form of consensus in terms of ethical-political principles that can never be rational or fully inclusive, and can only exist "through many different and conflicting interpretations that make room for dissent and for the institutions through which it can be manifested."[28] In this sense, we should strive for a type of historical literacy that will function as a catalyst in helping the United States to learn and understand what makes us citizens, what it means to live in a cultural democracy—a historical literacy that will break through the common sense of "supplied" facts by rupturing the current conservative discourse. This form of historical literacy will challenge static ideas of what is worth being historical, will prompt interventions, and create opportunities for questioning a society's own institutions. The role of pedagogy is crucial in this endeavor.

PUBLIC MEMORY AS RUPTURE: A PEDAGOGICAL PROJECT

School curricula have had enormous success in shaping and reproducing the American doctrine that insulates U.S. history and society from the messy, less linear citizenship of a global transnational world. Despite the advent of critical pedagogy and education to raise consciousness, educational curricula are still embracing a nationalistic ideal that anaesthetizes students' perceptions of the "other." The current "crisis" of history is, in reality, not a crisis of ignorance but rather a crisis of American society's growing indifference toward the very political culture of the United States. Public memory should be intimately connected with the question of democratic representation. That is, narratives of memory should necessarily enable people to read the world and position themselves in it, make the appropriate choices, and assume responsibility for themselves and the societies they live in. Along these lines, the educational dimension of public memory has to bear relevance to students' lives and histories today. It should function as a stimulant that incites them to raise critical questions rather than paralyzing their thinking. As Butler argues, "if we paralyze our thinking, ... we will fail to take collective responsibility for a thorough understanding of the history which brings U.S. to this juncture. We will, as a result, deprive ourselves of the very critical and historical resources we need to imagine and practice another future."[29]

Hegemonic history, as it is taught in schools, becomes a powerful tool that regulates the way people live and provides paradigms for mimesis rather than creating structures in which new social and cultural spaces are able to emerge. It works to conserve the past rather than as a means of insight into the past. It aids the creation and shaping of what is considered to be common sense to the degree that it imposes conceptions that are accepted and lived uncritically. History and its multifaceted constructed memories should move beyond a superficial level of remembering and celebrating the past, or parroting the "official history," as is done with the celebration of Columbus Day or Thanksgiving among other important, albeit fragmented, presentations of historical events.

Cornelius Castoriadis notes that "We live in a society, that has instituted with the past a type of relationship that is entirely original and unprecedented: total disinvestment. ... The relation to the past is, at best, touristic."[30] Given the approach to history largely promoted by the conservative agenda, it is of paramount importance to question the versions of history that are deemed worthy to be taught in schools, as well as the broader cultural and political context that disarticulates the present from questions about the past. This disarticulation is inextricably related to the increasing irrelevance of politics in people's lives as well as the erasure of the social "as a constitutive category for expanding democratic identities, social practices, and public spheres. In this instance, memory is not being erased as much as it is being reconstructed under circumstances in which public forums for serious debates have been eroded."[31]

A critical analysis of history is perceived as being so irrelevant to the present that it blocks out, as Maclear points out "difficult questions … questions about how today's social 'order' is constituted through commemorations that marginalize testimonies bearing witness to ongoing social crises and violence."[32] For example, when, as Zinn recalls, "Jewish organizations lobbied against a Congressional recognition of the Armenian Holocaust of 1915 on the grounds that it diluted the memory of the Jewish Holocaust. Or when the designers of the Holocaust Museum dropped the idea of mentioning the Armenian genocide after lobbying by the Israeli government." Zinn adds that "to remember what happened to Jews served no important purpose unless it aroused indignation, anger, action against all atrocities, anywhere in the world."[33] In other words, remembering becomes problematic when it privileges some histories at the expense of others, considering them less worthy or less atrocious. Rearticulating the past with a view to making the present political is a great teaching challenge because it offers possibilities to make the past-present-future relationship meaningful.[34]

History, in its dominant version, is always about the far remote past. It is conveniently positioned at a time so distant that it creates a comfort zone between the event and the individual. Occasionally, it gets so lost in the midst of time that it seems it should simply be left alone, that it has now gained a form of autonomy that disarticulates it from anything else. There is no call to question or problematize history. The further we go back in time, the safer it is to "remember." However, the lessons of history should be unsettling; memory should not be perceived a refuge, but rather as an open arena of struggle. Unearthing and articulating dangerous memories should contribute to our notion of political agency in that it would force us to move beyond a depoliticized comfort zone. Historical narratives should be detached from their safe and permanent character and should become a counter-memory, an "unfinished, ephemeral process"[35] that involves opposing views and ideas that are subject to critique and questioning. A dynamic comprehension of history serves as a precondition for agency, ruptures the rigid forms of determinism, and acknowledges that "in this consciousness. … the very possibility of learning, of being educated resides."[36] When history becomes distant or disconnected from the present, remembering becomes nostalgic instead of critical. The temporal/spatial dimension of history raises a number of questions. Why are history and remembrance so tied to the notion of temporal distance?

What does it mean then to remember something that happened fifty years ago while conveniently forgetting its direct link to events taking place now? In other words, how can we remember and commemorate the Holocaust while simultaneously forgetting the current atrocities of Israel against the Palestinian people and the way Holocaust memory has enabled the Jewish State "to employ the tragic memories as the certificate of its political legitimacy, a safe-conduct pass for its past and future policies, and above all as the advance payment for the injustices it might itself commit?"[37] In this sense, how can we mediate events through public memory and use disturbing memories to produce a kind of ethical referent for explaining the world without justifying it? How can disturbing memories serve as a translative tool for understanding the conditions that shape our present existence in the world? Furthermore, how can we conceptualize social history in other societies without having to recur to some sort of transparent language of truth and without having to use our own imaginary cultural constructions as a canon?

Against a static and disarticulated view of the past we should position historical memory as a pedagogical force that according to Giroux, "makes claim on certain histories, memories, narratives and representations."[38] In this instance, history is not the predetermined sequence of the determined, but "the emergence of radical otherness, immanent creation, [and] non-trivial novelty,"[39] and therefore remembering should rupture history's successive character. Through the prism of history, remembering should become less about commemorative practices and closure and more about knowing and creating spaces. History opens up the possibilities for a kind of transformative learning and an ensuing discourse of possibility. Under such conditions, the questions that need to be addressed would necessarily include: What is it in learning about other societies in other times that would enable us to understand our current historical social and cultural location, and how would this understanding or remembrance ultimately lead to our exercise of agency? How can remembering encompass a superficiality of celebration or mourning to become the axis of our transforming agency? How are we as agents to reinvent a language of critique for the past and possibility for the future that would unmask the conservative discourse and break the stagnancy of a contrived common sense?

Addressing the above questions implies viewing history as the means to an unlimited self-questioning of the individual, the society, and its institutions. Historical literacy, as intervention in the world, positions public memory as a political and pedagogical project that unfolds identities, struggles, and desires that can mobilize the present. Public memory as a set of lived experiences, representations, histories, and identifications creates space for subjective or individual positions that are not fixed spatially or temporally. While we cannot speak about a common history as a set of common identifications and images shared by everyone, we can nevertheless talk about knowledge of the past that is open to all. Within this framework, agency "becomes more than the struggle over identification, or a representational politics that unsettles and disrupts common sense; it is also a performative act grounded in the spaces and practices that connect people's everyday lives and concerns with the reality of material relations of values and power."[40]

Obviously, we cannot change what has been, but we can change how we gaze upon it, and knowing—instead of merely remembering—these histories, we can create new histories that are less exclusionary, less violent, less unjust, and more humane. It is in this rejuvenative examination and creation of what has occurred that our role as autonomous human beings should focus. By ceasing to be "tourists," "visitors," or "spectators," and instead becoming authors of our own post-memory, we can begin raising questions about our agency and subjectivity. We can begin to question and explore these topics as more than a replication of the past. This relation to the past would enable us to locate ourselves in reference to memories and histories and thus make sense of our own contemporary reality. By contesting history's memory, we would create a new memory for ourselves. Along these lines, Horkheimer suggests that "fidelity to the old is not proved by repeating it but by giving it new expression in word and deed at each historical juncture."[41] This observation implies that we should not take history as a set of transparent events representing the Truth, but rather as a set of significations that lend themselves to exploration, rupture, redefinition, and reappropriation. It also implies that "it is an error to imagine that civilization and savage cruelty are antithesis ... both creation and destruction are inseparable aspects of what we call civilization."[42] Therefore, history is essentially creation—creation and destruction—and it is incumbent upon us to decide whether to create or to destruct, because as autonomous beings we have the option to choose.

The value of "remembering" through history, that is, penetrating a different socio-historical construct lies not only on its shared, public nature, which makes it necessarily political and thus pedagogical, but also in its ability to serve as an antidote to the social and historical amnesia that results from the loss of agency. Reclaiming a politics of public memory necessarily implies reclaiming politics "as a progressive force for change within the cultural sphere."[43] The real challenge is to reconstruct the pedagogical role of history, moving beyond the limits of the discipline and creating a discourse that underlines the importance of keeping dangerous historical memories alive as a requirement for a substantive democracy. A critical perspective on public memory would consider both the politics of remembering and forgetting, and would lift the heavy yoke of positivism imposed by political will that presently distorts the manufacture of historical memories.

History as possibility must invariably be understood pedagogically so as to be relevant and meaningful. It is precisely the pedagogical and political nature of history that was succinctly understood by Paulo Freire who reminded us that "we know ourselves to be *conditioned* but not *determined*. It means recognizing that History is time filled with possibility and not inexorably determined—that the future is *problematic* and not already decided, fatalistically."[44]

NOTES

1. Norman Fairclough, *Critical Discourse Analysis: The Critical Study of Language* (London: Longman, 1995).
2. Lynne Cheney, "Teaching Our Children about America," Dallas Institute of Humanities and Culture, Dallas, TX (October 5, 2001).
3. "Losing America's Memory: Historical Illiteracy in the 21st Century," American Council of Trustees and Alumni, February 16, 2000.
4. Edward Said, Global Crisis, *ZNet*, March 17, 2003.
5. Lewis Lapham "Cause for Dissent," *Harper's Magazine*, (April 2003), p. 36.
6. You're either with us or against us, http://www.cnn.com/2001/US/11/06/gen.attack.on.terror/at CNNCom (November 6, 2001).
7. Antonio Gramsci, *The Antonio Gramsci Reader*, edited by David Forgacs (New York: New York University Press, 2000), p. 343.
8. Stanley Aronowitz and Henry A. Giroux, "Schooling, Culture and Literacy in the Age of Broken Drama: A Review of Bloom and Hirsch," *Harvard Educational Review*, 58.2 (May 1988): 175.
9. Donaldo Macedo, *Literacies of Power: What Americans Are Not Allowed to Know* (Boulder, Colorado: Westview Press, 1994), p. 65.
10. Aronowitz and Giroux, "Schooling, Culture and Literacy," pp. 65 & 66.
11. Ibid., p. 66.
12. See American Council of Trustees & Alumni (ACTA), "Losing America's Memory: Historical Illiteracy in the 21st Century," February 2000. www.goacta.org.
13. "Teaching Our Children About America"—Dallas Institute of Humanities and Culture, Dallas, Texas, October 5, 2001.
14. James Loewen, *Lies My Teacher Told Me: Everything Your American History Textbook Got Wrong*. (New York: New Press, 1995), p. 87.
15. Howard Zinn, Unsung Heroes, in *Rethinking Schools* (Fall 2000).
16. For an elaborate analysis on how historical events are misrepresented in history textbooks, see James Loewen, *Lies My Teacher Told Me: Everything your American History Textbook Got Wrong* (New York: New Press, 1995).
17. "Losing America's Memory: Historical Illiteracy in the 21st Century," p. 3.
18. For a detailed list of U.S. military interventions see ZNET, "A Century of U.S. Military Interventions: From Wounded Knee to Afghanistan."
19. ACTA Survey, p. 3.
20. Donaldo Macedo, *Literacies of Power: What Americans are Not Allowed to Know* (Boulder CO: Westview Press, 1994), p. 45.
21. See http://www.ed.gov/
22. "Paige Announces 49.6 Million in Grants to Improve Teaching of American History," *United States Department of Education News*, October 2, 2001. Availably at <http://www.ed.gov/PressReleases/>.
23. Ibid.

24. Ibid.
25. *Teaching American History Program,* Grant Information, available at <www.ed.gov/>
26. Zygmunt Bauman, *In Search of Politics* (Stanford, CA: Stanford University Press, 1999), pp. 136–137.
27. Chantal Mouffe, "Rethinking Political Community: Chantal Mouffe's Liberal Socialism," in Race, Rhetoric and the Postcolonial, edited by Gary A Olson and Lynn Worsham (New York: State University of New York Press, 1999), p. 169.
28. Chantal Mouffe, "Which Ethics for Democracy," in *The Turn to Ethics,* edited by Marjorie Garber, Beatrice Hanssen, and Rebecca Walkowitz (New York: Routledge, 2000), p. 92.
29. Judith Butler, "Explanation and Exoneration or What We Can Hear," *Theory & Event,* 5.4 (2002): 11.
30. Cornelius Castoriadis, *Time* (Athens, Greece: Ypsilon Publications, 2000), p. 98.
31. Henry Giroux, *Public Spaces Private Lives: Beyond the Culture of Cynicism* (Boulder, CO: Rowman & Littlefield, 2001), p. 10.
32. Kyo Maclear, Beclouded Visions: Hiroshima-Nagasaki and the Art of Witness (New York: New York University Press, 1999), p. 121.
33. Howard Zinn, "A larger consciousness," *ZMagazine* (October 10, 1999).
34. Excellent work towards this direction is done by *Rethinking Schools* through an array of publications. For more information see http://www.rethinkingschools.org.
35. James Young, *At Memory's Edge* (New Haven & London: Yale University Press, 2000), p. 2.
36. Paulo Freire, *Pedagogy of Freedom: Ethics, Democracy and Civic Courage* (Boulder, CO: Rowman & Littlefield, 1998), p. 66.
37. Bauman, *In Search of Politics,* p. ix.
38. Giroux, *Public Spaces Private Lives,* p. 22.
39. Cornelius Castoriadis, *The Imaginary Institution of Society* (London: Polity Press, 1998), p. 184.
40. Henry Giroux, *Impure Acts: The Practical Politics of Cultural Studies* (New York: Routledge, 2000).
41. Max Horkheimer, *Critique of Pure Reason* (New York: Seadburry, 1974), p. 156.
42. Zygmunt Bauman, *Modernity and the Holocaust* (Ithaca, New York: Cornell University Press, 1989), p. 9.
43. Giroux, *Impure Acts.*
44. Freire, *Pedagogy of Freedom,* p. 26.

Section IV. Promising Practices Based on Praxis

CHAPTER SIX

Critically Examining Beliefs, Orientations, Ideologies, AND Practices Toward Literacy Instruction: A Process OF Praxis

KAREN CADIERO-KAPLAN

> It was neither text nor instructional processes that led to the mastery of Standard English communication skills, but the nature of teachers' beliefs regarding their prior educational experience and the nature of their current relationships with children.
> (HOLLINGSWORTH & GALLEGO, 1996, P. 271)

Effective teachers are professionals who know their students and understand the types of work in which they should engage to acquire the literacy skills they need to be successful in school. Many effective teachers are also reflective individuals, but as Richardson (1994) points out "teachers make decisions on the basis of a personal sense of what works; but without examining the premises underlying a sense of working" (p. 187). That is, teachers very often engage in practices that they inherently know will "work" or are "effective," but they rarely are provided opportunities to have conversations around what theories and ideologies inform their practice and how they come to know what works. In addition, even teachers deemed effective or successful have few opportunities to interrogate curricula and "best practices" authorized by school districts and state policies.

In this chapter, I share one bilingual teacher's reflective and self-inquiry process regarding possible links between her language arts teaching practices and her beliefs about what constitutes "literacy" and effective pedagogy for linguistically and culturally diverse students. Throughout this reflective process, the teacher came face-to-face with the connections between her beliefs regarding the unjust greater society's hierarchical social order and her classroom work with low SES English language learners. Using a reflective questionnaire protocol of my design, I successfully assisted the teacher in understanding if and how her ideology about the greater social order was being replicated or challenged in her classroom via her teaching approaches. Ideology is a concept from which most teachers shy away as it is seen as a "technical" or "academic" term reserved for only those who work in the academy. However, ideology is what forms the basis of how we understand our world, which further informs our teaching practices. Ideology will be defined here as "the production and representation of ideas, values, and beliefs" (McLaren, 1998, p. 180). Ideology informs not only the knowledge of the individual but also the knowledge they present and represent both personally and professionally. For example, it is thought that in teaching our actions are neutral, but in reality all that we do in the classroom is informed by our own experiences, which are connected to specific ideological positions (i.e., conservative, liberal, conformist, nonconformist, and so on). In essence, we act out our ideologies, but we rarely name the ideologies that inform our practice.

In the context of literacy instruction, a teacher's ideology is rarely examined especially in terms of understanding what learning theories and assumptions undergird a teacher's best practice. In this chapter, I am concerned with how we, as educators, reflectively examine our beliefs about linguistic minority students and what constitutes effective literacy instruction for them. I describe how one teacher juxtaposes her ideological beliefs with her actual language arts instructional practices and the curriculum. The reflective process that this bilingual teacher underwent illustrates the importance of helping teachers recognize how unspoken ideological orientations influence the ways in which they teach, interact with students, and utilize curricular materials. One end goal of this reflective process is to help the teacher begin to understand the potential implications particular literacy ideologies and practices may have pedagogically, socially, and politically in classrooms in particular and in society in general.

As a former high school teacher and now as a university professor, I continually see how teachers and teacher educators rarely consider or discuss their beliefs about literacy instruction from a political or ideological perspective. What typically occurs when educators do get the opportunity to discuss their own beliefs about literacy and language development and about what they know works pedagogically, they may not readily notice that their stated practices or beliefs are not reflected in the materials or teaching methods presently adopted and held up as models of "best practice" by the State or the schools.

Without opportunities to reflect and critically analyze state mandated materials and their own beliefs and teaching practices, teachers are caught up in an endless loop continually uncritically reacting to curricula shifts and materials, methods, or practices. I propose here that readers engage in a process of praxis.

Praxis is defined as dialogue, action, and reflection (Freire, 1993). It is only in praxis with others that we can engage in dialogue, speaking by naming the world and processes in which we engage, then take action in the form of questioning, teaching, interrogating, and so on. After the action, take up reflection and examine the outcomes and what has been learned. This activity in turn informs a deeper dialogue, thus perpetuating the unending cycle of praxis. Teachers engage in this cycle when they develop a teaching lesson or idea, talk about it with others to see if it makes sense and is workable, thus starting the initial "dialogue." After the lesson is developed, the teacher will teach the lesson or "act." Following this action, teachers frequently reflect on the outcomes with their students or colleagues. This reflective dialogue is deeper than the initial planning dialogue and results in a new "action" and the continuation of the cycle of praxis.

I illustrate the process of praxis through the case study of one teacher using questions and reflective activities that take the reader through a similar reflective process. The goal of this process is to move toward what Bartolomé calls ideological clarity, where individuals work to identify both the dominant society's explanations for existing literacy curricula, the societal and political hierarchy that informs it, as well as our own beliefs and practices. Bartolomé (2000) states:

> Ideological clarity requires that a teacher's individual explanations be compared and contrasted with those propagated by the dominant society. It is to be hoped that the juxtaposing of ideologies forces teachers to better understand if, when, and how their belief systems uncritically reflect those of the dominant society and support unfair and inequitable conditions. (p. 168)

By engaging in a critical examination of the politics and ideologies that inform literacy practices, teachers can then begin to understand that they either "maintain the status quo, or they can work to transform the sociocultural" definitions of what it means to be a literate person and a teacher of literacy (Bartolomé, 2000).

CLARIFYING IDEOLOGIES THROUGH PRAXIS

According to Keller (2002), an immediate need exists to construct and define research processes that critically engage teachers in examining not just what they teach, but what they do in the name of literacy education through classroom discourses and practices. In this section, using the Literacy Word Web (Figure 1) that I developed and utilized with my target teacher, Eva, I will take you through a process of praxis, which I hope will also assist you in clarifying and identifying the personal ideologies that inform your own beliefs about literacy.

120 | IDEOLOGIES IN EDUCATION

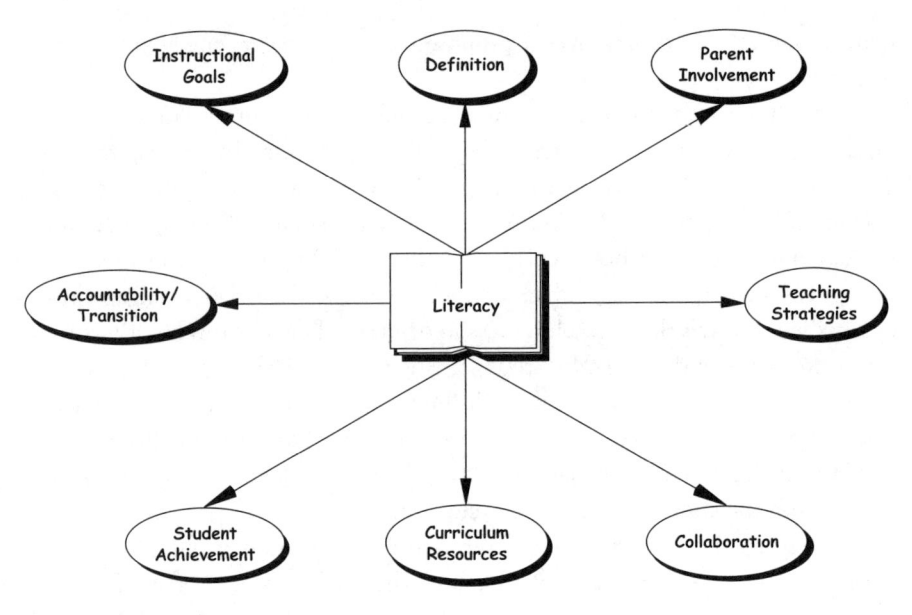

Figure 1. Literacy Web.

The aim of this reflective process is for teachers to express their beliefs about literacy instruction and how they do or do not perceive the operationalization of their beliefs in their teaching practice. To begin this critical dialogue, teachers must first reflect on their own beliefs about literacy using the Literacy Web depicted in Figure 1. The web was created based on eight themes reflected in the literature as areas that influence and impact the teaching of literacy in schools regarding definition, strategy, curriculum, and the process of "literacy," which is the center of the web (Cadiero-Kaplan, 2001).

The eight themes include:

1. Definition of Literacy: Come up with a personal definition, one not based on school programs or curricula, but derived from experience, family, community, and school contexts.
2. Parent Involvement: Define the role of parents as related to their beliefs about literacy and how teachers view parental involvement as part of their students' literacy/language development.
3. Teaching Strategies: Identify those teaching strategies that are most effective, based on personal/professional practice with learners in school contexts.
4. Collaboration: Consider here individual and group avenues for relationships that are most important in supporting literacy development inside

and outside of the classroom. Identify the collaborations that teachers deem necessary.
5. Curriculum Resources: Identify those material and personnel resources that are most important to literacy development based on professional knowledge and experience.
6. Student Achievement: Consider student outcomes, identify what students need to achieve as part of the literacy and/or language program.
7. Accountability and Transition: Specify the tools that are most effective and useful to measure literacy growth and progress based on standards, i.e., what are teachers ultimately held accountable for.
8. Instructional Goals: Identify the benchmarks and standards related to curriculum and instruction that are indicators of student success and achievement.

This reflective process and discussion of the above eight key themes can provide teachers with a tool to use in conversation with others in working toward ideological clarity. Through such praxis, individuals can begin to reveal the sociopolitical contradictions between their beliefs and their practices. This critical dialogue allows teachers to think and reflect in a concrete manner regarding their own and the school's curricula's ideological perspectives, thus providing the space to understand how ideology shapes our views of self and the world (Cadiero-Kaplan, 2004).

PRAXIS: DIALOGUE, REFLECTION, AND ACTION

After engaging teachers around their definitions and views about literacy, I typically ask them to respond to questions such as those listed in Table 1, the Literacy Web Questions. The purpose of these questions is to deepen the reflection begun individually with the web and to go deeper to discuss actual classroom processes with others. As teachers enter into dialogue, it is crucial to realize that simply bringing this knowledge out into the conscious realm is insufficient unless it is also supplemented by an awareness of the ideological construction of our consciousness and the education and political results of such construction (Kincheloe, 1995, p. 81). Thus, we first must understand the world and the way it is shaped in order for it to be transformed (Kincheloe, 1995). In this case, "world" refers to the everyday practice we engage in as teachers. As such, personal reflections on literacy practice followed by dialogue constitute a first step on the path toward ideological clarity. In this context, theories of literacy are informed not just by our beliefs, the curriculum, and teacher practice, but

TABLE 1. Literacy Web Questions

- What is your definition of literacy?
- What form of literacy do you feel is most important for your ELLs?
- How would you define bi-literacy?
- How do you put into practice your ideas of literacy and illiteracy in your classroom?
- What do you expect your ELL students to accomplish by the end of the semester? School year? By graduation?
- What are your instructional goals for the school year for your ELL students?
- To achieve these goals, identify the curriculum resources and teaching strategies you utilize?
- How do you value professional development? What has been the most beneficial form of professional development you have received?
- How are you held accountable for the progress of your students?
- What forms of assessment do you use? How often?
- How do you determine a student's readiness to transition?
- Do you think parent involvement is important? If so, how do you accomplish this?
- What contributions do parents make to the literacy development of students?

also by key literature on pedagogy and practice. Therefore, in order to achieve praxis, teachers need to examine their beliefs and practices in the context of the literature and school literacy ideology.

As part of this reflective process, teachers will also need to go further and identify areas of congruency and incongruency. For example, I ask teachers to consider if and how their literacy practices connect to specific ideologies that are reflected in their actual classroom practice? The school curriculum? The district standards? This part of the process requires identifying the ideology of instructional practice and curriculum alongside personal ideology.

USING THE REFLECTIVE WEB TO DEFINE ONE'S LITERACY BELIEFS AND PRACTICES

An example of how Eva, my target high school bilingual teacher, completed her web is illustrated in Figure 2, Eva's Literacy Web. This web reflects her initial responses in considering the various dimensions of literacy in relation to school factors (Cadiero-Kaplan, 2001). For example, Eva's initial assessment in defining literacy is students' ability to communicate in their native language and English. This response became the starting point for our conversations to further interrogate her perspective on what it means to be able to communicate in two languages. Initially, Eva felt that her current school followed a model of bilingual education that was different from the one at the school where she had worked the previous year. Based on her responses and my classroom observations, this different approach to bilingual education in her present context does

A PROCESS OF PRAXIS | 123

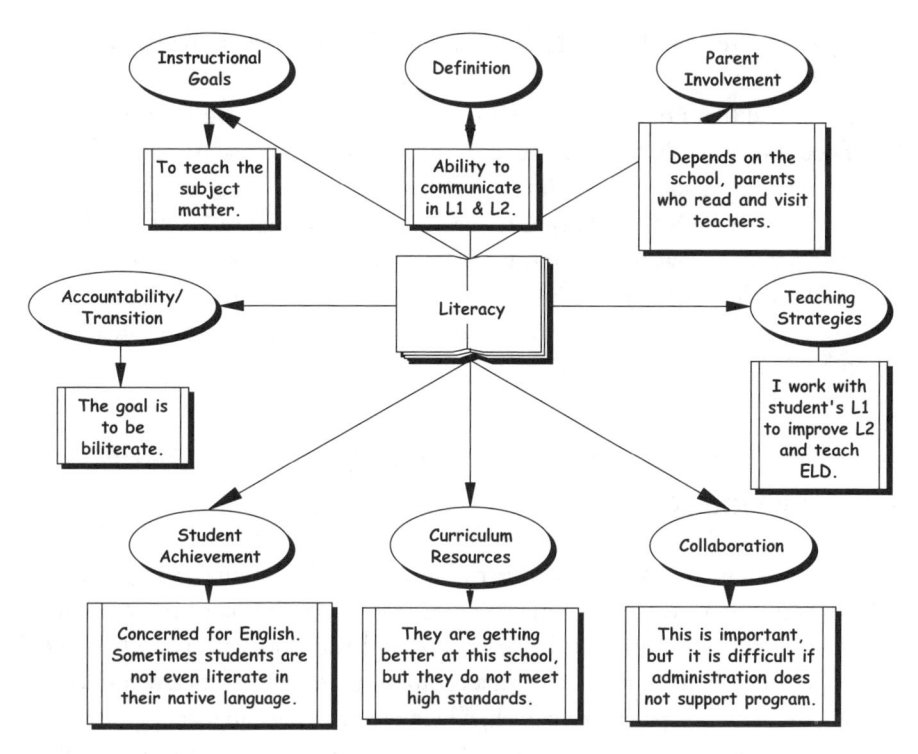

Figure 2. Eva's Literacy Web.

not support bilingualism and biliteracy as its goal, which is a key outcome that Eva values. However, Eva neither readily recognizes this difference in approach nor realizes that it is in conflict with her own ideological orientation and bilingual practice. During our conversations, Eva seems to be under the impression that the school's model of bilingual education supports her biliteracy goals. Even so, she documents various weaknesses in the program: English and the L1 are used inconsistently; English is not taught intensively; students are allowed to lose their L1; inferior materials in L1 are used; the school system resists assuming accountability for rendering students academically and linguistically underprepared, and students, through no fault of their own, end up paying the price for ineffective educational experiences. This process of praxis unveils the incongruencies between Eva's beliefs and the practice of the ideological orientation of the curricula and the programs of her current school.

After considering Eva's responses, take a moment to review Figure 2, and contemplate how you would complete your own Literacy Web. Reflect on these themes as they relate to what you believe about practice regarding literacy development for students and yourself. The point of the web is to provide a focus and context for the conversations that follow. For example, if you defined literacy as "being able to read and write to communicate," explore what you mean by this in practice.

Eva noted that literacy is the "ability to communicate in two languages." This belief could potentially reflect a progressive, cultural, or critical ideology depending on how she made connections from this definition to her practice. As you reflect on your own web and begin to dialogue, refer to Figure 1 and identify the teaching practices that match your beliefs and/or practice and then connect it to the ideology that you see best informs your practice. In the next section, I share the work I carried out with Eva, in our struggle to develop greater ideological clarity.[1]

EVA MONTOYA: A BILINGUAL HIGH SCHOOL TEACHER'S REFLECTIVE JOURNEY

Eva is a Latina bilingual, Spanish/English English Language Development (ELD) high school teacher. At the time of this study, she had been a bilingual teacher for six years. Eva is in her early 30s and was born and attended school (K-12) in the same southern California community in which she now resides and works. She grew up speaking Spanish, which is her native language. Eva did not recall if she attended a bilingual or an English-only mainstream program when she was in elementary school, but she remembers starting school without speaking English. Eva possesses a B.A. in Spanish and an M.A. in education. She presently teaches "beginning ELD" and "intermediate ELD," intermediate Spanish for Spanish speakers, and a college preparation class for English language learners. During our conversations, she focuses on her work as an ELD teacher and her role within the school's bilingual education program.

Eva recently transferred to Fountainview High, a school in an upper middle-class community with an English Language Learner (ELL) population of 11.5% and with 44.1% of the population being Latino. Eva's previous years in the district were spent at a low performing school in a lower socioeconomic community with an ELL population of 44.5% and a Latino population of 82.4%. Eva's beginner ELD class, observed for this study, is made up of 21 ninth and tenth graders, who have all been in the United States for one year or less. Eighteen of the students speak Spanish and are from Mexico, two speak Japanese, and one speaks Korean.

Eva was interested in participating in this study for her own professional growth and development. Since finishing her master's degree, she has not had the benefit of having an outside person come into her classroom and provide her with feedback and opportunities for self-reflection. When we met, Eva was concerned with her ability to reach those students in her class who struggle with English oral language acquisition and seem to develop English at a much slower rate. She asked that when I observed her teaching that I focus on the oral English development methods she presently uses and how she could change her teaching to better meet the needs of all the students in her class.

EVA'S LITERACY BELIEFS: REVEALING SYSTEMIC INCONSISTENCIES

When Eva and I met for the first interview, my first question to her was, "What was the first thing that came to your mind when you started to do this [work with the Literacy Web, Figure 1]?" She indicated that the first two areas she started with were "accountability" and "teaching strategies." She explained,

> How you're held accountable for, you know, what you're going to be doing in the classroom; it's something that's been *told*, like, forever.

She emphasized the word *told* with a tone of futile capitulation, suggesting that this pressure for accountability seemed very present in her thinking. I persuaded Eva to not think in terms of the school or district views of accountability, but in terms of her own accountability toward her students. She then stated that accountability for *her* was "to have students be biliterate by the time they graduate." When I asked to define biliteracy, she stressed student mastery of academic discourse in both languages,

> It's the ability to dominate both languages, not just, you know, being able to speak the language but also to communicate in other ways: writing, reading ... They [the students] have to have the ability to communicate—not just in reading and writing—but you know ... in math, they have to be biliterate in all ways ... in many ways of communication.

Being a bilingual learner herself, she recognized the value in being biliterate and, most importantly, to be able to succeed academically in both languages. She expressed these values with a sense of urgency and questioned how students could get to high school level and still be in ELD classes. She questioned why students were not fully bilingual and biliterate at this stage of their schooling. Eva continued, "I can think of one student that was told when she was a junior, that she would not graduate high school no matter what she did" [this student could speak English and Spanish, but lacked academic English skills]. Eva asked, "How can you have a student ... in the school system here in the United States since like third grade or fourth grade. How can you let that happen to a student [not become fully bilingual and biliterate]?" She indignantly questioned how it was possible for students, who spent eight to nine years in U.S. schools, not to develop academic language and literacy skills in both English and Spanish.

I asked her how she viewed bilingual classes, considering that the school at which she had taught previously—for most of her teaching career—offered bilingual classes in the core content areas of math, science, and social studies for Spanish speaking ELLs while they simultaneously studied English in both language and content classes. Conversely, her present school Fountainview does not have a fully developed bilingual program but does offer a few content bilingual classes for students who are not ready to transition to English-only classes. (In these so-called bilingual classes, ELLs are taught subject matter such as social studies in both their native language and in English but somewhat inconsistently.) I found her comments to be a little unclear. This quote is a continuation of her previous comment:

> I know that when I talk to my students, I say, "Well that's a bilingual class and then, what languages does the teacher use?" And then they'll just say, you know, their home language, which is Spanish. And to me, that's really not a bilingual class. You know, of course I know that they need to get their ... content in their [primary] language so they'll understand it. Well that's a bilingual class.

Eva was referring to the fact that teachers and students who are in the bilingual classes often solely utilize the native language, Spanish, to teach and learn content subject matter (i.e., history, math, and so on). She realizes it is important to use the primary language to teach effectively, but her concern is that little to no English is being taught. Eva correctly points out that "bilingual" refers to instruction in two languages—the native language and English. Thus, she views the classes as primarily "Spanish" language classes but not authentically bilingual because English is not used. Eva questions whether a haphazard bilingual program that offers Spanish-only instruction can render students bilingual and biliterate.

Eva asks important questions, and they cause me to reflect on what Eva understands "bilingual education programming" to be. I believe that her previous school experience with a well-developed and coherent bilingual education influences her thinking here. She seems to be under the assumption that her current school follows the same program as her previous school but is doing a poor job of it. Eva's previous school follows a transitional bilingual education model where students transition from a majority of their instruction in their native language to instruction in English.

In that school, the ELD classes, Eva's responsibility, supported the bilingual classes in content and writing processes. In this setting, the content readings in Spanish, used in the bilingual content courses, are supported further in ELD classes where she connected thematically in English to the content and vocabulary development. That is, in ELD Eva attempted to connect literacy strategies (i.e., writing, reading, vocabulary) to assist students in making connections between what they knew and were learning in Spanish to English in order to help facilitate transition. At her current school, the content area teachers teach primarily in Spanish with no connection to ELD or the English they will need to succeed in mainstream classes.

As a result of her past experience, her conception of a bilingual class is one where the teacher is, of course, fluent in L1, in this case Spanish. However, the teacher should also utilize the L2 (English)—both in speech and materials when appropriate—to assist with the transition to English. This method of course resembles a "maintenance"[1] or dual language model,[2] neither of which is a program in her present school. As mentioned earlier, the program at Eva's current school follows an "early transition" model. In this model, students are in content bilingual courses with the goal to transition as quickly as possible to English content courses. However, despite her insistence that Spanish language development is important, I noticed her concern was still with the students' ability to use English, not their first language, Spanish. It is possible that at Eva's previous school, there was little concern about Spanish because it was consistently focused on and developed. At the new school, Eva could not assume that the L1 would be developed, yet she continued to assume a teaching role identical to the one she had in the previous school. Eva did not appear to recognize the different sociocultural and curricular contexts in which she found herself in the new school. She was not able to reconcile her new school's use of Spanish dominant bilingual classroom with her new need to change her role into one where she taught predominantly in English without a connection to what students were learning in their bilingual content classes. In addition, she felt pressure to get students to be fluent in English as quickly as possible, thus going against her belief and training that literacy in L1 provided a foundation for transition to English.

A second tension Eva experienced related her new school's bilingual education typology was the lack of collaboration between ELD teachers and content area teachers. Eva explained that at this school her students received English instruction in separate ELD classes, and bilingual instruction in content classes conducted solely in Spanish. Her description rang true of a transitional model, except that in this school's transitional programming, transition occurred without communication between ELD and content area teachers. Ideally, as was the case in her previous school, ELD teachers work collaboratively with content science and social studies teachers to know what content concepts and themes are being taught. The ELD teacher can then focus English language instruction to connect with content area concepts.

Thus, while pedagogically the bilingual program was transitional and set up technically as such, Eva felt that teaching pedagogy was not reflective of the program's intent: to connect content to English. Her belief, based on her experience, was that since there was no communication between the ELD and content area teachers, the students viewed their content and ELD classes as separate, unrelated, and mostly unequal. Her "solution" then, was focused on one of two options: first, to improve the transition process by having the bilingual teachers provide some of the transitional support in English and, second, to support collaboration between ELD and content area teachers. Eva strongly believes that the school is not providing a true bilingual program to students and, as a result, they are not becoming proficient in English by graduation.

What Eva does not readily recognize is the different value placed on biliteracy between her former and present school. In her previous school the goal was complete biliteracy for bilingual students, yet this is not the goal at her present school. The goal at her present school is simply to get the students into English as soon as possible with little effort to retain and teach the primary language. Thus, her real tension is that if the bilingual program is not being used to teach and use the primary language, then more needs to be done to ensure student success in English. If English-only literacy is the goal, she reasons, more effort needs to be put into developing and teaching English in the content areas (once again contradicting her articulated pro-bilingual education orientation).

Eva clarifies these issues in the following excerpts. When speaking about teacher-teacher collaboration, she states:

> It [collaboration] is difficult if the administration does not support the program [bilingual program]. ... So, what I see is that, first, it has to start with administration. If they support teachers, then the teachers will get what they need to be able to work with the students.

Eva states here that without support from the administration for collaboration, including the space and time, then it most likely will not occur. Her belief is that teachers need to come together and meet to discuss programming for EL students and that this needs to occur in an environment where administrative support is available and consistent. Even in her own experience as an ELD teacher, she found that as much as she wanted to make connections between content themes and her ELD classes, she just did not have time to do that. Eva continues to discuss the potential for collaboration and how it could be brought about:

> After that, the Social Science teacher will talk to the ELD teacher and the ELD teacher will talk to the math and to the science [teachers]. That's collaboration: teachers working by asking questions like, "What are you guys talking about?" You know,

for this unit [i.e., social studies, math] and then you [the teacher] can use that in the ELD class. And actually, I do it, *but instead of going to the teachers, I talk to the students.* I think that if teachers connect first, then the students know that, you know, we're a team. And that we know what they're doing in their other classes and we are there to help them, you know with their English part.

Here, for Eva, the salient issue related to providing quality literacy instruction to ELLs hinges on administrative support for both the bilingual program and English language content area instruction. More importantly, though, she makes the case that if teachers have conversations about what they are teaching when they share students, then the students will see that all their teachers are concerned with their education and progress. It also gives the perception to students that ELD instruction is important and relevant to their academic program and progress, thus highlighting the need for quality materials in both English and Spanish,

By supporting, I mean having the curriculum there, having the textbooks, and then having good textbooks. Sometimes you see the regular [English language] text books and then you see the text books for the bilingual students, you know which are in Spanish, or their native language, and it's so watered down. You know, and of course the teacher supplements and all that but—still just by looking at the textbook the— I don't think it's, you know, equal. I saw … a social science book, and the regular [English] book was, thick, and it had, uh, more information and I just kind of flipped through the other one [in Spanish]. And that's not even my subject area; I was just looking at a student [book]—a student had a book and I was, "Oh, let me see it." And it was all in Spanish, but it was really watered down, you know. It didn't even compare to the other [English] one.

Eva notes that the Spanish textbooks and materials are inferior to the English books and materials for subject matter instruction. This inequality of language and materials was not evident at Eva's prior school, yet she does not seem capable of recognizing or discussing the different outcomes of different bilingual education programs, in particular, her new school's program. She seems to be at the initial stages of learning about the ELL curriculum and program at her current school, yet she acts as if they were identical to that at her previous school.

These teacher excerpts and reflections point to the complexities of ideology of Eva's beliefs, her experiences, and knowledge of pedagogy related to bilingual education and English language development. Her view of literacy appears progressive, and her orientation to questioning the program is critical. She believes in working with colleagues and students to understand content and processes of teaching, but the questions she asks of how programming is determined, its goals and outcomes reflect a more critical stance. Eva also passionately shares her concerns regarding the administration's support or lack of support of the bilingual program and the facilitation of teacher collaboration. Her concerns reflect some of the tension I felt in interviewing Eva. She teaches from a curriculum model that is functional—given its focus on English grammar and reading skills with little support for transitioning and collaboration, processes she learned as "pedagogically" sound, but they do not reflect her experiences.

Referring both to her previous work in a school with a supported bilingual model, and presently in a school without such a model, she finds contrasting ideologies. On the one hand, Eva cites the need for "accountability," the responsibility of individual teachers, while on the other hand, she recognizes a clear lack of support for collaboration between teachers and weak curriculum materials, both of which could assist in student achievement and enhance it, too. The tension here is between a functional ideology of teaching language and literacy basic skills, and Eva's personal progressive stance, reflected in her concern for collaborative processes and questioning the system supported by administrators.

In reflecting on my conversations and work with Eva, it became clear that her conflict was related more to the orientation of the programs in which she worked, rather than to her teaching approach. That is, in her former school she was able to enact more collaborative processes not only with colleagues, but with students as well. The bilingual program at her previous school also supported her views on biliteracy. Thus, there was greater congruency between her ideology and practice in her previous school setting. However, at this point Eva could not see that because she seemed to place the responsibility for student achievement solely on her own shoulders.

When I asked Eva what caused differences in student academic progress and English language development rates, she highlighted the importance of fully developing the students' primary language. Eva stated it was "their … home language. Their strength of Spanish [that positively affects academic achievement and English language development.] And that's it." I pointed out the comments she made earlier regarding the lack of quality L1 materials and the lack of support for teacher collaboration and asked whether working with the bilingual teachers would help with her students' primary language development and academic achievement in English. She seemed to perceive my questions as criticism of her work and her use of English because she responded in an upset tone, "But I tried to! I don't use any other language in the ELD class [only English]." She seemed to mediate the tension between a desire to meet students' individual needs, while struggling to work within her new school's curricula and bilingual education model—a model that neither supported her bilingual and biliteracy goals nor provided pedagogical support.

This tension is important to note as it may signal a starting point for gaining ideological clarity. That is, despite her six years of teaching experience and after receiving not only a teaching credential but a master's degree as well, Eva has had little experience in engaging in dialogue related to what she truly believes about literacy development, ideology, and practice and how such beliefs have been impacted by the previous and current school and district policies and curricula. It is also surprising that, given her experience and education, Eva has not been able to recognize that it is the lack of a coherent bilingual program and language policy at her current school, and not her practice as an individual teacher, what is shortchanging ELLs' bilingual and biliteracy language development.

The quote that follows came toward the end of our dialogue and provides the most insight into Eva's commitment to her students; along with the frustration she has regarding her new school's inconsistently implemented bilingual education. We were discussing parent involvement when Eva brought up a story about a young woman who was told by school counselors that she would not graduate from high school "no matter what she did" despite the fact that this student had acquired a tremendous amount of English without the benefit of developing Spanish, her primary language. This student had evidently attended U.S. schools all of her life and learned as much English as was possible in her years in ELD classrooms. Eva seemed to criticize the school's inability to effectively teach English as well as its practice to allow students to lose their first language rendering them in her words, "almost mute." Eva offered this example of a case where the student pays the consequences for the school's failure to educate her and prepare her to be a bilingual and biliterate academically competent student. When Eva tells this particular story, she gets very emotional and her tone reflects her frustration with the system. This discussion also ignites within her a passionate concern for this particular student but focuses her anger on the situation created by the school system but unfairly shouldered by the students. Eva explained that a counselor stated to the student that she was just going to have to go to adult school or just wait until she was over 18 and go to Peak Community College because she was not going to get a high school diploma Eva indignantly recalled,

> Now, this student was in my ELD 1 [class] ... and she had the [English] language, she had the vocabulary. She was able to understand everything that I said in English. And she would have conversations with me. It's just that her writing was horrible. You know, her writing wasn't [strong] and she was never in Spanish for Spanish Speakers. So, I don't even know if her Spanish was okay, but probably not. She was able to communicate with me. She would speak to me [although] of course sometimes, you know, she had grammatical mistakes.

Clearly disturbed by the situation of this student, she further elaborated,

> It was throughout her career as a student, you know. What happened to her in elementary school? I mean, if you're in a bilingual program, and you only have thirty minutes of English, well why isn't that student literate in Spanish, then? At least! If she [the student] is going to be in ELD 1 when she's in ninth grade, tenth grade, eleventh grade, then her Spanish should be, you know [fluent, proficient at an academic level]. ... But it wasn't. That's the thing. It wasn't. So then what? What's going on? And that really bothers me.

It is important to note that when Eva brings up issues of inequity and programming concerns, she does not do it in a complaining fashion, but rather in a questioning mode. When she asks—"How can we let it happen? I mean, how can we let students just fall through the cracks?"—she is not blaming, but problem posing, which can be part of critical reflection. Her response to her own questions is that the schools are not implementing bilingual programs that fully develop students' cognitive academic language skills (CALPS)[3] in either English or Spanish. Her frustration comes, I believe, from seeing a discrepancy between the "theory" that is supposed to inform bilingual pedagogy and the fact that theory was not being implemented in practice fully at Fountainview and was lacking clarity in the larger system for the majority of ELL students who attended the school at which she had taught previously. Thus, to answer the question regarding Eva's view of literacy, I found that when discussing biliteracy programming, bilingual education, and administrative support, her views were progressive and critical. Her stance was reflected in her comments regarding the responsibility districts had to meet the needs of all students, including her student who was advised she could not graduate.

DISCUSSION AND CONCLUSION

What Eva and the other teachers with whom I worked shared was their commitment to empowering their students and to improving their professionalism. Eva, like others engaged openly in this study, displayed a willingness to reflect on their own practices. Cochran-Smith and Lytle (1993) state that such participation should be commended as this process "requires considerable effort by innovative and dedicated teachers to stay in their classrooms and at the same time carve out opportunities to inquire to reflect on their own practice" (p. 20). These researchers further highlight the difference between K-12 and university based research, where university level research "occupies an unquestioned position at the center of the institution's mission" (p. 20). Brisk (1998) states that the goal of quality education, is "to educate students to their highest potential" (p. xix), where English is only a part of the educational goal. Eva believes that "bilingual learners access knowledge not only through English but through their native languages" (Brisk, 1998, p. xix). She further recognized and valued students' cultural experiences and knowledge. Although Eva's methods for teaching students were incongruent with her beliefs, her view of education for the students in her class and herself reflected a quality-based model over a compensatory model of education. More precisely, a quality model focuses on the achievement of student academic success as opposed to seeing students with deficits that need to be "fixed." This is a crucial point because many teachers start out with views of teaching all students to their "fullest potential," but then learn, and often times accept, from district mandates, curricula changes, adoptions, staff development, and other forms of "lockstep methodologies promulgating unexamined beliefs and attitudes" (Bartolomé, 2000, p. 167) as the correct and "best" approaches to reaching students who are struggling learners or speak a language other than English.

In this process, it is even more disheartening that teachers passively accept school and district-level changes rather than critically analyze them, understand them, and then change them. The more common response, similar to Eva's, is that teachers begin to doubt their passion and strong beliefs about what works. Most importantly, they doubt their own professional expertise and skills. As a result, teachers often start to feel less empowered, more frustrated, and oppressed by the very system they became a part of, a system they entered with the goal to empower and engage their passion for teaching and awaken in students a passion for learning.

Teachers need to be given the opportunity and, more importantly, the language to critically analyze the sociopolitical agendas linked with certain ideologies, pedagogy, and teaching processes and to respond accordingly on an individual basis, to struggle for ideological clarity. However, without the space to explore such critical issues, without support from school administrators, and without critical teacher education classes and programs, such processes are not likely to occur unless teachers, teacher educators, and even students, parents, and community members actively seek these avenues. It is through reflective tasks such as the one I developed that can begin to facilitate this necessary and crucial dialogue.

NOTES

1. In this bilingual program students receive a portion of their daily instruction in their native language to support literacy development in L1 until the student is ready to transfer to an English-only program.

2. A bilingual program that supports L2 acquisition for both non-native and native speakers of English with the ultimate goal for biliteracy for both groups of students.
3. BICS refers to Basic Interpersonal Communication Skills and CALPS is cognitive academic language proficiency skills. The point is that programs address BICS, but they do not adequately engage CALPS in either L1 or L2 for these students.

REFERENCES

Bartolomé, L. (2000). Democratizing bilingualism: The role of critical teacher education. In Z. F. Beyknot (Ed.), *Lifting every voice: Pedagogy and politics of bilingualism*. Boston: Harvard Education Publishing Group.

Brisk, M. (1998). *Bilingual education: From compensatory to quality schooling*. Mahwah, NJ: Lawrence Erlbaum Associates.

Cadiero-Kaplan, K. (2001). Literacy ideology and practice: Teachers' beliefs and practices for English language learners at the secondary level. Doctoral Dissertation, Claremont & San Diego, CA: Claremont Graduate University & San Diego State University.

Cadiero-Kaplan, K. (2004). *The literacy curriculum and bilingual education: A critical examination*. New York: Peter Lang.

Cochran-Smith, M., & Lytle, S. L. (1993). *Inside/Outside teacher research and knowledge*. New York: Teachers College Press.

Freire, P. (1993). *Pedagogy of the oppressed*. New York: Continuum.

Keller, S. (2002) *Women('s) teacher(') literacy (ies) practice(s) and policy (ies)*. Toledo, OH: Dissertation submitted to University of Toledo.

Kincheloe, J. (1995). Meet me behind the curtain: The struggle for a critical postmodern action research. In P. L. McLaren & J. M. Giarelli (Eds.), *Critical theory and educational research*. Albany: State University of New York Press.

McLaren, P. (1998). *Life in schools: An introduction to critical pedagogy in the foundations of education*. New York: Longman Press.

Richardson, V. (1994). Teacher inquiry as professional staff development. *Teacher research and educational reform: The Ninety-third yearbook of the National Society of the Study of Education* (pp. 186–203). Chicago, IL: University of Chicago Press.

CHAPTER SEVEN

Sharing the Wealth: Guiding All Students Into the Professional Discourse

STEPHANIE COX SUÁREZ

More than five years have passed, and I still wonder why I was not able to connect with Joyce. She was an African American graduate student from the south who had moved to New England to attend graduate school. She struggled with writing formal reports for my course; we met individually many times; she submitted many more drafts than her peers. Eventually, she did produce a document with which I was satisfied, and I was confidently able to pass her as a teacher. In the end, she was bitter with me because she felt that I had given her a lower grade than was fair. She had not completed a minor assignment despite multiple reminders and extended deadlines. My feeling at the time was that I must stick to my "standards" and have all my students meet all the course requirements. I was perplexed that she found this expectation unreasonable, and yet it was a requirement my other students could meet. It was this struggle with Joyce that started me on a quest to understand better how I teach students and to question what I bring personally to the classroom.

As an assistant professor in education, I require from my graduate students a variety of written assignments. I expect my students to write cohesive, concise, professional papers that help prepare them for their new role as teachers. It is this term *professional* that I now realize can cause confusion—entering a new profession requires a mastery of that profession's discourse. On the face of it, we seemingly know what teaching is—what it looks and sounds like—since we have all been in schools for so many years. However, it is the more invisible qualities of the culture of professionals that I am learning is not easy for my preservice teachers to master. Even defining the term *professional* is difficult. Over the years in my own professional development I have learned that there is an implicit image of a professional based on how one presents in their dress, speech, actions, and values—something that personifies an educated, accountable, and ethical human, who is employed and trusted in the service of others. The focus of my work as described in this chapter is my role as a cultural mentor to the profession of teaching, and my struggle to help students, particularly those from the non-dominant culture, to enter a professional discourse (Bartolomé, 2003).

Multicultural educators challenge teachers at all levels to consider their personal culture (race, ethnicity, class) and to consider how these affect their pedagogy. Nieto (1999) asks teachers to reflect and learn from their practices, attitudes, and values in order to understand how these affect and promote student learning. Nieto describes this process of self-reflection as the heart of multicultural education. As I work to move students into the profession of teaching, I ask, what it is about my struggles, my education, personal culture, my personality, and my ideological predispositions that influence both my teaching and my students' learning?

This chapter explores my personal culture and how my origins as a Mexican-American woman from a working-class background influence the decisions I make as a teacher. I share what I have learned over the past ten years from teaching students (preservice teachers) the specific skill of writing an educational report. I include four of my students' voices as they describe our learning and teaching process. Finally, I offer explicit strategies that I have developed over the years in a semester-long course, Special Education Assessment, and how I shift roles between "teacher as gatekeeper" to "teacher as cultural mentor" to enable all of my students to successfully establish themselves in the professional culture as special educators. In this course my students learn how to administer formal, standardized achievement and diagnostic tests, as well as to develop informal classroom assessments in order to evaluate the learning progress of a child, with a particular focus on children with special needs. In addition, the students must be able to communicate these assessment results both orally and in writing to their pupils' families and school administrators and teachers. This written educational evaluation is a public document for distribution to other professionals and families. It was not until I interviewed my students that I realized just how anxious they had been about writing such an assessment report. This written document becomes a public, permanent representation of each student's professional self.

LITERACY AND A CULTURE OF POWER

How do students learn to write? Why do some students come to graduate school with strong writing skills while others do not? Delpit (1995) describes the successful presentation of self to mainstream society (orally or in writing) as a necessary skill that is learned naturally at a young age by those within the "culture of power." This "culture of power," in the United States, is the current mainstream (White, middle class) with strong influences on literacy, personal presentation, and how schools are organized to confirm and perpetuate this dominant culture. I wonder where students who are not from this culture of power can learn the mysteries of success in writing. How can teachers demystify writing and find accessible, nonthreatening ways to teach their students to write?

For students socialized outside the mainstream culture, there can be significant adverse consequences imposed on them by schools and by the greater society. Delpit (1995) argues that there are linguistic codes or rules that outline success in institutions (schools and workplaces). These codes "relate to linguistic forms, communicative strategies, and presentation of self; that is, ways of talking, ways of writing, ways of dressing, and ways of interacting" (p. 25). Students from middle- and upper-class mainstream families are unknowingly socialized into these codes at an early age and thus equipped, through no effort of their own, to utilize expected language forms in their classrooms. Other families who are not as familiar with the culture of the school (not middle-class, not from the mainstream, dominant culture) are not as comfortable or adept with the codes. Bourdieu (1986) described this early learned linguistic ability as an example of cultural capital. Cultural capital refers to the acquired tastes, values, languages, dialects, and the educational qualifications that mark a person as belonging to a privileged social and cultural class. Those from the culture of power hold vast wealth in cultural capital. Do we as teachers recognize that some of our students in high school, college, or graduate school may not possess enough cultural capital to succeed? How do adults from nonmainstream families learn the codes? When we meet an adult student who struggles to write and present himself or herself in the expected formal and academic ways, what do we do? What are our responsibilities as teachers to these students? How can we create ways to help them acquire and benefit from cultural capital?

As a Latina from a working-class background, I have spent a lifetime trying to decipher what is needed to succeed in academic contexts, as well as how to present myself professionally, both orally and in writing. By the very process of self-reflection and writing this chapter, I realize that because my background is not mainstream (White, middle-class), I am very sensitive to my students who also appear to come from outside the mainstream. Perhaps being an outsider explains why my antennae are raised when I think I see students in my courses trying to enter into and navigate through this "culture of power," and experiencing challenges similar to those that once faced me.

Considering literacy (writing and speaking) from an ideological perspective enables me to understand how some of my students have learned to negotiate, as I have, within a culture of power with minimal cultural capital, and have successfully managed to enter a profession, such as becoming a teacher. Gee (1991) frames literacy as a "discourse" that is a socially accepted way of using language, thinking and acting within a specified social context. Discourse for students in a graduate education program will naturally be different from that of a law school, software company, or a street gang in Los Angeles. Gee (1991) outlines critical features of a discourse, the first being that "discourses are inherently ideological" (p. 4). This ideological perspective of a discourse involves a set of values and viewpoints that dictate how one speaks and acts in order to be a valid member. Gee (1999) views literacy as a social practice; he analyzes literacy based on the sociocultural perspective of the communicator reflecting his or her individual characteristics (i.e., class, race, culture, profession). Gee in his later writing came to capitalize the word *Discourse* to identify this sociolinguistic approach to literacy. Gee, Hull, Lankshear (1996) challenge Delpit's view of static linguistic norms and argue that there are multiple forms of literacy and they take the positive pluralistic view that non-mainstream people can "become a new 'mainstream' a new center of social power, in the larger society" (p. 14). To honor new and varied discourses would be a significant goal for multiculturalism.

Academic institutions, however, tend to operate around an ideology that values a middle-class discourse and perpetuates these values by promoting students who can write, speak, and act as members of the middle class. Mitchell and Weiler (1991) define this ideology from the middle-class stance as "exclusionary literacy," regarding itself as the universal model for how one should speak and act (p. xviii). In other words, exclusionary literacy regards any other discourse outside the boundary as being "other, alien and troubled, lawless and frustrated, and marked by an inherent failure to learn to read and write, and an inability to use language appropriately" (p. xviii). Exclusionary literacy therefore excludes those individuals who have a mismatch with the discourse structures typically expected in schools. Students from non-mainstream backgrounds, poor and working class, non-white, and English language learners are all underrated by schools; the discourse they bring from their respective communities is not recognized or valued.

If educators and sociolinguists collaborate to understand the ideological and socio-cultural perspectives of literacy, teachers could be challenged to identify narrow personal ideologies that may frame their practice. Moving from an exclusionary literacy model would enable educators to acknowledge the multiple forms of discourse that come through their door. I recognize that the ideology I operate within my graduate classroom includes the requirement that my students develop a professional discourse regardless of their individual discourse. The challenge for me is to understand how to respect the discourse of individual students and yet bridge two cultures, if necessary in order to adopt and master the discourse of the professional.

There is a debate whether teachers should require writing in formal, standard English. The standard language is the language spoken and enforced by the cultural groups in power (Bartolomé, 1998). Sociolinguists argue that a standard form of a language is not superior to non-standard languages. Educators need to recognize that no language or set of life experiences is inherently superior (avoiding the stance of exclusionary literacy), yet our social values in the mainstream reflect our preferences for certain language and life experiences over others. I recognize this tension, but as one who prepares teachers, I have made the decision to require Standard English to ensure that the writing is both identified and respected by the teaching profession. I assume responsibility for explicitly assisting my students through the editing process to ensure the use of a standard language. Too often students who struggle with writing or those learning English as a second language do not receive the explicit instruction they need in order to master the professional discourse needed to participate in their chosen profession within the dominant culture.

EARLY ASSUMPTIONS ABOUT MY STUDENTS

When I first started to teach graduate courses, I assumed that my White middle-class students were well prepared to write research papers. I assumed that they would be able to use correct grammar, accurately cite sources, and to analyze and synthesize data. I assumed that the mainstream students had received lifelong coaching in the use of academic discourse—and were well prepared to present themselves both orally and in writing in a manner befitting a "culture of power." I assumed that my students of color, who may have spoken in non-standard English, or for whom English was a second language, would write as they spoke. I sometimes made false assumptions that students of color would have difficulty with writing; I assumed they shared some of my experiences, such as an incongruence between their home and school culture. However, each year, my assumptions often prove wrong. Until recently, I had never taken the time when the course was completed to individually interview some of my students to find out what worked for them in the course and what did not. I wanted to find out how they learned to write, what obstacles they met in writing, and whether there were some aspects of the graduate course that helped them to overcome some of these obstacles. What I learned is that the discourse theory and the advantage for those from the middle class were defied by two of the students of color I interviewed. These individuals came from poor working-class families as new immigrants and yet formed their own bridges to the profession with hard work and help from mentors.

LISTENING TO STUDENTS

I interviewed four students specifically to get their perspectives about learning to write. Two are Black women (from Bermuda and Haiti), one is Latina from Guatemala, and one is Caucasian and who was born in the United States, and who identifies herself as Irish from New England. Two of the students I interviewed learned English as a second language (the students from Haiti and Guatemala). I selected these women to interview because—whether or not they found writing difficult—each one of them defied some of my assumptions about writing ability, race, English language learning, and class. I met individually with each student after the course was completed; the sessions were tape-recorded, and open-ended questions were asked. Student names have been changed. Questions included:

- Tell me about your family and your ethnic identity. If born in another country, how old were you when you immigrated to the United States? What was the socioeconomic status of your family? Where did you grow up? What was your education like for you?
- What did you find most challenging about the assessment course?
- What was most helpful to you in learning to write assessment reports?
- How confident do you feel about starting your teaching position and being able to produce assessment reports?

Alisha is a Black woman who emigrated to the United States from Haiti at age seven. She was the youngest of ten children; she described her family was poor; her father completed 8th grade and her mother 5th grade. They moved to the United States seeking a better life, and Alisha looks back at her life now—a teacher with a master's degree and owning a new home—and acknowledges the positive impact on her own life because of her family's decision to move to the United States. Even so, her early years in elementary school were not easy. Alisha remembers:

> My mother discouraged me to speak Creole in school. I was teased about being Haitian. I remember being told to go back to Haiti. The prejudice, even the teachers too, I could sense the prejudice from them.

A first- and a fifth grade-teacher stood out for Alisha in elementary school, and it was the luck of a lottery that allowed her to be part of a new pilot program in high school that offered college preparatory courses.

> When I first came here, I was in a bilingual program which was not helpful. ... my first grade teacher ... taught me everything, she taught me English. ... Because of my fifth grade teacher, everything I learned I learned from her. ... she inspired me to be a teacher. ... She was very strict about everything. She really pushed. I just remember spending hours doing homework in her class. I'm still learning how to write formally. ... I think a lot of it comes from the things I learned in 5th grade and from my teaching. I was in a pilot school when I went to [high school]. The classes were tracked so I took a lot of intermediate or standard courses and for some reason the Haitians were in the basic classes all over the school. In the pilot program I could take classes outside the program. The whole philosophy of the pilot program was college prep and the courses got you ready for college. It was a lottery to get to the program.

Alisha described her struggle to learn to write in college:

> In college I took a course ... that really helped me a lot. *The Little Brown Handbook* was like my Bible. I learned English formally by practicing and writing lots of papers in school. I always spoke Creole or French at home ... I always think in Creole first and then I translate it. In my papers I find mistakes. I find the verb in the wrong place, it just doesn't sound right. It may not sound right because I am translating it directly from Creole. It's a little awkward.

Alisha was a student who defied my expectations as I found her writing to be as strong as that of her peers who appeared to be from the dominant culture. Alisha had taken every advantage afforded her and followed an older brother's lead to take more advanced college preparatory courses in the high school pilot program and to realize that she needed a small college with small classes to ensure her success. Alisha made significant progress in her writing of an assessment report and responded to specific feedback I provided described below.

Linda emigrated at the age of twelve from Guatemala. She described her family as being poor/working class; her parents completed a fifth-grade education. Upon arrival in the United States, she attended public school and was placed in a bilingual program. She commented about her first school experience in the United States in middle school and learning to write English.

> In middle school English I was in ESL (English as a Second Language). In English [class] I was told, "You don't have to do this, it is fine." It was a shove-under-the-rug attitude. What did I know?

Because she was in the process of just learning to speak English as a second language, this young woman missed out on academic English writing instruction.

In middle school she was told her writing was "fine"; it was good enough, and she was not pushed to meet a standard of writing comparable to that of her native English-speaking peers. She met similar attitudes in high school until she met a mentor in a program designed to help students prepare for and apply to college.

> He did push me. I remember he did the training for the SATs. ... He gave me the moral support that I can do it. When I wrote my essay to get into college, he read it and edited it. He treated us like we were in college, which was the difference. He pushed us to do well in school. If we didn't get above B he didn't want us in the program. You needed the grades to get into college.

When asked about her undergraduate experience in learning to write Linda said,

> I felt I was cheated in undergrad. ... I was never really corrected. They knew it was my second language, so it didn't matter? ... There were a couple of courses, literature courses ... but I don't think I was pushed to write critically, to expand my thoughts, get in depth and to really say what I mean. ... I think my last year in undergrad I was pushed in some ways. I think it depends on the professor and where they come from.

Linda felt she was not given a strong base in spelling and grammar in middle school and high school and felt her thinking was not pushed to deeper levels in college. It was not until she reached graduate school that she was told she needed to improve her academic writing. I asked whether Linda felt intellectually challenged and pushed to develop writing skills.

> Yes, I think I was pushed, and I am glad I was pushed. I was pushed to think exactly what I was writing and what I mean; to really examine my writing and to think of ways to improve my writing; to sit down and think. ... But I have to remind myself that English is my second language. I think the hardest thing is that I would be so amazed when my peers would tell me that they wrote the paper last night and it was right, it came out nice and flowing. I would have to remind myself that I didn't have their education and their type of English the day I was born. I had to think that I couldn't just do it overnight.

Both of the English language learner students I interviewed identified the impact of a teacher who pushed them to excel. Alisha's first- and fifth-grade teachers made such an impact on her life that she was inspired to become a teacher. Linda's high school mentor had high expectations and demanded that she maintain good grades and provided her with critical support in writing that motivated her to pursue college.

Rachel is White from a middle-class background. I could not understand why, given her middle-class background, she found writing the assessment reports so difficult. I assumed that she had attended good suburban schools and had received quality writing instruction that matched with her home culture. In fact, she reported that her parents were college educated and that her father had proofread her papers throughout high school and college. Nevertheless, Rachel found writing for this course extremely challenging.

> Writing assessments were difficult. I did better on the second one than the first one. ... When I re-wrote it, I spent a lot of time going through it and seeing how I could change it. I re-read every comment you wrote four or five times [as well as the comments you] made on my paper. What you said earlier—if someone had to read it, I felt terrible if it wasn't written well.

Rachel presented herself in a manner that was both physically and orally typical of teachers one may meet in a school. She appeared to have the cultural capital but felt a huge deficit in the area of writing. It was important for me to understand that Rachel was anxious about writing a public document. I had emphasized to my students that a grammatically correct, carefully crafted document summarizing a child's progress would be related to the amount of confidence a family member or administrator might feel about the content of the report. I did not expect that someone like Rachel would be nervous about this specific aspect of her teacher preparation. I falsely assumed that Rachel would not require particular help beyond what I provided to the general group. In fact, Rachel needed and actively sought my assistance to edit her writing and to coach her through the process.

Kerry is a Black woman from Bermuda who came to the United States as a young adult to attend college. She was probably ten years older than the other students I interviewed. She described herself as a confident writer; her college professors had agreed. She described her challenge in writing the assessment reports for the course.

> It was challenging because as for myself I wanted to write professionally. And trying to look for those words [terms] that were "every day" in order for parents to understand but also to be professional. ... So that was a challenge, what were the right words to use? Sometimes I would have a word in my head and go to the thesaurus just to see which word would fit better in order to make the report professional.

Kerry and Rachel both recognized the impact of a public document to be understood by parents and to appear "professional" to the family and other teachers. Kerry was a student whose spoken and written language was eloquent.

My students happen to be at the end of their formal education and preparing for a professional career. It is possible that like me, they too realize that this is their last chance to learn and hope that their instructors take on the challenge with them. I want *all* my students to be effective classroom teachers. Although some of my non-mainstream students do not come equipped with cultural capital, I have learned to explicitly point out how to speak, write, and act successfully in a school environment.

MY PERSONAL CULTURE

I am a woman of second-generation Mexican descent and the first in my immediate family to attend college. I grew up in a working-class family with limited cultural capital. As I consider my personal history, two themes emerge that have shaped me as a learner and teacher—assimilation and low expectations.

Both of my parents came from working-class families. They graduated from high school, but neither of them contemplated college nor was it considered a choice. My mother's family is from Sonora, Mexico—they immigrated to Tucson, Arizona, in the 1920s. In Tucson my mother and her family were surrounded by other immigrant and first-generation Mexican Americans. My father is White with an English background and proudly reminds me that he is also part Native American. My father was an enlisted man in the Air Force whose assignments forced us to uproot ourselves several times, particularly when I was in the junior and senior high school years. Because my father's parents were not pleased with his decision to marry a Mexican Catholic woman, we had very limited contact with his family. Our only real roots were with my mother's family from the southwest.

Growing up in different parts of the country, particularly outside of the southwest, meant that I was often questioned about my ethnicity (i.e., Italian, Jewish, Lebanese). My mother's response to our ethnic heritage was to insist that we call ourselves "English" or "Spanish," and I came to understand that this was my mother's quiet way of avoiding racial conflicts and unwanted notice. I learned to take on my mother's reticence about my identity and discovered that I could be a sort of ethnic "chameleon" depending on my current social group. I had learned from my mother that the "armor" I needed was to assimilate and perhaps be unnoticed.

The second theme relates to low expectations, cultural capital, and the limited number of choices I felt I had. My parents were loving but had a rather fatalistic approach to life. If something was meant to happen, it would happen. I did not understand what was needed to attend college and had no one with whom to discuss my options. My parents thought college attendance was beyond our scope and made me feel sometimes that I would never make it. "*Ojala que ...*" or "*if God wills it,*" were the phrases I heard whenever I brought up the topic. My parents had no sense of entitlement, and they did not have savvy about how to negotiate the system. They could hardly imagine the ways of a professional culture much less teach my siblings and me how to negotiate our way through it.

I figured out what was needed to succeed at school and managed to move beyond what seemed to me my parents' limited educational expectations. As did other low-income and minority students in the mid-1970s, I benefited from federally guaranteed loans, affirmative action, and minority recruitment (Gándara, 1995). I received a federally funded government position for high school graduates who needed steady summer employment for four years as a supplement to financial aid for college as part of the President's Opportunity Program. It felt like pure luck when I overheard an announcement over the intercom in my rowdy 12th-grade homeroom one morning. I have always known that my luck in hearing that fuzzy announcement made the difference in my ability to attend college. I was able to put together multiple jobs and loans to pay for my own schooling and expenses.

My point in describing my personal history is to illustrate how the "multicultural stew" in each of us affects how we teach and understand how our students learn. I can look back at my personal history and point to the times when I did not receive the cultural capital that would have been helpful for me to excel as a student, perform well on standardized tests, learn more about the outside world, negotiate and feel a sense of belonging in schools and other institutions. These examples are particularly poignant as I currently raise my own children and see the difference in cultural capital that I provide for them and the striking difference to my own childhood. Although I felt like an outsider growing up, now that I am a professional in a middle-class environment, I have a perspective about two sets of cultures—working-class and middle-class.

HOW DOES MY STORY AFFECT MY TEACHING?

I believe there are some distinct advantages in being a teacher who does not come from a mainstream background. I see that my background affected the range of educational and social opportunities available to me. I want other non-mainstream students to benefit fully from as many educational opportunities as are available. I want to be explicit in helping others to decipher the academic discourse. Ladson-Billings (1994, 2001) and Foster (1997) describe teachers of color and their positive effect on diverse students. Foster outlines distinct characteristics of these teachers: Good teachers demand respect, have high expectations of students, work hard to prepare for class, and likewise expect an equivalent preparation from students.

It would be ideal if all teachers embraced an attitude that everyone *can* learn and teachers were willing to explore their own cultural and racial identity, question their biases, and look critically at how their attitudes might affect their students' learning and their relationships with students. Ladson-Billings (2001) describe this process as "cultural competence," which means that teachers understand the complexity of culture, particularly when they work in a school culture that is different from their own. Those of us who do not come from the mainstream quite possibly have more insight into our non-mainstream students because we have experienced the incongruent juxtaposition of home and school cultures and are conscious that our students may be experiencing a similar incongruence. It is possible we have developed some cultural competence because we have had to navigate between our home culture and the mainstream culture and achieved success in each. We have learned to be bicultural in order to bridge the dominant and non-dominant cultures as we enter a professional discourse. This navigation includes dealing with competing ideologies and ways of seeing the world.

LESSONS LEARNED: TEACHER AS CULTURAL MENTOR AND GATEKEEPER

There is a dynamic tension between the roles of cultural mentor and the role of gatekeeper. On the one hand, I am dedicated to bringing my students into the professional culture. On the other hand, I have the power to block their entry into that culture. I can provide nurturance, support, and modeling as a teacher up to a point. I need to decide when to let go and allow the student to stand independently and demonstrate his or her skills as a teacher. The question is how much coaching is reasonable to provide? This is the most challenging balancing act in my teaching: When is enough enough? Elbow (1986) discusses the contrary roles of a teacher—the tension of developing trust between a student and a teacher to take risks and connect to the material and the teacher's commitment to be loyal to knowledge and society. The latter requires maintaining a critical eye on standards and student performance. The teacher is a gatekeeper to the profession and is accountable for taking a demanding stance in evaluating papers, exams, and student performance.

I will highlight several strategies that I have developed over the past ten years and offer insights from the students I interviewed. These suggestions are presented within a particular context to enable graduate students to produce well-written educational evaluations. It is my hope that these suggestions can be translated by other educators to their respective written products and the ultimate outcomes for their own students. My focus is on my role as a cultural mentor and the strategies I use to develop a professional discourse of speaking and writing.

THE CULTURAL MENTOR ROLE

For me the cultural mentor role, the coach, is the most important. I have learned to be bicultural, to straddle the dominant and non-dominant cultures as I became a professional. It is now my passion to enable graduate students to enter the field of teaching. Our country is in urgent need of well-trained special education teachers, and if I can also enable more teachers of color or those from non-dominant cultures (not from White or middle-class backgrounds) to enter the field, then perhaps some of our nation's children will find their own cultural mentors much earlier in their school careers.

After the opening speech the first day of my course, I describe my role as coach. Until writing this paper, I had never described the coaching role as "cultural mentor"; this description now seems like a more fitting term as I begin to understand why I have worked so hard over the years to be so explicit with my students about being professional. I now understand that my role is to mentor my students in order to acquire the cultural capital they need to enter a new culture—the professional discourse.

My students learn quickly that I have high standards and expectations. My job then is to convince them that I will mentor each of them to reach these standards. In a group of 15 to 20 graduate students, perhaps 20% come from a non-dominant culture. I know that I cannot possibly meet everyone's personal cultural and learning styles, but I have seen how certain approaches to my coaching role have helped students. This cultural mentor role includes providing written and face-to-face feedback on writing, multiple drafts, and in-class practice on the oral discourse.

First I need to admit to a huge assumption that I make about student motivation at the beginning of each new course that must influence the effectiveness of my coaching role. I assume that my students will have as strong a work ethic as I have. I expect that my students want to work hard and that they want to earn an A in the course, and that this well-deserved grade genuinely reflects not only their effort but the actual final product that we can point to—a well written educational report. I always appreciate it when students admit they are having difficulty learning, but that they are willing to work with me to achieve success in the course. This scenario is the easier one for a teacher. Through this research I have learned, however, that not all of my students feel comfortable telling me of their learning or writing issues, or that they have other obligations or complications in their lives that limit how much effort they can really put into a graduate course. Either way, I need to respect these decisions and meet students where they are willing to meet me.

1. Written Feedback

A critical feature of my teaching style is my commitment to provide detailed written feedback. This written feedback is my way of communicating with each student in a one-to-one written format, very specific details on the use of professional language, grammar, interpretation, and analysis of data, and the synthesis of this information in order to understand and diagnose children's learning issues. Because this information is so central to the education of a child, I think this feedback is critical. At first I tried to write my feedback in the margins of the students' papers, but I found that there was not enough space to say everything I needed to say. Instead I provide typewritten feedback, following a particular protocol.

I frequently struggle over how much written feedback is appropriate. As in all developmental learning, I have to make a judgment about how much information a student can process and learn at any given time. I have been known to return a student paper with several typed pages of comments—almost equal to the amount of writing they originally submitted! For strong writers I find that I can include enough comments on "fine tuning" their draft in order to move the writing to a more sophisticated level of analysis. For the students who are struggling to write, I am careful to not overwhelm them with too much feedback; I prioritize features of the paper that are most critical for improvement. I may ask for additional drafts specifically in order to provide additional opportunities for feedback.

I typically include two headings in the written feedback: *What I liked about your report* and *Things to consider for your next report*. Below is an excerpt of written feedback for Kerry's final report; the complete feedback can be found in Appendix A.

What I liked about your report:

- Your writing was clear and professional.
- The tables you included are excellent.
- Excellent introduction to the Discussion section. Introductions and summary statements are excellent to include as much as possible—they help the reader stay on track with all this material.
- You did a nice job combining information about subtests into one paragraph—a sign of true growth and development in report writing. You were able to do this with 4 or 5 passages from the Qualitative Reading Inventory and with the math subtests from the Woodcock-Johnson Tests of Achievement.
- Nice job comparing test results and sometimes also comparing to reading performance.

Things to consider for your next report:

You'll probably never have the time to put together such a comprehensive report again unless, of course, you decide to be an evaluator professionally. But, as a classroom teacher, your evaluation reports will probably not realistically be so complete. But, you now have the template for an excellent report.

Kerry was the Black student who emigrated to the United States from Bermuda to attend college. The example I provide here is one where her work was fine-tuned; there were no major areas of concern. She was able to apply what she learned from one written report to the next. She was a confident student and writer who commented about the written feedback:

> I think the written feedback was good for me because … it helped me to be more concise with the writing. … I mean I relied on that feedback to help me with the next report. … It wasn't something that I just disregarded; I used it to help me for the next steps.

My response to her written work was to push her toward deeper understanding about children's learning and to reflect this in a concise, succinct manner that would also be accessible to family members.

In the syllabus I require that students write at least three educational reports. Each assignment is crafted in order to add a new layer of complexity. Students like Kerry were able to read the written feedback and apply it to the next assignment. The written feedback I provided for a student like Kerry was generally effective, but this was not always the case for all of my students. Some students could not integrate all of my suggestions; I often noted and repeated these suggestions in the next assignment. Because I keep my written feedback on my computer, I can re-read my notes to individual students, particularly if I notice that they did not apply the feedback, and I do not see significant progress in a follow-up report. I also look back to reassess what I have written. Was it too much information? Was it upsetting, too demanding, too strict? Was the feedback sufficiently clear? Is the student motivated?

When I write feedback on the penultimate paper, I feel the pressure of time as I race against a semester-long clock. I want to move my students to achieve an A because I feel a professional responsibility that these final reports must be excellent. This final report is one ticket for the student to enter the professional discourse. In the end, students have told me that they felt they had a solid template for the report with my feedback and would continue to make progress once on their own. I often get emails from former students telling me how helpful the course has been for them and that they often go back to the written feedback and their old reports as guides for the assessments they write now as special educators.

Rachel was one student who had difficulty at first with the written feedback. Rachel's reaction to her written feedback came in stages; at first she felt that the feedback seemed too critical, but when she took time to re-read the comments, she found that she could move away from responding to the feedback as criticism toward making concrete changes to her next report.

> I'm a firm believer in feedback. At first it seems like it is criticism, but then I change this into feedback. I learn best when someone says: Can you think about it this way,

or think about that? In the past I've had people say it in a negative way, that doesn't help me at all. You can take this and change that to make it more tight—that is more helpful. My father used to do that for me.

Rachel needed to adjust getting over her discomfort after shifting from a parent's feedback style to a professor's. This level of discomfort, and her search for support, is evident in Rachel's following comments:

> It was very helpful when you would write "good description" or "excellent" or "nice job." Because as much as I needed to know about what I needed to work on it was also nice to know what you thought I had done well on. But when I went to write the second report, I went page by page and read every comment and said okay, you said here "need more description." Then I would go there and add more description. Then I would tick it off and go comment by comment. It was really helpful for me, because you as my instructor were pointing out to me what I had missed and what I could improve on. If you hadn't written that I would not have known where to go.

It is interesting to wonder about the involvement of Rachel's father and to consider how striking it is to have a parent so involved with a graduate student's education. Rachel, from a middle-class background, arrived at graduate school with a clear congruence between home and school cultures. My students from non-dominant cultures never mention a parent involved in the proofing of their written work. The non-dominant students seem to depend a great deal on their teachers for guidance. In fact, in my interviews with Kerry (Black student from Bermuda) and Alisha (Black student from Haiti), both commented how they remembered very specific details about my written feedback, months after the course ended. They had clearly taken this feedback seriously.

2. Face-to-Face Meetings

One clear finding from these student interviews was that written feedback seemed more effective than a face-to-face conference. Rachel specifically identified how relieved she was to have the written feedback first. She was very anxious about her grade and her performance. She felt that she would not have been able to listen effectively if she had to meet with me to discuss her paper in person. Her anxiety would have prevented her from hearing the feedback—both negative and positive. She reported carefully studying my written comments until she understood the salient points—and it gave her confidence to then approach me in person to discuss her questions or concerns. Rachel commented:

> I think that if I was sitting in front of you with my paper it would have been embarrassing for me. To sit there with you, who knows more than me, and look through my

paper that was not very good, that would have been more difficult for me; that would have been embarrassing. But the [written] comments were extremely helpful. I think it's only going to improve what you have done. It was very helpful. I went through them all. It really helped me to see that, okay, this is what I need to do next ...

I have found that White students like Rachel, who may be accustomed to congruency between home and school cultures, are not afraid to ask for help from their professors. On the other hand, I have often found that my students of color or students from non-dominant cultures hold back and seem to be more reticent to ask for help. I can certainly relate; I have often felt reluctant to ask for help from my superiors because of fear that my "cloak of competence" will be lifted and reveal my inadequacies at a critical moment. Perhaps a student like Rachel was given both the permission and the model from an early age to ask for help from her family and teachers. I receive frequent emails and requests for help from my White students for even the most minor questions about an assignment. This dynamic has almost never been the case for my students from non-dominant cultures. My students from non-dominant cultures often act very formal with me, perhaps calling me "professor" while my White students call me by my first name, which is typically the protocol at the college. My non-dominant students rarely email or ask for help, and I have found that often when they finally do, it reflects dire circumstances such as a personal crisis or fear of failure of the course. Now that I recognize this discrepancy, I need to build into my cultural mentoring role a place for "face-saving" opportunities for check-in and feedback with all of my students. Since students reported that they appreciated first receiving written feedback, perhaps I would build into the course structure a requirement that all of the students meet with me individually to review the feedback and to prepare for the final educational written report. This individual meeting by mid-semester may be the necessary invitation for my non-dominant students to make a personal connection with me and allow us some time to develop a learning relationship.

3. Multiple Drafts and Peer Editing

I find it helpful to require multiple drafts of a final project before the final grade is given. Reviewing drafts for students allows me to wear the "coach" hat without the obligation of giving an evaluative grade. I take the opportunity with students' draft to truly coach them with specific advice on how to proceed with an assessment plan and what revisions to consider. In this writing process, first I ask students to write a proposal for the required educational report, and I provide specific recommendations on how to proceed. Then students are asked to find a peer coach (another student in the class) to read and give feedback on an initial draft.

Students then submit this revised draft to me for my comments and feedback. Students also submit the feedback that they received from their peers. I like to see the kinds of comments their peers offered. I have found that my written feedback on earlier required papers may influence students in the quality of the feedback they provide to their peers. Peers edit for content rather than only looking at grammar or style. They ask questions, seek clarification, and make suggestions regarding an analysis. I have been satisfied to see the depth of this peer editing, and perhaps my written feedback on earlier papers has influenced this level of editing. This is an example of new professionals practicing the discourse together! Alisha remembered that the peer editing went beyond exchanging a draft and that students also found each other in the library to work together.

> This is what I like the most, working together. I don't know if you really encouraged it. The drafts, that was really excellent and was helpful for us. Julie reading mine, we would exchange it via email. I forwarded my report to her and she did the same thing. I know that the scoring of the tests ... we would meet at the library and go over the scoring. They [students] were not all in my section and we would just meet and they were very nice and I would just join them and we would score together. That really helped me a lot. I definitely think you should encourage that, it was so much easier.

In addition to requiring multiple drafts, I make a commitment to grade or edit papers within one week of receiving them. Because time is short within a course and assignments are meant to build off of one another, I want students to get immediate feedback while the writing is fresh in their minds. Optimally, students will then know how to proceed as they begin the next assignment and benefit from a cycle of writing, learning from feedback, and further writing.

4. Opportunities to Practice the Oral Discourse

In recent years I have found it helpful to provide regular opportunities for students to practice the oral discourse of a special education teacher. Each student is required to present a case study at least once in the course. Students bring in samples of children's work, information about the child's strengths and skills, and their own questions about the learning. We follow a protocol to structure the conversation, and I model ways that a team of teachers could collaborate and wisely use their time to discuss student issues. I ask students to base their conversation on concrete evidence—the children's work samples—and I listen and provide feedback on how children's skills and abilities are described. Sometimes students do not know the correct term used in the special education profession and this is my opportunity to coach them in this discourse. For example, students describe a child's behavior but do not necessarily know the applicable terms such as *receptive* and *expressive language, visual perception,* and *low muscle tone.* Students also need practice in describing a child's behavior using objective, non-judgmental language that is both descriptive and informative. At the end of the course, we conduct mock team meetings for a child's Individual Education Plan (IEP). Students organize themselves in teams of six to eight and take roles as administrators, teachers, and family members. One half of the class participates in the role play while the other half observes and takes notes. Students report that these mock meetings have been helpful, and I use this role play as an opportunity to discuss how important it is to use professional but clear language for families.

FINAL THOUGHTS

I have learned to be bicultural and to move across borders between the non-mainstream, working-class discourse of my background to the mainstream, middle-class, professional discourse of teachers and schools. I am as precise and explicit as I can be in helping all of my students join the professional discourse of teaching. My role as cultural mentor is one of guide or coach as I work to enable students, particularly my students from the non-dominant cultures to cross this border. Piper (1995) speaks to the obligation those of us have who have crossed this border, and yet some professions, such as her profession of psychology, tend to ignore the real-life dilemmas of people from the poor and working class.

> I think that those of us who have experienced the oppression of being marginalized and have worked our way through the educational system to be able to engage in the dominant discourse have a responsibility to illuminate the effects of class oppression. It is important that we all, in our own teaching and professional work, speak to this issue and work toward helping others understand how broader social forces affect people's lives. (pp. 295–296)

I wonder if, in my role as cultural mentor, I could be even more explicit with my students about crossing borders into a new professional discourse: Could I help students from the non-dominant cultures more clearly find and follow their path across the borders? I want to not only confirm and respect what my students already bring to the classroom, but also to support their consciousness of the journey as they learn the new skills that will allow them to negotiate the dominant discourse. Making this path between borders visible might enable students to respond positively to the value of adding new skills—in contrast to a deficit model that only encourages self-doubt and retreat (Bartolomé, 2003). There is no real mystery in academic writing or preparing a sound educational report—what it does take are opportunities for feedback, practice, and review of exemplars.

All teachers can provide this explicit information, particularly when there is an attitude (an ideology) that all students have the right and capability to learn, regardless of their cultural and socioeconomic background. All teachers must reflect on the ideology and values that shape how they respond to the students who enter their classrooms.

 I still sit with my dilemma of not able to fully connect with Joyce, my student who initially set me on this quest to reflect on my teaching. Joyce is now a teacher in California—she presumably learned the skills she needed to succeed, even though she left the graduate program annoyed with a low grade I had given. I do believe in equity and standards and feel that these are not antithetical terms—I hold high expectations for my students and I provide coaching to help them meet those expectations. I am convinced, however, that I must continue to explore different coaching or mentoring styles to reach different types of students based on their culture, personality, and learning styles. I certainly am not always successful with all of my students, and I am grateful that I have Joyce to remind me to look for new ways.

 After listening to some of my students' stories and writing my own, I am impressed with the "luck" that seems to occur for students from the non-dominant culture to access opportunities in higher education—the fuzzy announcement I heard on the school's public address system, Linda finding a mentor in a special program in high school, Alisha winning a lottery to get into a pilot high school program for college preparation. We cannot operate on luck to locate, encourage, and move students from nondominant cultures to successful academic careers and professions. Those of us without the inherited cultural capital and the social and professional networks that come with this wealth need to have a clear way to get our share of the capital. It is my hope as a teacher to find and share this wealth—to be explicit and point to the learning that I see needs to be made in order to succeed in a graduate program and to enter the gate to become a professional.

APPENDIX: WRITTEN FEEDBACK

Final Assignment: Educational Evaluation and IEP

Name: Kerry
Total Points: 22 out of 25 points

What I liked about your report:

- Kerry, you are thorough! Nice work.
- Your writing was clear and professional.

- The tables you included are excellent.
- Excellent introduction to the Discussion section. Introductions and summary statements are excellent to include as much as possible—they help the reader stay on track with all this material.
- You did a nice job combining info about subtests into one paragraph—a sign of true growth and development in report writing. You were able to do this with 4 or 5 passages from the QRI and with the math subtests from the WJ-III.
- Nice job comparing test results and sometimes also comparing to reading performance.

Things to consider for your next report:

You'll probably never have the time to put together such a comprehensive report again unless, of course, you decide to be an evaluator professionally. When you are a classroom teacher, your evaluation reports will probably not realistically be so complete. However, you now have the template for an excellent report.

Background Information and IEP Student Performance Profile

- This info should read like a Student Profile. You need brief statements about her current performance levels in math and reading, particularly. This same info is also needed in your IEP under Student Performance Profile. Give at least ranges of grade level abilities, based on your observations in the classroom. If you look on the second page of your IEP under Student Strengths and Key Evaluation Results Summary—again this is where specific grade level info would be helpful. Here you could include the actual assessment data based on your results. Give as specific info on performance abilities as possible so that the next year's teachers have a better idea on where to begin.

Current Levels of Performance

- Give more specific examples of performance. Include samples of work, i.e., for writing. Include these samples in the Appendix. In the text of the report, analyze the work sample—what do you understand about Alexa's writing based on this sample?
- The math skills section is more specific and helpful.

156 | IDEOLOGIES IN EDUCATION

General Observations

You mention Alexa's anxiety but you do not clearly state if a particular session or test was invalid. You do mention this test anxiety repeatedly in the report, particularly when you are surprised that her scores are low. Recommend that she be re-tested to confirm your results and to note her performance at a better level.

Discussion of Results

Try to compare test performance with classroom performance as much as you can. I know you did this at several points in the report. I was most interested to hear about your observations of classroom reading comprehension abilities since this was such a difficult area for your student.

- Appendices—refer the reader to an exact page or item number in the appendix to make it most useful.
- Try to complete more of an item analysis. What kinds of problems did Alexa get correct and incorrect?
- Before completing the Discussion section—go back to your assessment questions. Did you answer them? Summarize your discussion by answering your questions and then move on to the final summary. Or use this info to help prepare the summary section.

Summary

- Good summary. Add more standardized scores, at least highlight the Broad Math and Broad Reading Scores from the WJ-III, the Total Test scores from the Key Math (include the standard scores and percentile ranks).

Recommendations

- Recommend repeating some of the testing to obtain a more optimal performance from Alexa.
- Repeat the QRI-3 and use look backs to determine what she needs to comprehend materials and at what grade level.

IEP Objectives

- On several of your objectives, you used the phrase "Given the opportunity." This is too vague and not appropriate for a learning objective. You must state the conditions for learning that are appropriate. For example, "Given 4-6th grade reading materials, Alexa will develop comprehension strategies such as predicting, summarizing, etc."

Rating Criteria (Total of 35 Points)

(See complete rubric on pages 15-16 of the syllabus.)

What it looks like	Earned
1. Presentation and complete information (2 points)	2

What it reads like	Earned
1. Professional language (5 points)	4
2. Present Level of Educational Performance Level (3 points)	3
3. General Observations (2)	2
4. Discussion of Results (5 points)	4
5. Summary (3 points)	2.5
6. Recommendations and IEP (5 points)	4.5
TOTAL POINTS	22

REFERENCES

Bartolomé, L. (1998). *The misteaching of academic discourse: The politics of language in the classroom.* Boulder, CO: Westview Press.

Bartolomé, L. (2003). Beyond the methods fetish: Toward a humanizing pedagogy. In A. Darder, M. Baltondano, & R. Torres (Eds.), *The critical pedagogy reader.* New York: Routledge Falmer.

Bourdieu, P. (1986). The forms of capital. In J. Richardson (Ed.), *Handbook of theory and research for the sociology of education* (pp. 241–258). New York: Greenwood Press.

Delpit, L. (1995). The silenced dialogue: Power and pedagogy in educating other people's children. In *Other people's children: Cultural conflict in the classroom* (pp. 21–47). New York: The New Press.

Elbow, P. (1986). *Embracing contraries in the teaching process.* New York: Oxford University Press.

Foster, M. (1997). *Black teachers on teaching.* New York: The New Press.

Gándara, P. (1995). *Over the ivy walls: The educational mobility of low-income Chicanos.* Albany: State University of New York Press.

Gándara, P. (1999). Staying in the race: The challenge for Chicano/as in higher education. In Moreno, J. (Ed.), *The elusive quest for equality: 150 years of Chicano/Chicana education* (pp. 169–196). Cambridge, MA: Harvard Educational Review.

Gee, J. (1991). What is literacy? In C. Mitchell & K. Weiler (Eds.), *Rewriting literacy: Culture and the discourse of the other* (pp. 3–11). New York: Bergin & Garvey.

Gee, J. (1999). *An introduction to discourse analysis: Theory and method.* New York: Routledge.

Gee, J., Hull, G., & Lankshear, C. (1996). *The new work order: Behind the language of the new capitalism.* Boulder, CO: Westview Press.

Ladson-Billings, G. (1994). *The dreamkeepers: Successful teachers of African American children.* San Francisco: Jossey Bass.
Ladson-Billings, G. (2001). *Crossing over to Canaan.* San Francisco: Jossey Bass.
Mitchell, C., & Weiler, K. (1991). *Rewriting literacy: Culture and the discourse of the other.* New York: Bergin & Garvey.
Nieto, S. (1999). *The light in their eyes: Creating multicultural learning communities.* New York: Teachers College Press.
Piper, D. (1995). Psychology's class blindness: Investment in the status quo. In C. Dews & C. Law (Eds.), *This fine place so far from home: Voices of academics from the working class* (pp. 286–296). Philadelphia: Temple University Press.

Section V. Gaining Greater Ideological Clarity

CHAPTER EIGHT

"I'm White, Now What?" Setting A Context FOR Change IN Teachers' Pedagogy

PAULA S. MARTIN

Deeply imbedded in American society, coloring virtually all cross-cultural interactions is racism, a system of privilege and power based on race that typically goes unacknowledged by those who benefit from this system: Whites in general and White teachers in particular. In education, it is particularly important that White teachers develop an understanding of this system of privilege especially when they work with non-White students (Wellman, 1993). The majority of urban school teachers no longer teach White culturally homogeneous student bodies. Despite the changing student population, White teachers are typically not prepared to effectively respond to their multicultural and multilingual students' needs. More importantly, White teachers are not aware of their White race privilege and the role this privilege may play in their work with minority students. In this chapter, I describe the results of a study conducted with 125 White K-12 teachers, who participated in a 36-hour graduate level antiracism course developed to increase their racial identity awareness to improve their work with minority students.

INTRODUCTION

According to the U.S. Department of Education National Statistics: Digest of Education, 17% of students enrolled in K-12 public schools are Black (1999, Table 45). The 1996 *Digest of Education* also reports that 90.7% of the teachers in the United States are White, compared to 7.3% of teachers who are Black. Seventy-four point four percent of the White teachers are female and 25.6% are White males. From these statistics we can infer that the vast majority of Black children in the United States public school system are instructed by White teachers.

Perhaps one of racism's most observable and enduring expressions is the "Black-White achievement gap." As educators, we know that academic performance of all students can depend on the quality of teacher student relationships. Therefore, we must acknowledge that poor-quality interactions between White educators and Black students can adversely affect these students' academic performance. When White teachers are queried about racism in their classrooms, some claim "not to see color" and say they treat all children the same irrespective of racial background. In these cases, when White teachers who believe and act on their beliefs that students' cultures and experiences are irrelevant to teaching—actively choose to treat all children "the same," the classroom culture and teacher-student relationships may be negatively affected. In other words, teachers who supposedly treat all the students "the same" may actually be communicating to the children, "I see you as White; therefore, I will treat you as a White child, and expect you to behave and to learn as a White child." Helping teachers recognize and overcome this covertly racist practice are the focus of the present research.

A body of educational and psychological literature exists that contends that White teachers must develop ways of talking about racial identity, racial privilege, and racial discomfort as a way to improve their work with students of color (Cochran-Smith, 2000; Lawrence & Tatum, 1997; Tatum, 1992; Titone, 1998). Teachers must become aware of their ideological beliefs around race, as well as their expectations and personal beliefs—especially those that can have a negative impact on the academic achievement of Black and other minority students. I contend that through professional development efforts that are explicitly anti-racist and anti-White supremacist ideology, teachers can begin to develop clarity of thought regarding racism and White supremacist beliefs, as well as their possible effects on their teaching. As Mills (1998) so aptly expressed, "The white eye can thereby learn to see itself seeing whitely" (p. 9), recognizing that as member of the dominant White culture they contribute to and reinforce hegemonic thinking and a continuance of the cycle of oppression. hooks (1989) eloquently reminds us:

> When ... Whites fail to understand how they can and/or do embody white-supremacist values and beliefs even though they may or may not embrace racism as a prejudice or domination, they cannot recognize the ways their actions support and affirm the very structure of racist domination and oppression that [many] profess to wish to see eradicated. (p. 113)

Antiracism education produces change in White teachers' awareness of Whiteness and White privilege. For example, only recently in a new teacher orientation I asked the question, "How many of you walked into this room and thought, 'It's really *White* in here?'" Only the four teachers of color in the room raised their hands; the remaining 56 White educators had not noticed the disproportionate number of White educators in the room. The privilege of not noticing, or not having to notice, that the room was primarily White carries over into the classroom. (I continue to be amazed by the number of White educators who do not recognize their majority privilege.) This blindness leads to not noticing the children of color and thereby not placing them at the table as contributors in class. In other words, their cultural capital is ignored and not valued. Antiracism education engages White teachers in dialogues and activities that enable White teachers to see their privilege. Antiracism education can potentially help White educators to develop a positive White racial identity devoid of its White supremacy dimensions, and, most importantly, translate their greater awareness to more effective instructional practices.

PRECEPTS, PRINCIPLES, AND PRACTICES OF ANTIRACISM EDUCATION

Peggy McIntosh (1989) explains that White people benefit from privileges both earned and unearned, and that people of color, especially Black people, do not. Further, White people are not educated to see the links between their privilege and racism. For example, White women can always expect to find makeup in their skin tone, or pantyhose in their flesh tone at any retail establishment, but Black women must always consider where they shop in order to secure the same products in their skin tones. For most White people in the United States, the connection between privilege, membership in the dominant group, and their role as oppressors is not evident. Most White people do not see the connection between their personal membership in the White race as a benefit. For example, White people do not walk into a meeting and say, "This group is too White for me. I'm leaving." White people are not conscious of the fact that another perspective is missing from the group (McIntosh, 1989). Sidanius and Pratto (1993) suggest that individual discrimination refers to the values one individual places on another individual primarily on the basis of perceived group membership. Furthermore, this value placement is driven by the need for a positive self-identity such as the need to feel good about oneself. Social dominance theory is consistent with systems of privilege and power in that it supports group-based inequities linked to personal and institutional behavior, assigning privilege and power to one group, while assigning low status and other "penalties" to another group.

Many antiracist education researchers contend that White school administrators and teachers must change their perceptions of themselves as racial beings and recognize how they contribute to the cycle of oppression perpetrated by the dominant culture so as to gain a better understanding of Black and other minority students' social and academic experiences in dominant culture school environments (Howard, 1999; Rios, 1996; Tatum, 1997). Tatum (1992) suggests that professional development programs in K-12 schools take the lead in initiating change in teacher thinking and beliefs. In other words, how can a White teacher come to recognize that being White shapes her thinking about other cultures and helps to form her belief system, which may ultimately affect her behavior toward those groups? (The pronouns "she" and "her" will be used throughout this chapter for consistency.) It is not surprising that current research has failed to determine which models of antiracist teacher education are most likely to affect positive change in White teachers' predisposition toward Black and other non-White students and the extent to which any anti-racist teacher training model can influence White educators' instructional practices and beliefs and thus improve the academic success of Black and other historically underachieving minority students. Absence of antiracist education models served as the impetus for my study.

My research focus concerns how White teachers change as a result of experiencing one particular model of antiracist teacher education that focuses on White racial identity development and White privilege awareness. Such a model assists White teachers in recognizing and interrogating their power and privilege as members of the dominant cultural group in the United States. The focus on White racial identity is meant to help White teachers consider adopting an antiracist posture and seriously interrogating attitudes, beliefs, and actual practices that challenge hegemonic White supremacist ideology. Unless White educators are willing to take the first step toward improving their relationships with culturally and linguistically diverse students in general and with Black students in particular, racism will continue to afflict teacher student relationships, unduly hampering the efforts to improve academic achievement among all students. The principles of antiracism education aim to help teachers in general and White teachers in particular, to critique the dominant discourse of racism and to understand how racism and racist attitudes on the part of teachers can potentially adversely affect the classroom culture.

I further suggest that after experiencing this type of White awareness antiracism education, White teachers are better prepared to adopt the posture of antiracist educators, a posture that illuminates the set of attitudes, expectations, and behaviors that challenge racism, and places the White teacher and other-race students on the same footing. More to the point, after experiencing White

Awareness antiracist education, White teachers can potentially become allies in the struggle against racism as opposed to becoming adversaries in the struggle to maintain it.

PRIOR RESEARCH AND REVIEW OF RELEVANT LITERATURE

Literature on teacher-student relationships, when conjoined with the emerging literature on White teacher attitudes, beliefs, and behavior suggest the possibilities for positive change in teacher pedagogy (Hollins, 1996; Nieto, 1996; Seller & Weis, 1997; Tatum, 1997). Teacher education programs have not been sufficiently effective in addressing the problem of racism, although, to be fair, they have not exactly ignored the issue either. As a way to combat racist ideologies' and practices' negative effects, school educators have embraced various curricular interventions that expose students to socially diverse cultures. Often, through the somewhat superficial use of food, festivals, holidays, heroes, and multicultural education, teachers attempt to bridge the gap between White and non-White cultures. However, this approach has typically served to reinforce common stereotypes of non-White cultures while paying little if any attention to the intellectual and societal contributions of those groups.

According to Howard's (1999) social dominance model, the roles White teachers assume are typically one of three: fundamentalist, integrationist, or transformatist. A *fundamentalist* role refers to a role that White teachers assume when they deny or ignore Whiteness as a power construct and White supremacy as a racist ideology of dominance. White teachers who take on this role tend to self-identify as French or Italian or other European ethnicity, rather than see themselves as White—as a member of the dominant racial group in the United States. When teachers assume this fundamentalist role, they do not recognize themselves as racial beings. Alternatively, teachers who assume the role of *integrationist* see racial injustice as the victims' fault. For instance, they acknowledge that slavery existed. However, they feel that since Blacks were eventually freed, they were able to pursue the advantages of being free and equal members of society. Teachers assuming an integrationist role cannot readily perceive that even after slavery was abolished, economic and political access for Blacks was and continues to be limited. Teachers at the *transformatist* stage seek to understand diverse points of view. They acknowledge the collective reality of White complicity in dominance and oppression, the construction of racism and are willing to probe deeper into racial identity to become self-reflective, authentic, and antiracist in their understanding of Whiteness. These teachers often ask—thus, the title of this chapter—"OK, I'm White, now what?"

Titone (1998) notes that White teachers who assume a purely intellectualist role have steeped themselves in the educational literature concerning racism and academic performance of children of color and speak as though they understand the context of race, racism, and antiracism, but fail to understand how to apply theory to practice. For example, they are often not clear regarding what action is necessary to make transformative changes in schools. Action is the key to moving preservice as well as in-service teachers away from the intellectualized stance to that of an authentic White ally role, which is the desired outcome of antiracist education. The White ally role is action-orientated. However, Paulo Freire (1972) warns us about uninformed action. It is not enough to be action oriented without reflection, and it is not enough to be an armchair intellectual. "Praxis" is a concept that he introduced that captures the importance of reflective-action—teachers reflect and then act. Once they act, they reflect. Praxis refers to the unending cycle of reflection-action and action-reflection.

In general, traditional multicultural education's central focus is on celebration and the appreciation of cultural difference. It assumes:

1. Racism is absent in the teaching process
2. The classroom is not a microcosm of the world influenced by racism and power dynamics and problems of a diverse society
3. Solutions to problems in a diverse society rely on merely obtaining a greater understanding of diverse cultures
4. The key to improving cultural understandings is on emphasizing individual attitudes and values
5. The focus in on celebrating differences
6. Educational equality is the focused value (Mier & Mizell, 1996).

In contrast, antiracist multicultural education acknowledges the role of White supremacist ideology and its systematic effect on the infrastructure of the educational system. The antiracism component identifies *structural racism as an active component of teaching pedagogy*. The antiracism component also provides a global perspective in that it recognizes that schools and classrooms are a reflection of the larger society and the problems of society, such as racism, also exist within the schools on structural and systemic levels. The antiracist perspective acknowledges that the major problem affecting our society—especially our education systems—is systemic racism and its resulting numerous harmful beliefs and practices.

This is significant in that antiracist education makes explicit for teachers the effect of racism on their lives, inside and outside their classrooms as the findings from my study suggest. Lawrence and Tatum (1997) examined teacher beliefs in an antiracism professional development program. Their study found that educators who participated in a semester-long explicitly antiracist professional development course changed their behaviors. For example, they were able to actively engage in conversations about race and racism with the students in their classrooms, and they were able to distinguish between incidents that were generated by race and those that could occur between any students regardless of race.

Similarly, Martin (2000) used the Helms and Carter (1994) White racial identity model to determine the extent to which an antiracism education course affected the racial identity development of White teachers. Her findings reveal that the participants underwent significant and statistically positive changes in three of five racial identity stages. This study demonstrates that by increasing educators' White racial identity awareness through professional development, they take concrete action to reduce equalities and improve the school climates at their respective schools. In one school, teachers who took this course returned to their suburban middle school and established a one-to-one mentoring program for the Black students in their school. Another group of teachers at a high school started a book and discussion group on racism, while another group of teachers and administrators conducted an action research study to investigate what the Black students in their school district saw as the conditions for academic success or failure for them. What is significant is all of the initiatives were conducted by graduates of one particular model of an antiracist course, which I researched.

Keith and Martin (2002) in a discussion on privilege and homophobia suggest that it is difficult for members of dominant cultural groups to become aware of their privilege because it is usually taken for granted and seldom consciously acknowledged. The author likens unacknowledged racial privilege to heterosexual privilege. Keith states,

> If you are a member of the majority culture you never have to make excuses because you see your job as maintaining the status quo and perpetuating the social and cultural myths which keep marginalized people outside of the accepted sphere of influence. Heterosexual privilege is a little like White privilege ... if you can't see it, you can't acknowledge it. If you can't acknowledge it, then it doesn't exist and if it doesn't exist, you can easily change the subject and talk about something else because it becomes a non-issue. To truly understand heterosexual privilege, one must understand racism, which is about power and privilege, the same privilege exercise by a dominant culture over another culture. When you get that then you see clearly how heterosexual privilege is played out in current culture. This is about a social/cultural/historical attitude among a dominant culture (p. 3).

As Keith's quote alludes, White educators must have the willingness to abandon White supremacist ideology and move toward the development of a positive White racial identity in which membership is recognized, and privilege is acknowledged as a maintenance function in the cycle of racial oppression. Very simply: White teachers who undergo an antiracism training experience that includes a racial identity component typically experience positive change in their attitudes and beliefs about racism and their own White privilege.

STUDY OVERVIEW

In this section of the chapter, I provide an overview of my theoretical framework: the White Racial Identity Model (Helms, 1984), my method of data analysis, the antiracism course used in the study, and the findings. My study focused on a particular antiracist education model with the underlying assumption that responsibility for equality and equity in the classroom and the reduction of the achievement gap between Black and White students relies on the adult professionals who may either consciously or unconsciously act in ways that collude with an institutional environment that some consider inherently racist (Scheurich & Young, 1997). This particular antiracist education class focused on developing teacher clarity regarding the roles they may play in either promoting or subverting racist policies, thus providing both a basis for teachers to develop a common language around racism and a means for the creation of instructional practices that promise to benefit all children. This thirty-six-hour graduate course was composed of four sections which met on a bi-monthly basis. Three of the classes were full day, 8:30 a.m. to 3:30 p.m., while the remaining five classes met from 3:30 to 5:30. In fact, this course continues be offered to educators.

WHITE RACIAL IDENTITY MODEL

By building on her observations of counseling situations, Helms (1984) framed the problem of improving interracial relations in terms of helping Whites develop greater awareness of their White racial identity. Her model offers five racial identity stages that White people may move through: 1. Contact—a stage of racial identity during which Whites express naiveté and a lack of awareness of their sociopolitical significance of racial-group membership in the dominant racial group in U.S. society. 2. Disintegration—a stage during which Whites experience confusion and self-disorientation with respect to their membership in the dominant U.S. racial group. In addition, Whites at this stage of racial identity awareness often feel ambivalence toward the implications of race membership for other racial groups. 3. Reintegration—a stage during which Whites both passively and actively endorse White superiority and Black inferiority. 4. The Pseudo-Independence stage is characterized by an intellectualized acceptance of one's

Whiteness and quasi-recognition of the sociopolitical implications of racial difference. 5. Autonomy—a stage during which Whites experience racial humanism from a positive White (nonracist) orientation.

This racial interaction model is suitable for use within the field of education, as both fields, counseling and education, function under didactic power relationships (e.g., counselor-client, teacher-student, and parent-child). Note that the term *stage* was changed by Helms (personal conversation, April, 2002) to *schema* to avoid the generalizations that the stages of racial identities were set. Schema represents fluidity according to Helms. Although the term has changed, the content of the five stages remain consistent. I will use the terms *stages* and *status* interchangeably as they reflect the language of the study.

WHITE PRIVILEGE ANTIRACISM EDUCATION

Teachers in the course met weekly for two and one-half hours. The enrollees were educators from ten Northeastern suburban school systems. The course required all participants to complete a series of tenacity challenges. For example, participants were asked to: first, identify an issue concerning a student of color in their classroom or school and develop a plan to assist that student in achieving success; second, undergo a minority experience during which the educators would place themselves in contexts where they would not be the dominant culture or race. A majority of the participants in the course were White, although some classes also included teachers of color. However, for this study, all participants in the four sections of the course were White teachers.

The course is generally made up of three components: personal, experiential, and implementational. The *personal* component reflects the first three sessions during which teachers are introduced to the working definition of racism primarily through Peggy McIntosh's (1989) article on White privilege, and Janet Helm's (1984) racial identity development theory and five-stage model of racial identity. Supplemental readings, in-class discussion, and reflective writing are also integrated into this component as well as throughout the course.

The *experiential* component takes up the next three classes. During this second component, participants become active in their antiracism work. In addition to writing reflection papers, participants are required to participate in a minority field experience where White participants themselves are placed in a situation where they are the only White person or in the minority situation (e.g., Black neighborhood, Hispanic store, Asian community).

In the last four classes, during the third and final component of the course—the *implementation* component—participants examine the hiring practices and pedagogy of their school districts through an antiracist lens, determining the steps necessary for increasing the teachers of color population and reviewing the hiring policies in their respective school districts. The course participants also develop a pedagogical action plan, a document that states how they will interrupt some cycle of oppression or racism that occurs in their school system.

DATA ANALYSIS

I utilized a pre-test, post-test design to investigate the effects of a model of antiracism education which focused on the White racial identity and White privilege awareness of White teachers from a collaborative team of ten Northeastern suburban school districts. Helms and Carter's (1994) White Racial Identity Attitude Scale (WRIAS) provided the means to measure attitudes related to the five stages of White Racial Identity along a five-point Likert scale that ranged from strongly disagree, disagree, uncertain, agree, and strongly disagree. A paired sample t test ($p < .05$) was performed for the pre-test and post-test sub-scales, I used a paired-samples t-test (Green, Salkind, & Akey, 2000) to evaluate whether the mean of the difference between pre- and post-test WRIAS scores were statistically significant. To evaluate the qualitative themes (e.g., awareness of White privilege, acknowledgement of White Privilege, intent to take action to abate racism), I employed a content analysis technique.

FINDINGS

This study determined that, after taking a 36-hour graduate level antiracism course in which White Racial Identity was a focus, White teachers showed a variance in their post-test scores. The findings of this study showed a positive significant variance ($p < .05$) at the reintegration stage, and $p < .01$ at the pseudo-independence stage. Subsequent qualitative data suggest that as a result of participation in this particular antiracism education curriculum, White teachers experienced a change in their racial identity development, which led to an elevation in their White Privilege Awareness (WPA). Not all changes on the White attitude sub-scale were statistically significant. However, I present excerpts from teachers' reflection papers to augment and clarify the education significance of the data in this study. To protect the anonymity of the subjects, I use feminine pronouns, although the teachers providing the quotes could be either female or male.

Contact. A White teacher at this stage of racial identity development may be characterized as being unaware of her own Whiteness and privilege and may perceive racism as being an individual as opposed to an institutional phenomenon (McIntyre, 1997). Helms (1990) opines that such a person may enjoy being a racist more than Whites at the other stages simply because this individual has not faced any racial confrontations such as being called a racist by a Black student. The length of that time an individual remains in the Contact stage is dependent upon the kind of experiences she has with racial issues. As such, the individual at this stage does not demonstrate conscious awareness of her racist or White supremacist posture. Qualitative data taken from the participants enrolled in the class suggest a change in the level of their awareness concerning their identity and privileged status. In the following excerpts, students express how initially unaware they were concerning the issues of racism. One student pointed out racism's presence in everyday life:

> Many people including myself naively felt that racism *was not a big issue in society anymore*. Often times when we think of racism, the violence and segregation in the 60s, the Ku Klux Klan, and inappropriate language may come to mind. Many of these scenarios are not as common today compared to back then. Not to talk about what is today is very hard to prove. Many White people don't recognize it and sometimes, even people of color. (emphasis added)

Another student expressed how she never had to think about being White or how deeply racism was entrenched in U.S. society.

> At the start of the course I *had never thought about being white, about racism and how entrenched it is in the systems of our country*, or about the fact that I have a role in perpetuating racism. I think this course has helped me to gather some of my here-there-forays into some of the issues included in the *concept of racism* under a *larger umbrella* and has forced me to face some of the unpleasant realities of racism in an intense way. (emphasis added)

A third student recognized her own personal racism and White supremacy as evidenced in the need to feel safe outside of the diverse community in which she lived.

> I live in a diverse neighborhood in Somerville. My neighbors speak mainly Portuguese or Spanish. I didn't have much contact with anyone in my neighborhood before this class, but as a challenge to myself I have attempted to be open and friendly to everyone I see. Hard as it is to admit, I had never done errands in my neighborhood. I always *traveled out to someplace that I felt safe in* (of course, I didn't realize that I was doing this until I took the course!!) (emphasis added)

The next set of teacher responses capture the movement from the Contact stage toward the next stage, Disintegration.

Disintegration. Disintegration refers to an individual's conscious and sometimes conflicted acknowledgment of Whiteness and privilege. This acknowledgment often leads teachers to question what they were explicitly and implicitly taught about race and Whiteness as children and what teachings and beliefs are reinforced by the mass media and society. A catalyst for propelling White students into the Disintegration stage is the minority field experience which requires students to place themselves in various situations where they were not among a White majority. Rosenberg's (1960) group theory suggests that changes in the affective domain in turn can lead to changes in the cognitive domain. In other words, an experience that influences the way individuals feel about an issue can also change how individuals think about the issue. The following excerpts point to the heightened awareness of Whiteness and privilege that subjects experienced. The first teacher acknowledges that she was not ready to venture into sites that she knew were predominately Black, suggesting a level of discomfort with giving up her dominant posture and privilege.

> My minority field experience took place in downtown Framingham, MA. *I was definitely not ready for the Roxbury or Dorchester* [two predominantly minority communities in Boston] *experience so I chose a neutral place* for me. The experience was interesting and a little nerve wracking. ... I tried to shed my Lord and Taylor [high end clothing store] mind set and look at the store for what it was, not my misperceptions of what it should be. (emphasis added)

Another student reflected on a personal acknowledgment of privilege and the invisibility contained therein.

> Describing racism in terms of unearned or White privilege was a new way of thinking about it for me. This, as a definition, makes it very clear what one means when talking about racism. I was never taught to consider that there were invisible systems at work all around me. (emphasis added)

A third teacher expressed realization of her privilege and acknowledgment of its existence.

> In terms of White privilege, I had never used the term before this class, and *I had never really thought about myself as being privileged because of my race.* One of the key realizations for me, which was made clear as we watched the video contrasting the experiences of a man of color and a White man, is that the main privilege of my race is that *I do not have to think about race.* (emphasis added)

Another student expressed her lack of awareness about race for most of her life.

As I reviewed my experience in this course I listened to the tape I had recorded before the course began. My biggest realization was simple one of awareness, *the awareness that for most of my life I simply haven't thought about race.* (emphasis added)

Finally, another student recognized the unequal power relations between White and non-White ethnic groups and their manifestation in the privilege of being White and the subsequent lack of privilege and low status of being non-White.

The definition of White privilege has helped me to understand *the system of disadvantage that People of Color face daily.* Whether it be waiting to be served in a coffee shop, choosing where to sit in a cafeteria, or finding a new job, race makes a difference. *Although often unspoken, a person's race carries stereotypes and assumptions with it. White privilege is what mainly European descendants have whether they realize it or not.* Whether it be an Aryan beauty or speaking the English language, favoritism towards these qualities still exists today. *It's what is dominant and what society prefers.* (emphasis added)

Student reactions at both the Contact and Disintegration stages of racial identity demonstrate their growing awareness and acknowledgment of White privilege. However, the desire to act on this awareness is not clearly evident. Although the White educators' attitudes toward White privilege and racism are becoming clearer, reactions to such change on the part of members of their group (e.g., colleagues, family, and friends) is often negative and may cause the teachers to regress to earlier stages where racism and White supremacy are negated and ignored. Faced with colleagues' negative feedback, White educators often react by expressing anger and frustration toward Blacks and other non-White racial groups and blaming them for the existence of racism. Others respond, as Katz (1960) observes, with a conscious desire or commitment to change racist conditions in schools and society.

Reintegration. Reintegration refers to active and passive endorsement of White superiority and Black inferiority. Helms (1984) notes that this stage is characterized by participant feelings of anger and discomfort. I believe that it is also the stage wherein White educators begin to seriously acknowledge their privilege and recognize, on a visceral level, that their newfound awareness and desire for change can come in direct conflict with the ideology of their White group. In other words, they experience tension and conflict recognizing that any action they take may signal to other Whites their abandonment of White privilege hegemonic beliefs.

Many of the teachers express frustration at this stage. One key challenge at this stage that our White participants cite is trying to work with White colleagues who have not adopted or been exposed to antiracist precepts regarding race or

White privilege. These colleagues often make statements that anger our White participants. For example, they make statements laced with phrases such as, "those students," or "*they* won't change," or "why do you spend so much time on *them*." The teachers in the reintegration stage often do not know how to respond to those statements and often admit that they say nothing, thus adding to their discomfort. To develop a positive White racial identity, white teachers must move within or from the Reintegration stage. Movement occurs when White teachers "let go" of all negative information that they were taught to believe about Black people and other non-White groups and exercise a willingness to step outside of their dominant White racial group. The findings show significant positive subject movement in the reintegration stage. This teacher's comments reflect the conflicts she feels at the Reintegration stage. The context for her comments relate to her experience at an airport and her observation regarding the treatment of a family of color in the same situation. She describes the airline's staff attempts to accommodate her when her flight was cancelled

> The staff really bent over backwards. They gave me several calling cards so that I could call my family and inform them of the changes. They even booked me on first class. *The people next to me were a Family of Color. I became acutely aware that they were not being given the same courtesies that I was.* They left without a new flight, without calling cards, and no first class. *As I left feeling uneasy* I questioned was it because I have a preferred flyer card? Was it because I was traveling alone? *Or what it because I was White? I left feeling guilty but not guilty enough to question it on that busy, crazy day because I got what I needed and wanted that day.* I am aware now of how I benefit every day. *I am trying to change my own behavior ... I am trying to notice my own privilege and question when unfair practices occur.* (emphasis added)

This teacher took a risk and made explicit her feelings and thinking about her own White privilege and the obvious discrimination she observed against the family of color in the same situation. Her statement suggests movement toward the pseudo-independence stage.

Pseudo-Independence. The pseudo-independence stage is characterized by the abandoning of White supremacist ideology. During this stage, the White person has an intellectual understanding of the unfairness of White privilege and recognizes her personal responsibility for dismantling racism. Whites at this stage of race identity development will often distance themselves from other Whites and seek out relationships with people of color, as if seeking congruence with their changed attitudes and belief systems. The educator at this stage might respond to the question, "Why are all the Black kids sitting together" by saying, "It's important for Black kids to have and create affinity with each other. It's important for their racial identity development." I once asked a group of educators, "Why are all the [White] kids sitting together …?" There was a very pregnant pause as they struggled to answer my question. Finally, one teacher ventured a response, "Because it's normal." This teacher had to acknowledge that White was perceived as normal, therefore, not worthy of attention. When the students were asked to reflect on their progress and to identify where they felt they were in their identity development, most of them responded that they believed they were in the pseudo-independence stage. Not surprisingly, it is the more enlightened status to achieve. Because the White racial identity model and its stages were explicitly taught in the course, students were aware of the various stages of racial identity development. The desire to be enlightened may have led some subjects to see themselves at a "higher" stage of racial identity rather than reveal their actual stage.

One student expressed an intellectual awareness indicative of the pseudo-independence stage when she began to make a connection between the impact of social dominance and the need to expand her awareness of her own White privilege. The teacher went on to explain that the onus of responsibility for eliminating racism and discrimination lies with Whites.

> At the beginning of the course, I stated that I felt Whites and Blacks have to work together to end racism. Now I believe it is more the *White people that have to recognize their own privilege and work to break the cycle. White people are the ones who created it.* (emphasis added)

A second student goes a step further and states that she must take action. Although she did not describe the specific action, her statements were nevertheless action-oriented.

> In some ways my journey has just begun. *While I have been able to identify past and present racist practices, I need to look at how I benefit from this.* I know that there is privilege attached to being White and that there is a racial hierarchy, keeping people of color on the bottom. Having learned about racial identity development, I now understand where anger and frustration comes from people of color. *Color does make a difference in the way we are treated. I have seen it most of my life but never thought about how I was personally benefiting from it.* As I mentioned in class one day, *I can no longer be a bystander. I have to say or do something whenever I witness racism in any way shape or form. To ignore racism is to allow it to continue.* (emphasis added)

The comment below by the following student sums up the key findings in this study and illuminates the possibilities for change in White teachers' attitudes, beliefs, and behaviors.

> At the beginning of this course I felt "Racism doesn't apply to me, I'm not a prejudiced person, and there's not much I can learn here. Now, however, looking back on the past

few months, I can't believe how wrong I was and how grateful I am ... for opening up my eyes enabling me to examine racism in a whole new light. I had always believed that as long as I didn't treat people of color with any disrespect or racial prejudice, that was enough and I was doing my part against racism. But [I know] that if I am not a part of the solution then I am part of the problem. I always felt that racism only affected people of color when they were around White people ... racism was a much deeper problem than I had ever realized. I didn't comprehend how racist attitudes by white people so strongly affected people of color. I realized that most white people aren't aware of white privilege as well as how they benefit from it at other people's expense. I even had thoughts myself of how I only now just barely make ends meet and if it weren't for the few benefits of White privilege that I receive, where would I be now. It scared me to think of where I would be if I didn't have it. Then I thought to myself, "How horrible can you be, it is never morally right to benefit from something at someone else's expense. Racism is a moral issue and does everyone in society an injustice. (emphasis added)

Autonomy. Autonomy refers to the stage where racial humanism is expressed from a positive White (non-racist) orientation. This level is represented by those individuals (similar to the one quoted above) who choose to leave their White supremacist culture and work toward eradication of racism and interruption of the cycle of oppression. White people who participated in the Civil Rights movement of the 1960s could be characterized as possibly having been in an autonomy stage of racial identity. Teachers in this study did not self-report in any of their writing that they were in the autonomy stage. However, some teachers' writings suggested that they were moving toward this awareness level.

DISCUSSION AND CONCLUSION

White teachers, who undergo White privilege antiracism training, experience some change in their attitudes and beliefs about racism. Evident in their writings are the willingness to change, a willingness to abandon White supremacist ideology, a willingness to take steps toward the amelioration of racist practices in the classroom and in society, even at the risk of being branded a "race traitor" (Ignatiev & Garvery, 1997) by other White group members.

This study demonstrates that a change in attitudes of White educators is possible, leading to the development of a positive White racial identity, which can become evident in their practice, curriculum, and teaching pedagogy. The study also suggests that positive movement within the stages of White racial identity development is contingent on active deconstruction and reconstruction of a non-hegemonic group identity. This dynamic involves a willingness to abandon White supremacist ideology and move toward the development of a positive White racial identity in which membership is recognized and privilege is acknowledged but only as it interrupts the cycle of racial oppression. An antiracism education model that incorporates a White racial identity component appears to be a promising next step in transforming White teacher attitudes, beliefs, and White supremacist ideology. The White educator who assumes an antiracist stance moves toward becoming a White ally who works to interrupt situations of racism whenever they occur and works to actively prevent overt or covert acts from re-occurring. Antiracism education seeks to provide a formal and structured teacher education curriculum through which preservice/inservice White teachers can examine their attitudes and beliefs regarding racism and White supremacy using a racial identity development framework. Key to antiracism education is the change in White teachers' beliefs and attitudes that lead to the development of a positive White racial identity devoid of White supremacy and shows itself in their practice, curriculum, and teaching pedagogy. White privilege awareness is a function of White racial development. In essence, it is the positive movement within the stages of White racial identity development that recognizes that White privilege is based on membership in the dominate group in the United States, and the active deconstruction and reconstruction of a non-hegemonic [White] group identity.

White teachers may move through the contact and disintegration racial identity statuses without formal guidance, as evidenced in the findings. However, effective transition into formulating a positive White racial identity (e.g., movement through reintegration) requires individuals to take deliberate action precipitated by their acknowledgment of White privilege through a structured curriculum of White identity/White privilege antiracism education. Finally, this study showed that a desire for change must be present. In the case of educators, accountability related to standardized testing and site based management can serve as motivators in that their teaching will be assessed in accordance with the performance of all children.

Critical to the success of antiracism education is the inclusion of Black, Latino, Asian, and Native American identity development. Although social dominance serves to reinforce White supremacist ideology, it is nonetheless critical to also examine the consequences of hegemonic maintenance through the perceptions and experiences of people of color. White teachers teach the majority of Black children in the United States. As members of the dominant-hegemonic culture, White teachers bring into their classrooms perceptions, stereotypes, and active or passive racist actions that affect all children, especially Black children. I am confident that White identity/White Privilege Antiracism Education, can affect change for White teachers in White-led school systems, and the hegemonic White supremacist culture. Racism is everybody's problem; however, the impetus for change must come from the dominant White culture.

I recently attended a seminar with five African American women. Interestingly, the focus of this seminar was positiveness. During a break between speakers, we remained at our table talking amongst ourselves. In the midst of our conversation a White woman who was passing by stopped, leaned in between two of my friends, and interrupted our conversation by saying, "I know *you* people!" Needless to say we were shocked to the point of silence. She continued, "I met all *you* people before … in Watts!" She went on to say, "I was a teacher there, and I really got to know *you* people. I really like you!" My friend who was sitting next to me leaned over and whispered, "Let it go, she doesn't get it!" My friend observed my ire and realized that I was about to call the woman to task. The White woman said something else and left. We looked at each other, shaking our heads still at a loss for words.

Several issues regarding that interaction struck me. First, that this White woman would exercise her White privilege and assume that what she had to say would interest a table of African American women to an extent that she felt that she had to "interrupt" us to say it. Second, the phrase, "you people" smacked of White supremacist thinking as if, "you people are different from me." Third, I shuddered to imagine what negative and harmful messages she, as a White teacher in Watts, conveyed to the Black and other minority children she taught. Finally, I realized that, as my friend said, "She didn't get it." I thought of my research and concluded that this woman's behavior and language represented a "Contact" level of awareness. She did not recognize that her behavior was being perceived as racist, and that, as an educator, her inappropriate way of interacting can negatively impact the development of Black and other non-White children. In one respect it was sad, but in another, it helped me to realize the importance of my research.

As educators, we are called to a higher purpose and continually must examine ourselves to ensure that we do not infect the children we teach with negative racist ideologies, attitudes, and behaviors, which continue the legacy of dominance and oppression amongst racial groups. White educators in particular must work to recognize their participation in the cycle of dominance and oppression and then take active steps to abandon White supremacy.

REFERENCES

Cochran-Smith, M. (2000). Blind vision: Unlearning racism in teacher education. *Harvard Educational Review, 70*(2), 157–190.

Freire, P. (1972). *Pedagogy of the oppressed.* New York: Continuum.

Green, S. B., Salkind, N. J., & Akey, T. M. (1997). *Using SPSS for windows: Analyzing and understanding data* (2nd ed.). Upper Saddle River, NJ: Prentice-Hall.

Helms, J. E. (1984). Toward a theoretical explanation of the effects of race on counseling: A black and white model. *The Counseling Psychologist, 12*(4), 153–165.

Helms, J. E. (1990). *Black and White racial identity: Theory, research, and practice.* Westport, CT: Greenwood Press.

Helms, J. E., & Carter, R. T. (1994). White racial identity attitude scale (WRIAS). *Journal of Vocational Behavior, 44*(2), 198–217.

Hollins, E. R. (1996). *Transforming curriculum for a culturally diverse society.* Mahwah, NJ: Lawrence Erlbaum.

hooks, b. (1989). *Talking back: Thinking feminist, thinking black.* Cambridge, MA: South End Press.

Howard, G. R. (1999). *We can't teach what we don't know.* New York: Teachers College Press.

Ignatiev, N., & Garvery, J. (1997). *Race traitor.* New York: Routledge.

Katz, D. (1960). The functional approach to the study of attitudes. *Public Opinion Quarterly,* (24), 165–204.

Keith, A. I., & Martin P. S. (2002). *Talking about privilege.* Unpublished manuscript.

Lawrence, S. M., & Tatum, B. D. (1997). Teachers in transition: The impact of antiracist professional development on classroom practice. *Teachers College Record, 99*(1), 10–12.

Martin, P. S. (2000). The effect of antiracism education on the racial identity development in white teachers. Unpublished Pilot study (qualifying paper), University of Massachusetts Boston, Boston, MA.

McIntosh, P. (1989). White privilege: Unpacking the invisible knapsack. *Peace and Freedom, 49*(4), 10–12.

McIntyre, A. (1997). *Making meaning of whiteness.* Albany: State University of New York Press.

Mier, & Mizell (1996). *EMI training manual.* Empowering Multicultural Initiatives. Lincoln, MA.

Mills, C. W. (1998). *Blackness visible: Essays on philosophy and race.* Ithaca, NY: Cornell University Press.

Nieto, S. (1996). *Affirming diversity: The sociopolitical context of multicultural education* (2nd ed.). White Plains, NY: Longman.

Rios, F. A. (Ed.). (1996). *Teacher thinking in cultural context.* Albany: State University Press.

Rosenberg, M. J. (1960). A structural theory of attitude dynamics. *Public Opinion Quarterly, (24),* 309–340.

Scheurich, J. J., & Young, M. D. (1996). Coloring epistemologies: Are our research epistemologies racially biased? *Educational Researcher, 26*(4), 4–16.

Seller, M., & Weis, L. (1997). *Beyond black and white.* Albany: State University of New York Press.

Sidanius, J., & Pratto, F. (1993). The inevitability of oppression and the dynamics of social dominance. In P. M. Sniderman, P. E. Tetlock, & E. G. Carmines (Eds.), *Prejudice, politics, and the American dilemma.* Stanford, CA: Stanford University Press.

Tatum, B. D. (1992). Talking about race, learning about racism: The application of racial identity development theory in the classroom. *Harvard Educational Review, 62*(1), 1–24.

Tatum, B. D. (1997). *Why are all the black kids sitting together in the cafeteria? And other conversations about race.* New York: Basic Books.

Titone, C. (1998). Educating the white teacher as ally. In J. L. Kincheloe, S. R. Steinberg, N. M. Rodriguez, & R. E. Chennault (Eds.), *White reign: Deploying whiteness in America.* New York: St. Martin's Press.

U.S. Department of Education National Center for Education Statistics. 1996 digest of education tables and figures. Retrieved August 31, 2002, from http://nces.ed.gov/programs/digest/d96/.

Wellman, D. L. (1993). *Portraits of white racism* (2nd ed.). Cambridge, UK: Cambridge University Press.

CHAPTER NINE

Reflections FROM Beneath THE Veil: Mainstream Preservice Teachers (Dis)Covering Their Cultural Identities

NELDA L. BARRÓN

> ... urban schools and teachers are defining a majority of their students as children who have problems that exceed the typical classroom teacher's ability to educate them. How is it possible for schools and teachers to define a majority of their children as people who should not be there, or people they are unable to help?
>
> (HABERMAN, 1995, P. 49)

It is the fifth week of the semester and the twelve student teachers, all of them White, are discussing this week's experiences in their urban classrooms. I hold back during this part of the seminar to give them room to share, complain, and vent without censoring their words, perspectives, and emotions. Usually, they manage to forget I am in the room. As one of the student teachers finishes recounting a particularly challenging day, she suddenly exclaims with frustration:

> I don't get it! How am I supposed to teach José [a pseudonym] given all the problems he has? He is below grade level in reading, he doesn't do math so I don't know what level he is there. He lives with his aunt and uncle—I don't know why, and he never seems to follow what we're teaching. When I try to talk with him about his work he acts like he doesn't even care! It's not my fault he doesn't want to learn. He doesn't belong in fifth grade, and I heard they just moved him up to the next grade because of his age.

She pauses, looks directly at me, and then quickly adds, "Are you going to tell me that I am missing something about José's culture? Don't! He's American and he doesn't act any different." I pause as I consider whether to respond. Then I ask, "'Any different' from what?"

The look of frustration fades from her face as she declares with a hint of laughter in her voice, "I did it again didn't I? I walked right into it. ... I was thinking about me! I don't see him as acting any different from me when I was a ten year old kid ... which is why I like him so much. I know you think I am missing something. You are probably right. Why don't I talk to you after class and you can take me to dinner and tell me everything I am doing wrong, ok?" This exchange may not seem particularly significant at face value. However, this student teacher's willingness to consider that part of the issue might lie in her perceptions of José's experience is an indicator that Jen (not her real name) has begun to recognize that her cultural lens frames and influences her teaching.

Getting Jen to this point has been a long and arduous journey that began three years ago when she entered my introductory education class exploring issues of race, culture, and oppression. Jen resisted almost everything I tried to teach her about culture, race, cultural identity, and oppression, and she worked hard to rally other students, faculty, and even an administrator or two against me and the course. She accused me of being biased against White students, offensive, insensitive, unfair, anti-American, and even "clueless" about my subject area, and she had no qualms about sharing her opinion with anyone who might listen. By chance, after hearing her complaints, an administrator invited her to a talk by Peggy McIntosh about White privilege. With two days remaining in the course, Jen came to the next class with tears in her eyes and said, "You tried to teach me about all this, and I couldn't hear it from you because I wanted to believe you had a chip on your shoulder because you are a minority. I was so rude and disrespectful, and all I can feel is shame and guilt and I don't know what I can do about racism, but I just wanted you to know I've been a pain and I am sorry." That admission led us to this point today in our third course together. In the past three years, Jen convinced me to supervise her during pre-practicum, fought to be placed in my practicum seminar, and cried when she discovered I would not be her practicum supervisor. We have an honest and authentic relationship in which I tell her about herself without too many holds barred, and she credits me with witnessing and experiencing the only two occasions she has been embarrassed and ashamed of herself during her college career. I cannot seem to get but so far away from Jen despite my wishes at the end of that first class to never deal with her again.

Today, Jen is sometimes able to recognize when she is imposing her own cultural lens and experience on others, and she is willing to admit she does not know or understand much about the low-income, immigrant, and students of color in her urban fifth-grade classroom. Even so, she has a long way to go before I would begin to see her as culturally competent in working with the population of students

I care so much about. Jen is barely able to see that the issue with José is not just about him and his culture but about *her* and her cultural identity and the school system in which she teaches. At this point, Jen cannot see that the ideological frameworks from which she unconsciously and uncritically operates and which reflect a dominant White, European-American, English-speaking, middle-class mainstream belief system, compound José's struggles in her classroom.

Jen challenges me, enlightens me, and reminds me that out of the most uncomfortable, painful, and seemingly hopeless (which is how I often felt about her ability to understand culture, race, and oppression) teaching experiences a window of possibility can open. I have spent countless hours trying to figure out how to help Jen "get it" and met with limited success. Nevertheless, she keeps coming back and asking the important questions. Student teachers like Jen remind me once again that sometimes the simple act of pulling back just one layer or "veil" can begin to expose the socialization that keeps many White, European American, English-speaking middle-class, preservice teachers from becoming the effective, culturally competent teachers they could be. Jen keeps me asking the question: How can interrogating cultural identity[1] help teachers like Jen become the practitioners they need to be with diverse student populations?

Jen is not unlike the hundreds (and maybe thousands) of young women who enter teacher education programs each year. In order for teachers to develop the necessary cultural competency and responsiveness for working effectively with urban students of color and other disenfranchised populations, teacher educators must recognize and understand the fundamental belief system—ideology[2]—already in operation for these preservice teachers. This preservice teacher ideology requires conscious and deliberate *"uncoverage"* for teacher education programs to begin to adequately prepare developing teachers with the necessary skills and dispositions they need to better serve racially, ethnically, linguistically, and economically disenfranchised students.

THE POLITICS OF TEACHING

Teaching is political work. However, a large number of prospective teachers enter teaching believing that this is not the case. They have chosen teaching because they view it as a neutral act borne out of a love for children (elementary teachers), a passion for content (secondary teachers), or some combination of both. Visions of focused, happy, quiet students hanging on the knowledgeable, charismatic, and engaging teacher's every word are not uncommon in the minds of many preservice teachers. Even when confronted with the real work of teachers through pre-practicum and practicum experiences, many preservice teachers believe the problems they encounter are particular to that school, class, teacher, or group of students and will not exist once they have their own classrooms. Few teachers-to-be see themselves at the center of a political struggle for the minds and lives of their charges and even fewer are equipped with the appropriate and necessary tools to survive, much less thrive, in the myriad of often contradictory and politically motivated national, state, and local mandates, time-consuming bureaucratic requirements, questionable institutional support, constant disruptions during instructional time, large class sizes, dilapidated facilities, inadequate instructional resources, and resigned, disillusioned or disengaged colleagues. Preservice teachers face these conditions before they ever encounter whatever personal circumstances, special needs, or learning challenges students may bring into school each day.

Haberman (1995) noted that urban schools are likely to use terms such as *at-risk* to describe their students who are English language learners (ELL) of color, poor, and/or immigrants. He believes this labeling is so prevalent that it is not uncommon for teachers in urban schools to identify all of their students as being "at-risk." Haberman (1995) indicated that with the 11% of students with disabilities, 25% of students living in poverty, and the children whom teachers label as unable to learn despite not being labeled as "special needs," the number of children who are viewed as failing in schools "exceed 50% in almost every urban school district" (p. 49). He then asks: "How is it possible for schools and teachers to define a majority of their children as people who should not be there, or people they are unable to help?" (p. 49). Haberman's question begs for immediate action on the parts of teacher education programs invested in preparing effective teachers for urban contexts. What work do teacher education programs need to do to position teachers to be more effective with culturally diverse students?

In my work as a teacher educator I have been interested in research that focuses explicitly on pre-service teachers' experiences with students of color and how courses that address race, culture, identity, and oppression influence teachers' beliefs about urban, ELL, low-income, immigrant, and students of color. Some researchers have sought to uncover teachers' beliefs and attitudes toward "cultural diversity" and the impact of their beliefs on teaching. In general, these studies have tended to identify teachers' personal dispositions and experiences as they relate to:

1. *understanding* cultural "others"
2. *working with* cultural "others"
3. *responding to* multicultural education courses, which they often perceive as being for the benefit of cultural "others."

This research provides a context for my assertion that teacher education needs to directly and explicitly expose the prevailing ideological foundations from which

White mainstream teachers operate and then work to change them. Though well-intentioned and caring, these teachers have not developed their beliefs, attitudes, and perspectives in isolation. Their cultural identities have been shaped by social, historical, and political factors that perpetuate social inequities, unequal power relations, and White, European-American supremacist ideologies. Teacher education must recognize, name, interrogate, and challenge these teachers' beliefs and attitudes as ideologies, rather than as individual beliefs, attitudes, and dispositions. When we do this, teacher education programs may be better positioned to prepare teachers for the political nature of teaching.

UNDERSTANDING CULTURAL "OTHERS": THE SIGNIFICANCE OF STUDENTS' CULTURAL IDENTITIES

While many variables impact a child's school experience and achievement, multicultural education researchers have found that the teachers' experiences, expectations, knowledge, personal beliefs, and understanding of oppression, all influence her interactions with students, her teaching practice, her curricular choices and her students' success (Irvine, 1990, 1991; Rios, 1996; Nieto, 2000; Sleeter, 2001; Tatum, 1997). A recent survey of U.S. schools, colleges, and departments of education showed that 86% of the people enrolled in education programs were White (Ladson-Billings, 2001). Furthermore, although many White teacher candidates realized they would work with children from racial, ethnic, linguistic, and economic backgrounds different from their own, they had very limited cross-cultural experiences, knowledge, or understanding (Barry & Lechner, 1995; Gilbert, 1995; Larke, 1990; Schultz, Neyart, & Reck, 1996; Su, 1997; Nieto, 2000). While preservice teachers may "expect" diversity, given the public attention to changing demographics, they have yet to internalize this reality as anything more than a change of hues and skin tones or different family configurations. They may anticipate noticeable cultural differences such as "unusual" names, ethnic foods, varied family celebrations, multiple language backgrounds, single parents, extended families, and other such tangible elements of culture.[3] However, they have little to no understanding of the significance and impact of the underlying beliefs that inform the behaviors, expectations, and attitudes of their students and their families.

The realities of today's urban classrooms—parents working around the clock, extended families, single parents, students with serious family responsibilities, primary languages other than English, use of "non-standard" English, learning strategies, communication styles, special education needs, broad ranges of skills and preparation, student disengagement, lack of visible or familiar patterns of parent involvement, and students who do not exhibit European American, middle-class behavioral norms (e.g., social engagement, competition, independent thinking, discussion, self-perceptions)—are a far cry from what many teachers anticipate. When these teachers encounter these differences, they often fail to recognize the dominant ideologies that have allowed them to acknowledge these differences, while simultaneously clouding their interpretation of them. These ideologies deny the contributing inequalities and prevent well-intentioned teachers from what Sleeter (2001) calls "thinking in terms of alternatives, even when there is plenty of evidence that the alternatives exist." The result is teachers who mistakenly locate the *systemic* "problems" their students encounter in their *individual* students' backgrounds, motivations, behaviors, and cultures rather than questioning the role of teachers, schools and educational systems in creating or contributing to the issues.

WORKING WITH CULTURAL "OTHERS": BECOMING CULTURALLY COMPETENT EDUCATORS

White mainstream teachers must stop viewing their disenfranchised students' cultural backgrounds as detriments to learning and recognize that the discontinuities between students' home cultures and the realities of schools contribute to children's low academic achievement. In recent decades, multicultural education theorists have called for culturally responsive teaching[4] practices that reflect and draw upon students' cultural strengths (Delpit, 1995; Gay, 2000; Ladson-Billings, 1992, 1994; Nieto, 2000), bridge home and school cultures when mismatches exist (Gay, 2000; Nieto, 2000; Law & Lane, 1987; Villegas & Lucas, 2002), and use culturally relevant communication, learning, and management styles (Irvine, 1990, 1991; Delpit, 1995; Gay, 2000). Irvine (1990) noted that depending on the teachers' beliefs, teachers who do not share their students' cultural backgrounds, no matter how well-intentioned, often misunderstand students' behaviors, language, and capabilities. Ladson-Billings (1994) found that teachers' beliefs about students are often based on negative and erroneous misperceptions about their non-mainstream students. Equally significant is the fact that teachers who consciously or unconsciously act upon these misperceptions are more likely to locate perceived issues in the student rather than to consider that the challenge might actually be a "teaching issue" resulting from the teacher's flawed methodology or beliefs. These misconceptions, along with White preservice teachers' general ignorance of oppression and unequal power relations among cultural and social groups (Avery & Walker, 1993; King, 1991; Su, 1997) dramatically affects what a teacher does, or does not do, in the classroom.

To become effective urban educators, teachers must confront their misconceptions and assumptions about students (Villegas, 1991; Rios, 1996) and cultivate dispositions and skills that will allow them to recognize, acknowledge, and contend with the realities of today's classrooms. However, focusing exclusively on cultural competency creates gaps in that it does not address the influence of teachers' cultural perspectives and experiences on their work as teachers. Teachers cannot continue to operate from romanticized notions of who the students are, what teaching entails, what school systems are like, and who teachers are supposed to become if they are going to effectively serve urban students. Teachers will need to first acknowledge that their cultural frames of reference cause them to interpret much of what they see in their students, which differs from their own upbringing and school experiences, as obstacles, impediments, deficiencies, hindrances, or inconveniences to student learning. They will also need to confront their assumptions about low-income, immigrant, ELL, and students of color as being culturally disadvantaged people who must adopt the values, beliefs, norms, and behaviors of the White (English-speaking, European American, middle-class) mainstream[5] in order to become successful learners. Second, teachers must understand that it is impossible to teach in a way that is not value-laden, bias-free, or political. They must be willing to view teaching as a revolutionary process that requires all persons involved to look critically at the world in order to recognize their social reality (Freire, 1986) and work to change it and free society from the systems, including the educational system, which keep some social groups in dominant positions over others. Teachers will need to challenge academic rationalist positions that view knowledge as a codified body of work that holds the core "truths" of that discipline or area of study and students as "receptacles" of knowledge as imparted by the teacher. Freire (1986) notes that teaching and learning are intertwined and require achievement of deeper levels of understanding as both students and teachers contribute to the "unveiling of reality, the emergence of consciousness, and critical intervention in reality" (Freire, 1986, p. 68). Finally, teachers need to develop a consciousness and awareness of how their own socialization in a White mainstream culture cultivates ethnocentric, White supremacist thinking that impacts their work with urban, low-income, immigrant, students of color. This inherited ethnocentric, White mainstream thinking is also inconsistent with a desire to effectively serve all students. Preservice teachers must also be willing to embrace the power and authority they have as teachers to actively counter the hegemonic ideologies that schools and curricula help perpetuate. Finally, they must be willing to critically reflect on themselves, their students, their practice, and the educational system, and apply what they learn from experience while still acknowledging that there is more than one "best way" to be, learn, and teach. Until teachers can be at peace with this reality and embrace their own necessary perpetual state of inquiry, they will be limited in their effectiveness with students who are (dis)placed outside the White mainstream culture by choice or circumstance.

FOR THE "BENEFIT" OF CULTURAL "OTHERS": TEACHER PREPARATION AND MULTICULTURAL EDUCATION

Various researchers have noted that teachers are better prepared to address cultural differences that manifest in their classrooms (Ladson-Billings, 2001; Nieto, 2000; Sleeter, 1993; Zeichner, 1992) when teacher education programs provide preservice teachers with opportunities to interact in meaningful ways with diverse communities, learn about multicultural curricula and pedagogy, and explore issues of oppression, power, pedagogy, and racial and cultural identity. While much has been written about pre-practicum and practicum opportunities for teachers to interact in meaningful ways with diverse populations and learn about multicultural curriculum content, curriculum design, and instructional strategies, there are fewer studies that document effective ways to explore issues of oppression, power, pedagogy, racial, and cultural identity with preservice teachers.

In many multicultural education courses, teacher educators sometimes juxtapose and dichotomize preservice teachers' lived experiences with those of their culturally diverse students by presenting information about "others'" learning styles, cultural values, and experiences with discrimination and prejudice. Thus, preservice teachers enter these courses with perceptions that they are there to learn about cultural "others" in order to better serve these cultural "others," and they are not disappointed. This approach reinforces the message that multicultural education is about and for so-called "others." In a sample of 350 preservice teachers, Lien (1999) focused her attention on the tendency among White mainstream students to view themselves and their culture in opposition to so-called "others." She proposes that until courses challenge this dichotomized thinking, White students will continue to consider multicultural education as compensatory education for students of color and places to learn about "others." She also noted their tendency to see an examination of institutional racism and cultural hegemony as personal attacks of their own European-American cultural identities and their deeply held beliefs about the United States as an equitable meritocracy. Gomez (1993) concludes that preservice teachers often left multicultural education courses with contradictory ideas or limited understanding of the information they had uncovered with regard to race, culture, and oppression.

In teacher education courses, prospective teachers need to explore how their own race and culture, along with existing preconceptions, affect their teaching practices as well as their interactions with, attitudes toward, beliefs about, and expectations for, students (Ladson-Billings, 2001; Irvine, 1990, 1991; Allen, 1999; Banks, 1994; Daniel & Benton, 1995; Irvine, 1990; Kincheloe, 1993; Ladson-Billings, 2001; Lawrence, 1997; McIntyre, 1997). Spindler and Spindler (1994) note that "Teachers carry into the classroom their personal cultural background.

They perceive students, all of whom are cultural agents, with inevitable prejudice and preconception" (p. xii). If this is true, then much of the initial work in multicultural education courses should require preservice candidates to engage in self-examination of their cultural identity if they are going to be positioned to critically examine its influence on their own actions and effectiveness as teachers of diverse populations. It is this focus on uncoverage of teachers' cultural identities, including their beliefs and attitudes, and the influence of their ideologies that is of primary interest in my current work with prospective teachers.

BECOMING THE "OTHER": UNCOVERING PRESERVICE TEACHERS' CULTURAL IDENTITIES

Some researchers have found that teachers' beliefs about race, culture, and oppression perpetuate White mainstream supremacist thinking and become obstacles to their development of cultural competencies along with perpetuating the underachievement of disenfranchised students (Ahlquist, 1991; Hyland, 1998; Agee, 1998; Lien, 1999; Marx, 2000). Ahlquist (1991) found that her preservice students initially believed that oppression was "over," yet when engaged in explorations of racism, sexism, and classism, they recognized that these forms of oppression existed all around them. However, they did not believe they were engaged in or responsible for oppression because they were not directly engaged in racist or sexist practices and did not intentionally discriminate against anyone. When she attempted to teach them about institutionalized oppression and offered a critique of White mainstream culture, their resistance to understanding the significance of racism increased as they began to realize that their attitudes about "the reality they wanted to believe in" were in conflict with reality and this perpetuated feelings of fear, guilt, powerlessness, and denial about the significance of the issue. Hyland's (1998) case study of one veteran teacher found that she was willing yet uncomfortable discussing racial issues. In addition, she was unable to see the role of systemic racism in her students' underperformance. Hyland (1998) and Marx (2000) also found that the teachers in their studies focused heavily on their dispositions of care and concern for their students. In both instances the researchers found their "missionary-like concern" to be paternalistic, grounded in racial superiority and hegemony.

Once researchers identify these perceptions and beliefs, we can begin to focus on ways to change these beliefs and help teachers develop what Villegas and Lucas (2002) call sociocultural consciousness which is "awareness that one's worldview is not universal but is profoundly shaped by one's life experiences" (p. 27). Gomez (1994) studied a variety of programs, including field experiences, designed to change teachers' perspectives about the cultures of their students. She concluded that teachers' beliefs are difficult to change and change is difficult to measure. Other researchers have noted that White teachers are unwilling to change their beliefs and would prefer to ignore racial, ethnic, and cultural differences between themselves and their students and their potential role in maintaining oppression at the systemic level, even if it means accepting deficit model explanations for their students' lack of academic success (Cochran-Smith, 1995a, 1995b; Agee, 1998; King, 1991; Sleeter, 1993, 2001).

This research clearly indicates that we must begin with the teachers themselves as they enter education programs. It also tells us that changing beliefs and values is difficult, and we should expect resistance. Finally, it identifies particular values, attitudes, beliefs, and perceptions that teachers have about diverse student populations. It is not made as explicit in this research that ideologies are embedded within their personal and cultural identities that must be uncovered, interrogated, challenged, and changed if White mainstream teachers are to be effective with disenfranchised student populations. It is this set of beliefs about identity, race, oppression, and culture that I have begun to investigate in an attempt to make explicit and concrete those ideologies with which teachers enter the profession.

I have taught education courses that introduce teaching candidates to sociocultural issues and conceptions of race, culture, identity, and oppression for the past eight years. These courses examine the sociocultural and sociopolitical context of schooling. I have witnessed the struggles of many primarily White, middle-class, female preservice teachers as they try to make sense of culture, race, and oppression. I have encountered many students who view these issues as relevant to their students of color, but not themselves and their teaching. For example, one preservice teacher recalled that a Latino child's cultural values may place family above all else, including school and that this attitude may affect his attendance and homework completion. Nevertheless, she was unable to see that her own cultural socialization prioritizing individual achievement and responsibility impacted how she perceived that family's values and therefore allowed her to justify her practice of not extending homework deadlines in the interest of "fairness" to all students. This teacher located the "problem" in the family's "choice" to not value education rather than her "choice" to not value family above the individual. In this case, she never considered that her view is grounded in a White mainstream cultural and ideological frame that elevated her cultural values above those of her student.

In some of my courses, a small number of preservice teachers noted that the process of recognizing that they were "cultural beings" was an important and meaningful experience, and they expressed a belief that this awareness would help them better understand their students. Other teachers, preservice and in-service, indicated that understanding race and racism gave them the language and understanding of oppression and their role, as teachers, in a system of oppression. With this new understanding, teachers reported that they felt prepared to meet the needs of their students of color. Given the research that supports the value of this type of teacher awareness, I set out to explore in greater detail the particulars of how some prospective teachers articulate, define, describe, and interpret the impact of this awareness and how these teachers use this understanding once they are no longer immersed in coursework requiring self-exploration and examination.

THE CONTEXT FOR EXPLORING PRESERVICE TEACHERS' CULTURAL IDENTITY

Inspired by Jen and students like her, I began my efforts at uncovering preservice teachers' ideology by working with six former students following their participation in an education course I taught in their first semester in an elementary education master's program. The course focused on culture, identity, race, and oppression and had an explicit goal of engaging students in self-reflection and self-exploration of their own socialization as cultural beings. Participants volunteered for the study after the course, in which they had completed an initial 60 to 75 minute self-interview of their knowledge, attitudes, and beliefs about race, culture, and oppression, ongoing written reflections and journal entries, an essay on the legacy of oppression and the socialization of different racial and ethnic groups, and a second paper discussing "Whiteness" as a state of being. The final paper required that they describe their responses to their initial knowledge and understanding of course concepts and discuss their end of semester understanding of race, identity, cultural socialization, and oppression. The two figures below summarize the participants, course context, and data collection timeline (see Figure 1 and Figure 2).

After reviewing the participants' written work from the course, I conducted two follow-up interviews two months and eight months after the course ended. Because I was primarily interested in how the participants themselves discussed their knowledge of their own cultural identity and conceptions of race, culture, and oppression, I asked broad, open-ended questions using language that was familiar to them and never asked them to speak about the impact of the course (see Figure 3). Given that I had been one of their instructors, I wanted to minimize the degree to which students would feel compelled to discuss my influence, my teaching, or my expectations. Some questions were as follows: "Discuss your understanding of race and how this has evolved over time," "How do you describe your cultural identity?" "Could you discuss what you know about oppression and racism and how you

Participants	Course Context
6 White, middle- or upper middle-class, suburban women	13 week semester 13 class meetings (2 ½ hours each) Team-taught by Latina/White experienced teaching team
Between 22 and 34 years old	Focus on race, culture, identity, and oppression through self-examination of one's cultural background, social identities, race, and sociocultural experiences.
Preservice candidates in the same section of their first graduate course in education	Students generated approximately 30 to 40 pages of writing through journal entries, precourse self-interview, two 5 to 8 page papers focusing on the historical legacy of oppression in the United States and on "whiteness" and a final paper reflecting upon the influences on their own culture, race, identity, and their knowledge of oppression.
Volunteered for study AFTER completing the course	(See Figure 2 for additional details)

Figure 1. Participants and course context.

gained this knowledge," and "How does your culture and cultural identity influence your work in classrooms?" I asked participants to discuss their knowledge and understanding of a concept, their recognition of where that understanding had come from, how it had changed over time, and if and how it was significant in their current lives. At the end of the first interview, I clarified any questions I had about their written work and audio-taped self-interviews and reminded them of their right to withdraw from the study at any time. Participants received transcripts of their initial interviews in order to provide member checks, and they were asked to clarify any points they wished to make on the transcripts. For the second interview, I used the same questions and added one question asking participants to raise any other points or issues they thought I should have asked about and then asked them to respond to that question.

"LIFTING THE VEIL"

> Veil. 1: Something that conceals, separates, or screens like a curtain:[6] 2: to obscure, or conceal 3: make undecipherable or imperceptible by obscuring or concealing[7]

In examining how interrogating cultural identity in preservice education programs can position prospective teachers like Jen to be effective with urban students from diverse backgrounds, I was primarily interested in identifying patterns in preservice teachers' thinking and beliefs about identity, culture, race, and oppression. I sought to uncover ways in which these six preservice teachers' beliefs were

Timeline	Course Assignments/Data
September	• Enrollment in the course • Audio-taped self interview on initial understanding of diversity, race, culture, identity, and oppression • Journal Entry: "What is culture and why is culture important?" • Journal Entry: "Reflection on audio-taped self interview, including identification of cultural group(s) you are affiliated with. What does it mean for you to be associated with this group? If you had trouble coming up with and/or describing your cultural group affiliations, why do you think this was/is the case? Also discuss your most meaningful and important values and beliefs, where you "got" them and how they impact your identity."
October	• Journal Entry: Social Identities Activity discussing the significance of each of 12 social identities (race, sex, ethnicity, class, religion, language, sexual orientation, and so on) in shaping your identity. Discuss the 3 to 5 most important in shaping who you are today. • Journal Entry: "Using the readings from Tatum, Sleeter, and others on ethnic and racial identity describe your own racial/ethnic identity development with examples for each stage of your development." • Journal Entry: "Everything I know about racism and where I learned it." • Journal Entry: "One course book is entitled, White Privilege: Essays from the Other Side of Racism." Write about "the other side of racism." In other words, the only way we know that some people are disadvantaged, discriminated against, viewed as different from the "norm" in terms of race and/or ethnicity, and that they are "minority" is that some people (or groups of people) are advantaged and/or viewed as the "norm" and not identified as minorities."
November	• Journal Entry: "Describe the 'quintessential American' including significant behaviors, beliefs, attitudes and values of Americans as a group." • Journal Entry: "After viewing the video True Colors discuss your personal reactions and your understanding of prejudice, stereotype, discrimination, oppression, internalized oppression, internalized dominance, and privilege using examples from the reading and the video." • 5 to 7 page paper addressing the significance and legacy of Americanization, deculturalization, segregation, acculturation, assimilation, resistance, and political activism on the histories of 3 racial and ethnic groups in U.S. society. • 4 to 6 page paper answering the question: What Is Whiteness?
December	• Final project assignment. Part I. Students listen to their audio-taped self-interview and write about the thoughts, feelings, ideas, and patterns they notice in their initial discussion of core course concepts. Student also discussed what they uncovered from listening to their self- interview. Part II. Students discuss the influences (individual, family, social, historical and political context) on their own cultural identity, their understanding of their own racial identity and racism as an individual, cultural, and institutional form of oppression, understanding of whiteness and privilege and discuss barriers to confronting racism, sexism, and other "isms" beyond issues of personal stereotyping and prejudice and remaining questions.
January	• Participants recruited for participation in research project • Listen to audio-taped self-interviews and reviewed all written work
February–March	• Interview #1 with participants
September	• Interview #2 with participants

Figure 2. Course assignments and data collection timeline.

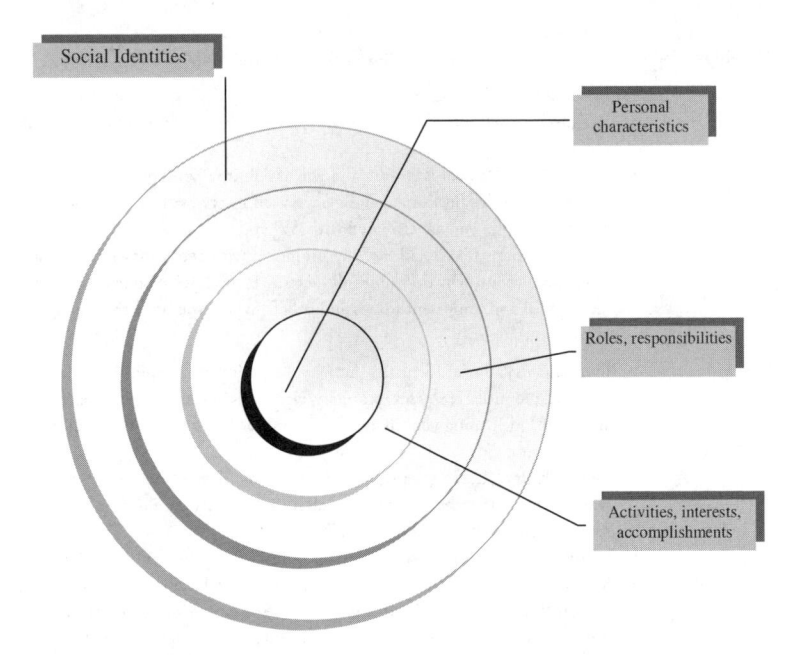

Bull's eye diagram with concentric circles labeled:
- Social Identities
- Personal characteristics
- Roles, responsibilities
- Activities, interests, accomplishments

Figure 3. "Bull's Eye": Visual description of identity characteristics.

challenged and their ideological frameworks disrupted following their engagement in a course focusing on an examination of these concepts as they related to their own lived experiences. I paid particular attention to their ability to lift their cultural veil to uncover and examine their deeply held beliefs and attitudes about identity, race, culture, and oppression.

There are three overarching findings from my study that I will highlight in this chapter. First, I identified shared beliefs and patterns of thinking about identity, race, culture, and oppression among the study's participants. These patterns provide the basis for preservice teachers' ideological foundations that must be acknowledged by teacher educators if we are going to prepare teachers to be effective in today's schools. The second finding was the role cognitive dissonance played in helping the participants maintain, disrupt, and discover their own existing ideologies. Cognitive dissonance created discomfort and destabilized their existing beliefs, allowing them to tolerate ideological disruptions and sustain a heightened consciousness. The third finding relates to the space created by capitalizing on the participants' cognitive dissonance which led to the emergence of a shift in their beliefs and their ability to identify and articulate this shift. These findings will be briefly described in order to illustrate the possibility that interrogating teacher ideology can effectively lead to the development of critical consciousness and what Bartolomé (1999) terms ideological clarity.[8]

SHARED BELIEFS AND PATTERNS OF THINKING ABOUT IDENTITY, CULTURE, RACE, AND OPPRESSION

As a group, these preservice teachers shared a number of beliefs, attitudes, and perceptions that served as an ideological foundation from which they approached anything related to identity, race, culture, and oppression. This shared framework of ideas included the following beliefs:

1. They were non-judgmental, non-prejudiced, and open-minded about "diversity." (*"I guess I am lucky my parents taught me to be open-minded at a young age."* Another observation: *"Even though we grew up in a homogeneous community, I was raised to be open-minded."*)
2. In today's U.S. society, everyone is equal.
3. Individualism and individual identity are more salient than social group memberships (*"we are all individuals," "I see people as individuals," "I treat everyone as an individual,"* and *"I don't want to be seen as a girl, I want to be seen as a person"*).
4. They did not consider themselves to have much of a culture because they did not have strong ethnic affiliations. (*"when I think of culture I think of people speaking a different language, exotic foods, and music or art that shows them doing ... cultural things ... Or maybe Spanish people or Italians."*)
5. Race did not matter in their own lives, and this was proof that race was insignificant to *anyone's* lived experience. (*"I never saw him [an African American friend] as different and I don't think he ever felt different"* and *"My race is not important to me so I don't understand why it is important to them."*)
6. Race was a biological, genetic, or physiological condition only.
7. Color blindness was good, noticing/naming race was bad (and "racist") and elimination of the racial categories/classifications would effectively eliminate whatever racism remained. *"I don't care whether someone is black, brown, green or purple, it's what's on the inside that counts"; "My generation doesn't really care what skin color someone has"*; and *"don't you think if we stopped calling people Black or White or whatever, then racism would disappear?"*
8. The United States was a meritocracy, a melting pot, a land of immigrants, culturally superior, multi-cultural, and diverse. (*"We open our doors to everyone!" "We are the best country in the world, even if we have some problems"; "[we] accept people from around the world";* and *"People choose to come here because they want what we have."*)
9. There was no tangible "American" culture, and there were no identifiable shared American beliefs and values because the United States was made up of diverse individuals. (*"You cannot call anything an American*

value because all of our values as individuals are American"; and "*There is no quintessential American*").
10. Racism, sexism, classism, and other forms of oppression exist at the individual level and manifest themselves as individual acts of meanness. ("*... For example, the majority of students in this class are White, and I am sure that no one in this room has been cruel or mean to someone because of their race.*")
11. It is a matter of personal disposition and character if one allows oneself "to be kept down" by people or incidents involving discrimination. ("*I didn't dwell on it*" [*when someone treated her differently because she was a woman*] *and "Everyone has been discriminated against at one time or another, so it isn't only about race but about how you handle it."*)
12. Racism is a thing of the past (the negative), and we should focus on the progress (the positive) the United States has made.
13. They themselves did not benefit from white privilege. ("*I have never felt privileged because of my skin color*"; and "*we should talk about people of color privilege like with affirmative action.*")

Initially, the participants comfortably owned these beliefs, both privately and publicly, and felt validated when they discovered that these beliefs were overwhelmingly "shared" by nearly all members of the class. This belief system operated as a screen or veil that concealed the significance of race, culture, and oppression in their lives and in the lives of their students. When these beliefs were contradicted and exposed as "rationalizations" due to cognitive dissonance, students were left with little choice but to accept this pre-existing cognitive dissonance as a point of inquiry.

THE ROLE OF COGNITIVE DISSONANCE

Cognitive dissonance results from the act of holding two incongruous or incompatible beliefs or attitudes at the same time. The resulting discomfort compels the person to acquire new thoughts or beliefs, in order to minimize the amount of conflict between these two opposing ideas. Festinger (1957) suggests that people avoid information that is likely to increase dissonance by associating with people who are like us, engaging in activities that support our beliefs and when we encounter an inconsistency, we seek to eliminate it to decrease discomfort. Festinger (1957) also observes that there are three ways to eliminate cognitive dissonance; one can reduce the importance of dissonant beliefs, add more consonant beliefs to outweigh the dissonant ones, or change the dissonant beliefs so they are no longer contradictory.

For these preservice teachers, cognitive dissonance played a significant role in their process of understanding the significance of race, culture, and oppression on a deeper level. Throughout their lives, the participants had engaged in countless acts of creating new thoughts in order to dissipate cognitive dissonance and reconcile contradictory beliefs or ideas with the realities of race, culture, and oppression they witnessed, encountered, or read about. For example, early in the course participants wrote about their being taught or raised to believe that "everyone is equal," and in the same writing they recall examples of schoolmates of color or low-income backgrounds being treated unequally and being judged as inferior. In some cases, these ideas were perpetuated by the same parents who "taught" them everyone was equal. It was also clear that they had little cognizance of their engagement in the process of reconciling opposing ideas as a way of maintaining the veil due to the cultural socialization process they had undergone that seemed to rationalize the existing social order thereby maintaining a white supremacist, Eurocentric ideological orientation.

Cognitive dissonance created discomfort and destabilized their existing beliefs and allowed the participants to sustain a heightened consciousness about race, culture, and oppression and actively seek information about these topics. For example, initially all of the participants saw race as personally insignificant (although significant to people of color) and prided themselves on being "color-blind." One woman who had been adamant in her belief that noticing someone's race was "racist" indicated that she had begun to realize this was not the case. However, in the post-interviews she described her continuous struggle with this particular notion because she intellectually understood that it was not racist to notice someone's skin color, but she "felt" racist anyway. In the interviews following the course all of them noted that one of the most significant belief changes in their thinking was the belief that color blindness was no longer synonymous with equity. They had come to recognize that color blindness was something they had adopted because they thought it was expected of them and they had operated in this manner for so long that it was difficult to change. One participant noted that she found it liberating to be able to drop the façade she had maintained because she thought it was "politically correct," while two others spoke of being able to see how their holding on to the idea of color blindness kept them from seeing something (racial identity) that was important to their students. Only one student seemed to long for a time when she was still color-blind because she felt her confidence in her ability to work with students of color was shaken by the knowledge that she should not treat them "the same as White students," and she still did not know how she should treat them instead.

IDEOLOGICAL SHIFTS: A BEGINNING

Cognitive dissonance and its accompanying discomfort created opportunities for the participants to shift some of their earlier beliefs. For example, initially the participants viewed social identities such as gender, class, and race as "labels" that had little personal significance in shaping their own identities and experiences. In the follow-up interviews, it became clear that each of them was more inclined to highlight specific social identities in her self-descriptions and had come to recognize that a particular social identity (or two) was important in ways she had not previously realized. They all articulated ways in which their understanding of race and gender had changed, and they were clear about discussing its influence on how they interacted with others and how they viewed themselves. For example, one said "I am more aware of myself as a woman and how that has influenced some of the career and personal choices I am making." Another woman noted that she found herself asking "am I saying this because I am White" and "do I think this way because I am a woman or because I really believe this." This sentiment was echoed by yet another participant who talked about her first day in practicum and noticed that the teacher was the only other White person there. She casually asked the teacher if she was uncomfortable being the only White person in the room. The cooperating practitioner's surprised expression quickly resulted in the student teacher "wishing the ground would open up and swallow me," but she left thinking that it was surprising that the teacher had not thought of this before given that she had been worrying about this ever since she realized she would be placed at that particular urban school. She went on to discuss her sense that being White was a very important part of how she saw things and she could not understand how there could be (White) people in that school who did not think the way she did.

Throughout their course, participants noted having encountered numerous occasions, in which they were forced to confront and challenge a prior belief or idea about themselves or about the way U.S. society operated with regard to race and culture. For example, in an early course activity about identity, five of the participants labeled themselves as "open-minded." In the follow-up eight months later, only three of the participants noted "open-minded" as a personal characteristic. When asked about this, two participants indicated that they felt less open-minded now that they understood their identities better than when they started the course. One said, "I know how hard it is to be open-minded now; so I am not sure I am as open-minded as I want to be."

Initially all of the preservice teachers had difficulty describing their culture and how it might influence their identity. In the post-interviews, most could articulate this initial challenge and stated that they now had a better sense of their cultural influences and why they might highlight specific aspects of their cultural identity. They freely admitted that initially they had never considered that they had been socialized into particular cultures, that they had a culture beyond some sense of their ethnic heritage, and that everyone did not have the same cultural socialization that they did. Some of them began to see that what they often thought of as "normal" or human nature might actually be cultural and not universally shared. Initial beliefs in a desire for cultural superiority as being "natural" and "human nature" for individuals, groups and/or nations because "everyone wants to be the best or number one" or "everyone competes to be on top but only one can be the best" were questioned and in a couple of instances, discarded.

With regard to racism there were several significant, competing, and complex shifts in thinking among the preservice teachers. During the post-interviews, all of them demonstrated an intellectual understanding of racism and oppression as systemic and institutionalized (beyond individual acts of meanness), and they recognized that, although their life circumstances did not make them "feel" privileged, they all benefited from racial privilege and lacked privilege based on gender. All six participants were better positioned to discuss racism from both an individual and institutional level. They now recognized racism and other forms of oppression as being more than stereotyping and prejudice and individual acts of discrimination. This was not the case when they entered their education program. Participants seemed to feel empowered by being exposed to a discussion of institutionalized oppression and were more inclined to consider the possibility that racism, and other forms of oppression, was at play in their schools and other institutions. For example, one participant seemed highly conscious of the racial and gender composition of the "low-level" reading groups in her pre-practicum placement. She wondered whether racism and sexism were involved, even as she sang the praises of her mentoring teacher. She noted:

> My cooperating teacher ... she's amazing and she loves these kids so much—she's been at the school for 13 years. ... I have noticed that she seems to like the two White boys more than the girls or the other boys and it's not that she's mean or anything, but she just ... makes me wonder why she spends so much time with them in their reading group while she leaves the low-level readers, who are all black, to whoever is around—me, the preprac student—and they need more of her help. I also notice that in that reading group, the boys always seem to do the reading and the two girls just sit there. ... I started to wonder if she notices that she does this or if maybe it's unconscious racism and sexism. Don't get me wrong ... she's a great teacher, and I probably wouldn't have noticed it if there were more White boys and girls ...

While she could "see" the possibility that her teacher was acting in discriminatory ways, her understanding of the possibility that other factors beyond the teacher's individual actions might also contribute to her cooperating teacher's actions.

Two participants also noted that they had the privilege of not having to experience racism and were more aware that children of color might enter their classroom having experienced racism. However, both believed that as teachers, they would be able to show their students that "not all White people are racist."

This last statement indicated a continued centralization and privileging of their own feelings as individuals and as Whites over the lived experiences of their students of color (McIntyre, 1997). Such statements suggested that they still had a limited ability to recognize the manifestation of racism and oppression at an institutional level and retained a view that the individual, rather than institutional, elements or dynamics would be more significant in their teaching. However, for three of the participants, there did seem to be a greater understanding and acceptance of the responsibility they had for countering institutional oppression, although they still seemed at a loss as to what to do even when they recognized it.

IMPLICATIONS

I believe my findings can inform teacher education programs' abilities to create meaningful opportunities for teachers to engage in this process of understanding the impact of cultural identity and oppression on the teaching and learning process. It also helps to identify the ways in which teacher education candidates interested in becoming effective urban educators can also work to reconstruct their cultural identities as a result of the opportunities to reflect on their backgrounds in their teacher preparation coursework. This reconstruction would require an active choice to critically examine the impact of their own White, European-American mainstream ideology on their sense of themselves as individuals, as teachers, and their teaching practices, and then discarding those elements that work against their ability to be effective with students. For example, if a teacher has been socialized to believe that English is the only language for success in the United States and that English is the language all Americans should speak, she might justify a decision to ban the use of other languages or dialects in her classroom for her students' "own good." However, if she recognizes that this notion of success and English dominance is rooted in White supremacist thinking that serves to distance some students from their communities and families, she might be willing to adopt a "both/and" stance rather than an "either/or" position. Such a position does not require that she abandon her recognition of the power of English in the United States, but it does require that she see English as a tool her students can access without needing to discourage the use of her students' home language(s). Furthermore, she would then reconstruct her cultural identity as a monolingual English speaker as being both a strength (she uses the language of power) and a deficit (she only speaks one language compared to her bi/multilingual students), and, therefore, she reconstructs her cultural identity to include a recognition of both the superior and the inferior language group status she can no longer own as simply "normal." She is now in a position to make conscious and deliberate choices in her teaching practice; she can acknowledge the advantages her students will have because they can speak and read English, while simultaneously recognizing the advantages of speaking multiple languages despite the "deficit perception" multilingual students often face in schools. This reconstruction supports Lien's (1999) position that preservice teachers' reconstruction of their identities should include a vision of themselves and "others" in a pluralistic, democratic society without the "self" and the "other" having to operate in a competitive relationship.

These findings indicate that it is important to understand teachers' perspectives, beliefs, and values as they enter teacher education programs before we structure learning opportunities about issues of race and culture. They also indicate that attention to racial and cultural identity issues in a structured, self-reflective context can have constructive outcomes. Oftentimes, instructors shy away from direct discussion of attitudes and beliefs about race, culture, and oppression because of the fear that it will cause discomfort, raise resistance, or put faculty "on the hot seat." While all of these are valid points, it is also possible, and arguably essential, to structure opportunities for teaching candidates, and others, to explore these issues in a meaningful way and to capitalize on the influence of cognitive dissonance in changing perspectives and beliefs. In curriculum and methodology courses, we need to foster opportunities for teacher candidates to reflect upon these influences of racial and cultural identity on their own practice, so they develop the skills to continue to critique their own assumptions. Such an opportunity would be particularly useful if we can support teaching candidates' sharing their observations of one another with a critical, race-conscious, and culture-conscious lens.

Another implication that I would like to address more explicitly in subsequent research is the "lasting power" of this learning experience and the nature of follow-up learning opportunities for building on the work that was initiated in the course. Keeping preservice teachers actively engaged in exploring and addressing these issues throughout their program is paramount, or we risk having them be "out of sight and out of mind." For example, following the course all the participants recognized the homogeneity of their friendship circles throughout their lives despite opportunities, particularly as undergraduates, to diversify these groups. As they recognized this homogeneity, they articulated a strong desire to diversify their friendship circles (which were almost exclusively White and middle class). However, to date, none of them had done anything to change this situation. They seemed to be waiting for people of color to enter their lives but had not sought out situations that would increase the likelihood of this scenario. Teacher education programs need to explicitly bolster teaching candidates' discovery of their own cultural identity as consisting of particular racial and cultural subjectivities and understandings. They also need to promote White mainstream teachers' recognition that their cultural perspectives are just one among many in this society.

CONCLUDING THOUGHTS

The participants in this study show that ideological shift is possible. Considering the shared patterns of thinking with which preservice teachers start their training, it is imperative that teacher education programs that seek to train teachers to be effective in urban settings consciously structure an interrogation of teacher ideology. As the "Jens" of teacher preservice programs can show us, there is much to study beneath the veil, and this inquiry can give a teacher pause: pause for reflection, consideration, and choice that can lead to revolutionary change and clarity in teacher practice and ideology.

NOTES

1. "Racial identity," "ethnic identity," and "cultural identity" are often used interchangeably and are perceived to mean the same thing. A discussion of the distinctions and overlap among these is complex and far beyond the scope of this chapter. However, it is important to note that in this chapter, *racial identity* refers to a dynamic, multidimensional sense of belonging, awareness, knowledge, acceptance, attitudes, and collective identity that is partly determined by how one thinks about one's race and how society views one's racial group. *Ethnic identity* refers to a multidimensional, dynamic sense of group or collective belonging based on one's perception that he or she shares a common ancestry, heritage, language, kinship, or place of origin with a group. (See Phinney, 2000, 2003, for more information.) "Cultural identity" refers to an individual's (or group's) sense of distinctive identity that is influenced by the person's belonging to and socialization by an identifiable group that shares common frames of reference, beliefs, norms, values, behaviors/rituals, and characteristics. Cultural identity is generally constructed by associations with different social groups including, but not limited to, gender, class, ethnicity, race, nationality, sexual orientation, geographical location, educational/professional status, and so on. The combined influences of these groups result in the foundational elements of one's cultural identity, which is also influenced by the group's social context and positionality in a given society.
2. Ideology is generally defined here as a set of beliefs that provide the frameworks through which people make meaning of their social worlds, even in the face of contradictions. For example, the "American Dream" is an ideology that helps people make sense of the inequities in U.S. society by "explaining" that those who are dominant and privileged arrived there through hard work and natural talent. Thus, those who are subordinate and poor could simply work more, or possess fewer natural gifts and therefore are in the appropriate (and less dominant) position. Hegemonic ideologies refer to the widely held and pervasive social beliefs that reflect the privileged and dominant mainstream's cultural views about what is right and what is wrong. One need not be a member of this dominant mainstream in order to hold these dominant ideologies.
3. For the purposes of this chapter, culture is broadly defined as "the accumulated sum of symbols, ideas, and material products associated with life in a social system; the symbols and rules that comprise language; the beliefs, values, attitudes, and norms that form the core from which we perceive, think, feel, and behave" (Johnson, 1997, p. 18). Furthermore, the role of culture in people's everyday lives and its influence in their perceptions requires that one think of culture simply as "the lens through which we view the world and interpret our everyday experiences" (Hidalgo, 1993, p. 100).

4. Culturally responsive teaching is defined here as teaching that recognizes the importance of including students' cultural references to impart knowledge, skills, and attitudes in all areas of learning (Ladson-Billings, 1992, 1994) and uses the cultural knowledge, experiences, communication and learning styles of students as important strengths that contribute to student learning (Gay, 2000). Gay (2000) also stresses the importance of teaching that bridges home and school experiences and academic abstractions and lived sociocultural realities to make learning meaningful. Furthermore, culturally responsive teaching acknowledges the legitimacy of the histories of different groups, both as legacies that affect students' dispositions, attitudes, and approaches to learning and as valuable content to be taught in the formal curriculum.
5. White (English-speaking, European American, middle-class) mainstream is used here to connote not only the particular characteristics based on race, language, national affiliation, and class groupings—White, English-speaking, European American, middle-class—but the unique nature of the combined influences of all of those groupings to form a mainstream "American" cultural identity that is presumed by many members of those groups to be either shared or desired by all peoples who make their home in the United States either through immigration, naturalization, or continued presence in this country. This interpretation also connotes an ethnocentric view that cultural capital and social power naturally should reside in those who subscribe to this mainstream worldview. Throughout this chapter "White mainstream culture" will be defined as including these characteristics noted above as distinctive from a simple racial categorization of white-skinned people as culturally White.
6. *Merriam-Webster's Medical Dictionary* (2002) Merriam-Webster, Inc.
7. WordNet ® 2.0, (2003) Princeton University.
8. Ideological clarity refers to "the process by which individuals struggle to identify both the dominant society's explanation for the existing societal socioeconomic and political hierarchy as well as their own explanation of the social order and any resulting inequalities" (Bartolomé, 1999, p. 141).

REFERENCES

Agee, J. (1998). Confronting issues of race and power in the culture of schools: A case study of a pre-service teacher. In M. Dilworth (Ed.), *Being responsive to cultural differences: How teachers learn*. Washington, D.C.: Corwin Press.

Ahlquist, R. (1991). Position and imposition: Power relations in a multicultural foundations class. *Journal of Negro Education, 60*, 158–169.

Allen, R. L. (1999, April). *The hidden curriculum of whiteness: White teachers, white territory and white community*. Paper presented at the annual meeting of the American Educational Research Association, Montreal, Canada.

Avery, P. G., & Walker, C. (1993). Prospective teachers' perceptions of ethnic and gender differences in academic achievement. *Journal of Teacher Education, 44*(1), 27–37.

Banks, J. (1994). *An introduction to multicultural education*. Boston: Allyn & Bacon.

Barry, N. H., & Lechner, J. V. (1995). Pre-service teachers' attitudes about and awareness of multicultural teaching and learning. *Teaching and Teacher Education, 11*, 149–161.

Bartolomé, L. (1999). Beyond the methods fetish: Toward a humanizing pedagogy. In D. Macedo & L. Bartolomé (Eds.), *Dancing with bigotry: Beyond the politics of tolerance*. New York: St. Martin's Press.

Cochran-Smith, M. (1995a). *Knowledge, skills, and experiences for teaching culturally diverse learners: A perspective for practicing teachers*. Paper presented at invitational conference on Defining the Knowledge Bases for Urban Teachers. Emory University, Atlanta, Georgia.

Cochran-Smith, M. (1995b). Uncertain allies: Understanding the boundaries of race and teaching. *Harvard Education Review, 65*(4), 541–570.

Daniel, P. L., & Benton, J. E. (1995, November). *Involving pre-service teachers in discussion of diversity.* Paper presented at the annual meeting of the Mid-South Educational Research Association, Biloxi, Mississippi.

Delpit, L. (1995). *Other people's children.* New York: Teachers College Press.

Festinger, L. (1957). *A theory of cognitive dissonance.* Stanford: Stanford University Press.

Freire, P. (1986). *Pedagogy of the oppressed.* New York: Continuum.

Gay, G. (2000). *Culturally responsive teaching: Theory, research and practice.* New York: Teachers College Press.

Geertz, C. (1973). *The interpretation of cultures.* New York: Basic Books.

Gilbert, S. L. (1995). Perspectives of rural prospective teachers toward teaching in urban schools. *Urban Education, 30,* 290–305.

Gomez, M. L. (1993). Prospective teachers' perspectives on teaching diverse children: A review with implications for teacher education and practice. *Journal of Negro Education, 62,* 459–474.

Gomez, M. L. (1994). Teacher education reform and perspective: Teacher's perspectives on teaching "other people's" children. *Teaching and Teacher Education, 10,* 319–334.

Haberman, M. (1995). *Star teachers of children in poverty.* West Lafayette, IN: Kappa Delta Pi.

Hidalgo, N. (1993). Multicultural teacher introspection. In T. Perry & J. Fraser (Eds.), *Freedom's plow: Teaching in the multicultural classroom.* New York: Routledge.

Hyland, N. (1998). *One high school teacher's unexamined pedagogy of race.* Paper presented at the annual meeting of the American Educational Research Association, San Diego, California.

Irvine, J. J. (1990). *Black Students and school failure: policies, practices and prescriptions.* New York: Greenwood Press.

Irvine, J. J. (1991). *Black students and school failure.* New York: Praeger.

Johnson, A. G. (1997). *The forest and the trees: Sociology as life, practice and promise.* Philadelphia: Temple University Press.

Kincheloe, J. (1993). *Toward a critical politics of teacher thinking: Mapping the postmodern.* Westport, CT: Bergin & Garvey.

King, J. (1991). Dysconscious racism: Ideology, identity, and the miseducation of teachers. *Journal of Negro Education, 60*(2), 133–146.

Ladson-Billings, G. (1991). Beyond multicultural literacy. *Journal of Negro Education, 60*(2), 147–157.

Ladson-Billings, G. (1992). Reading between the lines and beyond the pages: A culturally relevant approach to literacy teaching. *Theory into Practice, 31*(4), 312–320.

Ladson-Billings, G. (1994). *Dreamkeepers: Successful teachers of African American children.* San Francisco: JosseyBass.

Ladson-Billings, G. (2001). *Crossing over to Canaan: The journey of new teachers in diverse classrooms.* San Francisco: JosseyBass.

Larke, P. J. (1990). Cultural diversity awareness inventory: Assessing the sensitivity of pre-service teachers. *Action in Teacher Education, 12*(3), 23–30.

Law, S., & Lane, D. (1987). Multicultural acceptance by teacher education students: A survey of attitudes. *Journal of Instructional Psychology, 14,* 3–9.

Lawrence, S. M. (1997). Beyond race awareness: White racial identity and multicultural teaching. *Journal of Teacher Education, 48*(2), 108–117.

Lien, H. N. (1999, April). *A challenge toward binary racial epistemology: The reconstruction of cultural identity in multicultural teacher education.* Paper presented at the annual meeting of the American Educational Research Association, Montreal, Canada.

Marx, S. (2000, April). *An exploration of preservice teachers' perceptions of second language learners in the mainstream classroom.* Paper presented at the annual meeting of the American Educational Research Association, New Orleans, LA.

McIntyre, A. (1997). *Making meaning of whiteness: Exploring racial identity with white teachers.* Albany: State University of New York Press.

Nieto, S. (1995). *From brown heroes and holidays to assimilationist agendas.* Albany: State University of New York Press.

Nieto, S. (2000). *Affirming diversity: The sociopolitical context of multicultural education* (3rd ed). New York: Longman.

Pang, V. O., & Sablan, V. A. (1998). Teacher efficacy. In M. E. Dilworth (Ed.), *Being responsive to cultural differences* (pp. 39–58). Washington, DC: Corwin.

Phinney, J. (2000). Ethnic identity. In A. E. Kazdin (Ed.), *Encyclopedia of psychology* (Vol. 3) (pp. 254–259). New York: Oxford University Press.

Phinney, J. (2003). Ethnic identity and acculturation. In K. Chun, P. B. Organista, & G. Marin (Eds.), *Acculturation: Advances in theory, measurement, and applied research* (pp. 63–81). Washington, DC: American Psychological Association.

Rios, F. (1996). Introduction. In F. Rios (Ed.), *Teacher thinking in cultural contexts* (pp. 1–22). Albany: State University of New York Press.

Schultz, E. L., Neyart, K., & Reck, U. M. (1996). Swimming against the tide: A study of prospective teachers' attitudes regarding cultural diversity and urban teaching. *Western Journal of Black Studies, 20,* 1–7.

Sleeter, C. (1993). How White teachers construct race. In C. McCarthy & W. Critchlow (Eds.), *Race, identity, and representation in education* (pp. 157–171). New York: Routledge.

Sleeter, C. (2001). *Culture, difference & power.* New York: Teachers College Press.

Sleeter, C., & Grant, C. (1988). An analysis of multicultural education in the United States. *Harvard Educational Review, 57,* 421–444.

Spindler, G., & Spindler, L. (Eds.). (1994). *Pathways to cultural awareness: Cultural therapy with teachers and students.* Thousand Oaks, CA: Corwin.

Su, Z. (1997). Teaching as a profession and as a career: Minority candidates' perspectives. *Teaching and Teacher Education, 13*(3), 325–340.

Tatum, B. D. (1994). Teaching White students about racism: The search for White allies and the restoration of hope. *Teachers College Record, 95*(4), 462–467.

Tatum, B. D. (1997). *Why are all the Black kids sitting together in the cafeteria? And other conversations about race.* New York: Basic Books.

Villegas, A. M. (1991). *Culturally responsive pedagogy for the 1990's and beyond.* Princeton, NJ: Educational Testing Service.

Villegas, A. M., & Lucas, T. (2002). *Educating culturally responsive teachers: A coherent approach.* Albany: State University of New York Press.

Zeichner, K. (1992). *Educating teachers for cultural diversity.* East Lansing, MI: National Center for Research on Teacher Learning.

CHAPTER TEN

Mapping the Terrain(s) of Ideology in New Urban Teachers' Professional Development Experiences

PAULA ELLIOTT

PRELUDE

This chapter describes my journey, as teacher educator, of learning to map the terrain(s) of ideology and ideological influences in schools. My journey evolved from participating in a professional development project that initially did not name or intentionally assert particular ideologies to later formally and explicitly incorporating the study of ideology into the professional development activities and assignments. This pilot professional development project provided support to sustain new teachers in urban schools. Approximately 50 elementary, middle, and high school teachers joined this project over a three-year period. Some stayed for three years, and new ones joined when others left. The participating teachers had no more than three years of teaching experience in urban schools and were seeking ways of becoming more effective.

The professional development project planners and higher education faculty believed it was essential to directly address educational equity for culturally diverse students in urban schools as a critical component for supporting new teachers concerned with student achievement. Over time, the project's programming focused on developing a professional community of peers with increased motivation and capacity for critical self-reflection and inquiry focused on issues of race, culture, and teacher identity.

I am one teacher educator involved in this project, who became interested in examining the nature of new teacher ideology as it related to race, racism, culture, and identity. My exploration focused on a critical conceptual examination of the ideologies[1] reflected in new teachers' questions, expectations, and beliefs about teaching, learning, and schools. A related story is the preparation of higher education faculty to support K-12 teachers' engagement with an authentic analysis of the sociopolitical context of schools and schooling. This account is meant to make a case for creating more opportunities for new urban teachers to examine the sociopolitical nature of schooling and the influences of teachers' ideologies on their beliefs and practices.

In planning relevant professional development activities, the faculty asked these new urban teachers the following questions: What types of support do you need? What support do you get? Where does support come from? What support can higher education offer? The following vignette, drawn from one of their "Teacher Talk" sessions, provides an entry point to their immediate concerns and experiences. In this discussion, five new teachers share the demands of using a standards-based math curriculum that requires them to think differently about teaching elementary mathematics. The teachers are discussing this math curriculum's effectiveness and relevance. They are expected to use it in a prescribed and scripted manner, and they face many in following the district's daily schedule of sequential activities.

> The teachers talk about their ambivalence when they have to move on, "I know so many students still don't get it. You're set up dealing with their frustrations ... but what are the alternatives? If you stay on it until more get it, then it's the scramble to catch up." The compromises are hard to manage for teachers and students. Another teacher inquires, "Doesn't NCLB require the high stakes tests?" Another teacher observes "Yeah, the curriculum has to cover what's in that test." They know that "people teaching in schools with low test scores are afraid of losing their jobs." Then the conversation shifts ...
>
> A teacher suddenly declares: "Students should still be taught the basics. Students need specific calculation skills. They need to know procedures and content like memorizing multiplication tables and knowing how to divide." The teachers continue talking about the value the math curriculum places on students knowing different ways to solve problems and represent mathematical concepts. Then someone notes: "Where is the time to teach the basics?" As another teacher adds, "*and* not get your hand slapped for doing so."
>
> They also talk about pressure from the parents because "so many believe their kids have to know how to multiply and divide" and to the parents, "that's what it means to know math, and that's what should be taught." Another teacher declares, "At least some parents speak up. I really don't know what many of my parents care about for

their kids, about math or anything else." They return to the impact of school administrators. Some teachers see principals as "only interested in the test scores going up, and looking like the curriculum is being taught right." Others see their principal as being supportive, willing to listen, but no one is taking the time to consider: "what math content should be taught?" Besides, someone asks, "Who knows the students better? Who should make decisions on what their students need to know?" They continue to talk about who knows more about how to teach the students, the politicians and bureaucrats, district specialists, the manufacturers of the curriculum, or the teachers who see and work with them everyday? Then a voice from the front of the room announces: "'Teacher Talk' has two minutes to wrap up."

INTRODUCTION

The vignette presents these teachers' everyday questions and concerns as they work to be effective instructors for their students. "Start where they are at" is an adage amplifying the value in recognizing learners' prior knowledge and relating to their views of the world around them. This glimpse of where these teachers "are at" allows us to "eavesdrop" on their discussions and interpretations about teaching and working in their schools. The new teachers wanted practical strategies and sure-fire methods that would help them figure out, "What am I going to do on Monday?" They voiced chronic concerns about administrative expectations, busy schedules, being prepared, and the need for students to see the relevance of school in their lives; they voiced fears of being marginalized for being too public with any critique. The visceral nature and immediacy of their dilemmas, questions, and challenges was readily apparent. At times their practical and pragmatic concerns appeared to dominate their attention. However, if addressed only at face value, the pragmatic issues could obscure recognition of their deeper, more complex concerns about working in schools and being effective in the classroom.

This vignette highlights their daily struggles and competing challenges. At the same time, it offers a glimpse into some of their underlying beliefs and assumptions about teaching in urban schools and the prominence of dominating social forces that have shaped their beliefs, values, and perceptions of the world around them. The professional development project goals and curricular and instructional choices were greatly informed by starting where the teachers "were at." The project planners began to draw upon the teachers' questions and concerns as a starting point to create space and time for them to explore issues related to their sociocultural and sociopolitical contexts. As teacher educators, we worked to create experiences and protocols for the teachers to engage in emotionally, conceptually, and politically challenging discussions about personal beliefs, values, and expectations, and their related ideologies in light of their needs for practical and concrete instructional support.

An examination of the influences of ideology can start by recognizing the sites where one's educational and societal beliefs, values, and norms reside. The next step would be to map their connections to social and historic systems of beliefs. These ideological influences emerged in the teachers' statements about what is important for students to know; their questions about who decided what should be taught; and their concerns about how decision-making authority is assumed and granted to some people and not to others. Their beliefs about which parents' voices were important and needed to be listened to and which could be ignored without administrative consequences reflected ideological influences as well.

Ignoring the impact of dominant[2] ideological influences in teachers' lives and daily classroom decisions constrains their ability to use the very methods, approaches, and strategies they claim to seek. These teachers knew conventional practices were not working for too many urban students. They wanted to learn about and effectively use methods and approaches that increase opportunities for student achievement. However, in order for them to meet their goals, a compelling case had to be made for them to interrogate the political and ideological dynamics that shaped their beliefs and drove their practice.

New teachers must recognize and appreciate the essential questions about what is to be known and why some knowledge is legitimated while another form of knowledge is unrecognized, devalued, or dismissed. By not exploring and delineating the terrain of ideology, the historic antecedents and current influences of dominant ideas and beliefs are taken for granted and appear immutable. Denial of the intimate relationship between teacher beliefs and practice undermines teachers' abilities to become the effective educators they wish to be.

PURPOSE OF THIS CHAPTER

Teachers' views of the role of schools in society, the purposes of schooling, and their beliefs and values about their role as teachers contribute mightily to their actions in classrooms. Freire (1974) called for humanistic educators to seek "the emergence of consciousness and critical intervention in reality" (p. 68). Critical analysis of the relationship between belief and practice is fundamental to teaching, yet many educators do not see it as imperative. Critical consciousness is not systematically encouraged in teacher preparation programs or in the dominant socialization experiences for many people. In light of these realities, an important question is: What encourages teachers to sustain critical reflection and analysis of both their practice and their underlying motivations and goals? The new teachers involved in this project initially neither demonstrated the consciousness implied by Freire nor the capacity for critical interventions in the realities of their schools. Collectively, they neither displayed disciplined inquiry nor recognized the value of posing questions that could provoke more comprehensive understanding of the "problem(s)" before seeking to change their strategies or yielding deeper insights into the sociopolitical nature of schooling. This critique is not an indictment about these teachers. The purpose of critique is to inform educators who work in pre-service and in-service settings.

This chapter proposes that new teachers working in urban schools can and should deliberately consider the mediating influences of ideologies—their own and those that inform schools and society—as significant in teaching and learning. For new teachers to engage in a critical examination of these ideologies, they must have opportunities to reconsider their assumptions of schooling as neutral and value-free and probe their understanding of the role of schools in society. As they come to see schooling as typically reproducing societal inequities, new teachers will have to reconcile the conflicting contradictions. They will also have to consciously make choices to comply with existing practices or be willing to view their work in schools as politically directed toward the advancement of democracy and social justice.

Higher education can play an essential role in helping teachers interrogate the influence of dominant ideologies by providing professional development and new teacher induction programs designed explicitly for extending teachers' capacity for critical analysis. In support of this vision for new teacher development, this chapter addresses the following issues:

1. The relevance of professional development supporting new teachers in urban schools to address sociopolitical context and ideology;
2. The identification of challenges and opportunities in creating professional development that addresses sociopolitical context and ideology;
3. The lessons to be learned from a professional development project that attempts to address sociopolitical context and ideology while acknowledging teachers' needs for practical, pragmatic, and instructional support.

WHY IT IS IMPORTANT TO NAME IT: IDEOLOGY AND THE SOCIOPOLITICAL CONTEXT OF SCHOOLING

Professional development with an explicit sociopolitical framework may give teachers the opportunity to see their work as servicing democratic principles and upholding high academic standards. It directs teachers to challenge forces that sustain patterns of underachievement among African Americans, Latino Americans, and Native Americans. For example, greater knowledge of the political nature of school initiatives and conditions that adversely impact the educational achievement of their most vulnerable of students might broaden teachers' questions about external initiatives imposed on their schools. For example, the Federal and State administration of the No Child Left Behind Act (NCLB)[3] has profoundly impacted teachers' preparation, work, and determinations of qualifications and effectiveness. The implementation of NCLB has been criticized on multiple levels by those who see the gap between its purported ideals and the impact of its practices (Cochran-Smith, 2004a). Teachers entering school systems, whose populations are significantly and adversely impacted by these initiatives, must have the capacity to recognize the role of dominant ideological systems of beliefs in educational policies that sustain unequal power relationships and limit educational achievement for culturally diverse students in urban settings.

New teachers are often subjected to societal messages that normalize the perspectives of White middle-class teachers while relegating those of low income and students of color to the realm of "Other" which is often equated with being deficient. In particular, the socialization experiences of teachers of color and their personal familiarity with discrimination may compel them to challenge the ways lower expectations are directed to students based on race, language, and economic status (Bartolomé, 2004). There is substantial evidence that teachers' beliefs, which are influenced by race, class, culture, and other social group memberships, directly impact their practice and are extremely difficult to change (Cochran-Smith, 1997). Providing greater knowledge and understanding of teachers' ideological positions can help counter dominant belief systems and the negative consequences resulting from the preponderance of messages that validate the experiences of some groups of people at the expense of others.

The goal of sustaining effective teachers in urban settings cannot be realized through training of decontextualized "best practices," methods-orientated, professional development (Bartolomé, 2003; Cochran-Smith, 1997). A preliminary review of the literature on new teacher mentoring and induction services (Alkins, Banks-Santilli, Elliott, Guttenberg, & Kamii, 2006) and a review of case studies of six exemplary induction programs around the country (Alliance for Excellent Education, 2004) indicate some attention being given to developing effective practices for diverse learners based on language, culture, and ability, but there is no evidence of attention to ideology and teaching in a sociopolitical context. Characterizations of "best practice" and new teacher support systems interpreted with an ideological analysis may help teachers assess the strengths and limitations of induction programs so they can seek additional supports that are more congruent with their understanding of their roles as teachers. When new teacher professional development programs provide explicit attention to the sociopolitical context of schools, teachers' socialization experiences, teacher belief systems, and the conditions of teachers' work and professional life, they increase the likelihood of sustaining an invigorated work force that sees schooling as a location for enacting justice. Cochran- Smith (2001) notes, "Underlying most arguments for teaching social justice or social responsibility ... the assumption that teaching and teacher education are fundamentally political activities and that it is impossible to teach in ways that are neither political nor value-laden" (p. 3).

During the three years of this professional development initiative, the new teachers were encouraged to reassess their understanding of their identity, their role in classrooms, perceptions of students' communities, their explanations of school failure, and their willingness to view teaching in a political context. In the process of doing so, it was hoped that they would become more self-conscious of their decisions, the interests served by their choices, and the consequences of those choices. Motivation for the analysis in this chapter stems from Bartolomé's (2000, 2003, 2004) work that compels teacher educators and teachers to seek ideological clarity and political clarity[4] in how they live in the world and do their work in schools. In seeking this clarity, teachers' desire and capacity may intensify to assess their existing practices and recognize those that are socially just and transformative and those that are not.

Seeking this clarity will propel teachers to expect more from students than proficient test scores and help them view achievement in reference to enlarging students' emancipatory capacity and possibilities. This clarity allows teachers to make instructional decisions so that all their students can cultivate critical skills and dispositions to co-construct curricula that are relevant to their world. Teachers can support students to learn that they are not dependent on having access to the canon and knowledge legitimated by others. A commitment to seek clarity helps teachers define student achievement that provokes understanding of the content, context, and purposes of standardized test requirements, as well as purposes of a more just society. So equipped, their students can then make ethical and responsible choices in terms of how they want to live their lives and how they want to contribute to society at large.

IDEOLOGY FOR PROFESSIONAL DEVELOPMENT FACULTY AND NEW TEACHERS: WHAT DOES IT MEAN AND WHAT ARE THE CONSEQUENCES?

What comes to mind when you think of ideology? To initiate discussions about ideology, professional development planners should understand the various interpretations and connotations of the concept and the role of ideology in one's personal judgments and teaching practices. When beginning a conversation about ideology, choosing to use the term or not may be a worthwhile option to consider. The focus of the discussion should be on how people come to embrace a set of beliefs or an ideological framework of thought that helps them make sense of their world. Consciously or not, personal ideologies provide psychological assurance of the place persons have in the world based on their holding of a particular idea, belief, or stance.

Many people perceive ideology as a force external of themselves, asserting a particular point of view that is unrelated to how people have come to assume ways of being. They are not aware of the personal meaning-making role of ideologies. McLaren (2003) notes that ideology "refers to the production of sense and meaning. It can be described as a way of viewing the world, a complex of ideas, various types of social practices, rituals, and representations that we tend to accept as natural and as common sense. It is more than political ideologies of communism, socialism . . ." (p. 79). Burbules (1995) refers to ideology as a dynamic "conceptual chameleon" that "reveals as well as conceals aspects of social and political life" (p. 53). By helping teachers see how ideologies impact life on both the micro and macro levels—those that dominate, structure, and sustain social inequalities—they can begin to develop an appreciation of how their own teaching decisions are influenced by ideologies residing both within and outside themselves.

For example, many people have come to firmly believe that anyone who works hard enough or is smart enough can make it in this society. Most of us know some teachers who have visual reminders on their walls that state that making a real effort is what counts and working hard brings about the desired results. The set of beliefs are grounded in the meritocratic ideology that informs many of the values and beliefs Americans espouse. In this country, the idea that those who succeed deserve to succeed based on the merit of their actions and attitudes is a powerful and lasting influence. This idea is often used to explain success or failure in schools and society. In fact, it justifies decisions about the types of consequences doled out to people who have failed or not measured up. The consequence of this belief in education is high when seen as a justification for denying a high school diploma to students who do not or cannot pass high stakes tests. This justification of low passing rates allows people to locate the problem within the student and not consider the circumstances surrounding the students as a significant factor in success or failure. When confronted with the expectation to reassess the validity and purposes of long-held belief systems, people are likely to need time and support. For instance, people holding the beliefs that value acquiring particular mathematic skills may see that knowledge as providing their students greater opportunities, responsibilities, and choices in life. As an example, let's take a closer look at the vignette that opened this chapter, which provides an example of ideology at work: "of course, everybody should know times-tables and division!" The statement infers value placed on knowledge associated with a mathematical-logical thought process. The statement may also indicate value ascribed to positivistic ways of knowing and an epistemological stance on what knowledge is to be known. Instructional ideas related to this statement may also include a preference for memorization of multiplication tables. This method suggests a particular way of knowing—rote memorization—that is consistent with positivist beliefs of knowledge external to self to be deposited and consumed as is by the student. Therefore, the statement infers the type of knowledge and ways of knowing that has legitimacy for the speaker. This philosophical paradigm has framed the dominant approach to inquiry for decades. For many teachers, the ways of scientific inquiry is assumed to be so legitimate that they are not aware that they are excluding other ways of knowing.

Dominant ideologies appear as normal in ways that can be taken for granted and therefore be rendered invisible. The invisibility of "taken-for-granted" norms of behavior and expectations gives ideology its power and significance. Bartolomé and Trueba (2000) note, "Better understanding of the politics of education and the power of ideologies that ultimately silence oppressed groups are of central importance" (p. 277). In the math example above, understanding the limitations of positivistic frameworks, specifically the assertions of universal truths, and inattention to context and dynamics of power, may be sufficient critique for considering alternative frameworks more congruent with the holders' stated goals for their students. For teachers, ideological clarity is required in our understandings and judgments on the role and purpose of schools in society. As people begin to seek clarity, feelings of fear and trepidation are likely to occur. They should be viewed as a normal accompaniment to realizing greater possibilities for freedom. People learn to live in a world "made of the tensions between the certain and uncertain" (Freire & Macedo, 2003, p. 361).

Darder, Baltodano, and Torres (2003a, 2003b) recognize a relationship of ideology to a person's beliefs, attitudes, and opinions, with systems of beliefs often represented as being individually constructed by one's unique socialization experiences. Teacher education texts may reference ideological positions of individuals or institutions, but they do not typically frame the evolution of teachers' belief systems in the context of dominant ideologies or those that counter patterns of dominance and support a counternarrative. Bartolomé (2004) notes the limitations of studies on effective teachers that locate the impetus of their practices in their individually held beliefs without recognizing the ideological frames for those individually held beliefs. The Bartolomé and Trueba (2000) position is that beliefs should not be viewed simplistically and as apolitical and decontextualized. They note that teachers should "interrogate their ideological orientations" (p. 282), for example, their internalization of the value of assimilation, ethnocentrism, and deficit beliefs about linguistic and ethnic groups. They insist that recognizing the significance of shared understanding of belief systems evolves over time.

The literature on ideology's relationship to schools, teaching, and learning has received limited consideration as a rationale to intentionally structure explicit attention to ideology in teacher education (Bartolomé, 2004) and new teacher professional development experiences. Bartolomé (2004) notes several reasons explaining why explicit attention is not given to ideology. One important reason is that professional development planners and teachers are not prepared to overtly critique the legitimacy of the existing social order. Another rationale is that teachers, K-12 and in higher education, do not have the tools and capacity to recognize and critically reflect on beliefs, values, and norms they hold that are upheld by the dominant society.

Calling attention to the validity for new teachers to generate the skills, character, and commitments to sustain critical reflection is one of the purposes of this chapter. The story and discussion that follow, taken from a professional development project, illustrate some lessons for educators interested in developing the competencies and dispositions to interrogate social and educational ideologies in themselves and in the world around them.

SUPPORTING SOCIAL JUSTICE: EXAMINING ONE PROFESSIONAL DEVELOPMENT[5] INITIATIVE FOR NEW TEACHERS

QUEST (Quality Urban Education and Support for Teachers) was initially conceived as a mentoring and support program focused on teachers and teaching in urban schools. Significant in the program's initial development was the Feiman-Nemser and Parker (1992) research on mentoring and cultivating the role of the teacher as an agent of change. A decision to locate the mentoring services outside of a school, not endorsed in the mentoring literature, was made to avoid replicating services already provided by the districts. This choice supported building community as a multi-district professional network among the teachers. Feimen-Nemser and Parker's work on teacher inquiry and problem posing skill development, for the purposes of change, was maintained as planners looked for frameworks that addressed dynamics of race, culture, and power. The explicit social political/social justice framework began to evolve from the work in Ladson-Billings's *Crossing over Canaan* (2001), using instructional tools by Enid Lee[6] and developed based on the research of Cochran-Smith, Nieto, and Bartolomé.

QUEST then evolved in its design to support new teachers' capacity to address the question: "What do I need to know and be able to do to provide an equitable and just education in an urban school for my culturally diverse students?" QUEST's goal was to cultivate teacher capacity to advance equity and justice in schools. Teacher participants could expect mentoring from higher education faculty and instructional resources/activities to

1. promote reflection on one's self and self in relation to others;
2. examine issues of racism/oppression/social justice within the context of classroom practices and management;
3. examine state-mandated professional standards and exemplars of social justice;
4. build a community of colleagues; sessions were scheduled approximately every other month during the academic year.

After reviewing the feedback from participants of the project, planners initially structured the sessions to include segments for:

1. "Teacher Talk";
2. Examination of case studies of teaching and QUEST participants' experiences;
3. Investigation tools to examine classroom interaction and knowledge about students' lives;
4. Teachers' personal histories and circumstances that led them to become teachers.

The theme of self-reflection became more focused through activities designed to encourage writing their "Teacher Autobiographies." During the second year, with the exception of the participant-directed "Teacher Talk" sessions, attention to the dynamics of race, culture, and linguistic differences were beginning to become an explicit element within each component. During the third year, QUEST project staff decided that consistent attention to issues of race, culture, oppression, and identity to be formally and explicitly integrated into the planning process. My role as a mentor was then extended to support all the mentors' efforts to cohesively infuse these concepts in the program. In the third year, we extended "Teacher Talk" time and refined the previous structure and routine to include segments that focused on "Putting Race on the Table," developing and analyzing their autobiographies and examining and interpreting state standards through a social justice lens. "Homework" drawing from their classroom experiences was assigned and used for discussion and analysis.

TEACHERS' QUESTIONS, CONCERNS, AND REFLECTIONS ABOUT RACE, ETHNICITY, AND IDEOLOGIES

The first year's needs assessments did not indicate that the participants wanted to examine the sociopolitical context of their schools or their own social identities (e.g., race, class, culture, and so on). However, it was clear that they wanted to examine "teacher identity" and "student/teacher relationships." Keeping the teachers' declared interests in mind, project planners nonetheless believed that the participants would benefit from exploring their own cultural identities and issues of race, oppression, and social justice. Thus, explicit attention was given to including activities on these themes. As teachers gained confidence in exploring these topics, they began raising questions about the role of race and culture in the process of teaching and learning in post-session feedback. Some of their questions included the following:

1. Why is it that people of the same race (skin color) seem to have an instant bond when they begin talking to each other, whereas people of different colors seem to need to bridge a gap before they can feel comfortable?
2. I wonder how I incorporate race into my thoughts. Do I ignore it? Do I have subliminal thoughts?
3. Do my students see how my actions and reactions may be a result of my White upbringing? How do they feel about it? Is this a bad thing? Would I have reacted differently to the scenario if I were a Hispanic or a Black woman? Would she feel the same way as I do? Would she react the same as a White teacher?
4. Are race and culture important considerations in subject matter or are they limited to how you interact with students on a personal (teacher/student) level?
5. How is the role of academic teacher viewed across various ethnic and cultural segments?

Their questions shed light on teachers' assumptions, questions, and tensions about the role of race and culture in the context of teacher/student relationships and their conceptualizations of curriculum content, instruction, and achievement. The questions could allow planners to make tentative assessments of their insights about race and culture. The teacher concerns (questions 1–3) revealed apprehensions of holding prejudices, stereotypes, and beliefs that reflected the influence of racism. They made note of self-segregation patterns among people of color (question 1) and Whites and their description of race, as "skin color," could mean defining race as a biological construct (question 1). The teachers also appeared to consider the possibility that their students' race and culture were influencing curriculum, (question 4) instruction, (question 5) and perceptions of the teacher (questions 3 & 5).

In terms of ideological influences, the feedback surfaced views of color blindness, the denial of race as having significance: "I wonder how I incorporate race into my thoughts. Do I ignore it? Do I have subliminal thoughts?" They showed concerns and ambivalence about recognizing racial differences, as well as how people of other racial groups perceived them as White. The comments implied that White teachers were perceiving people of other races in this racially, culturally, and linguistically diverse setting as different from themselves. "If I were X racial group, would I react or feel differently? The issue here is the increased likelihood that people, racially different from White, are often perceived as having lesser status than Whites. The earnestness of their questions demonstrates the teachers had little opportunity, prior to QUEST, to examine the socialization experiences shaping perceptions and beliefs about social group membership. Racist ideologies maintain unequal relationships to power between racial groups by infusing dominant cultural messages in the society of racial superiority or inferiority. Attributions of the superiority of Whiteness, within the context of oppressive ideologies, endorse perceptions of inferiority and deficiency that then justify the denial of power and privilege to persons, cultural representations, traditions, ways of knowing, and ideas that are not White.

Along with issues directly related to race, these teachers raised concerns about "maintaining the values that brought them into teaching" "and questions about teacher identity." QUEST responded to their queries by integrating an "autobiography" activity that allowed them to examine their socialization experiences and begin to see how some of their belief systems—ideologies—were driving their practice.

TEACHER AUTOBIOGRAPHIES: LINKING PERSONAL SOCIALIZATION WITH BELIEFS

Review of the development of this assignment highlights its conceptual alignment to an examination of concepts and connotations related to ideology. The use of autobiography as a vehicle for individual and collective inquiry has been linked to teacher development initiatives (Cochran-Smith, 2000; Nieto, 2003a).[7] The conceptual construction of this activity related to Nieto's (2003a) assertions about teaching as: Evolution, Autobiography, Intellectual Work, and Democratic Practice.[8] Cochran-Smith's (1997) professional development framework provided very specific guidance in developing the structure for interpreting teachers' autobiographies. "Successful urban teaching is not dependent on method, but is dependent on a confluence of interpretations, ideology and practices" (p. 92). This framework identifies sites where ideological influences of perceptions of self and others are most significant in working with diverse students.

The QUEST autobiography curriculum begins with a focused examination in the first domain of Cochran-Smith's framework "Interpretations." Within that domain she locates the sites of interpretations within: "Teachers' beliefs, images, and knowledge/understandings of self, particular the self-as-teacher; beliefs, images, and understandings of knowledge itself-both generally and subject matter knowledge specifically; beliefs, images, and knowledge/understandings of culture, cultures and cultural differences" (1997, p. 30). The focal points to examine teachers' interpretations, listed in Table 1, identify specific sites of teachers' assumptions, knowledge, values, and beliefs significant in working with culturally diverse populations.[9] The autobiography reflection included questions developed as inquiry guides, addressing each of these sites, and to remind teachers of this examination as part of a larger scheme of teacher development that named connections among beliefs, ideologies, and practices (see Table 1).

The QUEST participants worked on this autobiography over a period of 18 months. During that time, they were continually encouraged to consider the sources, i.e., family members, classroom experiences as students, games, traditions, rituals, and so on, and their significance in shaping the teachers' assumptions, beliefs, values, and norms about teaching. In their discussions, the need to clarify particular terms became apparent. To support their continued autobiography reflections, session activities clarified understanding of race, ethnicity, culture, nationality, stereotype, prejudice, oppression, and so on. Many of the participants were appreciative of the time taken to clarify for themselves the similarities and distinctions among these terms. They came to realize that their interpretations of these concepts influenced their practice with diverse students. Many of the teachers noted how much they valued working on this project. One noted, "I adore the teaching autobiography [assignment]. It has allowed me to

1. tap into my own head and heart;
2. assess my teaching;
3. envision the future;
4. sit with unanswerable questions."

Another teacher indicated: "The 'autobiography' assignment is helping me to think more deeply about why I am teaching and if this is really what I should be doing. It's helping me to learn more about myself and why I'm here."

The autobiography assignment was instrumental in helping teachers uncover their socialization experiences; to begin to recognize the sources of beliefs and values, norms of being that often, unconsciously shape what teachers do and do

TABLE 1. Inquiry guideposts & reflective questions

Where, in these particular sites, might I look more closely to find my beliefs, values, assumptions and knowledge?	*Using the questions as inquiry guides, how does, or might, my autobiography reveal my beliefs, values, assumptions, and knowledge; where in my response do I reveal the source(s) of my beliefs, values, assumptions, and knowledge?*
Autobiography and [forming] Alliances	• What have I come to think and believe about people like and unlike me? • In what ways do I have alliances with people like me and not like me?
Efficacy and Agency	• Under what circumstances do I believe I am an effective teacher: when do I feel I am not?
Inquiry Stance	• Under what circumstances will I share my questions and concerns about my school and classroom?
Knowledge of Subject matter	• What subject matter do I have a "passion" for teaching; what circumstances, attitudes, and beliefs ignited that feeling? What subject matter do I not have a passion for teaching; why do I not? • How does the presence, or absence, of that "passion" affect the quality of my teaching?
Image of Culture, & Image of Difference	• What is my conception of "culture"; what do I believe and assume about cultural differences?
Classrooms as Cultures/Home and School Culture	• What are my explanations for failure in my school and in my classroom?

not say and do. Over time, we hoped the new teachers could find new meaning in Nieto's observation of teacher evolution, "Excellent teachers don't develop full-blown at graduation; nor are they just 'born teachers.' Instead, teachers are always in the process of 'becoming'" (Nieto, 2003a, p. 125).

THE SIGNIFICANCE OF INQUIRY: IDEOLOGICAL CHALLENGES AND PEDAGOGICAL CONSIDERATIONS

The QUEST experience prompted awareness of some challenges and opportunities for new teachers' development of inquiry in general and, related to ideology, as "a stance on teaching and learning that is both critical and transformative"

(Cochran-Smith, 2004a, p. 14). The vignette at the beginning of the chapter casts light on some of the challenges for new teachers to appreciate and cultivate the capacity for personal and collective inquiry. In talking about their challenges using the math curriculum and their ambivalent feelings, the teachers opened the door to discussing numerous other issues. They noted that they have to move on with covering the content despite awareness that students "still don't get it" and despite pressure from parents and principals who are "only interested in the test scores going up." A closer examination of their comments raises several types of dilemmas. One cluster of teacher concerns has to do with the standardized math curriculum's rationale, relevance, and constraints of its structure as well as its impact on student achievement, classroom management, and parent involvement. Another cluster of dilemmas has to do with the teachers' conceptualization of "basic math" as characterized as procedures and specific content to be memorized, presented, and reinforced, accompanying the standardized sequence of math activities.

Teachers are clearly aware that all of their students are not being adequately served academically. They see how the mandated math curriculum tolerates children being left further and further behind, and they recognize top-down policies for scripted "teacher-proof" curricular requirements as problematic. They witness the concerns of parents, students, and teachers neither being solicited nor taken seriously by administrators and curriculum developers. They question the ways parents, students, and teachers can become part of a conversation about what it means to be an educated person. They also question what the formally sanctioned process of "becoming educated" should include. They know the insights they hold about teaching have value, so they question why their ideas are dismissed and devalued.

The practical and pragmatic questions and concerns teachers raised were often responded to by their peers without benefit of a more complete understanding of the "problem." Therefore, well-intended efforts to be helpful were less likely to be so than intended, because the responder held incomplete information. The person posing the problem would also miss the chance to get deeper insight into the issues and be able to solicit and receive more comprehensive or focused recommendations. The lessons needed among educators who get limited or incomplete answers to their problems are within the challenges and opportunities for individual and collective inquiry processes. For the person posing the problem, the value of this inquiry process is that it unveils more insights into the "problem(s)." Observations over time demonstrated that as a group these new teachers did not have a conscious problem-solving framework or organized approach for analyzing their concerns and problems. They were not in a position to see teaching as "a complex activity that occurs within webs of social, historical, cultural, and political significance [nor understand that] [a]cross the life span, an inquiry stance provides a kind of grounding within the changing cultures of school reform and competing political agendas—a place to put one's feet, as it were, as well as a frame of mind" (Cochran-Smith, 2004, p. 14). The following quote, taken from participant feedback, illustrates the teacher's consciousness of a relationship between her beliefs and practices, and the mediating influence of dominant ideologies. It is too soon to say whether this consciousness positions them to conceive of the act of teaching in the sociopolitical context that Cochran-Smith endorses.

> Starting to formulate an autobiography (or prepare myself to begin it) will be helpful to me. I have tried many times to write a philosophy of teaching, which is strongly grounded in my autobiography, but I find my philosophy of teaching changes daily to meet the needs of my students. Talking about culture, ethnicity, exclusion, [my autobiography] is really helping to highlight my evolving ideology and practices. I am beginning to let myself get to a place in my philosophy where I stress myself out less with MCAS/Standard-based expectations to move towards a more aware/empathetic approach to teaching responsibility.

The intention of the autobiography was to stimulate awareness of relationships among beliefs, now interpreted as ideologies of teaching and practice. QUEST's program design was intended to provoke individual and collective inquiry. While it is premature to determine any cause and effect relationships, I see the above quote as a source of hopefulness in that an inquiry stance also provides a foundation for teachers taking individual and collective action positioned within the sociopolitical context in which teaching exists. It is possible that teachers' need to define their role in the classroom can be served and they can see the value in using this approach. New teachers' capacity for critical inquiry cannot and should not be assumed. It is a capacity that needs to be cultivated over time.

CONCLUSIONS

In the Prelude and Introduction sections of this chapter, I started where teachers "were at." I then asserted that aspirations for emancipatory teaching and learning in schools should be endorsed through new urban teacher professional development. In the beginning, QUEST's planners knew focusing on sustaining effective practice in urban settings required attention to issues of race, culture, and difference. We encountered well-intended, hard-working teachers. Many of them showed little experience with critical inquiry skills and dispositions of practice or awareness about their own socialization experiences and the influence of these experiences on their beliefs and practices. Initially, many of them neither viewed schools in a sociopolitical context nor understood the dynamics of oppression in classroom decisions about what was important to know and do. Some appeared eager to develop this understanding and were appreciative of efforts to validate the relationship between teaching and the practice of justice. To support this work, we, teacher educators, relied on research that addressed the sociopolitical context of schools that also complemented the literature on new teacher induction programs and mentoring.

Over three years, QUEST provided a venue in which we could learn how to infuse the ideas, beliefs, values, and ideologies that worked toward equity and justice and supported new teachers. We applied principles of equity and justice in the autobiography assignment, in the examination and use of district standards, and through investigative tools and resources for their classrooms. Teachers used these tools to examine what they knew, believed, assumed, and did not know about their students. They used the resources to examine their practice and its consequences. Although we did not explicitly name or study ideology, we did present principles, concepts, analytical frameworks, and practices of critique that are essential to any interrogation of educational and societal ideologies.

Until a formal assessment of the impact of QUEST can occur, we can draw upon some early feedback. It suggests that QUEST responds to teacher needs identified in the first year such as their need to reduce feelings of isolation and the need to cultivate a professional network of peers, as well as provide them with time and encouragement to assess the beliefs, values, and experiences that brought them to teaching. Their need for support was addressed by providing a venue, time, structure, and a climate to question contradictory, conflicting, and contested values and beliefs with those pervasive in the school. The value of the QUEST experience, in the short term for professional development planners and mentors, is its role as an incubator for exploring curriculum and instruction that can later be reviewed for its explicit relevance for the study and analysis of both personal and societal potentially discriminatory ideologies. The willingness of faculty to question and probe typically taken-for-granted ideas created conditions that allowed previously unnamed ideologies to surface. This chapter offers some of the initial lessons, considerations, and implications as it enthusiastically endorses continued work.

The tentative lessons from QUEST are to encourage resources in higher education to continue developing this type of work. New teachers deserve validation for raising larger, philosophical, and ideological questions arising from their day-to-day encounters. Supporting new teachers to recognize and interrogate personal and societal ideologies, and critically assess their professional goals, ethical standards, and the conditions in which they work may heighten clarity of the role of a teacher in advancing social justice. That vision coupled with a critical community of peers may help them stay in the profession and beat the odds "burn out."

Perhaps they will be better positioned to see the ideological and political contexts of schools. Perhaps they will use this vantage point to challenge the disastrous patterns of degradation in schools that stifles human potential and screams out the contradictions in a society that claims equal access to opportunity is available for all. It is in all of our self-interests and the nation's for them to do so.

CODA

A prelude in music functions as an introduction to the main theme of a song. A singer uses the coda at the end of a song to reiterate and punctuate the song's main theme. This coda is directed toward higher education faculty wishing to support this chapter's vision for new teacher professional development. It is to encourage teacher educators to question "where they are at" and to consider the consequences of the beliefs and values they bring to their practice. Scrutiny of one's ideological orientations becomes an imperative in managing the challenges of the "overwhelming presence of Whiteness" (Sleeter, 2001a) and recognizing the costs for the underwhelming presence of people of color in teacher education. Because expectations of social and intellectual discourse are defined by dominant ideologies of White supremacy, it is hard for people who are White to recognize when ideologies of White supremacy are operating. In a process of self-examination, the conditions of Whiteness can be challenging to manage for higher education faculty, more likely than not to be predominantly White, and who have been socialized primarily in racially homogeneous settings.

For instance, professing the value of color blindness indicates an orientation to deny the relevance of race and, in some cases, ethnicity for people of color. Thus, to determine not to see people as Black, Latino, or Asian Pacific Islander overlooks important aspects of their personhood. Holding beliefs that "race doesn't matter" and that "people are all the same" are typically intended to avoid the possibility of imposing any perceptions of inferiority on that person or racial group. However, holding these beliefs is to deny the significance for persons typically asserting this position of the privileges of their social location. While the intention may appear to be honorable, the impact of color blindness, as belief and ideology, is to deny the consequences of racial group membership, for members of groups targeted, and those advantaged by racism in this society.[10]

Higher education faculty, from all racial groups, need to probe dominant ideologies such as color blindness, meritocracy, individualism, competition, and so on that sustain deficit representations of "Other" and social and economic inequities. How have these ideologies drawn, colored, and shaped the terrain of one's beliefs, values, and assumptions? While these ideologies are directed to all members of society, attention to the particular and challenging experiences of people of color learning and working in schools and higher education must not be ignored or underestimated (Elliott, 1996). There are more lessons from the QUEST experience that may help colleagues—both white and of color—on this pathway. It is a goal to present those lessons in the future. For now, this coda is to encourage others to do their own work and be mindful of their settings so they can add to the knowledge base from their own experience.

NOTES

1. Ideology is used in this paper to refer to "the framework of thought constructed and held by members of society to justify or rationalize an existing social order" (Bartolomé, p. 97).
2. Recognizing and examining the dominant status of ideological ideas and beliefs is an essential aspect in this analysis. "The dominant ideology [sometimes referred to as hegemony] refers to patterns of beliefs and values shared by the majority of individuals." Like culture, ideological formations are taught through socialization and daily interactions. Like culture, it is so pervasive and deeply embedded in the unconscious for reasons mentioned above that it is extremely hard to extricate for examination. McLaren's examination of ideology includes finding "which concepts, values and meanings … obscure[s] … and clarify [ies] our place within networks of power, and understanding of the social world" (McLaren, 2003, p. 81).
3. No Child Left Behind (NCLB) is the name of federal legislation framing school reform and teacher licensure in terms of accountability through standardized tests, limited and problematic interpretations of teacher quality in terms of content knowledge related to standardized test requirements, and as competition by creating alternative teaching and learning structures via privatization (Cochran-Smith, 2004a).
4. Bartolomé advocates explicit teaching, which implies recognizing and responding to the ways ideology operates in relation to power and is evident in positions taken by individuals and in the symbols and language of schools and society. She defines political clarity as "the process by which individuals achieve ever-deepening consciousness of the socio-political and economic realities that shape their lives and their capacity to transform such material and symbolic conditions" (2004, p. 98). Ideological clarity "refers to the process by which individuals struggle to identify and compare their own explanations for the existing socioeconomic and political hierarchy with the dominant society's (2004, p. 98). In her study, she finds among four teachers ideological perspectives that challenged the dominant frameworks. They questioned "the myth of meritocracy, deficit views of minority students, and superiority of White mainstream culture" (p. 116).
5. Professional development is conceived as cultivating conditions for an inquiry stance (Cochran-Smith & Lytle, 1999; Cochran-Smith, 1997, 2004a). Cochran-Smith's definition of inquiry as stance is used "to describe the positions that teachers and others who work together in inquiry communities take toward knowledge, its relationships to practice, and the purposes of schooling." (2004a, p. 14). By interpreting inquiry as a stance, Cochran-Smith assumes teachers are considering the consistency or inconsistency of their political positions. The conceptual work on teachers' capacity to reflect and see the exchange of ideas among colleagues as generating growth remains salient when explicit attention to ideology is expected. This position is contrasted with conventional interpretations of new teacher induction, which is the provision of district policy

information, support services, and mentoring. These features are often used to orient and equip new teachers for work in their schools (Alliance for Excellence in Education, 2004). The work in this chapter should encourage and guide closer scrutiny of the conventional ways new teacher induction and professional development has been and could be conceived.
6. Information on these tools can be found at Enid Lee's Web site, Enidlee.com.
7. This activity, based on work in Nieto's *What Keeps Teachers Going?*, was co-developed by Nelda Barrón and myself while working with student teachers. I modified it for the QUEST's new teacher participants.
8. In "Teaching as Evolution," Nieto shares her professional journey in beginning to confront the sociopolitical context of education. "Most of us have been trained to think of dropping out or failing to learn to read ... as simply personal problems caused by short comings of individual students. ... The problems do not develop out of the blue, but are at least partially a result of the social, political, and economic context in which schools are rooted" (p. 19). In "autobiography," it is "remembering what brought them to teaching" (p. vii). In "Teaching as Intellectual Work" she quotes Giroux, "[I]n order to function as intellectuals, teachers must create the ideology and structural conditions necessary for them to write, research and work with each other ... As intellectuals, they will combine reflection and action in the interests of empowering students ... to be critical actors committed to developing a world free of oppression and exploitation" (p. 76). Democratic Practice "can mean many things ... teaching students a fuller more complicated history; it can mean being more inclusive. Making certain that silenced voices are included in the telling" (1998, p. 100).
9. For a complete explanation of this framework see Cochran-Smith (1997).
10. Research about the experiences of people color in k-12, higher education, and professional development settings are noted in the references, as well as studies on whites' resistance to examining color blindness and related issues of race, multiculturalism, and diversity are offered as resources for further examination.

REFERENCES

Alliance for Excellent Education. (2004). *Tapping the potential retraining and developing high quality new teachers*. Washington, DC: Alliance for Excellent Education.

Bartolomé, L. I., & Trueba, E. T. (2000). Beyond the politics of schools and the rhetoric of fashionable pedagogies: The significance of teacher ideology. In L. I. Bartolomé & E. T. Trueba (Eds.), *Immigrant voices in search of educational equity* (pp. 278–292). Lanham, MD: Rowman & Littlefield.

Bartolomé, L. I. (2003). Beyond the methods fetish: Toward a humanizing pedagogy. In A. Darder, M. Baltodano, & R. Torres (Eds.), *The critical pedagogy reader* (pp. 408–429). New York: Routledge Falmer.

Bartolomé, L. I. (2004). Critical pedagogy in teacher education: Radicalizing prospective teachers. *Teacher Education Quarterly, 31*(1), 94–122.

Burbules, N. C. (1995). Forms of ideology-critique: A pedagogical perspective. In P. McLaren, & J. Giarelli (Eds.), *Critical theory and educational research* (pp. 53–69). Albany: State University of New York Press.

Cochran-Smith, M. (1997). Knowledge, skills and experiences for teaching culturally diverse learners: A perspective for practicing teachers. In J. J. Irvine (Ed.), *Critical knowledge for diverse teachers and learners* (pp. 26–87). Washington, DC: AACTE.

Cochran-Smith, M., & Lytle, S. (1999). Relationships of knowledge and practice: Teacher learning in communities. In A. Iran-Nejad & C. Pearson (Eds.), *Review of Research in Education*, Vol. 24 (pp. 251–307). Washington, DC: American Educational Research Association.

Cochran-Smith, M. (2000). Blind vision: Unlearning racism in teacher education. *Harvard Educational Review, 70*(2), 157–190.

Cochran-Smith, M. (2001). Learning to teach against the (new) grain. *Journal of Teacher Education, 53*(1), 3–4.

Cochran-Smith, M. (2004). *Walking the road: Race, diversity, and social justice in teacher education.* New York: Teachers College Press.

Darder, A., Baltodano, M., & Torres, R. D. (Eds.). (2003a). *The critical pedagogy reader.* New York: Routledge Falmer.

Darder, A., Baltodano, M., & Torres, R. D. (Eds.). (2003b). Critical pedagogy: An introduction. In A. Darder, M. Baltodano, & R. D. Torres (Eds.), *The critical pedagogy reader* (pp. 1–23). New York: Routledge Falmer.

Elliott, P. R. (1996). *Testifying on racism: African American educations, racial identity and anti-racism professional development in schools.* Unpublished doctoral dissertation, University of Massachusetts, Amherst.

Feiman-Nemser, S., & Parker, M. B. (1992). Mentoring in context: A comparison of two U.S. programs for beginning teachers (pp. 699–718). Washington, DC: Office of Educational Research and Improvement.

Freire, P. (1974). *Pedagogy of the oppressed.* New York: Seabury Press.

Freire, P., & Macedo, D. (2003). Rethinking literacy: A dialogue. In A. Darder, M. Baltodano, & R. D. Torres (Eds.). *The critical pedagogy reader* (pp. 354–364). New York: Routledge Falmer.

Ladson-Billings, G. (2001). *Crossing over Canaan: The journey of new teachers in diverse classrooms.* San Francisco: Jossey Bass.

Macedo, D., & Freire, P. (2003). Rethinking literacy. In A. Darder, M. Baltodano, & R. D. Torres (Eds.). *The critical pedagogy reader* (pp. 354–364). New York: Routledge Falmer.

McLaren, P. (2003). Critical pedagogy: A look at the major concepts. In A. Darder., M. Baltodano, & R. D. Torres (Eds.). *The critical pedagogy reader* (pp. 69–96). New York: Routledge Falmer.

McLaren, P. L., & Giarelli, J. M. (Eds.). (1995). *Critical theory and educational research.* Albany: State University of New York Press.

Nieto, S. (2003). *What keeps teachers going?.* New York: Teachers College Press.

Sleeter, C. E. (2001a). Preparing teachers of culturally diverse schools: Research and the overwhelming presence of whiteness. *Journal of Teacher Education, 52*(2), 94–106.

Section VI: Ideologically Clear Teachers: Two Case Studies

CHAPTER ELEVEN

Developing Ideological Clarity: One Teacher's Journey

CRISTINA ALFARO

Discussions about how to best prepare teachers of language minority students typically revolve around teaching profession standards and linguistic and academic development best teaching practices. Whereas the focus on best teaching practices and standards is important, it is equally critical to interrogate the role ideology plays in how teachers work with language minority and other subordinated minority student groups. Ideology refers to a set of cultural beliefs, attitudes, fundamental commitments, and values about social reality that underlie and thereby, to some degree, justify and legitimate the status quo or movements for social change (Apple, 2004). Unless teachers engage in the process of consciously questioning the status quo, their own beliefs, and their classroom practices, they will, at best, become technicians that perpetuate the existing dominant ideology and social order. Bartolomé (2000) terms educators' ability to engage in ideological analysis, "ideological clarity," and explains:

> [I]deological clarity requires that teachers' individual explanations be compared and contrasted with those propagated by the dominant society. It is to be hoped that the juxtaposing of ideologies forces teachers to better understand if, when, and how their belief systems uncritically reflect those of the dominant society and support unfair and inequitable conditions. (p. 168)

It is precisely this ability to objectively compare and contrast ideologies that teacher preparation programs must teach. As a teacher educator, it has always been difficult to observe dynamic and enthusiastic teacher candidates who passionately claim, during their preservice work, that they have entered teaching to make a positive difference in the lives of linguistic minority students only to later see them, in their own classrooms, uncritically perpetuating the existing educational system they so strongly denounced initially. When I had witnessed this pattern repeatedly, I began to think about and re-examine my own historical experiences as an educator—as a prospective teacher, as a practicing classroom teacher, as a school administrator, and presently as a teacher educator. In so doing, it was not until I seriously began to critically analyze myself—my own ideology, based on Paulo Freire's work—that I understood the absolute necessity for teachers to begin developing ideological clarity concurrently with their studies of bilingual pedagogy and Spanish language development courses.

My encounter with discourses about teacher education and best practices intensified my own ideological scrutiny and that of other teachers. These discourses unveiled that the degree of teachers' courage, solidarity, and ethical commitment toward social change depends on their ability to examine, know, and name their ideological orientations in order to juxtapose them with those of dominant culture ideologies perpetuated by educational institutions. Teachers who engage in the process of developing ideological clarity come to realize that they are their own voices of activism.

This chapter presents a case study of Carlos,[1] a teacher education student who participated in the International Teacher Education Program (ITEP) within the California State University (CSU).[2] Although Carlos came into the CSU-ITEP with life experiences and predispositions that allowed him to recognize the political and ideological dimensions of education, it is evident from the data collected in this study that his level of understanding increased and that he became more sophisticated as a result of his participation in the program.

During the program, Carlos had the opportunity to work in Mexico within the public, private, and indigenous school systems. Exposure to such various school settings provided him with powerful ideological border crossing[3] experiences. Throughout his teacher preparation experience, Carlos demonstrated a keen ability to perceive discriminatory treatment experienced by children from low-status cultural groups in the various Mexican communities in which he lived and worked. For example, when he taught in the private school system, he quickly contrasted the curriculum and treatment of affluent students to that of the poor, working-class public school students. Furthermore, in his work with Native students in the indigenous Mexican school system, he quickly noted the political, linguistic, ideological, and pedagogical tensions this community encountered while fighting to maintain its sacred land, culture, traditions, and language.

Carlos adroitly compared and contrasted the experiences of low-status students in Mexico with those experienced by low status Mexican and Latino immigrants in the United States. Although Carlos experienced discrimination as a Mexican immigrant himself when he and his family immigrated to the United States, his return to Mexico, as an adult and as a teacher, put him in direct confrontation with racism and classism from and within a Mexican sociocultural context. As a result of this ideological border crossing experience, Carlos believes that he better comprehends how oppression takes on varied forms in dissimilar societies such as Mexico and the United States and how these ideologies often manifest themselves in a teacher's practice. Because he was able to enhance his insights about the different forms racism and classism take, Carlos believes that he has become a more effective teacher of low-status, linguistic minority students.

The implications of this case study are relevant to teacher education efforts. Clearly, in preparing teachers to work with low-status populations, it becomes important that they explicitly study dominant ideologies, better understand how dominant ideologies can potentially support racist and classist actions in school settings, and figure out ways to intervene and fracture harmful actions (Bartolomé, 2004; Macedo, 2003). It is my position as a teacher educator that in order for prospective teachers to seriously commit to teach for social justice and to work at equalizing unequal power relations in schools, teacher preparation programs must help teacher candidates develop ideological clarity along with pedagogical and linguistic expertise.

CALIFORNIA STATE UNIVERSITY-WIDE INTERNATIONAL TEACHER EDUCATION PROGRAM FRAMEWORK

In my role as the California campus director of the International Teacher Education Program (ITEP), I have made it my goal to provide a pathway for teachers to develop ideological clarity via their participation in this program. The CSU-ITEP is a one-year teacher education program with explicit situated learning experiences and coursework that immerse preservice teachers in diverse educational situation and spaces such as the private, public, and indigenous school settings in Mexico. The opportunity to teach in different sociocultural contexts with culturally heterogeneous student populations forces preservice teachers to experience cultural, pedagogical, and ideological dissonance, a sensation that appears to lead to increased ideological clarity (Alfaro, 2003). The pedagogical experiences are structured in such a manner that propels teacher candidates to juxtapose their personal belief systems with those of the dominant society in both Mexico and the United States. In this manner, teachers are constrained to critically examine the political and ideological dimensions of minority education on both sides of the U.S./Mexico border.

ITEP is a CSU system-wide bilingual credential program for elementary teacher candidates. The program was approved in 1994 by the Commission on Teacher Credentialing (CTC) and is administrated through the CSU International Programs office. The program, in its current form, brings CSU students statewide to San Diego State University for two summer "bookend" sessions of coursework and student teaching, while the fall and the spring of the academic year are spent in Mexico, also in coursework and student teaching. The program is situated in the city of Querétaro, Mexico. Besides CSU-San Diego State University, the program's spearhead campus, there are nine other CSU campuses that participate, including San José, Fresno, Hayward, Long Beach, San Bernardino, Sacramento, Sonoma, Bakersfield, and Fullerton.

Prospective teachers in the ITEP experience a one-year program in four different teacher preparation contexts or stages:

Stage 1: During this first stage, students begin their summer with an introduction to teaching in California, at San Diego State University, and end their summer teaching orientation in Mexico. This stage serves as an introduction to teaching and to the educational systems in the United States and Mexico. Most importantly, students are presented with ample opportunities to identify and interrogate their beliefs about teaching students from low-status populations. In addition, there are multiple opportunities during this phase for students to engage in numerous community building exercises to develop a cohesive and supportive student cohort. This initial orientation involves students in problem posing activities that force them to question their own biliteracy development as well as the ideological forces that propelled or inhibited their own level of biliteracy and bicultural development. Additionally, students are explicitly exposed to the California State legislative policies, program guidelines, and are challenged to consider the political, ideological, linguistic, and pedagogical implications of this legislation on the teaching of linguistic minority children. These activities establish a space for prospective teachers to reposition themselves and to begin to compare and contrast U.S. and Mexican standards of education.

Stage 2: During this stage, teacher candidates continue with methods courses and observe and teach in private schools followed by a more extensive student teaching experience in urban public schools in Mexico. The opportunity to observe and teach in private and public school contexts forces the students to recognize class differences in teachers' implementation of curriculum and treatment of students. It is during the teaching practicum where students begin to notice the contrasting lives of children in school: the better quality materials and curriculum as well as the teachers' more solicitous and respectful treatment of middle-class students versus what is experienced by school children who are from a lower socio-economic class. Teacher candidates juxtapose the one aforementioned "reality" with that illustrated by the meager supplies, large class size and teachers' often less considerate behavior in their work in working-class public schools. I will discuss Carlos's perceptions of this phenomenon in greater depth below.

Stage 3: During this stage, students teach in a rural indigenous school and live within the community setting in Mexico. In this teaching context, prospective teachers teach Spanish as a second language to one indigenous Mexican community. It is at this stage, given the classroom experiences, where prospective teachers begin to set side by side the cultural and linguistic hegemonic tensions that exist across borders, those geographical, political, and personal. More specifically, at this stage, they come to see how indigenous communities have been relegated to second-class treatment. At the same time, they learn to use the natural resources on which this community depends to promote authentic education. Most significantly, they analyze and dialogue about the manner in which the community negotiates and struggles to preserve their indigenous culture and language. This situated practicum forces prospective teachers to engage and observe, firsthand, the oppression and inequalities on the basis of class and race that exist in both societies and not just in the United States.

Stage 4: During the fourth and last stage of the program, students teach in a California public elementary, Spanish/English dual-language program in San Diego. In this U.S. context, prospective teachers typically begin to articulate their personal and professional transformative experience as a result of having taught on both sides of the Mexico/U.S. border. This is the last and most critical stage because students experience reverse culture shock. Given their close contact and work with educating linguistic minority low-status students on both sides of the border, they struggle to make sense of their acute awareness of asymmetrical power dynamics; they reflect on their experiences in Mexico, they miss the faces of their Mexican students, and ultimately, they struggle to articulate how all of their teaching experiences inform their current teaching ideology. In order to facilitate the process of critically analyzing dominant education ideologies, students engage in a seminar where the focus is to examine their student teaching in California English/Spanish dual-language programs. Students are assigned to work with dual-language teachers who have learned to navigate their way through the state/district required prepackaged, one-size-fits-all curriculum (Alfaro, 2003). It is during this last stage where these prospective teachers begin to use their lived experiences to identify the linguistic, pedagogical, political, and ideological contradictions that exist in both the Mexican and U.S. educational systems. Based on these four varied situated teaching and learning contexts, they begin to make the invisible visible and name the unnamed.

These four unique stages place teachers in different contexts where they can live and critically study the political and ideological dimensions of education necessary to increase their ideological clarity. Below I describe one teacher's, more specifically "Carlos's," development of his ideological clarity. This personalized case study depicts the rigorous process he undertook to gain greater clarity on issues related to teaching for social justice. Carlos came into the program with a predisposition (an open mind and heart) that allowed him to deconstruct, construct, and reconstruct his thinking about teaching and learning in a way that transformed him on a personal as well as a professional level.

IDEOLOGICAL CLARITY: ONE TEACHER'S JOURNEY IN THE ITE PROGRAM

This case study chronicles one teacher's response to the general question: "Did your experience in the international teacher education program affect your ideological orientation about and actual practice in linguistic minority education? If so, please explain how it affected your practice." This question was posed to 20 other program graduates during focus groups and individual interviews. In addition, I collected and analyzed students' journal entries and their anecdotal comments. I chose to focus on Carlos because he appeared to have benefited tremendously from his participation in this program. He came with a predisposition to "see" and recognize the ideological and political dimensions of minority education. According to Bartolomé (2004), teachers like Carlos, who have experienced marginalization in their own lives, often become sensitized to the degree that they are constantly on the lookout for it in their own work with low-status students. In this case, Carlos had plenty of personal experience on which to build. He arrived in the United States with his working-class, Mexican immigrant parents as an adolescent, struggled to learn English, and throughout his young life resisted the negative stereotypes of Mexicans in the United States. In addition, because of his darker skin color, Carlos understood firsthand what it felt like to be treated as inferior by others (both U.S. Whites and lighter-skinned Mexicanos) through no fault of his own. Later, as a young man, he became involved in the Chicano Movement[4] and acquired knowledge about the history of subordination of Chicanos/Mexicanos in the United States. Currently, Carlos teaches in a classroom with all "newcomers."[5] His students are precisely those that many mainstream teachers often define as an unwanted challenge to have in their classrooms because of their linguistically and academically diverse backgrounds, limited English proficiency, and their low social status in society. Carlos embraces these students and views his work with them as an opportunity to translate his progressive ideology to his classroom practice.

Carlos possesses a BCLAD Multiple Subject credential and is pursuing a master's degree in educational administration. Currently, he teaches in a fifth/sixth grade Newcomer program at Santana Elementary School[6] in Northern California. He works with predominantly Latino immigrant students who are new to California schools.

Carlos was born in Jalisco, Mexico, and many of his relatives still live there. He immigrated to the United States at the age of 13 and spent his teenage years in San Francisco, California. His parents are laborers and do not speak English. Carlos has six siblings, and he is the first member of his family to graduate from college. When Carlos arrived in California, he struggled as an English-language learner in schools that did not offer him a program that valued his native language or culture. He arrived in U.S. schools fluent in Spanish; however, the California educational system, as he puts it, "did a good job in diminishing that fluency." His personal educational and linguistic struggles served as the impetus for his desire to become a biliteracy educator. Carlos entered the teaching profession with an intense commitment to fully develop personally and professionally to better serve his students.

When I invited him to dialogue with me about his experience in the ITE program and his evolving teaching ideology, Carlos responded that he was honored to do so and went on to explain to me that he wanted to participate in my study because he felt a need for reflection and "thinking about his personal and professional growth." During our conversations, I learned that over the previous five years, his work as a biliteracy teacher has involved the same Latino immigrant community in Northern California in which he grew up after he immigrated. Carlos explained that he became a teacher with the definite intent to return and work with this particular Latino community. He is very active in his community and is profoundly committed to his students. Carlos is the type of teacher who opens his heart to all of his students in that he makes a special effort to understand each of his students' background, struggles, hopes, and dreams. In addition, he makes it a point to get to know his students' parents to work together with them in the education of their children.

Carlos confessed that he was presently very "disenchanted" with how things were going at his school in general and with the Latino students in particular. He felt that he needed to be very candid with me regarding his disillusionment with teaching. Despite his temporary dissatisfaction, Carlos continues to be active in his school and works closely with Latino parents. He is the leader of a county-level parent education group that offers parents and other community members workshops that inform them of their legal rights with respect to bilingual education and native language instruction. I began our conversation by questioning Carlos about his participation and professional development experiences in the ITE program.

COMING FACE-TO-FACE WITH CLASS AND RACE CONSCIOUSNESS

My goal was to find out whether as a result of his participation in the ITE program Carlos's ideological orientations about teaching linguistic minority students had changed or remained the same. During my interview with Carlos, he explained that he had originally come into the program with a personal understanding of classism and racism given his humble economic origins and dark skin, but he suggested that the program had amplified his initial limited understanding:

> *Pues que te dire* [Well, what can I tell you] ... since I was born in Mexico and raised there for a good portion of my childhood, I was aware, firsthand, of class and race issues. However, they were from a child's perspective. I knew that people of dark skin, like me "*prietito*" were considered lower class and treated as such. I came to California thinking that it was going to be great, and that I would leave that racism behind [in Mexico]. *Que* behind *ni que nada* [I did not leave that behind], quite the contrary. Here [in California], I was not only "*prieto*" but, I didn't speak the dominant language ... I know what it is like to be from the other side. (emphasis added)

Carlos's experiences were deeply embedded in what Villenas (1996) calls "Otherness." He came to the realization that he was an "Other" on both sides of the border. Having had the opportunity to return to his homeland in a different context, as a preservice bilingual teacher, presented Carlos with the opportunity to theoretically face and analyze the political dimensions of minority education in both countries At this point during the interview, he described his struggle to understand manifestations of inequality in Mexico and the United States so almost as he wanted to transcend his personal experience:

> After returning to Mexico as a teacher candidate, my lens illuminated the similar inequalities and linguistic and cultural equity issues that exist across borders. However, in México things are more blatant, *es como es* [it is what it is], and here in the United States things get sugar coated ... under issues like English for the Children[7] and No Child Left Behind.[8] As a result of participating in this program, and my experience as a classroom teacher, I am able to see how culture, language, and socioeconomic issues are at the heart of the politics in education across borders. (emphasis added)

In the above quote, Carlos articulates the unnamed ideological and political dimensions of education that, before entering the program, were somewhat visible to him, but he lacked the language with which to put his understanding into words. After exposure to critical pedagogy literature and varied classroom experiences in Mexico, Carlos recognized that racism and classism were evident in both societies but that they took on different forms. Making the invisible "visible" and developing a language for articulating this awareness constituted an important step in increasing Carlos's understanding of the inequalities in education. Carlos felt that going back to Mexico as a teacher candidate provided him with ample opportunities to clearly perceive classism and racism from a different angle and to recognize the diverse manifestations of the perpetuated oppression of low sociostatus groups across borders.

An incident that illustrates Carlos's predisposition for dealing with ideological and political elements of education occurred during the first month of the program in Mexico when university students in Mexico went on strike. I observed Carlos debate and engage in intense dialogues with Mexican students about their protest. During class he insisted that we address the issues that surrounded us, such as the strike, especially since we had been asked by university administrators not to heed the strike or the striking students' concerns. Carlos urged his colleagues to name the political issues related to the strike and to struggle to make visible those elements hidden by the university administration for their benefit. His peers initially considered Carlos "radical" because he dedicated himself to becoming knowledgeable about the strike and because, ultimately, he decided to stand in solidarity with the striking Mexican university students. Despite his peers' initial fearful response to Carlos's stance, they recognized his courage and his leadership qualities.

When I asked Carlos if he believed the ITE course curriculum and practicum prepared him to meet the pedagogical needs of linguistic minority students in his California classroom, he responded in the affirmative. Furthermore, Carlos highlighted the importance of being exposed to critical pedagogues who theoretically dealt with issues of inequality and oppression. He also emphasized the positive consequences of working with professors and teachers who similarly struggle to put theory to practice in their own work. He explained that

> [t]o have the opportunity to work with critical educators from Mexico that subscribe to Freire, Chomsky, and Vygotsky was intellectually and personally challenging and ideologically right on with what we need to know as teachers. It was an additional challenge to decipher (compare and contrast) the issues that transfer over to the California classroom ... not to mention that the majority of my students are from Mexico. After teaching in California classrooms for five years, I realize that the mission of the ITE program along with the coursework, readings, professors, and speakers all prepared me to better serve the community I presently teach.

Although Carlos appreciated the courage of ITE professors in honestly dealing with the political nature of education, he described the personal turmoil that he experienced when he started to critically analyze educational inequality both in Mexico and in California. Carlos repeatedly mentioned how "hard he was hit" when he realized that oppression and mistreatment of poor and non-White kids occurred in both countries. Given his experiences with discrimination only in the United States, Carlos did not readily understand that around the world individuals from low-status groups are mistreated and marginalized (Ogbu, 1992; Skutnabb-Kangas, 1981). Given the ITE curriculum and teaching practice, Carlos was forced to recognize that discrimination on the basis of class and race exists in both societies, not just in the United States as he had initially believed given his personal life experiences. Carlos learned that the issues related to oppression and inequality are complex, yet he remains committed to teaching for greater social justice. He attributes his clarity of thought and commitment to having participated in the ITE Program. Carlos pointed out the never-ending challenge of "walking his talk":

> I have got to stay strong in my position as a teacher and continue to fight for what is right for children ... the hard part is living out your philosophy, *tu sabes la politica* [you know the politics] ... our California professors were also on the same philosophical page. It [the Mexico experience] highlighted the harsh realities of the children we face in our classrooms. I truly believe that this program offers what no other campus program can attempt to duplicate! (emphasis added)

In the above quote, Carlos makes reference to the opportunities to live in Mexico and California and to be exposed to students from various cultural and social groups. He likened living and learning in Mexico, no matter the brevity of the experience, to the experiences of Mexican immigrant children whom he encountered in California classrooms. He often discussed the high level of dissonance and reverse culture shock he felt upon returning to the United States and likened it to what immigrant children go through but recognized that, while he always had the option to leave the discomfort of living in Mexico, his immigrant students do not have the choice to leave the United States. Carlos emphasized the significance of exposing U.S. teachers to a variety of teaching contexts in order to make bare in their own school sites the unequal power relations and resulting inequalities they read about in coursework:

> The life lessons I learned when I lived and student-taught in Mexico, I utilize in my classroom today. The infrastructure of the program provided me with the opportunity to question the inequities with the goal to create change. In this program we were expected to engage in projects of change. And as far as I am concerned, change is what is necessary, pero *que batalla* [but, what a battle]. (emphasis added)

Carlos highlights the four teaching stages and teaching contexts he experienced in the program (he refers to them as "infrastructures" in the quote above) that brought him face-to-face with four distinct student and teacher groups: private, public, and indigenous school settings in Mexico and Spanish/English dual-language classrooms in California public schools. In these four teaching contexts, Carlos witnessed the playing out of unequal power relations and the *mis*teaching of low social status and ethnic groups. The mistreatment of Mexican indigenous students and the deficit views of them held by mainstream Mexicans was especially enlightening to Carlos as his journal entries illustrated, specifically one that was written during his tenure working at the indigenous school in Oaxaca, Mexico:

> Indigenous education is sacred, not a paradise, despite all of the limitations imposed by the dominant ideology, it remains a space of possibility where teachers and community continue to labor for freedom. I have come to realize that education is a practice of freedom where we must continue to work around, through, and beyond boundaries.

In addition to interviewing Carlos, I have also analyzed his journal entries. His journal entries reflect many of the struggles and triumphs he experienced when working with the indigenous community in Oaxaca. The impact of how this indigenous community maintains its Native "worldview" despite pressures to assimilate (from the Mexican mainstream culture) helped him to make sense of cross-cultural and cross-economic class lived experiences. Carlos's ability to cross over to the indigenous worldview taught him how to work and teach in an authentic manner. His teaching and interactions with all the people around him illustrated his sensitivity toward others and the environment. For example, the Earth became his chalkboard, the leaves, streams, and wildlife became his science/literacy lessons.

One of Carlos's journal entries discussed a poetry lesson that he taught by a stream, adjacent to the indigenous school, where his students wrote about *El Sonido del Silencio* (The Sound of Silence) the title of his poetry lesson. The poems written by these 3rd and 4th grade students were telling of their oppressive yet hopeful reality with brutal honesty. It was during lessons such as these that Carlos discovered his cross-cultural and cross-social class strengths—strengths that continue to guide the discourses with his present students. He learned that he was able to cross ideological borders, to make his students' reality part of his reality. As a researcher, this was very impressive to me, because many of my students, given their close contact with students and their awareness of asymmetrical power dynamics, avoided becoming what Bartolomé (2000) calls, "unconscious voyeurs." *Unconscious voyeurs* refers to individuals who border cross into new cultures, but who never cease to view these cross-cultural and cross-economic situations through unacknowledged assimilationist and deficit ideological lenses. Instead,

Carlos and many other student teachers engaged in authentic "border crossing" as defined by Bartolomé (2002).

When I asked him to share an example of the effects of his increased ideological clarity on his teaching, Carlos quickly and passionately described a social studies lesson he developed for his 4th grade students in Mexico. He explained how he infused into this social studies unit the reality of classism and racism. His lesson grew out of the California History and Social Science Framework (California Department of Education, 1998), specifically out of the Historical, Political, and Economic Literacy Strands (California Department of Education, 1998). Carlos clearly understands that engaging students in critical literacy does not preclude his responsibility to address the California Framework and Standards (California Department of Education). It has been his practice to reject relying on prepackaged curricula because it is more motivating to students when he incorporates into lessons his students' relevant real-life experiences. He explained that his lessons work best when the curriculum is co-created with students. Carlos believes that a co-created curriculum ignites students' interest and desire to engage in critical thinking. In order to teach the Social Studies Economic Literacy Strand, Carlos developed an employment-phenotype chart to illustrate the relationship between type of employment position to skin color in both Mexico and the United States. Carlos utilized a visual display of how the most undesirable (manual labor intensive), "backbreaking" jobs, such as fieldworkers, restaurant dishwashers, and maids were occupied by people of color. In contrast, the more "respectable" jobs, such as professors, doctors, and scientists were occupied by White people. He brought into his classroom what Scheurich (2000) describes as racialized job patterns where the positions at the bottom of the hierarchy are filled by people of color and "[a]s you work your way up the hierarchy toward the better paid more satisfying jobs, the color slowly turns lighter, until by the time you get to the top, it is almost white" (p. 5).

Carlos's students were stunned by this lesson, yet they went on to make personal connections with the information on the chart. For example, many of them discussed how their father, brother, uncle, and other family members had gone to the United States for "better" employment opportunities but that they had never thought about the relationship between skin color and job type. All they knew was that their family members secured jobs in the United States and sent U.S. dollars home. Furthermore, they sadly recognized that the possibility of reuniting with their loved one was highly unlikely. Throughout the lesson the students offered the U.S. locations where their family members worked: Michigan, Oregon, Chicago, Los Angeles, and San Francisco. During Carlos's later activities in other content areas, his students would continue to make reference to this particular social studies lesson.

Carlos continues to teach this social studies unit because, as he states, "it is real," and the students "react very positively" to his courage in teaching the truth and the unmasking racism in the employment sector. Despite the young age of his students, Carlos discovered that they were capable of understanding and discussing classism and racism. Although many educators might criticize this teacher as unnecessarily exposing students to harsh realities appropriate for only adult learners, Carlos believes that minority students, no matter what their age and regardless of whether or not they have the "appropriate discourse" or language to discuss racism, have experienced discrimination (no matter how innocuous or implicitly expressed) and intuitively understand. Furthermore, by having a teacher legitimize and provide a language for what so many students experience, the teacher offers the students a tremendous service. Carlos described the results of the lesson and his students' reactions during part of the interview:

> After this powerful [lesson], my relationship with [the Mexican students] was one that I would describe as deep in that they knew that my lessons would always deal with real-world issues. At that moment I felt that I knew how to ignite their curiosity for learning in profound ways. The most amazing thing, though, was that I learned so much about teaching and learning ... through this process. ... I believe I began to develop ideological clarity ... it was only the beginning to my journey as a teacher with a clear purpose.

The results of this lesson confirmed to Carlos that to effectively reach and motivate students, his curriculum had to reflect his students' lives including the harsh realities such as their knowledge about racism and classism. There is no doubt that creating and teaching this particular lesson demonstrates Carlos's courage and commitment to ensuring his students' quality, culturally relevant instruction.

CARLOS'S POLITICALLY STRATEGIC AND SUBVERSIVE WORK

During our interview, Carlos described a second teaching experience that similarly served to increase his ideological clarity. This experience took place in his California school and exemplifies the prevalent covert racist attitudes of school administrators and classroom teachers when it comes to "schooling" immigrant children. For Carlos, this incident crystallized his role as a liberatory educator who must defend his students, even from teachers such as the Resource Specialist he describes in the next quote:

> Last year, when I took over this Newcomer class and in the middle of a chaotic first day of school, late in the afternoon a new student was brought to my classroom, and the [expletive] Resource Specialist, excuse my language, said to me, "This is as 'wet' as

they get, 'straight from the jungle.'" I dealt with her comment later as I was shuffling all of the paper work. *Tu sabes* [You know], what the system does to domesticate us. This young man [arrived with] unmatched socks, clothes that were too big for him, and uncombed hair. Yet he looked at me with this joy in his eyes, and said, "*Tu eras mi maestro en Oaxaca*," ["You were my teacher in Oaxaca."]. He was now a few years older and more mature looking then when I last saw him. At that moment I was not able to hold back the tears. (emphasis added)

Carlos explained that he cried because he could see in the Resource Teacher the same chauvinism and parochialism that can be seen at the U.S. national level and that opposes rather than joins border communities. This chance encounter with his former Oaxacan Mexican pupil put him tangibly in that "contact zone" experienced by immigrant students often at the hands of educators who, ironically, make the claim, based on their personal and academic/professional background, that they are "there" for "these" children (Pratt, 1990; Ríos, 1996). Macedo (personal communication, 2005) goes so far as to call such unsympathetic and antagonistic educators such as the one described by Carlos as "poverty pimps" because they make their living off the backs of the very students they disrespect and mistreat. Carlos explained why this particular occurrence constituted a significant event:

> You asked me about a significant event; it does not get more significant than this in my book. This [ITE] program positions us in a space that prepares us ideologically for the kind of students we must become advocates for [them] and embrace [them].

Carlos describes another result of having participated in the ITE program—learning how to keep "one foot in" and "one foot out" in order to become a strategic educator. Paulo Freire (1998a, 1998b) explains that for teachers to work effectively with subordinated student groups, they must learn to be strategic in order to keep their job while carrying out their revolutionary work. Freire maintains that in order to be an effective educator, one cannot be *wholly* an insider or an outsider. Carlos learned to strategically work within, through, and around the educational arena in order to systematically subvert an educational system that disrespects and mistreats low socioeconomic status and linguistic minority students. Carlos has come to understand that he must adhere to the state standards and teach to them, although he may not agree with a "lock-step" curricular orientation. Consequently, he has learned to be strategic in his pedagogical practices. Carlos explained how he balances meeting state standards with offering students a student-centered and critical education:

> First of all, to get it right, as in tenure, I must be very well informed of all the content area standards, and the California Standards for the Teaching Profession, *por que aquí*

es todo lo que les importa [because here that is all that matters]. But, you and I know that it goes way beyond the standards with my students and the space of freedom I have created in my teaching, I bring in their reality. I have come to see their reality as my own! Students need to understand *sus condiciones* [their conditions], and, most importantly, what they can do to change their position of low status.

Carlos realizes that to work for social justice is often difficult and painful, yet he is fearless when broaching difficult and controversial topics typically treated as nonexistent by most teachers. He is self-empowered, strategic, optimistic but realistically so, not in a "blind," irresponsible, and unreflective manner.

Carlos goes on to discuss his convictions about moving toward a more hopeful future by becoming a transformative intellectual teacher and, in the process, provides one more example of how he has learned to be politically strategic or "creative," as he calls it. He explains how he subverts his school's English-only mandate during the English language development[9] (ELD) period as if to ensure that English is comprehensible to all his students:

> I believe that to have a clear teaching ideology, I must have full knowledge of how the political educational system works and my role in it ... *por ejemplo* [for example]: I will not compromise what I know is good and right for my students such as biliteracy instruction, meaning comprehensible input for my newcomers. I have been told that [according to district policy] I am not to use Spanish when I am teaching ELD, [he makes hand gestures for "in quotes"] it is *English time* only. So I have established what we call *language brokers*,[10] in this manner I assign students to help each other. I will not compromise my students' cognitive understanding to an English-only ideology. So, I will not sell out my critical literacy ideology because I am afraid to lose my job. Instead, I became *creative*. I explain [problem pose] to my students the political language dilemma and as a community of learners we solve it. In addition to this, I also stay on top of the latest political issues and bring them into my lessons. I revolve my lessons, no matter what content area, around social political issues. (emphasis added)

Carlos reflectively and consciously works toward perfecting his strategic and subversive pedagogy to continue serving his students to the best of his ability. He reiterates the exhausting nature of his work yet maintains a tone of optimism when he states:

> As discouraged as I may get at times, like [I was at the time] when you first asked me to be part of this study. [At that time,] I felt like quitting this vocation. But, now I realize that I must get more strength from my strength to help create the change necessary for better conditions for our students.

In the above quote, Carlos addresses the reality of moments of teacher paralysis and inaction. However, he also understands that he must begin anew and continue being a strategic and subversive risk-taker. Thus, Carlos demonstrates impressive meta-cognitive awareness and reflective ability as he describes the struggles he experiences when he is tempted to give up the fight. He continues along this same vein stating:

> It is important that I begin to take more risks, *por que* [because] I have gotten to the point where my mind gets colonized and paralyzed, consequently not allowing me to follow through with what I know is right. I have been willing to take little risks, not big risks. I have developed strong convictions about my personal and professional values and the values of the school system that I work with ... standards, tests, and English-Only is their value system. Therefore this creates lots of tension. Reflection is another important factor, I learn so much from reflection. I have been working with my own students on the reflective process. They are so mature when they engage in reflection. I do this through a 'Socratic Seminar,' a teaching method, I was told by my principal, is only for *gifted* students [he makes hand gestures for "in quotes"]. When she told me this, I asked her what made her think my students were not gifted. Hey Cristina, maybe that is why my principal told you I am *too ambitious*.[11] (emphasis added)

SIGNIFICANCE OF CARLOS'S STORY

Carlos's journey reveals his courage to find another way of knowing that is in opposition to the domestication of teachers. Upon observing his classroom, all of the details that depict how he coherently walks his talk cannot be done justice in this short chapter. It is necessary to point out, however, that Carlos fully benefited from the ITEP because he came in predisposed to learn about the politics of education. He entered with an open mind and heart that allowed him to see oppression, racism, and classism more comprehensively and theoretically. Hence, he came to better comprehend how these mechanisms of oppression take on different forms in different contexts and across borders. He clearly realizes that he needs to be politically strategic and subversive in order to keep his job while working on behalf of his students. He practices "critical" culturally responsive pedagogy by incorporating his students' cultures into his curriculum. Indeed, he goes even farther in that he also includes the harsh elements of their lives, for example, racism. Similarly, he appreciates that he must be a reflective and strategic risk-taker to continually improve his students' academic opportunities.

Although I arrived at similar findings with other participants, it seems that those students who come in with personal experience, with experiences of marginalization, are better able to grasp the theory covered in coursework and to perceive it in classroom settings. The ITE program has prepared many highly effective bilingual teachers like Carlos. However, it is critical that we continue to search for ways to provide authentic experiences for students who do not come in with life experiences and knowledge about marginalization like Carlos.

CONCLUSION

This case study suggests that there is an urgency for both prospective and practicing teachers to develop ideological clarity to sustain and guide them in denouncing inhumane and discriminatory practices in the classroom. For the purpose of examining the implications from the perspective of teacher education, the findings have been clustered around a teacher's development with respect to his ideological clarity. Like the teacher in this study, realistic yet staying the course, Freire (1997) reminds us of how critical it is to identify the obstacles in order to create clear and realistic strategies to negotiate, navigate, and overcome them. Carlos's struggles toward ideological clarity illustrate the multiple issues imbedded in the epistemological journey of becoming a bilingual teacher with courage, solidarity, and ethical commitment.

To this end, teacher preparation should never be reduced to a form of training. Freire (1998a, 1998b) argues that besides technical skills, teachers must be equipped with the knowledge of what it means to teach with courage. Freire challenges us to denounce the inequities that oppress historically subordinated student populations by teaching with courage, solidarity, and ethics. Teacher preparation must go beyond the technical preparation of teachers and be rooted in the ethical formation of both selves and history. Teachers must become empowered through the realization that they are part of a greater human story of being and becoming. They must learn that they can expand their vision to include multiple realities, and they must know that their ideological clarity will be part of a greater story.

NOTES

1. A pseudonym was used as a way to protect the identity of my research participant. This case study was conducted over a period of 5 years after Carlos graduated from the ITE program.
2. California State University International Teacher Education Program (CSU-ITEP) is an international teacher education program that has been in existence since 1996. Web site: http://www.gateway.calstate.edu/csuienet/country.cfm?countryID=7004721.
3. Bartolomé (2002) defines "cultural border crosser" as "an individual who is able and willing to develop empathy with the cultural "other" and to authentically view as equal the values of the "other" while conscious of the cultural group's subordinated social status in the greater society. Border crossers are persons who will critically consider the positive cultural traits of the "other" and, at the same time, are able to critique the discriminatory practices of their culture that may be involved in the creation of the cultural "other" in the first place. In other words, a border crosser,

while embracing the cultural "other" must also divest from his/her cultural privilege that often functions as a cultural border itself" (p. 189).

Bartolomé's definition of a "cultural border crosser" differs from more conventional definitions that "merely focus on a person's ability to successfully interact and exist in an alternative social, economic or ethnic cultural reality without dealing with the real issues of asymmetrical power relations and subordination. Members of the dominant culture typically tend to border cross without compromising their position of cultural and social privilege. This type of border crosser can travel the world, study the 'other' in a detached and curious manner without ever recognizing that cultural groups occupy different positions of power and status and that many cultural perceptions and practices result from such power asymmetries. Often, these types of ideologically and politically 'blind' border crossers assume 'tourist' or 'voyeur' perspectives that are very much tainted by their unconscious deficit and white supremacist ideologies" (p. 189).

4. Villenas (1996) defines "Chicano" and "Chicana" as self-identified terms used by peoples of Mexican origin. They are political terms of self-determination and solidarity that originated in the Chicano liberation movement of the 1960s. Chicanos and Chicanas are members of a caste minority that share the same ethnic consciousness and regional and linguistic experiences.

5. "Newcomers" in Carlos's classroom are those students designated with limited English proficiency, have little experience with the American school system, lack academic preparation, and in some cases, are students who have experienced psychological and emotional trauma. Constantino and Lavadenz (1993) provide the rationale for Newcomer Programs: to respond to the needs of students with little schooling, educational interruption, trauma, and extreme culture shock. In their study they go on to describe the program designs and policies in use in California districts with Newcomer Programs, including the districts' intake criteria, program structure, exit policies, class size, curricula, and policies regarding language of instruction, teacher selection, staff development, and program evaluation.

6. Santana Elementary School is used as a pseudonym to protect confidentiality.

7. English for the Children (1998): Presented as California Proposition 227. An initiative that would end bilingual education in the state of California and institute an "English-Only" mandate for all K-12 school instruction. For more information, see: www.onenation.org.

8. No Child Left Behind Act (2002): Signed into law by President George W. Bush, it is the federal government's most drastic change to education. Its primary goal is to ensure that children receive the "best" education as defined by new federal government standards to be followed by each state. For more information, see: www.edgov/nclb/landing.jthtml?src=pb.

9. English Language Development (ELD): Explicit and systematic strategies to teach English to non-English speaking students, also referred to as English as a Second Language (ESL).

10. Language brokers are not simply "bilingual informants" but active agents operating within the complexity of a specialized social event. The advantage of the term "brokering" is that it focuses on the whole cultural meaning of such an event rather than just the translation, and reflects the dialogic complexity of such an intercultural transaction (Temple, 2002).

Carlos considers his language brokers to be highly gifted students. Language brokers develop their competence and knowledge of cultural and linguistic conventions, customs, and practices which support effective communication between two languages. This competence is extensive, both as language translators and interpreters, and in terms of social competence, has led one researcher to label the brokering behaviors of these children as "giftedness" (Valdés, 2003).

11. Before I visited Carlos's classroom, I followed protocol and explained my research to the school principal and asked for permission to observe his class. She stated at that point that Carlos was

much "too ambitious" with his students. When I entered Carlos's, classroom, I became aware of the principal's deficit view of Carlos's students, as well as the empowering climate Carlos created for the young people entrusted to him.

REFERENCES

Alfaro, C. (2003). *Transforming teacher education: Developing ideological clarity as a means for teaching with courage, solidarity and ethics.* Unpublished doctoral dissertation, Claremont Graduate University & San Diego State University.

Apple, M. (2004). *Ideology and curriculum.* New York: Taylor & Francis.

Bartolomé, L. I. (2000). Democratizing bilingualism: The role of the critical teacher Education. In Z. F. Beykont (Ed.), *Lifting every voice: Pedagogy and politics of bilingualism* (pp. 167–186). Boston: Harvard Education Publishing Group.

Bartolomé, L. I. (2002). Creating an equal playing field: Teachers as advocates, border crossers, and cultural brokers. In Z. F. Beykont (Ed.), *The power of culture: Teaching across language difference* (pp. 167–191). Harvard Education Publishing Group.

Bartolomé, L. I. (2004, July 16). Personal communication.

California Department of Education. (1998). *California history and social science frameworks and standards.* Retrieved July 15, 2005, from http://score.rims.k12.ca.us/Standards/grades/?g=4.

Constantino, R., & Lavadenz, M. (1993). Newcomer schools: First impressions. *Peabody Journal of Education, 69*(1), 82–101.

Freire, P. (1997). *Pedagogy of the heart.* New York: Continuum.

Freire, P. (1998a). *Pedagogy of freedom: Ethics, democracy and civic discourse.* New York: Rowman & Littlefield.

Freire, P. (1998b). *Teachers as cultural workers: Letters to those who dare to teach.* Boulder, CO: Westview.

Macedo, D. (2003). *Literacy for stupidification.* Paper presented at the National Council of Teachers of English Assembly for Research Mid-Winter Conference, February 21–23, 2003. The College of Education & Human Development, University of Minnesota.

Macedo, D. (2005, February 6). Personal communication.

Ogbu, J. (1992). Understanding cultural diversity and learning. *Educational Researcher, 21*(8), 287–429.

Pratt, M. L. (1990). Arts of the contact zone. *Profession, 91,* 33–40.

Ríos, F. A. (1996). Teachers' principles of practice in multicultural classrooms. In F. A. Ríos (Ed.), *Teacher thinking in cultural contexts* (pp. 129–150). Albany: State University of New York Press.

Scheurich, J. (2000). *White anti-racist scholarship: An advocacy.* Paper presented at the Annual Meeting of the American Educational Research Association, New Orleans, LA.

Skutnabb-Kangas, T. (1981). *Bilingualism or not.* Clevedon, UK: Multilingual Matters.

Temple, B. (2002). Crossed wires: interpreters, translators, and bilingual workers in cross-language research. *Qualitative Health Research, 12*(6), 81–93.

Valdés, G. (2003). *Expanding definitions of giftedness: The case of young interpreters from immigrant communities.* Mahwah, NJ: Lawrence Erlbaum.

Villenas, S. (1996). *The colonizer/colonized Chicana ethnographer: Identity, marginalization, and co-optation in the field.* Retrieved July 15, 2005, from http://www.edreview.orgharvard96/1996/wi96/w96front.htm.

CHAPTER TWELVE

Politicized Mothering: Authentic Caring Among African American Women Teachers

TAMARA BEAUBOEUF-LAFONTANT

AESTHETIC AND AUTHENTIC CARING

As many researchers and theorists committed to the educational success of poor, immigrant, and minority children have described, schools too often engage in social reproduction rather than social transformation. Through ability grouping, unexamined teacher attitudes, and overall school climates, distinctions, both overt and subtle, are made between dominant group students ("our children") and children from subordinated groups ("other people's children") (Delpit, 1995; see also Case, 1997; Gay, 2000; Kailin, 1999; Villegas & Lucas, 2002a). Consequently, many researchers identify educational reform as centrally requiring an examination and transformation of our identities and relationships as educators (Cochran-Smith, 1995; Nieto, 1999). As Lisa Delpit (1995) insists:

> [T]he teachers, the psychologists, the school administrators ... look at "other people's children" and see damaged and dangerous caricatures of the vulnerable and impressionable beings before them. ... What are we really doing to better educate poor children and children of color? ... What should we be doing? The answers, I believe, lie not in a proliferation of new reform programs but in some basic understandings of who we are and how we are connected to and disconnected from one another. (xiii, xiv, xv)

Delpit casts school failure as the logical manifestation of a "relational breakdown" (Ward, 1995), in which teachers see little in common or shared in purpose with their students. That is, the academic success of students from subordinated backgrounds lies very much in the quality of the relationships which their teachers establish with them, and in the form of caring they demonstrate.

Investigating the specific school contexts and teacher attitudes involved in the academic experiences of Mexican-immigrant and Mexican-American students, Angela Valenzuela (1999) focuses on teacher caring as the interpersonal source of the students' success and failure. She maintains that teachers are invested in an aesthetic caring when they value only those students who care about school-related "things and ideas" (which tend to have a strong assimilationist bent). For their part, students desire relationships based on authentic caring, with teachers seeing them as valuable, interesting human beings and not dismissing or derogating them based on societal stereotypes. Valenzuela asserts that feeling cared for in this way is the basic precondition for all students to sufficiently care about their education.

While not named as such, the practice of authentic caring is present in much literature focusing on African American teachers, from segregation to the present (Beauboeuf-Lafontant, 1999, 2002; Foster, 1993; Dempsey & Noblit, 1993; Siddle-Walker, 1996; Case, 1997). Although noted for its importance in the education of Black students in particular, most investigations do not analyze the nuances of such authentic caring to demonstrate the political and not simply cultural congruence that exists between the teachers, their students, and the local community. Furthermore, they are not sensitive to the fact that most Black teachers are women who draw on particular understandings of caring that are gendered as well as raced. As I explore in the next section, the concept of "politicized mothering" (Beauboeuf, 1997; Beauboeuf-Lafontant, 1999) reflects critical aspects of teachers' authentic caring—their maternal approach to students, the political awareness that shapes such maternal concern, and the transhistorical and communal vision of social change that sustains their commitments to children.

A MATERNAL APPROACH TO STUDENTS

The relationship of choice among exemplary African American women teachers as a guide for their interactions with students is the familiar and familial motherchild relationship. A public example of such teaching is that of Marva Collins, the founder of the renowned Westside Preparatory School in Chicago. Over the last 25 years, Collins has drawn out "extraordinary" capabilities from her students, who are "at risk" for school and social failure because they are poor African American children living in the neighboring housing projects. Reflecting on her frustration with the public school she left to begin her own academy, Collins explicitly connects her teaching visions to her sensibilities as a mother:

I couldn't escape the problem [of poor education], as a teacher or as a mother. These parts of my life were inextricably interwoven; at Delano I was fighting for the kind of education I wanted for my own children. As a parent I tended to be protective, and I always felt that same driving concern as a teacher. I could never walk out of Delano at 3:15 and leave the school and the students entirely behind me. Were my students going home or would they wander the streets? Were their clothes warm enough? Would their stomachs be full tonight and would they have sheets on their beds? (Collins & Tamarkin, 1982/1990, p. 73)

Collins views her inability not to mother her students as a matter of fact, and as a pedagogical strength rather than weakness. Indeed, in the Ten Teaching Commandments that she has developed for her own faculty, the first reads, "Thou shalt love the students as you would love your own children" (Collins, 1992, p. 178). Caring like a mother for her educationally underserved students focused her decision to take maternal steps—that is, to create an alternative structure in which she could educate her students and fortify them intellectually against adversity.

Such a maternal caring for students is also a central theme of a *People* magazine article entitled, "Momma knows best." Affectionately called "Momma Hawk" by her middle school students, Corla Hawkins began her own school, Recovering the Gifted Child Academy, after seeing too many poor children systematically failed by the public schools. Hawkins's teaching very clearly emanates from a vocation to extend herself, as a surrogate mother, to those children who needed her most:

I felt I could take the dysfunctional family structure these children were used to and replace it with a new family structure that stresses success, personal achievement and self-esteem. ... God gave me a dream—to take care of children of rejection. I literally saw myself going around the world hugging and loving children nobody else wanted. (Valente, 1996, pp. 45, 47)

Describing Momma Hawk, a board member of the school says, "Corla is so successful because she is so human. ... She's not on a pedestal. She feels things deeply. She hurts" (Valente, 1996, p. 46). At the same time, however, such emotional connection with her students does not preclude Hawkins from "run[ning] my school based on a corporate model" (p. 46), complete with a time clock and strict discipline.

For educators to emphasize and insist on having such an urgency about children demonstrates their belief that through aesthetic caring, teachers may be failing precisely those students considered to be failures. In the words of a high school history teacher, authentic caring contextualizes a teacher's role within the student's life:

You can tell a good teacher, because they keep talking about "my kids" ... [and] part of that is that *passion*. And saying, "my kids" means that when they walk through that door, you're accepting the responsibility that for the next nine months, what happens in your classroom, and what happens to those *children* is what you do with them. And you've got a precious life there. And if you mess it up, you're not just messing up a grade here or a grade there, that you're messing up a life. And that's an enormous responsibility. (Beauboeuf, 1997, p. 107; original emphasis).

Taking maternal responsibility for children means that one does not immediately delegate or outsource "problems": As Momma Hawk notes, when a student is disruptive, "the teacher's first reaction is to get him out of the class instead of saying maybe this child doesn't have anybody" (Valente, 1996, p. 44). Too often, in her opinion, teachers lacking a parental urgency (Jervis, 1996) take the easy, nonfamililal/nonmaternal way out difficult situations. They demonstrate aesthetic caring and reveal their inability or unwillingness to seek excellence in their students from subordinated backgrounds (Ladson-Billings, 1994).

The embrace of a maternal sensibility by such Black women reveals how mothering as well as teaching are influenced by the cultural expectations of women and the societal evaluation (or devaluation) of mothers. In her interviews with socially progressive Jewish, Catholic, and Black women, and retired White women, Kathleen Casey (1990, 1993) found that many of the White educators had a desire to "deconstruct the maternal." Mainstream, European-American, and patriarchal notions of teaching seemed to determine their discomfort with the maternal, even when they could recall ennobling models of women as mothers from their personal lives—models which resisted the patriarchal expectations of women. For the progressive White women, their commitments to social justice hinged upon their reworking of their professional relationships, as women, to both children/students and men/administrators: "Since the maternal relationship can leave a woman in our society so materially and psychologically vulnerable, it is no wonder that so many look for another metaphor to describe their connections with children" (1990, p. 313).

A strikingly different approach to the maternal emerged among the Black women teachers. They did not evidence a domesticated or European American view of womanhood or mothering in their reflections on educational philosophies and practice. In fact, the maternal served as a relational compass for their teaching. Unlike their colleagues, the African American women did not allow the school's appropriation of the maternal to circumscribe their own desire to relate to students in this familiar way. Rather, these teachers saw their maternal qualities and the mother-child relationship as central to their resistance to domination, both patriarchal and racial. Casey clarifies the Black teachers' maternal orientation to students:

> The relationship between mother and child is not exclusive and private, but is part of the wider family which is one's 'people'. ... [B]ecause of the social context out of

which this understanding has been constructed, the maternal is not seen as an individual burden, but as reciprocity among members of the group. Whatever nurture these teachers provide, it comes back to them; as one teacher says about her students, "they love your very soul." (1990, p. 316)

When a maternal approach to subordinated students is embraced by these educators, it allows them to recognize children's abilities and potential and to take (rather than avoid) responsibility for their development. In these classrooms, children find that they have not left Momma at home, that she is standing right here, in *loco parentis* (Beauboeuf, 1997, p. 76). Taking the role of a mother is not an effort to replace or subvert biological mothers, but a way of emphasizing a deep connection to the children. The idea of caring as a mother represents one of the most powerful ways the women know to reach out to children and take the teaching enterprise seriously. The maternal aspect of their caring is an insistent reminder that effective teaching depends of the quality of the relationships one establishes with students, and that teaching allows one to have a profound effect on a child's overall development. However, for politicized mothers, their version of authentic caring is not simply affective. Critical to their caring and effectiveness is their understanding of society and the way it distorts the lives of immigrant, poor, and ethnic minority children. They have political clarity.

POLITICAL CLARITY

Political clarity is the recognition by teachers of the structural relationships between schools and society that largely determine the successes and failures of students (Bartolomé, 1994). Political clarity contributes to caring by demonstrating the stakes involved in resisting societal imperatives not to care for subordinated children. For example, Marva Collins emphasizes the promise of her students, finding something admirable about each child every day. This habit is tied to her fundamental belief that good teachers "are willing to polish and shine until the true luster of each student comes through" (p. 6). In 'shining' her students, Collins does not sentimentally glorify them. She polishes them so that they may more effectively deal with a social reality that is unfair and which attempts to hide their true luster. As a politicized mother, the purpose of her teaching is to help children question reality along with her and to discuss its implications for them.

Because Collins's students are poor children from housing projects located in an urban ghetto, the social assumption (and perhaps desire) is that they will fail, both in school and in life. Rather than ignoring or minimizing the presence of such expectations, Collins makes the personal and political ramifications of their situations clear to them:

> If you throw away your life, you're just letting society have its way. ... You know, boys and girls, there are some people who look at places like this, neighborhoods like Garfield Park, and they say, 'Oh, children from there are not very smart. They aren't going to grow up to be anyone or do anything special.' If you decide to waste your lives, you are letting all those people be right. No one can tell you what you will be. Only you have the power to decide for yourselves. (Collins & Tamarkin, 1982/1990, p. 85)

While Collins speaks of her children needing to make choices that have lifelong implications, she also recognizes that they need guidance and sponsors, in their families as well as in their school. In expressing her maternal responsibility for the students' academic development, she commits herself to being a strong ally regardless of their home situations. As she repeats to her students, "I am not going to give up on you. I am not going to let you give up on yourself" (Collins & Tamarkin, 1982/1990, p. 87).

Very significantly, Collins lays bare the political realities that her students, all elementary-aged, are experiencing. Such honesty about the stakes of getting an education, particularly when one is marginalized and oppressed by society, is not common practice in our schools, whether at the secondary level (Fine, 1991) or in teacher education programs (Groulx, 2001; Kailin, 1999; Villegas & Lucas, 2002a). Teachers apparently fear (or falsely believe) that being truthful with minority children will demoralize them even further and seal their fate. From the perspective of these African American teacher-mothers, to withhold knowledge is to disempower those children.

Politically clear educators understand the necessity of seeing through stereotypes as false representations of children's realities and possibilities. As one communications teacher remarks:

> I teach you the way I perceive you to be. ... [Y]ou've got to start with a base level of understanding these kids as *human beings*. We're all subject to the stereotypes of our society, and we can't assume that because we're well-intended [chuckle], we don't carry with us all of that. You know, that sheltering, "Don't teach them that history." Or, "Don't tell them that." Or, "I feel so sorry for you. I *expect* you to be poor. I know you only have one parent. Your mother probably doesn't know how to be a mother" [all said in a gentle, yet condescending voice]. Hey, you've got to help them see within their own situation the strength and the richness. (Beauboeuf, 1997, pp. 122–123; original emphasis)

The politicization of these teachers emerges with their demonstration, in deed and in word, of their understanding of society, an understanding that does not shy away from the reality of domination nor from the existence of resistance struggles against oppression. In essence, loving students means discussing such insights with them, not withholding knowledge from them. Audrey Thompson (1998) describes the cultural significance of such openness: "[C]aring in the Black family has had to be, in part, *about* the surrounding society, because it has had to provide children with the understanding and the strategies they need to survive racism. ... [Thus] love and caring do not step back from the world in order to return to innocence, but step out into the world in order to change it" (p. 532; original emphasis). Being a politicized mother, and not simply a maternal educator, entails more than having a professed and global love for children: A politicized educator advocates for, and struggles with children—especially those considered "other" in society—out of a clear-sighted understanding of how and why society marginalizes some children while embracing others. In the words of a high school English teacher reflecting on her choice of placement during student teaching:

> The point is that I requested the remedial kids, because I knew most of the kids of color were there, and I really wanted to work with them. I want to help all students, all people, but I *do* have a special affinity towards helping people of color, because historically there's been such a disadvantage. (Beauboeuf, 1997, p. 80; original emphasis)

As politicized mothers, these teachers often have little patience with liberal, White savior attitudes that exist among co-workers. They bristle at practices that fail to see the parallels between ability grouping and segregation, and often are angered by teachers who enter urban schools without an examination of their motivations for teaching children of color:

> The fact that you can read and write is not sufficient. The fact that a white university gave you a piece of paper that said you had a legal right to work in our school is not sufficient either. Why should we allow you into our community? ... What specifically can you contribute? How do you know we can use it? What's in it for you beside a paycheck? Can you work anywhere else? If not, why would *we* want you? ... What of true value do Black and other people of color have that draws you to us and makes you want to learn, learn, and suffer with us? ... *What is it that you want so badly, you're willing to endure the challenges in order to get it?* (Berlak & Moyenda, 2001, p. 155; original emphasis).

In passionately caring for and being committed to marginalized students, politicized mothers do not suffer well those individuals who see their students/children as "other," who take a "self-righteous missionary [attitude] with the answers for others" (Howard, 1999, p. 14). At the same time, they are quick to commend the efforts of those educators who are certain rather than "uncertain allies" (Cochran-Smith, 1995) to children and teachers of color:

> You have some White teachers in [my] school, oh, girl, they work, they work, and work, and work, and work with these kids. They work with the kids, just as if ... the kids were White or that they were Black. I really must say this. Some of these teachers really *love* the kids and go out for them, and *work with them*. (Beauboeuf, 1997, p. 79; original emphasis)

Although political clarity and a maternal sensibility are central to the everyday practice of politicized mothers, their overall investment in the teaching profession emerges from something perhaps less tangible and visible—a focus on self as change agent. It is this view of self which provides politicized mothers with the moral fortitude and vision to persevere in their particular form of caring and teaching.

SELF AS CHANGE AGENT

Politicized mothers engage with oppressive realities in spite of their recognition that social injustice is deep-seated and not easily dismantled. They are not naïve about the problems in urban education and the social problems of poverty and racism that negatively and disproportionately impact the lives of students from marginalized backgrounds. What sustains these politicized mothers, however, is their view that their efforts contribute to something, a larger project of people working for change. They see themselves as "agents of change" (Villegas & Lucas, 2002b) and their classrooms as "locations of possibility" (hooks, 1994). They are mindful of how teachers and schools can work to develop individuals, communities, and the potential of all. In so doing, they believe they can make change through their teaching methods and approach to students; they also are not afraid of being changed by their teaching.

A key manifestation of this perception of self as change agent comes in the teachers' discussion of feeling "called to teach." While not all politicized mothers are religious people or draw from specific religious traditions, they do often see themselves and their work in spiritual terms. Thus, when Momma Hawk speaks of her dream of "tak[ing] care of children of rejection" or of her belief that "every child is a gift from God and our job as teachers is to find the gift in each" (Valente, 1996, p. 44), she frames her teaching as a commitment and sees herself as having the spiritual resources to undertake it. A similar belief in students and in one's self emanates from a high school English teacher's conviction that students "can be *great* achievers. It's so *much* in them, you know, but it takes a *skillful* teacher, it takes a skillful *woman* to draw it out" (Beauboeuf, 1997, p. 83; original emphasis).

In the words of a junior high school communications educator, teaching is best understood as a process of "manifest[ing] the divinity within you."

> And that means for me. ... I want to develop a *kindness* and a *love* and a *patience* ... [a] level of *understanding*, of *humility*, of *groundedness*, of *goodness*. ... I think that there's something really spiritual about being an educator, because I think the only reason to learn is to teach. (Beauboeuf, 1997, p. 126; original emphasis)

Seeing themselves as change agents is also rooted in the ability of politicized mothers to regard development as a quintessentially human activity. In the words of civil rights activist and community educator Septima Clark,

> You know, the measure of a person is how much they develop in their life. Some people slow down in their growth after they become adults. You can hardly tell they are changing at all. But you never know when a person's going to leap forward, or change around completely. Just think of how much Martin Luther King, Jr., grew in his life. That was the greatest thing about him. ... I've seen growth like most people don't think is possible. I can even work with my enemies because I know from experience that they might have a change of heart any minute. (Ayers, 1998, p. 255)

A belief in change challenges politicized mothers to believe in others and themselves, to see growth as the joyful outcome of working for social transformation. In her address to teacher education students, elementary school teacher Sekani Moyenda states, "You will inevitably exercise poor judgment in critical situations in your classroom; everyone does. If you let the effects of racist conditioning cloud your judgment, you will only compound your errors" (Berlak & Moyenda, 2001, p. 152). Important about politicized mothers is not that they are perfect teachers or individuals, but that they challenge themselves to grow and learn from their experiences. Their fundamental goal is to become better in the world and to help students do the same. They understand that a fear of mistakes is debilitating to both student and teacher alike. States Marva Collins, "If you can't make mistakes, you can't make anything" (Collins & Tamarkin, 1982/1990, p. 23).

When teachers believe in personal and social change, their commitments to working for social justice rest on a concept of self that is part of rather than apart from other people. From this sense of interdependence, politicized mothers often establish classroom routines or norms that model such mutual responsibility. Such routines are well described by educational researcher George Noblit (1993) in his ethnography of the classroom dynamics of an African American teacher. Pam created rituals with her second-grade students so that as they performed daily tasks—such as cleaning the board, sharpening pencils, and reading the calendar—they were "serv[ing] the collective good" (p. 29). Moreover, academically weak children were not left to themselves, and no one was ever singled out for praise at the cost of others. In her interactions with students who were unable to answer questions, Pam still held them responsible for acquiring academic skills; however, she allowed them to do so in a supportive environment filled with "a lot of coaching to get it right and a lot of room to figure it out for yourself" (p. 29). Even when asking a question and choosing one student to answer, Pam would try to include the whole class: She would "let the hands wave for a while—long enough to allow the maximum number of hands to raise ... smile and make eye contact with all she could" (p. 33). Regardless of whether the answer given was correct, "she would connect for a brief moment with her eyes, words, humor, and attention" (p. 33). Instructive about Pam's teaching is how she acknowledged, but did not resign herself to, the "difficult" students and parents: "She could laugh at a lot of the tribulations of classroom life because neither the events nor her enjoyment of her students threatened her authority. In many ways, they constituted her moral authority" (Noblit, 1993, pp. 27, 28).

As a junior high school history teacher explains, politicized mothering requires that teachers see both teaching and change as interpersonal processes.

> I mean, it's not that you have all the answers. ... I think you have to have the right attitude, the right outlook that, "I'm about change; I'm not perfect." ... And I think we've got to sort of remove it from being sort of a personal attack to like trying to help us understand who we are so that we can help our students understand better who they are. (Beauboeuf, 1997, p. 95)

Because they include self-change in the project of social change, politicized mothers are guided by humility in their teaching.

> To suggest "I'm going to change you," is to suggest, "I know everything, and I have the right answer." ... *People aren't victories.* It's about, "So, what have you got to tell me? So let's talk for awhile, let's keep the conversation going, and maybe we'll both be changed by the end of this." ... [Change occurs in] increments. It's little steps. And I value the process. ... It's the process through which we go that's often the time during which you learn the most. (Beauboeuf, 1997, p. 127)

Informed by a belief in change, politicized mothering encourages educators to see their action as a humble, yet essential, contribution to an extensive, collaborative, and enduring project of social change. For these women, teaching is literally a reflection of "who I am"—who they aspire to be, and hope to develop into. Feeling called to teach, they understand the growth involved as essential to the development of their gift to work with children. They approach their teaching with a sense that it plays a central role in helping them develop into people who are knowledgeable about their subject matter, sensitive to the needs of other people, and committed to ideas that will benefit humanity. Such a concept of development provides them with a dynamic rather than static view of themselves. As teachers, they accept the challenge to become what the children in their classrooms need—adults who help them grow into whole people, despite subordination.

CONCLUSION AND IMPLICATIONS

Politicized mothering as a form of authentic caring compels us to reconsider several assumptions we may make about women, teaching, and the larger project of education. First, it suggests that alternatives exist to mainstream notions of maternal caring, which is often regarded as interpersonal, dyadic, and apolitical (Polatnik, 1996). Such a form of maternalism is particularly detrimental to the teaching of minority children as it undercuts both the teachers' and the students' potential for political activism and social transformation. Protecting children from adversity is not the same as preparing them to effectively deal with such circumstances. Furthermore, to see children as innocent and incapable of wondering about the problems of our society is in fact to misapprehend their levels of curiosity and involvement in their social worlds. It is also to condemn them, through our silence and avoidance, to the same despair we have about our social ills. However, once we begin to see caring and mothering in larger, socio-historical realms, we can recognize how in sharing knowledge we can also share power.

For those women [and men] uncomfortable with the political nature of caring, we might ask, "Whose limitations are they embracing as their own? And to what end?" Noblit's (1993) admission of his own uneasiness with the authority and caring of Pam's politicized mothering is instructive here:

> I understood caring as relational and reciprocal. ... I, who saw power linked to oppression in everything, did not want caring to be about power, and thereby about oppression. ... I wanted the 'ethic of caring' to be pristine, to be somehow beyond issues of power that I considered to be essentially hegemonic and masculine. (p. 26)

By associating power with masculinity and oppression, and caring with femininity and liberation, Noblit acknowledges that he erroneously left no room to explain the pedagogy of Pam, a woman whose pedagogy combined both power and caring. However, as a result of being instructed in her methods as a participant-observer in her class, he realized that power in and of itself is not hurtful and that power is not the same as the exploitation or oppression of another person. He therefore concludes that the real task of teaching is to find ways of holding truth to power, of using power to promote rather than thwart human development. A key way of manifesting this "good" power, notes Noblit, is heeding Pam's "emphasis on collectivity ... as a corrective for the seemingly rampant individualism of Americans in general" (p. 37). Thus, the ends of the use or avoidance of caring and power are critical to understand and examine.

Furthermore, to subscribe to a form of mothering in which the nature and purpose of one's caring are not interrogated, out of the belief that good intentions necessarily result in good actions, is deeply problematic. Alice McIntyre (1997) describes the politically unclear caring of several White female students in a preservice teaching program:

> The observations that are made by the participants reveal several stereotypes about students of color (e.g., unkempt, violent, unprepared). Confounding that is the fact that the participants' perceptions of themselves as caring and benevolent teachers make it difficult for them to even recognize those stereotypes. ... Rather than expressing anger and rage at children coming to school with no coats and ' "not having" what "they have," the participants' discourse lacked a sense of urgency about the need to restructure educational institutions. The participants conceptualize the problem as being internal to their students. The solution then is to "save" them. (pp. 667, 668)

In resorting to such a missionary-like paternalistic pedagogy or what Sara Ruddick terms "maternal militarism" (1992), women fail to see or care about "others," those beyond their immediate families and communities. Under the guise of "saving" students from themselves, they want to fix the children rather than "nurture and support them, and sort of help them to figure out things" for themselves (Beauboeuf, 1997, p. 141). Furthermore, failing to see change as occurring in increments, teachers with a missionary zeal also run the risk of succumbing to self-righteous despair about the enormity of the social problems of poverty, racism, and general injustice.

Lastly, in its understanding of social change, politicized mothering offers heartening, yet sobering, information about the nature of social activism. It suggests that caring may not result in immediate, self-congratulatory successes. In fact, because the struggle is long and social in nature, one cannot egocentrically base one's commitment on seeing instantaneous change: One must have the faith, as Noblit (1993) writes of Pam, that "You'll love me more after you leave me." As a politicized mother, one must reconcile oneself to the paradox that "peace is the struggle"—that is, "life is [lived] on the edge, and that's when the best self emerges" (Beauboeuf, 1997, p. 150). Thus, politicized mothers see themselves as dynamic agents for social justice precisely because they define themselves as having a sense of connection with and responsibility to the human struggle for freedom and justice. In other words, politicized mothering keeps people from failing into the numbness and self-absorption of despair. From the standpoint of politicized mothering, we understand that oppression, as a misuse of power, occurs when there is a disconnection between people—when people refuse or fail to care for each other. As a result, politicized mothering offers ways to repair such relational breakdowns by emphasizing the following: the agency that each of us has to treat others as our own; the obligation we have to understand as fully as we can the world around us; and the responsibility we have to make sure that our actions contribute to the larger human goal of freedom for all.

Politicized mothers bring to teaching a large part, if not all, of who they are and who they wish to become in the world. As a result they come to their teaching not as people disconnected from their knowledge of relationships, power, and the human capacity for good. Rather, they bring to the profession their commitments to engage in personal and social change. Seeing potential in society, their students, and themselves, they embody a powerful example of authentic caring and a compelling alternative to deficit-driven pedagogical approaches to students from subordinated backgrounds.

REFERENCES

Ayers, W. (1998). "We who believe in freedom cannot rest until it's done": Two dauntless women of the Civil Rights Movement and the education of a people. In C. Woyshner & H. Gelfond (Eds.), *Minding women: Reshaping the educational realm* (Harvard Educational Review Reprint Series, #30) (pp. 249–259). Cambridge, MA: Harvard University.

Bartolomé, L. (1994). Beyond the methods fetish: Toward a humanizing pedagogy. *Harvard Educational Review, 64*(2), 173–194.

Beauboeuf, T. (1997). *Politicized mothering among African American women teachers: A qualitative inquiry.* Unpublished doctoral dissertation, Harvard University.

Beauboeuf-Lafontant, T. (1999). A movement against and beyond boundaries: 'Politically relevant teaching' among African American teachers. *Teachers College Record, 100*(4), 702–723.

Beauboeuf-Lafontant, T. (2002). A womanist experience of caring: Understanding the pedagogy of exemplary Black women teachers. *The Urban Review, 34*(1), 71–86.

Berlak, A., & Moyenda, S. (2001). *Taking it personally: Racism in the classroom from kindergarten to college.* Philadelphia: Temple University Press.

Case, K. (1997). African American othermothering in the urban elementary school. *The Urban Review, 29*(1), 25–39.

Casey, K. (1990). Teacher as mother: Curriculum theorizing in the life histories of contemporary women teachers. *Cambridge Journal of Education 20*(3), 301–320.

Casey, K. (1993). *I answer with my life: Life histories of women teachers working for social change.* New York: Routledge.

Cochran-Smith, M. (1995). Uncertain allies: Understanding the boundaries of race and teaching. *Harvard Educational Review,* i(4), 541–570.

Collins, M. (1992). *Ordinary children, extraordinary teachers.* Charlottesville, VA: Hampton Roads.

Collins, M., & Tamarkin, C. (1990). *Marva Collins' way: Returning to excellence in education.* New York: Putnam (Original work published 1982).

Delpit, L. (1995). *Other people's children: Cultural conflict in the classroom.* New York: The New Press.

Dempsey, V., & Noblit, G. (1993). The demise of caring in an African-American community: One consequence of school desegregation. *Urban Review, 25*(1), 47–61.

Fine, M. (1991). *Framing dropouts: Notes on the politics of an urban public high school*. Albany: State University of New York Press.

Foster, M. (1993). Other mothers: Exploring the educational philosophy of Black American women teachers. In M. Arnot & K. Weiler (Eds.), *Feminism and social justice in education: International perspectives* (pp. 101–123). Washington, DC: Falmer.

Gay, G. (2000). *Culturally responsive teaching: Theory, research, and practice*. New York: Teachers College Press.

Groulx, J. (2001). Changing preservice teacher perceptions of minority schools. *Urban Education, 36*(1), 60–92.

hooks, b. (1994). *Teaching to transgress: Education as the practice of freedom*. New York: Routledge.

Howard, G. (1999). *We can't teach what we don't know: White teachers, multiracial schools*. New York: Teachers College Press.

Jervis, K. (1996). 'How come there are no brothers on that list?' Hearing the hard questions all children ask. *Harvard Educational Review, 66*(3), 546–576.

Kailin, J. (1999). How white teachers perceive the problem of racism in their schools: A case study in "liberal" Lakeview. *Teachers College Record, 100*(4), 724–750.

Ladson-Billings, G. (1994). *The dreamkeepers: Successful teachers of African American children*. San Francisco: Jossey Bass.

McIntyre, A. (1997). Constructing an image of a White teacher. *Teachers College Record, 98*(4), 653–681.

Nieto, S. (1999). *The light in their eyes: Creating multicultural learning communities*. New York: Teachers College Press.

Noblit, G. (1993). Power and caring. *American Educational Research Journal, 30*(1), 23–38.

Polatnik, M. (1996). Diversity in women's liberation ideology: How a Black and a White group of the 1960s viewed motherhood. *Signs, 21*(3), 679–706.

Ruddick, S. (1992). From maternal thinking to peace politics. In E. Cole & S. Coultrap-McQuin (Eds.), *Explorations in feminist ethics: Theory and practice* (pp. 141–155). Bloomington: Indiana University Press.

Siddle-Walker, V. (1996). *Their highest potential: An African American school community in the segregated South*. Chapel Hill: University of North Carolina Press.

Thompson, A. (1998). Not the color purple: Black feminist lessons for educational caring. *Harvard Educational Review, 68*(4), 522–554.

Valente, J. (1996, November 18). Momma knows best: Chicago's Corla Hawkins simply won't let kids fail. *People*, 42-47.

Valenzuela, A. (1999). *Subtractive schooling: US-Mexican youth and the politics of caring*. Albany: State University of New York Press.

Villegas, A., & Lucas, T. (2002a). *Educating culturally responsive teachers: A coherent approach*. Albany: State University of New York Press.

Villegas, A., & Lucas, T. (2002b). Preparing culturally responsive teachers: Rethinking the curriculum. *Journal of Teacher Education, 53*(1), 20–32.

Ward, J. (1995). Cultivating a morality of care in African American adolescents: A culture-based model of violence prevention. *Harvard Educational Review, 65*(2), 175–188.

Afterword: The Importance of Ideology in Contemporary Education

JOE L. KINCHELOE

What a powerful and much needed book Lilia Bartolomé and her authors have put together on ideology and education. As Lilia so aptly points out in her introductory chapter, many educators see no connection between what is going on in schools and the powerful dominant ideologies that inscribe every dimension of the pedagogical act. Indeed, we live in an ideologically dominated era characterized by the efforts of the producers of dominant ideology to deny its existence. Thus, as Bartolomé puts it, ideology is rendered invisible. In fact, the more imperceptible ideology and other forms of power become, the more strength they gain—indeed, they acquire the influence to insidiously shape various dimensions of our lives.

Coming from similar theoretical traditions, Lilia and I have learned the definition of ideology from similar theorists: Antonio Gramsci, Terry Eagleton, and, of course, Paulo Freire. In this critical theoretical context, we are profoundly concerned with the need to understand the various and complex ways in which power operates to dominate and shape consciousness. Power, critical theorists have learned, is an extremely ambiguous topic that demands detailed study and analysis. A consensus seems to be emerging among criticalists that power is a basic constituent of human existence that works to shape both the oppressive and productive nature of the human tradition.

In the context of oppressive power and its ability to produce inequalities and human suffering, Antonio Gramsci's notion—as Lilia points out in her introduction—of hegemony is central to critical pedagogy and the ideological dimensions of education. Gramsci understood that dominant power in the twentieth century was not always exercised simply by physical force but also by social psychological attempts to win people's consent to domination through cultural institutions such as the media, schools, the family, and the church. Gramscian hegemony recognizes that the winning of popular consent is a very complex process and must be researched carefully on a case-by-case basis.

Central to the formation of hegemony is the production of ideology. If hegemony is the larger effort of the powerful to win the consent of their "subordinates," then ideological hegemony involves the cultural forms, the meanings, the rituals, and the representations that produce consent to the status quo and individuals' particular places within it. Ideology vis-à-vis hegemony moves critical inquirers beyond explanations of domination that have used terms such as propaganda to describe the way media, political, educational, and other sociocultural productions coercively manipulate citizens to adopt oppressive meanings.

These critical theory grounded definitions of ideology are central to *Ideologies in Education: Unmasking the Trap of Teacher Neutrality* because ideology has been traditionally defined in mainstream academia as merely a system of beliefs—the oppressive dimension was erased. Lilia and I are using the term in the critical context to denote something a little more complex. Dominant ideological activity in the context of critical theory involves the process of protecting unequal power relations between different groups and individuals in society. For example, dominant ideology sustains unequal power relations via the process of making meaning—in a sense by "educating" and "reeducating" the public. Applying the critical concept of ideology as we explore what is hidden in the current media scape and electronic information environment, we begin to understand how powerful groups shape people's consciousness in ways that will better serve the interests of dominant power. In such an ideological environment with its corporate backed power to persuade people of the worth of a corporatized privatization agenda, we can begin to see the interests such a policy would serve—and not serve. With neo-liberal, market-driven privatization efforts, for example, opportunities would be created for new ways for business to make billions of dollars of profit from for-profit schools and the child consumers who attend them. Right-wing free market ideology makes such capital production possible.

A central conceptual backdrop to Bartolomé's book involves the fact that it is easier to wield power in a privatized society than in a public one. Indeed, privatized power is accountable to very few, as most citizens have no say over who does what in a corporate run institution. Right-wing ideology has successfully produced a political climate where millions of people have come to believe that public ownership of social organizations is a manifestation of oppression, while private ownership is the ultimate marker of freedom. Interestingly, such representations of public ownership have been more successful in recent decades than during the Cold War when old conservatives equated public ownership of institutions such as the Tennessee Valley Authority (TVA) with communism. Questions concerning accountability of private organizations have been adeptly swept under the rug in such ideological representations.

Such right-wing ideological success has helped usher in a new political era in the United States—especially in education. In this new political era, the demands of the market always trump the needs of the larger society as well as the perpetuation of democracy and democratic institutions. In the new cosmos, government no longer intervenes to promote equity and protect the needs of those treated unfairly because of race, class, or gender. Indeed, in the brave new world of education, traditional conservative values such as local control of schools collapse in face of the dominant ideology of privatization. The federal government's role in twenty-first century education is to protect market needs by promoting a national agenda of standardization and privatization. Again, all this protection occurs in the name of political neutrality and the rejection of ideology.

Thus, when President George W. Bush signed NCLB into law on January 8, 2002, the federal government's role in K-12 schooling shifted from equity to guaranteeing simplistic and reductionistic forms of accountability. Such an assertion should not be taken as a rejection of school accountability; instead it is an assertion that the *types* of accountability mandated often reconstruct school purpose in a way that promotes low-level thinking skills and reduces education to the indoctrination of unchallenged "truths." The law's claim of increased flexibility and local control is misleading doublespeak, and its focus on teaching strategies that have been "scientifically proven" to improve instruction raises profound issues about the nature of knowledge production in a democratic society.

As for equity, the law does nothing to address the grotesquely unequal funding that separates schools and school districts in well-to-do neighborhoods and poor neighborhoods. In a public school system that gives lip service to an ideology of equality, the neglect of such equity issues shackles the progress of poor schools and the students who attend them. However, the ideological refraction promoted by right-wing rhetoric frames these ideological-driven reforms as the educational salvation of the dispossessed. Indeed, contemporary educational politics is best understood as a campaign of class disinformation. Many citizens, teachers, students, and parents are mystified by such ideological prestidigitation and are blinded to the real purposes of contemporary right-wing educational reforms. The authors of *Ideologies in Education* carefully document such malevolent ideological magic in their respective chapters.

Following its narrow ideological agenda, the Bush Administration has sought to undermine public education one piece at a time—always, of course, in the name of improving it. One of the major fronts of attack has been directed toward public school teachers. Over the last few years anti-public education groups had worked for the deprofessionalization of teachers. Such a movement had made little progress until the election of George W. Bush in 2000. As part of his larger plan for public education, Bush funded these groups with millions of dollars. With new support at the highest levels and funding proponents of deprofessionalization formed the American Board for Certification of Teacher Education (ABCTE) to promote a simplistic form of teacher certification characterized by few requirements. At the same time it claims that schools and teachers are failing and need higher standards to promote "educational excellence," right-wing ideologues throw their full weight behind efforts to undermine high standards in the professional preparation and certification of teachers. Such a schizophrenic scheme fits well the effort to produce standardized (ideologically "cleansed") curricula, reduce funding and support, test and measure, and then proclaim the failure of *public* education.

Once this ideology of privatization achieves success, the profound class differences that separate Americans in the last years of the first decade of the twenty-first century will expand dramatically. Access to education for the poor and racially marginalized will become harder and harder, for there will be few incentives for private for-profit schools to admit such students. A largely privileged, White corps of students will gain better access to the scientific, technological, and information professions, while poor and minority young people will be left with low-pay, low-benefits service sector jobs. Such a bimodal distribution of privileged and marginalized workers will not only cause suffering for the marginalized but will place great stresses on the American social fabric in the coming years. Such an inegalitarian future is dystopic as well as contrary to the social compact that the nation has given at least lip service to in the past.

In its understanding of power, critical pedagogy works to account for the ways hegemonic, regulatory, discursive, and, of course, ideological forces work to shape human beings and their ways of perceiving themselves and the world. Simultaneously, critical pedagogy carefully attends to the ways human beings can critique and resist such malevolent forces. This is what Bartolomé and her authors do so well in this volume. With the power of ideology in mind, the authors study the ways in which they can pursue human agency or self-direction as they make connections and forge relationships with the people around them. In this context, they pursue agency with the understanding that knowledge can be used as a weapon of dominant power—to those who control its production, knowledge is a warm gun. As a symbolic firearm Cartesian knowledge can keep away those who fall outside the group anointed by reason, sanity, and intelligence—the poor and those who are racially, ethnically, and linguistically different from the dominant culture. It is extremely important that critical educators understand the construction, use, and effects of ideological knowledge production in the society at large and in schools in particular. We are in part what we know. Indeed, our ability to act depends on what we know. In such a case the hidden ideological forces that shape what we know become even more important than we originally thought.

Thus, as Lilia points out, ideology is not some abstract, academic topic that makes good grist for discussion in doctoral seminars—it matters in the lived world, and it profoundly affects the lives of those it victimizes. Here rests the central importance of this book: It speaks to those dynamics that shape education and the lives of those teachers and students who operate in contemporary schools. We live in a dark, foreboding educational era where hope evaporates like a July raindrop on a desert rock. The concerns and the insights of Lilia Bartolomé and her authors renew our critical faith that things can get better, that the ideological motives of the right-wing reformers can be exposed, that teachers and students can engage in transformational, life affirming, and socially just experiences in the schools of the near future.

Contributors

Cristina Alfaro is Assistant Professor in the Department of Policy Studies in Language and Cross-Cultural Education at San Diego State University. She is also the California State University (CSU) Chairperson for the International Teacher Education Consortium (ITEC) and directs the CSU International Teacher Professional Development Program. Her research interests center on border pedagogy/cross-cultural languages and literacy practices. As a teacher researcher she examines the role of teachers' *ideological and political clarity* related to teaching practices with language minority and other subordinated student groups.

María V. Balderrama is Professor of Education at California State University, San Bernardino. She is a native of the Mexicali/Calexico Valleys (California) where she attended public schools. She earned degrees from Wellesley College, San José State, and a doctorate from Stanford University. For more than 25 years she has worked with teachers, parents and adolescents nationally and internationally in creating humane and equitable conditions for teaching and learning, including a presentation at the University of La Habana, Cuba. The impetus for her research and writing is applied sociology of education, focusing on social justice, bilingual and multicultural education, linguistic racism, and teacher preparation.

Nelda Barrón is Assistant Professor of Education at Wheelock College in Boston, MA. She has extensive experience as an educator working as an administrator in a K-8 school, counselor for 5th–12th graders, and curriculum director.

She has worked in both non-profit educational organizations and school settings and has been an independent consultant on issues of equity, social justice, anti-bias, cultural competency and multicultural organizational development. Her current research interests include teacher cultural competency, culturally responsive teaching, anti-racism, and the linkages between teachers' cultural identities, socio-cultural/socio-political consciousness and teaching practice.

Lilia I. Bartolomé is Associate Professor in the Applied Linguistics Graduate Program at the University of Massachusetts Boston. As a teacher educator, her research interests include the preparation of effective teachers of minority and second language learners in multicultural contexts. In particular, Bartolomé examines teacher ideological orientations around their work with linguistic-minority students as well as their actual classroom practices with this student population. She has published the following books: *The Misteaching of Academic Discourses*; *Immigrant Voices: In Search of Pedagogical Equity* (with Henry Trueba), and *Dancing with Bigotry: The Poisoning of Culture* (with Donaldo Macedo).

Tamara Beauboeuf-Lafontant is Associate Professor of sociology and education studies at DePauw University. Her teaching and research interests examine individual development within the social hierarchies of race, class, and gender. She has published articles focusing on how teachers negotiate discourses of race and gender in their identities and pedagogy in *Teachers College Record*, *The Urban Review*, and the *Journal of Teacher Education*. A second body of research explores the implications of normative expectations of Black womanhood on individual health and wellness, and has been published in *Gender & Society* and *Meridians*.

Karen Cadiero-Kaplan is Associate Professor at San Diego State University in the Department of Policy Studies in Language and Cross Cultural Education. Her research interests include literacy ideologies, the arts and technology, democratic practices for teacher development, and policy that impacts programming for biliteracy and English language development. Recent publications include her book, *The Literacy Curriculum and Bilingual Education: A Critical Examination*

Stephanie Cox Suárez is a mother and Assistant Professor in Education at Wheelock College in Boston. She teaches courses in curriculum and assessment and mentors graduate students in their urban, inclusive classrooms as they work towards licensure in special needs and elementary education. She was a classroom teacher for 15 years in public schools and the Perkins School for the Blind. Her current research interests include exploring ways to make learning visible for pre-service teachers and the children they teach as well as organizing and participating with faculty in understanding anti-racist practices in education. Stephanie also takes time to have fun with her two children, Samuel and Sophia.

Felicity Crawford is Assistant Professor of Special Education at Wheelock College. She also courses which examine the cultural, social, and political contexts of urban schools and the challenges that issues of racism and resistance in the classroom. To that role she brings the perspective of an experienced K-12 educator who has worked for many years in several racially and culturally diverse classroom settings. Her research interests include developing a deep understanding of the social context of urban special education and creating pathways to effectively transform the experiences of students from various racial, cultural and linguistic backgrounds in urban classrooms.

Paula Elliott is a third generation, African American, female Assistant Professor at Wheelock College. Prior to entering higher education, her professional experiences included: teaching in elementary and special education settings, directing a national school assessment program for independent schools, constructing curriculum and facilitating public school teacher professional workshops. Elliott's work in higher education has focused on infusing multicultural/anti-racist education and culturally responsive pedagogy into her undergraduate/pre-service education coursework. Her research interests, as in her teaching and consulting work, are directed toward an examination of the influence and consequences of race, racism, identity and oppression in various contexts of teaching and learning.

Ricardo E. Gonsalves received his doctorate in the area of Human Development and Psychology from Harvard University. He is currently a Child and Family Therapist at *Bienvenidos* Mental Health Services in East Los Angeles. Dr. Gonsalves also serves on the faculty of the California Graduate Studies Institute for Professional Psychology and is a founding member of the California Latino Psychological Association.

Panayota Gounari is Assistant Professor in the Applied Linguistics Graduate Program at the University of Massachusetts Boston. She holds a Ph.D. in Cultural Studies in Education from Pennsylvania State University. Gounari's primary areas of interest include language policy and linguistic hegemony, critical discourse analysis, language and the politics of difference, the role of language in social change and the construction of human agency and democratic spaces as well as its implications for critical pedagogy. She co-authored *The Hegemony of English* with Donaldo Macedo and Bessie Dendrinos (Paradigm Press, 2003) and *The Globalization of Racism* with Donaldo Macedo (Paradigm Press, 2006). E-mail: panagiota.gounari@umb.edu

Joe Kincheloe Joe L. Kincheloe is the Canada Research Chair in Critical Pedagogy in the Faculty Education at McGill University. He is the author of numerous books and articles about critical pedagogy, cultural studies, education and social justice, racism, class bias, and sexism, issues of cognition and cultural context. His books include: *Teachers as Researchers, Toil and Trouble, Critical Pedagogy: Where are we now?* (with Peter McLaren), *The Sign of the Burger: McDonald's and the Culture of Power, The Critical Pedagogy Primer, Rigour and Complexity in Educational Research: Conceptualizing the Bricolage* (with Kathleen Berry), and *Changing Multiculturalism* (with Shirley Steinberg).

Guadalupe López Bonilla is Professor at the Institute for Research and Educational Development at the Universidad Autónoma de Baja California in Mexico. Her current research interests focus in two areas: the literacy practices in two content areas (History and Literature), and the role literacy practices have in shaping adolescents' identities. She can be contacted at the Instituto de Investigación y Desarrollo Educativo, Universidad Autónoma de Baja California, Km. 103 carretera Tijuana-Ensenada, Ensenada, Baja California C. P. 22860, México, or by e-mail at bonilla@uabc.mx

Paula S. Martin is currently the Grade 7 House Administrator at the Pollard Middle School in Needham, Massachusetts, an adjunct professor at Framingham State College, and senior member of the Massachusetts Department of Education (MCAS) Massachusetts Comprehensive Assessment of Academic Skills Bias Review Committee. Dr. Martin received her doctorate from the University of Massachusetts, Boston and her research focuses on the impact of antiracism professional development on increasing White privilege awareness and racial development in White educators. Her current projects include a chapter in the book, *Racism in the Classroom*, her research project, "Our voices: Students speak about academic achievement," and an article, "Heterosexual and White privilege."

Index

ABCTE (American Board for Certification of Teacher Education), 268
ability grouping, 257
absence
    effects on learning, 57–58, 63
    expectations of, 58
    frequency of, 57
    mental, 58–59, 60–63
    physical, 58, 60
    teachers' facilitation of, 58–59, 60–63
    tracking of, 59–60
accountability, 267
achievement
    dependence on teacher-student relationships, 162, 251–52
    and discontinuity between home and school cultures, 186
    and meritocracy, 214
    see also underachievement
achievement gap, 162
    see also underachievement
ACTA. *see* American Council of Trustees and Alumni
action, individual, 14, 258–61
action and need for reflection, 166
Adler, A., 11
African Americans. *see* Blacks
agency, human, xxi, 258–61
Ahlquist, R., 5, 189
Alcorn, M., 20
Althusser, L., 13–14
American Board for Certification of Teacher Education (ABCTE), 268
American Council of Trustees and Alumni (ACTA)
    accusations of historical illiteracy, 98, 101–2
    agenda of, 106
    selection of history, 103–4, 105
    self-presentation of, 101, 102
    tactics of, 102, 103
    see also Cheney, Lynne
analysis, critical, 211
antiracist education
    and classroom behavior, 167, 168
    components of, 169–70
    effects of, 170–77

inclusion of identity development of
people of color, 177
movement within stages, 174
need for, 23
need for praxis in, 166
principles of, 164
as professional development, 164,
166–67
regression, 173
stages of, 168–76
White privilege awareness, 164
White racial identity development,
164, 167, 168–69, 177
and willingness to change,
176–77
see also multicultural education
Apple, Michael, xx–xxi
Armenian genocide, exclusion of, 110
assessment. *see* educational report
assimilationist ideology, xvii–xviii
"at-risk" students. *see* students, "at-risk";
students, minority/non-mainstream
attitude, definition of, 70n3
authority, challenge of professor's,
32–36, 40–41
autobiographies, teacher, 219–21, 223
Autonomy, 169, 176

Baltodano, M., 215
Bartolomé, L. I.
advocacy of explicit teaching, 226n4
on ideological border crossing,
241–42, 247n3
on ideological clarity, 119, 231
on lack of attention to ideology, 216
on need to understand politics of
education, 215
on need to understand power of
ideologies, 65, 215
on studies of effective teachers, 215
on teachers' experience with
marginalization, 236
Barton, D., 74
beliefs
difficulty in reassessing, 214
vs. knowledge, 76
bilingual education

allowing students to lose primary
language, 131–32
and development of primary
language, 130
ELD in, 126–27, 128–29, 130
ELLs in, 126, 128, 129
goals of, 122–23
need for high quality materials, 129
Proposition 227 (English for the
Children), 238, 248n7
teacher-teacher collaboration, 127,
128–29
transitional model, 127–28
use of primary language, 126
value placed on biliteracy, 128
see also biliteracy
biliteracy
Carlos's belief in, 245
Eva's definition of, 125
value of, 125
value placed on, 128
see also bilingual education
Blacks
effects of deficit ideology on, 65
in special education classes, 49, 51
stereotypes of, 56
teachers (*see* teachers, African
American; teachers of color)
teachers' attitudes toward, 63–64
teachers' explanation of
underachievement, 55–57
see also
students,
minority/non-mainstream
border crossing, ideological, 232,
241–42, 247n3
Bracher, M., 10
Brisk, M., 132
Bush, George W., 267, 268
Butler, Judith, 109

California
bilingual education in, 248n7
multicultural education requirements
in, 30
Newcomer Programs, 243, 248n5
Proposition 187, 45n7

INDEX

Proposition 209, 45n7
Proposition 227 (English for the Children), 238, 248n7
California State University International Teacher Education Program (ITEP). *see* ITEP
Camacho, Ms., 85–87, 90
caring, aesthetic, 253
caring, authentic
   and honest representation of realities, 256–57
   and political clarity, 255
   and power, 261
   practice of by African American teachers, 252
   see also maternal approach to teaching
caring, maternal
   alternatives to mainstream notion of, 261
   see also caring, authentic; maternal approach to teaching
Carlos
   assessment of ITEP, 239–40, 244
   background of, 232, 236–37, 239, 246
   disillusionment with teaching, 237
   experience in indigenous communities, 241
   experience in Mexico, 232–33, 240–41
   experience with marginalization, 236, 238
   experience with racism, 238
   as ideological border crosser, 241
   inclusion of classism and racism in classes, 242–43
   as strategic educator, 244–46
   subversive work of, 244–46
   see also ITEP
Carter, R. T., 167, 170
Casey, Kathleen, 254–55
Castoriadis, Cornelius, 109
change
   and antiracist education, 176–77
   belief in, 259
   and human agency, xxi
   influence of ideology, 232
   as interpersonal processes, 260

politicized mothers' understanding of, 262
resistance as precursor to, 22
self as agent for, 258–61
Chapter 766, 53
Cheney, Lynne, 98, 102, 105
   see also American Council of Trustees and Alumni
Chicanos/as
   perception of by dominant culture, 33, 34–35
   use of term, 248n4
   see also Latinos/as; Mexican community
civilization, western, 99, 105
Clark, Septima, 259
class differences and access to education, 268
classism
   and access to education, 268
   as existing in all societies, 240
   inclusion of in Carlos's classes, 242–43
   in Mexico, 232, 233, 235
   as sugar coated in U. S., 238
   teachers' perpetuation of, 66
coach. *see* mentor, cultural
Cochran-Smith, M., 132, 213, 219, 220, 226n5
cognitive dissonance
   and ideological clarity, 233
   and multicultural education, 196–97
collectivity, 259–60
Collins, Marva, 252–53, 255–56
color blindness, shortcomings of, 54–55, 225
Columbus, Christopher, 103
common sense, 100
compulsory education, 12
conflicted consensus
   absence of in U.S. society, 106
   need for in democracy, 108
conscious level, 19–20
consciousness
   ideological construction of, 121
   levels of, 17–22
   and power, 265

consciousness, critical
  definition of, 16
  development of, 17
  importance of for teachers, 210–11
  and moral dilemma, 17
  possibility for, 16
consciousness, individual, 14–16
consciousness, social, 14–16, *17*
consensus, conflicted. *see* conflicted consensus
conservatives
  selection of historical discourse, 100–101
  see also American Council of Trustees and Alumni
Contact, 168, 170–71
Corbin, J., 66–68
courage, teaching with, 247
critical analysis, 211
critical consciousness. *see* consciousness, critical
critical theory and dominant ideological activity, 266
critical thought, 15–16
cultural capital
  and culture of power, 137
  definition of, 137
  and educational opportunities, 144–45
  mentor's role in acquiring, 147
  writing as, 137
cultural competence, need for, 145–46
cultural identity
  definition of, 202n1
  preservice teachers' understanding of, 198–99
  QUEST's exploration of, 218–19
  reconstruction of, 200–201
  study of preservice teachers', 191–94
culturally responsive teaching, 186, 203n4
culture
  definition of, 202n3
  denial of by Whites, 31
  as relevant, 162
  White perception of, 31

culture, dominant
  collusion between individual and society, 18
  and consciousness, 14–16
  denial by, 11
  and dysconsciousness, 18–19, *22*
  enforcement of standard language, 139
  and maintenance of social order, 14–16
  oppression by, 164
  unawareness of privilege, 167
    (*see also* privilege)
  and the unconscious, 18
  and writing, 137
culture, personal, 136
culture, White mainstream, 203n4
culture of power and cultural capital, 137
curriculum, 208, 222, 243, 268
  see also American Council of Trustees and Alumni

Darder, A., xiv–xv, 215
DeBord, Guy, 15
defensiveness, 20
deficiency
  as explanation for failure, 49
  see also ideology, deficit
Delpit, L., 137, 251
democracy
  and conflicted consensus, 106, 108
  and public memory, 109
Democratic Practice, 227n8
Dendrinos, Bessie, xxi
denial, 4–5, 10–11, 12
difference, teachers' inability to understand, 49
Discourse
  in Mr. Gonzalez's interview, 83–84
  in Mr. Torres's interview, 88
  vs. discourse, 76–77
discourse
  critical features of, 138
  literacy as, 138
  in Mr. Gonzalez's interview, 83–84
  vs. Discourse, 76–77
discourse, oral, 152–53

discourse, professional
   need for mastery of, 135
   need for standard English, 139
   obligation to help non-mainstream students enter, 153
   and practice of oral discourse, 152–53
   students in study, backgrounds of, 140–43
   see also educational reports; writing
Discourse Analysis Technique, 68–70
discrimination, 163
disempowerment of Mexican community, 30
disengagement. *see* absence
Disintegration, 9, 168, 172–73
dispossessed, teachers as advocates for, 4
dissonance
   and ideological clarity, 233
   and multicultural education, 196–97
diversity. *see* multicultural education
dominant ideologies. *see* ideologies, dominant
dominant literacies. *see* literacies, dominant
dysconscious resistance, 18–19, *22*

Eagleton, Terry, xiv
education
   access to, 144–45, 268
   lack of honesty about stakes of, 256
   political and ideological nature of, xxviii
   politics in, 238
   sociopolitical context of, 227n8
education, antiracist. *see* antiracist education
education, bilingual. *see* bilingual education
education, compulsory, 12
education, inclusive, 65–66
education, Mexican. *see* public education, Mexican
education, public, xvii–xviii, 268
educational reports
   face-to-face meetings, 150–51
   multiple drafts, 151–52
   peer editing, 152
   quality of writing and confidence in, 143
   written feedback, 147–50, 154–57
   see also discourse, professional
Elbow, P., 146
ELD. *see* English Language Development
ELLs. *see* English Language Learners
English
   considered solution to disadvantages, xvi
   Proposition 227 (English for the Children), 238, 248n7
   use of, 200
   see also bilingual education; biliteracy; English Language Development; English Language Learners; language
English as a Second Language. *see* English Language Development
English for the Children, 238, 248n7
English Language Development (ELD)
   in bilingual education programs, 126–27, 128–29, 130
   definition of, 248n9
   language brokers, 245, 248n10
   see also bilingual education; biliteracy; English Language Learners
English Language Learners (ELLs)
   in bilingual education programs, 126, 128, 129
   expectations of, 143
   inapt of teachers on, 141, 142
   writing abilities of, 141–42
   see also bilingual education; biliteracy; English Language Development
Erikson, Erik, 12
Escuelas Normales, 79–80
ESL. *see* English Language Development
ethnic identity, 202n1
Europe, old *vs.* new false dichotomy, 99
Eva
   background of, 124–25
   beliefs regarding literacy, 127
   definition of biliteracy, 125
   definition of literacy, 122
   frustrations of, 131–32

inability to see different values placed on curricula, 128
inability to see different values placed on ELL, 129
Literacy Web, 122–23
on need for accountability, 130
problem posing, 132
role as ELD teacher, 126–27
on teacher-teacher collaboration, 127, 128–29
tension between ideology and personal stance, 130, 131
tension between practices and beliefs, 133
and value of biliteracy, 128
views of bilingual classes, 126
evaluation. *see* educational reports
experiential function. *see* field
explicit teaching, 226n4

face-to-face meetings, 150–51
failure
and aesthetic caring, 253
deficiency as explanation for, 49
expectations of for non-mainstream students, 255–56
of students, 184
teachers' influence on, 251–52
see also underachievement
Fairclough, Norman, 76, 77
Fanon, Franz, 18
Farley, John, xvi
feedback, written, 147–50
Feiman-Nemser, S., 216
Festinger, L., 196
field
definition of, 75, 77
in Mr. Gonzalez's interview, 83–84
in Ms. Osuna's interviews, 81
field observations, student resistance to, 37
Flemming, Leslie, 36
Flores, Barbara, xviii
Foster, M., 145
Freire, Paulo
concept of critical consciousness, 16
on intertwined teaching and learning, 187

on need to be strategic, 244
on need to seek emergence of consciousness in reality, 210
on need to uncover influence of ideology, x
on political and ideological nature of education, xxviii
on teaching with courage, 247
on uninformed action, 166
Functional System Linguistics (FSL), 75
see also field; mode; tenor
fundamentalist, 165

Gay, G., 23
Gee, J. P., 68–70, 76–77, 138
genocide
Armenian, 110
of Native Americans, 102, 103
Giroux, Henry, xv, 111
Gomez, M. L., 189–90
Gonzalez, Mr., 83–85, 89
grades as symbol of authority, 40
Gramsci, Antonio
on common sense, 100
definition of hegemonic ideology, xiii
on hegemony, 265–66
on ideology as lived social practices, xiv
Grant, C. A., 3, 44n6
grounded theory analysis, 66–68

Haberman, M., 184
Halcón, John, xi–xii
Halliday, M. A. K., 77
Hamilton, M., 74
Hawkins, Corla ("Momma Hawk"), 253, 254, 258
hegemonic ideology, xiv
see also ideologies, dominant
hegemony, 265–66
Helms, Janet, 9, 167, 168–69, 170, 171
Hispanics. *see* Chicanos/as; Latinos/as; Mexican community
Hispaniola, depopulation of, 103
historical illiteracy
conservative accusations of, 98, 101–2
see also American Council of Trustees and Alumni

historical literacy
   equated with American history literacy, 103
   items to include, 105
   as uncritical assimilation of facts, 101
history
   assimilationist notion of, 98–99
   beliefs about, 84–85
   conservative accusations of illiteracy, 98, 101–2
   conservative version of, 99, 100–101, 103 (*see also* American Council of Trustees and Alumni)
   as counter-memory, 110
   as creation, 112
   disarticulation of, 110
   groups missing from conservative version, 103
   homogenous notion of, 98–99
   illiteracy (*see* historical illiteracy)
   as means to self-questioning, 111
   in Mexican public education, 82, 84–85
   and national identity, 89
   need to reflect dominant and subjugated groups, 101
   pedagogical role of, 112–13
   perception of as irrelevant to present, 110
   primacy of western civilization in conservative view, 99, 105
   privileging of certain histories, 99, 105, 110
   redefinition of, 97
   remembering through, 112
   students' inability to view critically, 106
   Teaching American History, 107
   temporal/spatial dimension of, 110–11
   traditional version, 107–8
   version taught and funding of schools, 107–8
   as what Americans are supposed to believe, 99
   see also memory
history, hegemonic, 109

Holocaust, Jewish, 110, 111
hooks, b., 162
Horkheimer, Max, 112
Howard, G. R., 165
Howey, K. R., 12
Hull, G., 138
Hurtado, Aida, 36
Hyland, N., 189
hysterical blindness
   as defense of social identity, 11
   definition of, 5
   as ideological norm, 11
   and individual action, 14
   moving beyond, 16
   as repressed awareness of cooperation with state apparatus, 15
   see also denial; multicultural education, resistance to

identity, cultural. *see* cultural identity
ideological border crossing, 232, 241–42, 247n3
ideological clarity
   definition of, xix, 50, 70n2, 203n8, 226n4, 231
   dissonance and, 233
   explanation of, 119
   journey to (*see* Carlos)
   and reflective process, 133
   teachers' need for, 133, 213, 215, 231, 247
ideological norms, importance of, 76
ideologies, ability of humans to transform, xxi
ideologies, dominant
   absorption of in teacher preparation programs, xv
   and common sense, 100
   hysterical blindness in the service of, 11
   invisibility of, x, 215, 265
   need to examine, 226n2
   need to understand in school, xx–xxi
   perpetuation of, xiii–xiv
   and perpetuation of power relations, 266

preservice teachers' unawareness
of, 186
and prevention of thinking in terms
of alternatives, 186
reflection of in cultural practices, xiii
reflection of in symbols, xiii
and repression of critical thought,
15–16
and subversion of self, 15
teachers' need to interrogate, 211
and unconscious compliance, 18
see also ideology, assimilationist;
ideology, deficit
ideologies, hegemonic, xiv
see also ideologies, dominant
ideologies, negative, xii
ideologies, racist
and power, 219
see also racism
ideology
complexity of, xxi
definitions of, xiii, 70n1, 118, 202n2,
226n1, 231
distortion of reality, 39
effects of in special education, 64
hegemony as production of, 266
and hiddenness of privilege, 39
impact on institutional context
of language, 77
importance of, 210, 268
influence on practice, 214–15, 231
interpretations and connotations
of, 214
lack of attention to, 216
lack of examination of by
teachers, 118
lack of recognition of significance
of, xii
levels of operation, 14
as lived social practices, xiv
need to identify and question, xix
and social change, 232
and tension with personal stance,
130, 131
understanding of and reflective
process, 121
ideology, assimilationist, xvii–xviii

ideology, deficit
acceptance of, 190
and "at-risk" students, xviii, 49, 65
definition of, xviii
effects of in special education, 65
effects on minority students, 65
and perceptions of Latino/a students,
xviii
perpetuation of, xviii–xix, 49
inclusive education, 65–66
indigenous communities in Mexico,
235, 241
inequality, social, 12
inquiry, 221–23, 226n5
institutions
expectations of literacy, 74
value of middle-class discourse, 138
Whites' use of, 41–42
integrationist, 165
internalization of ideologies, xii
International Baccalaureate (IB),
78, 85, 86
International Teacher Education Program
(ITEP). *see* ITEP
interpellation, 13–14
interpersonal function. *see* tenor
Iraq war, dismissal of European
opposition, 99–100
Irvine, J. J., 186
Israel, 110, 111
ITEP (International Teacher Education
Program)
Carlos's assessment of, 239–40, 244
creation of dissonance, 233
description of, 233–36
see also Carlos

Jackter, Stephanie, 36
James, Frank, 102–3
job patterns, 242
Johnson, A. G., 70n3

Kegan, Robert, 7–8
Keith, A. I., 167
Keller, S., 119
Kincheloe, J. L., 34
King, Joyce, 14, 18

Kirkland, K., 23
knowledge *vs.* beliefs, 76
Koenigsberg, R., 14–15

Lacan, J., 11
Ladson-Billings, G., 145, 186, 216
Langer, Ellen, 18
language
    English dominance and White supremacy, 200
    Functional System Linguistics, 75
    ideology's impact on context of, 77
    Proposition 227 (English for the Children), 238, 248n7
    special education teachers' use of, 69
    standard *vs.* nonstandard, 139
        (*see also* discourse, professional)
    see also bilingual education; biliteracy; Discourse; discourse; English Language Development; English Language Learners; field; mode; tenor
language brokers, 245, 248n10
Lankshear, C., 138
Latinos/as
    effects of deficit ideology on, 65
    perceptions of, xviii
    in special education classes, 49, 51
    stereotypes of, 56
    teachers' attitudes toward, 63–64
    teachers' explanations of underachievement, 55–57
    see also Chicanos/as; Mexican community
Lawrence, S. M., 166
Lee, Enid, 216, 227n6
Lien, H. N., 188, 201
literacies, dominant
    criticisms of, 86, 90
    teachers' perceptions of, 75
literacy
    as a discourse, 138
    dominant literacies, 75, 86, 90
    Eva's beliefs regarding, 127
    Eva's definition of, 122
    events *vs.* practices, 74
    and expectations of social institutions, 74
    forms of, 138
    instruction (*see* literacy instruction)
    local *vs.* distant, 88
    as social practice, 138
    teachers' beliefs about, 75
    see also biliteracy
literacy, critical, 65
literacy, exclusionary, 138
literacy, historical. *see* historical literacy
literacy events, 74, 82
literacy instruction
    Literacy Web Questions, 121, *122*
    Literacy Word Web, 119–21
    for minority students, 118
    themes that influence and impact, 120–21
literacy practices, 74
Literacy Web, Eva's, 122–23
Literacy Web Questions, 121, *122*
Literacy Word Web, 119–21
literature
    importance of, 86
    in Mexican public education, 90
Lucas, T., 189
Lytle, S. L., 132

Macedo, Donaldo, 106, 244
Maclear, Kyo, 110
marginalization, teachers' experience with, 236, 238, 246
Martin, P. S., 167
Marx, Sherry, xv–xvi
Massachusetts, 53, 65
Massumi, B., 14
materials, need for high quality, 129
materials, state mandated, 118–19
maternal approach to teaching
    by African American teachers, 252–55
    Collins, Marva, 252–53, 255–56
    Hawkins, Corla, 253, 258
    as resistance to domination, 254–55
maternalism
    alternatives to mainstream notion of, 261
    Whites' desire to deconstruct, 254

math curriculum, 208, 222
MCE. *see* multicultural education
McIntosh, Peggy, 163
McIntyre, Alice, 262
McLaren, P., 214, 226n2
memory
    as arena of struggle, 110
    creation of, 112
    exclusion of certain histories, 110
    as pedagogical force, 111
    as rupture of history's successive character, 111
    see also history
memory, public, 109, 111–12
    see also history
mentor, cultural
    and acquisition of cultural capital, 147
    obligation to help non-mainstream students enter professional discourse, 153
    teacher educators as, 146–53
    vs. gatekeeper, 146
mentors for new urban teachers. *see* QUEST
meritocracy
    belief in, 214
    and lack of respect for culture and language of minority students, xix
    and responsibility for disadvantages, xvi
Mexican community in U. S., 30
Mexico
    Carlos's experience in, 232–33, 240–41
    classism in, 232, 233, 235
    indigenous communities in, 235, 241
    International Baccalaureate (IB) in, 78, 85, 86
    public education reform, 73–74
    racism in, 232, 233, 235, 238
    strike by university students, 239
    teacher training program, 79–80
    teaching in (*see* ITEP)
    Tijuana, 77–78
    treatment of low-status students in, 232, 235
    see also public education, Mexican

Mills, C. W., 162
minorities. *see* students, minority/non-mainstream
minority students. *see* students, minority/non-mainstream
Mitchell, C., 138
mode
    definition of, 75, 77
    in Mr. Gonzalez's interview, 83–84
Momma Hawk (Corla Hawkins), 253, 254, 258
Montoya, Eva. *see* Eva
moral dilemma
    change, 20–22
    and development of critical consciousness, 17
    difficulty in solving, 8–9
    moratorium, 19–20
    options for addressing, 19–22
    and possibility for critical consciousness, 16
    regression, 20
    resolution of, 17
mothers, politicized
    as agents for social justice, 262
    belief in change, 259
    engagement with oppressive realities, 258
    feeling of being called to teach, 258–59
    focus on self as change agent, 258–61
    teachers as, 257
    understanding of social change, 262
    uneasiness with, 261
    view of teaching and change as interpersonal processes, 260
mothers, societal evaluation of, 254
motivation, assumptions about, 147
Mouffe, Chantal, 108
Moyenda, Sekani, 259
multicultural education (MCE)
    antiracist, 166 (*see also* antiracist education)
    as being about "others," 188
    and cognitive dissonance, 196–97
    critical, 3–4
    and defensiveness, 20

effectiveness in changing attitudes and beliefs, 13
and ideological foundations of preservice teachers, 195–96
ideological perspective of, 38–39
and ideological shifts of preservice teachers, 197–200
importance in overcoming resistance, 16
insufficiency of one-semester course, 22, 24
introduction of alternative worldview, 16
lack of implementation, 24
and moral dilemma, 16, 19–22
need for focus on resistance, 23–24
need for follow-up, 24, 201
need to implement across curriculum, 24
and preconsciousness, 19
reconstruction of cultural identity, 200–201
requirements for in California, 30
responses to, 19–22
single-relations model, 38, 165, 166
stigmatization of, 24
traditional, 166
training of preservice teachers, 4, 188
understanding of cultural identity, 198–99
multicultural education (MCE), resistance to
as defense, 13
defensive reactions, 6
and denial, 4–5, 10–11
dual nature of resistance, 13
explanation of resistance, 7–8
importance in overcoming, 16
intensity of, 32
and moral dilemma, 8–10
need to focus on, 23–24
resistance at first sight, 32–36
and socialization, 13
students' emotional responses, 5–7
threat of self-knowledge, 10
see also resistance, student

multiculturalism, ACTA's attack on, 104
multiple drafts, 151–52

Native Americans, genocide of, 102–3, 104
NCLB. *see* No Child Left Behind Act
negative ideologies, xii
Newcomer Programs, 243, 248n5
Nieto, S., 136, 227n8
Noblit, George, 259–60, 261–62
No Child Left Behind Act (NCLB), 212, 226n3, 238, 248n8, 267
nonwhite linguistic minorities. *see* students, minority/non-mainstream

Of Plymouth Plantation, 102
oppression
attempts to discredit individual, 29
by dominant culture, 164
exclusion of from conservative history, 104
and political resistance, 21
and transformative resistance, 21
Whites as contributors to, 164
Osuna, Ms., 80–82, 85, 89

Paige, Rod, 107
Pam, 259–60
Paolino, T. R., Jr., 7
Parker, M. B., 216
pedagogy, critical, 268
peer editing, 152
Pennington, Julie, xv–xvi
Pilgrims' landing, 102–3
Piper, D., 153
political clarity
and authentic caring, 255
definition of, xix–xx, 255
of teachers (*see* teachers, politicized)
teachers' need for, 213
political power
and legitimacy assigned members of minority groups, 36
of Mexican community, 30
politics
in education, 40, 238
increasing irrelevance of, 110

schools' connection to, 40
    of teaching, 183–84
poor, teachers as advocates for, 4
power
    and caring, 261
    and consciousness, 265
    and dominant ideologies, 266
    and privatization, 266–67
    and racist ideologies, 219
    use of in teaching, 261
power, political, 30, 36
Pratto, F., 163
praxis
    definition of, 65, 119
    for literacy instruction teachers (*see* literacy instruction; Literacy Word Web; reflective process for literacy instruction)
    need for in antiracist education, 166
    need for in special education, 65
preconscious resistance, 19, *22*
privatization of schools, 266–67, 268
privilege
    acknowledgment of, 172–73
    hiddenness of, 39
    intellectual understanding of, 174
    need for awareness of, 162–63
    perceived loss of and resistance, 37
    preservice teachers' understanding of, 199–200
    social dominance theory, 163
    unawareness of, 163–64, 167
    and use of institutional mechanisms, 41–42
problem posing, 132
professional development
    and antiracist education, 164, 166–67
    Cochran-Smith's framework for, 219–20
    as cultivating conditions for inquiry stance, 226n5
    and extending teachers' capability for critical analysis, 211
    lack of attention to ideology, 216
    for new urban teachers, 207
    (*see also* QUEST)
    with sociopolitical framework, 211–13
    in special education, 53
professionals, 135
    see also discourse, professional
professors
    attempts to remove from classroom, 42
    challenging of authority of, 32–36
    ideological expectations of, 32–34
    respect for, 36
    titles of, 35–36, 44n5
Proposition 187, 45n7
Proposition 209, 45n7
Proposition 227 (English for the Children), 238, 248n7
Pseudo-Independence, 168–69, 174–76
public education
    assimilationist ideology in, xvii–xviii
    offered to nonwhite linguistic minorities, xvii–xviii
    undermining of, 268
public education, Mexican
    beliefs about history in, 82, 84–85
    criticism of, 87, 90
    dominant literacy in, 86
    history in, 89
    and International Baccalaureate (IB), 78, 85, 86
    literature in, 90
    national program, 88
    reform of, 73–74
    research study on, 77–79
    teacher interviews, 91–93
    (*see also* Camacho, Ms.; Gonzalez, Mr.; Osuna, Ms.; Torres, Mr.)
public memory, 109, 111–12

QUEST (Quality Urban Education and Support for Teachers)
    autobiographies, 219–21, 223
    conception and design of, 216–17
    exploration of cultural identity and race, 218–19
    goal of, 217
    planning of, 218–19

as responsive to teacher needs, 224
value of, 224

race, disregard for, 54–55, 225
race relations, exclusion of from
  conservative history, 104
racial identity
  definition of, 202n1
  of Whites (*see* White racial identity
    development)
racial identity stages, 168–69, 170–76
  see also Autonomy; Contact;
    Disintegration;
    Pseudo-Independence;
    Reintegration
racism
  and ability grouping, 257
  achievement gap, 162
  color blindness associated with
    equity, 197
  as existing in all societies, 240
  impetus of change, 177
  inclusion of in Carlos's classes,
    242–43
  in job patterns, 242
  in Mexico, 232, 233, 235, 238
  perpetuation of by teachers,
    xv–xvi, 66
  perpetuation of in special education,
    64
  preservice teachers' beliefs and
    understanding of, 199–200
  psychology of, need for course in, 23
  resistance to understanding
    significance of, 189
  in school administration, 243–44
  as sugar coated in U. S., 238
  teachers' experience with, 238
  value of understanding, 190–91
  and White ally, 166, 177
  Whites' responsibility for
    eliminating, 175
  White teachers' need to understand,
    161
  see also privilege; teachers, White
racism, dysconscious, 18

reality
  engagement with, 256–57, 258
  ideology's distortion of, 39
  seeking of emergence of
    consciousness in, 210
reflective process for literacy instruction
  aim of, 120
  and understanding of ideology, 121
  used to define beliefs and practices,
    122–24
reform of Mexican public education,
  73–74
Reintegration, 168, 173–74
remembering. *see* memory
reports, educational. *see* educational
  reports
resistance
  as defense, 7–8
  and defensiveness, 20
  in development of critical
    consciousness, 17
  as dynamic process, 20
  need for focus on in MCE, 23–24
  preconscious, 19, *22*
  as precursor to change, 22
  stages of, *17*, 18–22
  strategy to address, 23–24
  unconscious level of, 18
  see also multicultural education
    (MCE), resistance to
resistance, political
  psychological benefits of, 21–22
  use of titles, 44n5
resistance, student
  arrogance of, 37–38
  attempts to remove professor from
    classroom, 42
  challenge of grading system, 40–42
  continuum of, *40*
  and culture as superficial knowledge,
    38–40
  definition of, 44n1
  to field observations, 37
  and perceived loss of privilege, 37
  as political act, 35
  role reversal, 37–38

Shor on, 33, 34
  to social justice message, 38–40, 44n1
  and titles, 35–36, 44n5
  see also multicultural education,
    resistance to
resistance, transformative, 20–22
"Restoring America's Legacy" (ACTA).
  see American Council of Trustees and
  Alumni
Rumsfeld, Donald, 99–100

Said, Edward, 99, 100
Scheurich, J, 242
schools
  accountability, 267
  connection to politics, 40
  funding of, 107–8, 267
  history taught in, 107–8, 109
  lack of honesty about stakes of
    education, 256
  as mechanism of socialization, 13
  need to understand dominant
    ideologies in, xx–xxi
  privatization, 266–67, 268
  as reflection of society, 166
  and social reproduction, 251
  sociopolitical context of, 212
  and student failure, 184
  treatment of immigrant students, 244
self
  as agent for change, 258–61
  and interaction with Other, 9
  as part of other people, 259–60
self-knowledge, threat of, 10
sexism, preservice teachers' understanding
  of, 199
Shor, I., 33, 34
Sidanius, J., 163
Slater, Philip, 12–13
slavery, exclusion of from conservative
  history, 104
Sleeter, C. E., 3, 44n6, 186
social change
  and influence of ideology, 232
  politicized mothers' understanding
    of, 262
social consciousness, 9

social dominance, 163, 165
social identity, defense of, 11
socialization
  as coercive, 12
  and compulsory education, 12
  explanation of, 11–12
  and maintenance of social order,
    15, 197
  and resistance to multicultural
    education, 13
  schools as mechanism of, 13
  of teachers of color, 212
  teachers' role in, 12
social justice
  and belief in change, 259
  politicized mothers as agents for, 262
social justice model, resistance to, 38–40,
  44n1
social order
  justification of, xiii–xiv (*see also*
    ideologies, dominant)
  maintenance of, 14–16, 197
social practice
  ideology as, xiv
  literacy as, 138
social reproduction, 251
sociocultural consciousness, 189
Spanish. *see* bilingual education; biliteracy;
  English Language Development;
  English Language Learners
special education
  and absence (*see* absence)
  Blacks and Latinos/as in, 49, 51,
    54–57
  Chapter 766, 53
  department of at St. Augustine High,
    51–52
  effects of ideology, 64, 65
  and inclusive education, 65–66
  as informed by deficit model,
    49–50, 64
  lack of attention to race, 54–55
  need for appropriate knowledge and
    skills, 65
  need for praxis in, 65
  and oral discourse, 152–53
  perpetuation of racism in, 64

professional development, 53
research methodology, 50, 66–70
research questions, 50
teachers' description of Black and Latino/a students, 54–57
teachers' description of White students, 54
and teachers' inability to understand difference, 49
teachers in study, 52–53
teachers' use of language, 69–70
unpreparedness of teachers, 64, 69
standards and strategic educators, 244–45
"status anxiety," 33–34
status quo, teachers' perpetuation of, 231, 232
strategic educators, 244–46
Strauss, A., 66–68
students, "at-risk"
and deficit ideology, xviii
expectations of failure, 255–56
identification of, 184
see also
students, minority/non-mainstream
students, immigrant, 244
see also
students, minority/non-mainstream
students, linguistic minority
literacy instruction, 118
preparation of teachers of, 231 (*see also* ITEP)
public education offered to, xvii–xviii
teachers of (*see* Carlos; ITEP)
see also
students, minority/non-mainstream
students, low-status, 232, 235
students, minority/non-mainstream
dependence on teachers, 150
effects of deficit ideology on, 49, 65
expectations of failure, 255–56
lack of respect for culture and language, xix
misperceptions of, xviii, 186
patterns of underachievement, 212
and professional discourse, 153
relationship with teachers, 150, 151, 162, 251–52
reticence in asking teachers for help, 151
and social reproduction, 251
success of and relationship with teachers, 162, 251–52
underrating of, 138
writing abilities of, 141–42
students with disability, rights of, 65
success. *see* achievement
Sullivan, E.V., 21–22

Tatum, Beverly Daniel, 5, 8, 164, 166
teacher educators
contrary roles of, 146
as cultural mentors, 146–53
as gatekeeper, 146
need to interrogate ideological orientations, 225–26
teacher preparation programs
and absorption of dominant ideologies, xv
lack of honesty about stakes of education, 256
lack of study of ideology in, xv
in Mexico, 79–80
and multicultural education (*see* multicultural education)
need for course on psychology of racism, 23
need for critical literacy, 65
need to address ideology, 184–85, 231, 233
need to expose ideological foundations, 184–85
need to implement MCE across curriculum, 24
need to understand students' identities and beliefs, 200–201
and perpetuation of racism by teachers, xv–xvi
reconstruction of cultural identity, 200–201
see also multicultural education; teachers, preservice

teachers
- as advocates for poor and dispossessed, 4
- counter-hegemonic ideological orientations and success, xx
- dependence of non-mainstream students on, 150
- deprofessionalization of, 268
- effective, xx, 117, 186–87
- with experience of marginalization, 236, 238, 246
- exposure to variety of teaching contexts, 240
- gender of, 162
- lack of examination of ideology, 118
- need for critical reflection, 187
- need for cultural competence, 145–46
- need for ideological clarity, 133, 213, 215, 231, 247
- need for political clarity, 213 (*see also* teachers, politicized)
- need to interrogate influence of dominant ideologies, 211
- need to uncover cultural identity, 188–89
- from non-mainstream backgrounds, 145–46, 236, 238, 246 (*see also* teachers, African American; teachers of color)
- perpetuation of classism, 66
- perpetuation of racism, xv–xvi, 66, 189
- perpetuation of status quo, 231, 232
- political role of, 85
- as politicized mothers, 257
- professional development (*see* professional development)
- race of, 161–62
- relationship between belief and practice, 117–18, 133, 136, 210–11, 212
- requirements for effectiveness, 186–87
- role in socialization, 12
- role of, 76
- tension between practices and beliefs, 133
- value of understanding racism, 190–91
- *see also* teaching

teachers, African American
- maternal approach to teaching, 252–55
- Pam, 259–60
- political clarity of, 256–61
- as politicized mothers, 257 (*see also* mothers, politicized)
- *see also* teachers of color

teachers, Black. *see* teachers, African American; teachers of color

teachers, mainstream. *see* teachers, White

teachers, politicized, 256–61
- *see also* mothers, politicized

teachers, preservice
- beliefs about social inequality, 12
- and dissonance, 196–97, 233
- ideological foundations, 195–96
- ideological shifts of, 197–200
- lack of contact with non-mainstream people, 12, 185
- multicultural education courses for, 4, 188 (*see also* multicultural education)
- need to explore personal cultural background, 188–89
- politically unclear caring of, 262
- reconstruction of cultural identity, 200–201
- resistance to multicultural education (*see* multicultural education, resistance to)
- study of cultural identity, 191–94
- unawareness of dominant ideology, 186
- understanding of cultural identity, 198–99
- understanding of privilege, 199–200
- understanding of racism, 189, 199–200
- understanding of sexism, 199
- *see also* teacher preparation programs

teachers, White
- and antiracist education (*see* antiracist education; multicultural education)

as antiracist educators, 164–65
desire to deconstruct maternal, 254
intellectual role, 166
lack of contact with non-mainstream students, 185
need for awareness of White privilege, 162–63
need to recognize culture as relevant, 162
need to understand racism, 161
roles of, 165–66
unwillingness to change beliefs, 190
as White ally, 166, 177
teachers in urban schools, new
daily struggles, 208–9
development of inquiry, 221–23, 226n5
induction, 226n5
lack of problem-solving framework, 222
need to critically examine ideology, 211
professional development for, 207 (*see also* QUEST)
support for, 207–9, 211, 212–13, 224–25 (*see also* QUEST)
teachers of color
effect on diverse students, 145
socialization experiences, 212
see also teachers, African American
teacher-student relationships
aesthetic caring, 253
and authentic caring (*see* caring, authentic)
influence on school failure, 251–52
maternal approach, 252–55
role of race and culture in, 218
and success of non-mainstream students, 162, 251–52
teaching
with courage, 247
maternal approach to (*see* maternal approach to teaching)
as political, 183–84
use of power in, 261
teaching, culturally responsive, 186, 203n4
teaching, explicit, 226n4

Teaching American History, 107
tenor
definition of, 75, 77
in Mr. Torres's interview, 89
in Ms. Camacho's interview, 85
in Ms. Osuna's interviews, 81
text as evidence of beliefs, 77
textual function. *see* mode
Thompson, Audrey, 257
thought, critical, 15–16
Tijuana, Mexico, 77–78
titles, use of, 35–36, 44n5
Titone, C., 166
Torres, Mr., 87–89, 90
Torres, R. D., 215
tradition in conservative view of history, 107–8
transformationist, 165
transformative resistance, 20–22
Trueba, E. T., 215

unconscious compliance, 18, *22*
"unconscious voyeurs," 241
underachievement
of Mexican community, 30
patterns of among non-mainstream students, 212
teachers' explanation of, 55–57
see also achievement; achievement gap
United States
as extra-historical entity, 99, 100
founding of, 102–3

Valencia, Richard, xviii
Valenzuela, Angela, 252
Villegas, A. M., 189
Villenas, S., 238, 248n4

Wampanoag, 102–3
Weiler, K., 138
western civilization, 99, 105
White ally, 166, 177
White mainstream, definition of, 203n4
White Racial Identity Attitude Scale (WRIAS), 170
White racial identity development, 164, 167, 168–69, 177

Whites
　awareness/unawareness of privilege, 163–64, 167, 172–73, 174
　awareness/unawareness of Whiteness, 170–71, 173
　as contributors to oppression, 164
　endorsement of superiority, 173
　interethnic relations of, 9
　perceptions of Chicanos/as, 33, 34–35
　perceptions of culture, 31
　positive racial identity, 174, 176–77
　racial identity, development of (*see* White racial identity development)
　responsibility for eliminating racism, 175
　use of institutional mechanisms, 41–42
　view of womanhood, 254
　see also privilege
White supremacy
　within context of oppressive ideologies, 219
　difficulty for Whites to recognize, 225
　and English dominance, 200
　perpetuation of, 189

women
　cultural expectations of, 254
　respect for, 36
　tendency to blame selves, 43
　use of titles, 36, 44n5
writing
　abilities of ELLs, 141–42
　abilities of non-mainstream students, 141–42
　as cultural capital, 137
　and dominant culture, 137
　expectations of for ELLs, 143
　expectations of for mainstream students, 143
　face-to-face meetings, 150–51
　multiple drafts, 151–52
　peer editing, 152
　as presentation of self, 137
　of professional report (*see* discourse, professional; educational reports)
　written feedback, 147–50, 154–57
written feedback, 154–57

Zimpher, N. L., 12
Zinn, Howard, 103, 110

COUNTERPOINTS

Studies in the Postmodern Theory of Education

General Editors
Joe L. Kincheloe & Shirley R. Steinberg

Counterpoints publishes the most compelling and imaginative books being written in education today. Grounded on the theoretical advances in criticalism, feminism, and postmodernism in the last two decades of the twentieth century, Counterpoints engages the meaning of these innovations in various forms of educational expression. Committed to the proposition that theoretical literature should be accessible to a variety of audiences, the series insists that its authors avoid esoteric and jargonistic languages that transform educational scholarship into an elite discourse for the initiated. Scholarly work matters only to the degree it affects consciousness and practice at multiple sites. Counterpoints' editorial policy is based on these principles and the ability of scholars to break new ground, to open new conversations, to go where educators have never gone before.

For additional information about this series or for the submission of manuscripts, please contact:

> Joe L. Kincheloe & Shirley R. Steinberg
> c/o Peter Lang Publishing, Inc.
> 29 Broadway, 18th floor
> New York, New York 10006

To order other books in this series, please contact our Customer Service Department:

> (800) 770-LANG (within the U.S.)
> (212) 647-7706 (outside the U.S.)
> (212) 647-7707 FAX

Or browse online by series:
> www.peterlang.com